dark mother

M. Fonte
Jan 05

La Virgen del Barrio
Spanish Harlem, New York City
Painting by Elaine Soto

dark mother

african origins and godmothers

Lucia Chiavola Birnbaum

Authors Choice Press

San Jose New York Lincoln Shanghai

dark mother
african origins and godmothers

Authors Choice Press
an imprint of iUniverse, Inc.

For information address:
iUniverse, Inc.
5220 S. 16th St., Suite 200
Lincoln, NE 68512
www.iuniverse.com

ISBN: 0-595-20841-X

Printed in the United States of America

Alla memoria di mia madre Kate Cipolla Chiavola
E di mio padre Turiddu Chiavola,
And in the memory of my own godmother Mary Cipolla Pollaro

To Wally

epigraph

"The most radical thing is a long memory."
—Kalli Halvorson, *Herstar*, feminist scholar

"Lucia's work is unique among feminist scholars because she is unafraid to point
out African origins of humanity and African origins of the dark mother."
—Luisah Teish, poet, dancer, feminist scholar

"Many good wishes on your work, so original and so courageous."
—L. Luca Cavalli-Sforza, geneticist

"This book is a map of our own foreignness…interlayering history, folklore,
and religion…rewarded by a wave that swept me…right out into the long,
deep, dark history
of my own [Irish] grandmother's blood."
—Karen Smith, theologian, historian

"[Lucia's work} gives us a wonderful opportunity to examine what it means to
be
members of the human family
as we affirm our identities through ethnicity, gender, race, religion,
and the political, social, and cultural structures we create…
not only new ways of knowing,
but, new questions, perhaps the greatest contribution any scholar can make."

—Lillie Johnson Edwards, Director of Women's Studies and African Studies, Drew University

"…so important and holds such true integrity…so clearly articulate(s) the living presence of the ancient influences…."
—Rose Wognum Frances, painter, sculptor, scholar

"Her work is a source of intellectual pleasure and political hope."
—Donna Haraway, feminist scholar, History of Consciousness, U. C. Santa Cruz

"Daring and supra-disciplinary…a hope for our globe in these end times…one may recoil in outrage, face her disturbingly vital truths and/or suspend belief…. I bask in the chiaroscuri of her inexhaustible science and Lilithian poetry."
—Justin Vitiello, historian, Temple University

"Lucia's work is at the frontier of women's studies."
—Luisa Muraro, theologian, Libreria delle donne, Milano

"*dark mother* is exciting to me because it backs up what I say in my poetry…. As a working class southern italian/sicilian american pagan catholic… it's more than a joy, it's a life saver."
—Rose Romano, poet, scholar, editor.

"Her work is at the cutting edge of scholarship around liberation theology today."
—Harvey Cox, Harvard Divinity School.

"Lucia's feminist scholarship, grounded in prehistory with a commitment to
the women's movement,
is an arrow into the new millennium."
— Simona Mafai, sicilian feminist stateswoman and journalist

"Lucia's work is life-saving."
—Chickie Farella, playwright

"Her multidisciplinary, multi-ethnic approach is bringing a
desperately needed unguent
…providing a positive ground on which a healing discourse can begin."
—Adele LaBarre Starensier, art, Drew University

"…a transformative experience for me…groundbreaking…"
—Paola Chiarmonte, feminist scholar

"It is no exaggeration to say that [Lucia's work] is life-changing…"
—Dina Gerasia, sicilian educator

"As good as bread."
—Judith Grahn, feminist scholar, poet, educator, New College

"…allows the reader to understand that cultural and political action
can never be separated from spiritual perception."
—Vivian Deziak Hahn, feminist scholar

"Just imagine…
if everyone really understood
that their oldest mother is African and black."
—Corinne Innas, Chi Gallery.

contents

part three: comparative beliefs United States and Italy

part four: L'Ordine simbolico della madre

illustrations and map

Illustrations are not meant to convey a pictorial history of the dark mother, but to give a sampling of her many images, focusing on those less well-known and those that suggest she is everywhere. For more images, see books of Marija Gimbutas, as well as my *Liberazione della donna* and the U. S. and italian editions of *Black Madonnas*.

Tricia Grame's painting on the front cover superbly catches the meaning of this study, an african woman with first signs of the dark mother—ochre red and the pubic V—along with figures of godmothers, or comari, who carried her memory into the historic epoch.

Elaine Soto's painting of the black madonna of Spanish Harlem, the frontispiece, as well as Elaine's other images throughout the book, point to the dark mother's message of liberation. Lydia Ruyle's banners illustrate that the dark mother may be found in all parts of the earth. The end illustration, Eleanor Dickinson's pregnant dark mother, is a complex metaphor: the mother holding the earth in orbit and the world's long wait for deliverance.

Rose Wognum Frances' painting on the back cover, the dark mother of Catal Hoyuk giving birth, and girl unfolding hands with henna, carries theological, and personal, meaning. In June 1998, Rose and I, and many other scholars and artists of women's spirituality, participated in an international symposium at Catal Hoyuk. Afterward, we walked into town to witness the women's shelter that had been burned down. As we grieved among the ruins, a little girl came to the door and slowly unfolded henna palms. Rose and I gasped, both of us struck by the figure of the child signifying the dark mother's regeneration.

L. Luca Cavalli-Sforza gave me permission to reproduce his map of human migrations from Africa, the book's underpinning in genetics data of african origins of modern humans, and of world civilization. The 5300 BCE cliff incision of a dancer in the central arabian peninsula (reproduced as a sculpture by an artist and photographed by Wallace Birnbaum), is indebted to the image in Emmanuel Anati's archive of prehistory at Capo di Ponte, Brescia Italy. Monica Sjoo's painting of a black madonna (with african signs)of Malta, illustrates Sjoo's early intuition that everyone's ancestors are african.

Sharon Anthony gave me her stunning photograph of Magdalen, Pat Bennett her photo of the street sign of a cooperative art workshop of contemporary comari that we found in Syracuse, Sicily, and Max Dashu her paintings of a hebrew priestess, a witch, and a grandmother. Louise Paré sent photographs of black madonnas in Moscow, Elsa Polansky the postmodern black madonna of Prague, and Stefanie Romeo her sculpture pointing to a dark mother beyond gender. Wallace Birnbaum's and Jodi MacMillan DeMartile's images bring different perspectives to the story. I thank the Museo Archeologico Regionale "Paolo Orsi" for the image of the dark mother of Megara Hyblaea in Sicily. Molte grazie to Doug Latta whose glass sculpture of a pubic V with wheat carries the central theme— the dark mother as generatrix—throughout the book.

frontispiece

La Virgen del Barrio. Spanish Harlem, New York City. Painting, Elaine Soto

prologue

1. Map of human migrations, in Africa after 100,000 BCE and after 50,000 BCE to every continent of the earth may be found in *The Great Human Diasporas. The History of Diversity and Evolution* by L. Luca and

Francesco Cavalli-Sforza. Translated by Sarah Thorne. Reading, Ma. et al., Addison-Wesley Publishing Company, Inc., 1995.

part one: african origins, african migrations, case of Sicily.

Pubic V and wheat. Design, Doug Latta

chapter one

2. Venus of Laussel. France. 25,000 BCE. Banner, Lydia Ruyle

3. Venus of Willendorf. Austria. 25,000 BCE. Banner, Lydia Ruyle

4. Siberian dark mother. 20,000 BCE. Banner, Lydia Ruyle

5. Pubic figures and animals, 10,000 BCE Cava del Genovese, Egadi Islands, Sicily. Photograph, Wallace Birnbaum

6. Isis and Horus. Photograph, Wallace Birnbaum

7. Ashanti dark mother. Photograph, Wallace Birnbaum

chapter two

8. Woman dancer of Central Arabia. 5300 BCE. Archives of Emmanuel Anati, Centro Camuno di Studi Preistorici, Italy. Photograph of sculpture thereof, Wallace Birnbaum.

9. Hebrew priestess, Qadeshah. Painting, Max Dashu

10. Black madonna of Malta with african spiritmarks. Painting, Monica Sjoo

chapter three

11. Dark mother of Megara Hyblaea, Sicily. 600 BCE. Photograph, Wallace Birnbaum

12. Canaanite youth "with attitude," Mozia, Sicily. Photograph, Jodi MacMillan DeMartile

13. Sicilian Demeter at Enna. Banner, Lydia Ruyle

14. Black madonna of Adonai, Sicily. Photograph, Jodi MacMillan De Martile

15. Ochre red image of the christian madonna, Priscilla Catacombs. Rome. Photograph, Wallace Birnbaum

16. San Benedetto il Moro, Palermo, outside sanctuary of santa Rosalia. Photograph, Jodi MacMillan DeMartile.

acknowledgments

I thank all the scientists, artists, and poets who have enhanced this book. For their poetry (in the order in which it appears) Necia Desiree Harkless, Marlene Saliba, Nicolas Otieno, Edouardo Galeano, students of the 60s, Louisa Calio, Luisa Muraro, Luciana Polney, Rose Romano, Rob Brezny, Louise Paré, and Gian Banchero.

The California Institute of Integral Studies in San Francisco provides a teaching environment encouraging vision as well as academic rigor, an ambience created in large part by Joseph Subbiondo, president; Janis Phelps, dean; and Mara Keller, director of the women's spirituality program. Others to whom I owe a great deal are colleagues Angana Chatterji, Dorothy Ettling, Elinor Gadon, Joan Marler, Vicki Noble, Mayumi Oda, Arisika Razak, Cindy Shearer, Tina Stromsted, Tanya Wilkinson, and Alice Walker.

Especial thanks to Mutombo Mpanya and Richard Shapiro, with whom I co-teach a humanities seminar, who have helped me see this study in global context. And to my students who have helped me understand intercultural and intergenerational perspectives. Freud may have been right about sex, and Jung about art and religion, but the pervasive motivation I find among contemporary students is a passion to know the past from the beginning, their grandmothers' stories, and stories of all dark others. I am thinking, in particular, of students in the contemporary women's spirituality class I co-taught with Arisika Razak in the fall of 2000: Christy Amschler, Nicole Arkin, Karen Bricken, Ann-Marie Cory, Kathryn Crosby, Rona DeDecker, Jody DeMartile, Charmaine Ehrhart,

Penny Fellbrich, Rochelle Frehling, Sandra Hallsted, Ann Harrison, Michelle Herrera, Nicole Margiasso, Patricia McCormack, Shannon Reich, and Elizabeth Shillington. Students in my class on the dark mother in the spring of 2000 underlined for me how much teachers learn from their students: Joan Cichon, Kathryn Crosby, Patti Davis, Jane Marie DeMente, Donna Ray Erickson, John Heuser, Anna Joyce, Marguerite Rigoglioso, Deborah Grenn-Scott, and Mary Patricia Ziolkowski. Students I helped mentor in Elinor Gadon's CIIS cohort in the women's spirituality program were early guides on my journey, and are cited in the prologue.

Women in my Berkeley Women and Work group remind me of the nurturant and wise comari described in this book: Dorothy Bryant, Sydney Carson, Pat Cody, Clare Fischer, Estelle Jelinek Marge Lasky, Joan Levinson, Rachel Kahn-Hut, Alison Klairmont-Lingo, Celeste McLeod, Remi Omodele, Anne Machung, Rita Maran, Glenna Matthews, Maresi Nerad, Cecile Pineda, Ruth Rosen, and Renate Sandrozinski. So do the women in the Berkeley Organization for the Advancement of Women, particularly Karen Benveniste, Margaret Alafi, Johanna Harris, and Lynn Rees. Women who participated in my study tour to Sicily in the summer of 2000 have stimulated me to complete this book, which has been in process since 1993: Nina Aoni, Pat Bennett, Jean V. Demas, Chickie Farella, Joyce Lozito, Elizabeth Moran, Mary Beth Moser, Dee Poth, and Sandra Schnabel. As did participants in the Sicily summer 2001 study tour: Ardys De Lu, Jodi MacMillan DeMartile, Dina Gerasia, Shannon Reich, Marguerite Rigoglioso, and Mary Saracino.

Henry Farnham May, distinguished historian of the United States, early taught me to be a careful as well as imaginative historian. Ishmael Reed, writer and theorist, has been a beacon on the journey to a just world. I have been inspired by Patricia Adelekan's creative institution building, Renate Holub's intercultural scholarship, and by colleagues, not only in the women's spirituality program at CIIS, but in the analogous program at New College, San Francisco: Judith Grahn, Ani Mander,

Margaret Grove, and Dianne Jenett. And to that extraordinary role model of independent artist and scholar—Rose Wognum Frances.

I need to single out Rose Romano whose poetry parallels my journey to the dark mother, and Nzula Angelina Ciatu who reminded me long ago that we are all peoples of colors. Among those who have heartened me at critical junctures, I need to mention Kalli Halvorson, Jodi MacMillan DeMartile, Robin Davies, and Tricia Grame. As well as Sharon Anthony, Molefi Asante, James Atchison, Maria Cimino, Bence Gerber, Neal & Linda Birnbaum, Anne Bouie, Kris Brandenburger, Louisa Calio, Joan Clair, Diane Di Prima, Ida Dunson, Chickie Farella, Fred Gardaphé, Maria Gillan, Dianne Jenett, Deborah Grenn-Scott, Necia Desiree Harkless, Jean Rosenthal Harris, Yvonne Kohler, Willow LaMonte, Clarebeth Lo Prinzi-Kassel, Simona Mafai, Joan Marler, Betty Meador, Louise Paré, Pina Piccolo, Sara Poli, Francesca Roccaforte, Angela Romer, Karen Smith, Anthony Tamburri, Luisah Teish, Eula Thomas, Robert Viscusi, Emily Gruen White, and Barbara Natoli Witt.

This book remembers Dora and Harry Birnbaum. And my comari (godmothers), nonne, (grandmothers), and bisnonne (great grandmothers). My aunts Anne Connole, Jennie Di Simone, Pearl Burk, Concettina and Lillian Chiavola, Giorgia Monteleone, and Serafina Panettiere. My uncles George, Joe, Jim Chiavola, and Frank Cipolla. My cousins Tina and Louisa Chiavola, Lucy & Nino Giro, Mary Grantello, Anna Monteleone, and Jo Pollaro. And Gloria and Harold Klein, Irv Polansky, Cecilia Ross, Claudio Segré, Tito Hermida, Rena Vassar, and Claire Weisberg. This book, a bouquet to the generation of the 1960s, remembers, in particular, Susan Klein, Chuck Koloms, and Mario Savio.

Baci to my sister Joie Chiavola Mellenbruch, who plants wheat for me on December 13, and my brother Louis Chiavola, with whom I share a January birthday and a great deal else. And to other supportive siblings: Norman & Stella Birnbaum, Lonnie Chiavola, and Elsa Polansky. Especial love to aunts Rose Davis and Lottie Hermida, cousins Lucy Rice, Lucy Panettiere, Wanda Shockey, Edea & Rita di Benedetto, and Eve & Irv

Safir. And to all our nipoti, that italian word that embraces nieces, nephews and others in our extended jewish/italian family.

This book is for our children: Naury, who rescues my manuscripts when they are kidnapped to computer oblivion & Barbara, who gave me perspective when I had seceded from academia; Marc, who taught me italian, & Nancy, always there and radiant; and Stefan, whose editing and moral insights are superb. And for our grandchildren, who point to a better world: Josh, Sabrina & Jessica; Matt & Nicolas; and Courtney, Jake & Stefanie.

My deepest indebtedness is implicit in the dedication to my mother and father, and to my very own godmother. And to Wally, otherwise a physicist and computer scientist, who, for this and other books, has been logistics director, photographer, copy and graphics editor…and beloved life partner.

All translations, and all mistakes, are mine.

note on style

I have adopted contemporary italian style in removing capitals from as many words as possible, agreeing with italians that this is a step toward democratization of all institutions. Downcasing also reflects my dislike of mindless elevation of capitalized words to numinous status. Removing capital letters, in my view, encourages clearer thinking; e.g., god, goddess, dark mother, black madonnas, godmothers, africans, asians, europeans, americans, latin americans, canaanites, jews, catholics, everyday catholics, judaism, christianity, islam, moors, hindus, buddhists, capitalists, fascists, marxists, gramscian marxists, communists, democratic communists, democratic socialists, et al. I have retained capitals for places (e.g., Africa, Asia, Europe) but not for adjectives or peoples (e.g., Africa, african, africans; Asia, asian, asians; Europe, european, europeans). I have also kept capitals in initial letters of sentences, in first words of titles, proper names, and sometimes for comprehension. In quotations, I have left judgments about capitals to the writer.

prologue

premises and methodologies

In my sicilian/american childhood in Kansas City, Missouri, the favorite exclamation of my mother, grandmothers, and aunts was "bedda matri!" Origins of this invocation to beautiful mother—expressing wonder, astonishment, gratitude—did not become clear to me for a long time, not until the 1990s, when my research on italian feminists and black madonnas[1] coincided with rereading african scholars and studying western geneticists and archeologists[2].

The hypothesis of this book is that everyone's genetic "beautiful mother" is african and dark, and that she is the oldest divinity we know. At the beginning of the third millennium, the consensus among world scientists is that Africa is "the cradle of the most ancient living beings that paleo-anthropologists are willing to call Homo," and that Africa is the place of origin of modern humans, homo sapiens sapiens. In the paleolithic epoch, signs of our oldest mother were the color ochre red (signifying blood of childbirth and menstruation) and the pubic V painted in african caves.[3] After 50,000 BCE, migrating africans took these signs to all continents, where they may be seen today in the caves and cliffs of the world.

This study is an intercultural and interdisciplinary exploration of the african origin of the dark mother, and her continuing memory to the present. The first part presents contemporary findings of geneticists and archeologists. The rest of the book documents, in my research, and that of other cultural historians, the persistence of the belief in our oldest mother and in values associated with her—justice with compassion, equality, and transformation.

Belief in the african origin of world civilization, a civilization centered on a dark mother, was widely held in the ancient world, up until the first centuries of the common epoch when clerical and secular authorities destroyed her images and attempted to suppress her memory. Despite this campaign, her memory and values stayed alive in everyday and festival rituals of subaltern cultures of the world. In the late 20th century, the memory of the dark mother surfaced in writings of african and africanist scholars, in research of western scientists, and in women's movements of the world—particularly in that stream, becoming a river, called women's spirituality.

In the enterprise of rescuing the ancient belief in african origins of world civilization, the writings of Cheikh Anta Diop[4] in the 1980s are foundational, but many african, african american, asian, and other world scholars have participated, notably W. E. B. DuBois earlier and Asa Hilliard, Molefi Asante, Robert Thompson, Ivan Van Sertima, Runoko Rashidi, Danita Redd, Henry Louis Gates, and Cornel West in our time. The memory has inspired the writings of african american women, e.g., Audrey Lorde, Alice Walker, Toni Morison, and bell hooks. Luisah Teish has been pivotal in recalling the charms, rituals, and seasonal celebrations of african civilization, as well as the nuanced nature of gender in african understanding,[5] a theme evident in in contemporary flowering of lesbian and gay scholarship.

Two african american women who have been significant in rescuing the evidence of the african origin of world civilization are Drusilla Dunjee Houston earlier, and Matomah Alesha today. Their works exemplify african oral and nonverbal traditions, traditions that become powerful when complemented, as they are by Houston and Alesha, with other ways of knowing. In 1926 Houston wrote *Wonderful Ethiopians of the Ancient Cushite Empire,* exploring what scientists today confirm—the centrality and geographical breadth of early african civilization. In February 2001, as this book was being prepared for publication, Mara Keller referred me to a notice of the publication of Matomah Alesha's *The First Book of the Black Goddess.* Grounded in african oral and nonverbal traditions, as well as other ways of knowing, Alesha's book aims for wholeness.

In this spirit of wholeness, Matomah Alesha's book and this one—and hundreds of similar studies yet to be written grounded on african origins and african diasporas—may be considered complementary. Matomah Alesha writes in african oral and nonverbal traditions that are still alive. I am a sicilian/american woman recovering my suppressed sicilian ancestry, a journey that has taken me, via a circuitous route, to Africa.[6] A primary aim of this book is to inspire others to track their origins and their diasporas, which, in the hypothesis of this book, will lead them to Africa. The corollary to this hypothesis is that all humans carry the memory (often preconscious) of the dark mother and her values.

In the spring of 1988 I was a resident scholar at the American Academy in Rome, when I thought to go to Sicily to observe rituals of easter week. I took my professional attitude, my notebook, camera, and tape recorder to Trapani, where on Thursday of holy week I watched the procession of the black madonna. And was changed forever.

Trapani is located on migration and trade routes of what is called the "african coast" of western Sicily. As the sirocco, the hot wind that comes up from the african desert, sent my senses reeling, I watched the mesmerizing spiral dance of the procession of the black madonna. Looking about me I noticed that everyone along the route of the procession was in tears…and that I was in tears. In retrospect, this experience seems to me an overwhelming bodily memory of the ancient african dark mother.

When I returned to Rome, I dreamed of my mother as a black madonna—and the next day learned she was dying. In the next year and a half, while she was dying, I wrote *Black Madonnas.* That moment on the african coast of Sicily, and the dream of my mother as a black madonna, have motivated my research ever since, deepening my training in intellectual history with what we are coming to recognize as many ways of knowing.

In his 1963 study of prehistory to the conquest of Canaan, Emmanuel Anati, italian archeologist, and today premier authority on the rock art of the world, stated that the oldest religion we know centers on a woman. "A developed religion with all beliefs, rules and conventional rites appeared for the first time only thirty thousand years ago, as attested by repeated finds of mother goddess figurines and by the art in sanctuary caves."[7] In his 1995 book on the rock art of the world, Anati concluded, "All of us derive from this common ancestor."[8]

In the 1970s and 80s, Marija Gimbutas, lithuanian/american archeologist, gathered evidence in archeology and mythology that the earliest divinity of Old Europe was a woman.[9] In the anxious male backlash against feminism of the 1970s, 80s, and 90s, Gimbutas' work aroused hostile male response, as well as a following among women scholars, some of whom developed the academic study of women's spirituality.[10] In 1993 Elinor Gadon, art historian and scholar of the hindu goddess, founded the program in women's spirituality at the California Institute of Integral Studies in San Francisco.

In 1995, in a convergence of african, asian, and western women and men scholars, the *Journal of African Civilizations* stated, "modern humanity originated in Africa, African people are the world's original people." Further, "the light of Sumerian civilization can only be attributed to the arrival of Black migrants from Africa's Nile Valley." [11] In their book that same year on early african presence in Asia, Ivan Van Sertima and Runoko Rashidi concluded that earlier studies of african origins had now been confirmed by geneticists, that matrilineality characterized early african cultures, and that geneticists' confirmation in the DNA of african migrations to all continents was supported by material evidence of african presence in southeast Asia, on the eastern shores of the Black Sea, and the "jewel in the lotus," ethiopian presence in the civilization of the Indus Valley.[12]

Perhaps the greatest casualty of cultural and academic wars in the west of the last quarter century was a defensive turning inward that prevented beleaguered cultural groups challenging the dominant paradigm—white male supremacy—from seeing that there were allies across the lines. Women scholars did not realize that men scientists were confirming the presence in prehistory of a woman divinity who preceded a male divinity. The reluctance of some women scholars to acknowledge that the earliest woman divinity was african and dark may be attributed to the institutionalized racism of the west, as well as to unexamined premises of the now discredited multiregional theory of human origins.[13]

African origin of the mother divinity of prehistory was obvious to Cheikh Anta Diop. In his 1981 study, *Civilization or Barbarism. An Authentic Anthropology,* the senegalese scholar placed a photo of a contemporary south african woman alongside a figurine of a goddess found on a 25,000 BCE path of african migrants into Europe. Similarity of body type is striking.[14]

In 2001, many scholars across the world are recovering the evidence of a woman divinity in prehistory and history—joining a large grassroots movement of people who find the theory compelling. The hypothesis of a prehistoric woman divinity has stimulated new thinking, generated new questions, and may be the most fruitful research thesis of our time. The theme may also offer a unifying metaphor for the peoples of our troubled world.

In the south and east of the world, images of a venerated dark woman of a thousand names are commonplace. What may be new today[15] is women's scholarly interest in the subject, a good deal of it by western women who have lived in a dominant motherless culture for a long time. Women of the north and west of the world, struck by the implications of a woman divinity whose civilization preceded patriarchal world religions, pose questions which are not news to women of the south and the east of the globe. The subject takes on a momentum of its own. Women of the south and east, a little irritated by women of the north and the west "discovering" the subject, take a fresh look at what they consider everyday knowledge.

Interest in the woman divinity—whom "new age" and other theorists call "goddess," third world scholars call "mother," and I call "dark mother"—is particularly vibrant in the San Francisco Bay area. This is not to understate wide interest in this subject throughout the United States, and the world, but to offer a specific case. On the west coast of the United States, among those studying prehistory from a feminist perspective are Joan Marler, presently writing a life and times of Marija Gimbutas, Betty Meador, jungian scholar and therapist who has published a study of Inanna of Sumer, China Galland, who has written a highly popular study of Tara and the black madonna. The Serpentina series created by Dianne Jenett and Judith Grahn brings together grassroots as well as academic researchers, as does the Lilith series founded by Deborah Grenn-Scott, and books and workshops of Vicki Noble, Starhawk, Z. Budapest, and others. Elinor Gadon has followed her widely read *Once and Future Goddess* with research on the hindu goddess, and a study of the sacred male.

My own independent research, which began at the end of the 60s as a search for my sicilian grandmothers, has become a journey on which I encountered italian feminists, and wrote a book about them, then the experience on the african coast of Sicily impelled me to write a book on black madonnas. At the beginning of the third millennium, I am sending this book, *dark mother*, to the publisher, knowing that the questions she evokes are endless.

My research, and similar research by others, seem to me to tap an underground stream of submerged wisdom that is rapidly rising throughout the world. The nature of this phenomenon defies early definition, but its contours may be suggested in subjects of doctoral dissertations on women's spirituality. Some that I helped guide in Elinor Gadon's cohort of students at the California Institute of Integral Studies include Valerie Kack Brice on dolmens and menhirs: older women and veneration of saint Anne in Brittany; Margaret Grove on gender motifs in north australian aboriginal rock art; Miri Haruach on the ancient african queendom and contemporary relevance of the Queen of Sheba; Dianne Jenett on Pongala menstrual rituals of Kerala, South India; Judith Grahn on metaformic theory and menstrual rituals of Kerala; Holly Reed on the psychological implications of Inanna's descent; Katarzyna Rolzinski on daughters as caregivers of dying mothers; Michele Radford on the heart in hindu mysticism; Tricia Grame on spiritual autobiography inferred from her sculptures and paintings, Jennifer Colby on Tonantzin/ Guadalupe and transformational art. Dissertations in progress include Jean Demas on Pele of Hawaii, the U.S. constitution, and land rights; Louise Paré on bodily movement as transformative spiritual practice; Leah Taylor on spiritual autobiography as performance art of a jewish daughter; and Jan Marijac on the "end poverty now" initiative of an internet company.

Since 1999 I have been teaching in the California Institute of Integral Studies' women's spirituality program directed by Mara Keller, who has written a poetic and definitive scholarly study of the greater mysteries of Demeter and Persephone, and designed a challenging course of study for graduate scholars. The faculty of this program includes Arisika Razak who brings the african american oral tradition, the ancient wisdom of midwifery and the bodily wisdom of the dance to her classes in women's sacred arts, integral visions, and contemporary women's spirituality; I bring to my classes research on the dark mother, theories and methodologies of many ways of knowing, Sicily as a case of subaltern cultures venerating a dark mother, the dark mother as an emerging issue in the humanities, and the dark mother as symbol of transformation of the third millennium.

Also in this program, Joan Marler, intellectual heiress of Marija Gimbutas, brings this legacy to her classes in archeomythology; Eahr Joan has created Regenesis, a CD-Rom encyclopedia of women's myths and symbols; Charlene Spretnak teaches Mary and modernity and ecofeminism; Angana

Chatterji's anthropology classes study postcolonial themes and cross-cultural issues in social and environmental justice; Rina Sircar teaches spiritual transformation in buddhist psychology; Tanya Wilkinson, the psychology of women; and Jennifer Berezan, women's sacred liturgy. Workshop presenters at CIIS place the academic study of women's spirituality in the company of acclaimed writers, painters, and scholars, notably Alice Walker, Mayumi Oda, Riane Eisler, Susan Griffin, and Elinor Gadon.

In 2001, theses and dissertations I have, or am mentoring, suggest the reach (often into other programs) of the study of women's spirituality; e.g., Angeleen Campra on "persistent and insistent" Sophia; Susan Carter on the japanese sun goddess Amaterasu; Donna Erickson on the history and contemporary relevance of trance healing; Jayne DeMente on a gender and diversity balanced curriculum for our youth, Marguerite Rigoglioso on Demetra and Proserpina and the Lago di Pergusa in Sicily; Gail Williams on her spiritual journey and transformative art; Chandra Alexandre on Kali and black madonnas, and Deborah Grenn-Scott on the lemba, african tribe who keep jewish traditions.

In the program in women's spirituality at New College in San Francisco, Judith Grahn, Ani Mander, Dianne Jenett, Elinor Gadon, Margaret Grove and others teach archeomythology, art, poetry, metaformic theory, et al. At Sonoma State University, Dianne Jenett directs a weekend cohort in women's spirituality. At these schools as well as at CIIS, african americans and other scholars bring a double consciousness (ethnic and spiritual) to the subject; e.g., Ida Dunson documents the racism on U. S. census forms, and records voices of african/american women's spirituality. Ethnic consciousness informed by knowledge of prehistory has spread from african/american women to other ethnic groups. This double consciousness, a concept first articulated by W.E.B. Du Bois, is evident in the contemporary work of many scholars who bring an ethnic perspective, as well as awareness of multiple ways of knowing, to their research in women's spirituality.

Looking to my own italian/american ethnic group, a spiritual and ethnic double consciousness was early present in the Beat poetry of Diane Di

Prima, later in her *La Loba* series. A triple consciousness may be glimpsed today in the writings of Rose Romano, poet and novelist, who searches for her great grandmothers in Africa, her grandmothers in Sicily, and her mother in America. A many-faceted consciousness is apparent in the research of Marguerite Rigoglioso, who participates in archeological digs in Sicily and wrote an M.A. thesis at CIIS on Lake Pergusa at Enna in Sicily, relating world mythology to contemporary ecology issues. Louisa Calio's epic poem of her journey finds the "heart waters" of all humans in Africa. The dark mother informs Chickie Farella's plays, Giovanna Capone's poetry, Francesca Roccaforte's photography and writing, Diane Marto's performance art, and Joie Mellenbruch's biography of her sicilian/american mother. A double consciousness of african and sicilian inheritance has motivated Patrizia Tavormina to change her name to Nzula Angelina Ciatu. Not confined by gender boundaries, the dark mother has inspired the plays of Tommi Avicolli Mecca, paintings and poetry of Gian Banchero, poetry and scholarship of Justin Vitiello, and memoirs of Louis G. Chiavola. Louisa Calio suggests how the study of women's spirituality has deepened the social science mantra of race/gender/culture into profound understanding: "When love calls one past time, past place, gender or race/unto itself, we find our true self/our oneness again."[16]

We have learned to study women's spirituality, not with universal abstractions, but with attention to class, age, and beliefs, as well as variables of race, gender, and culture, coming to a deeper understanding of race as one human race, while keeping in mind the enormous importance of difference in "racial" experience, gender as largely socially constructed, and culture as many-layered, requiring the study of subaltern as well as dominant cultures. We have come to understand that class takes many shapes, that age and generational group inform experience, and that beliefs, including those not conscious, are central to understanding one's self, other people, one's culture, other peoples' cultures, and work for a better world.

Personal journeys, sometimes unexpectedly, lead to wider implication. Elaine Soto, artist and thealogian[17] (who has loaned her paintings of black madonnas to this book) searched in Puerto Rico for the black madonna for whom she is named; now she paints dark woman divinities of the world. I wrote a study of black madonnas of Italy, then was drawn to their origins in Africa and to research the theme of this book: prehistoric african migrants took signs of the belief in the dark mother to all continents, where the belief has persisted to the present in the art, folklore, and political hopes of subaltern cultures of the world...and perhaps in the submerged memory of all humans. Lydia Ruyle finds dark women divinities everywhere, sews their images onto banners, and takes the banners to enthusiastic audiences all over the globe.

Women's spirituality, a field of study with ancient roots, is changing the way we look at everything. Karen Smith, trained in women's spirituality at California Institute of Integral Studies, wrote a doctoral dissertation at the Graduate Theological Union in Berkeley on the pagan underpinning of veneration of saint Margaret. In Italy I am sometimes called a teologa, or woman thealogian, a startling term to me for my work as a historian tracking the the african dark mother from prehistory, through history, to the present.[18]

At the beginning of the third millennium, violence may cloud our vision, but I am heartened that men as well as women scholars of many cultural groups are embarked on similar journeys.[19] Stewart Brand, a leader of the whole earth movement of the 1960s, encourages us to think, as do many scholars of women's spirituality (and peasants the world over) in the perspective of the "long now," simultaneously embracing prehistory, history, the present, and responsibility for the future.[20]

O

Before separation into male, female, ethnic, and other academic enclaves of the 1970s, 80s, and 90s, as mentioned above, Emmanuel Anati, italian archeologist (whose name recalls the canaanite goddess Anat), confirmed in archeological evidence that the oldest divinity we know is a woman. In the 1980s and 90s, italian/american geneticist L.

Luca Cavalli-Sforza, and international colleagues, tracked the DNA of select populations of the world and confirmed origins of modern humans in sub-saharan Africa, the several "Eves" of Africa, and african migrations of homo sapiens sapiens to all continents after 50,000 BCE.[21]

Independently, in his archive of rock art of the world, Centro Camuno Studi Preistorici at Capo di Ponte in Italy, Anati confirmed Cavalli-Sforza's findings and documented that the richest prehistoric cliff art of the world is found in sub-saharan Africa, where modern humans emerged. Anati's scholarship also converged with scholars of women's spirituality, for whom the color red ochre is a sign of a venerated woman. Anati, a jungian, calls the color ochre red "the most ancient evidence of artistic creation in the world."[22]

Cathedrals of tribal peoples, for Anati, are not the massive monuments constructed by autocratic governments, like the acropolis of Athens and pyramids of Egypt, but rock paintings found in central and south Africa with a predominance of the color red or purple, and characterized by spirals, straight or wavy lines, petals, and concentric circles in series[23]—signs, according to Marija Gimbutas, of the woman divinity of prehistory. Holding the concept of archetypes, Anati points out that primordial art has "almost identical characteristics in the entire world," thereby implicitly confirming geneticist Cavalli-Sforza's concept of demic migrations, wherein people take their beliefs with them when they migrate.[24]

The boundary between religion and art, for Anati, is not clear. His timeline of the path of creative art in caves and cliffs of the world begins 40,000 years ago in central and south Africa, then into other parts of Africa; 35,000 years ago from Africa into Asia; 34,000 years ago from Africa into Europe; 22,000 years ago from Africa and Asia into the Americas (the oldest drawing is in Brazil); and 22,000 years ago from Africa and Asia into Australia. The dates closely follow those of african migrations in the world confirmed in DNA evidence. (see map). Primordial art has different expressions, but the "common matrix," for Anati, is Africa.[25]

The centrality of a venerated woman in folklore of Old Europe was uncovered in the 1980s by Marija Gimbutas in work linking archeology and mythology, a field she called archeomythology. Independently, Carlo Ginzburg confirmed the centrality of a woman in the folklore of the world. My work, and that of others, on the many images of black madonnas, points to the centrality of a dark woman in european folklore, converging with research of others on black madonnas and other dark women divinities of Africa, Asia, Europe, north and south America, and Oceania.[26]

The scholarship of these and other scholars provides the themes of this book—that in prehistory symbols of the african dark mother were carried across the earth by african migrants, then carried by migatory farmers from west Asia, and then in late antiquity by canaanite traders. In the common epoch, the memory was transmitted in stories and rituals associated with icons of black madonnas and of other dark women divinities. Yet, as we shall see, the story is very complex. Similar to a polyphonic melody, riffs sound notes of different cultures while the continuing bass resonance of the main melody carries the memory of everyone's dark african mother.

In this study, her memory is explored in everyday and festival rituals of dark *others* of Europe and the United States—women, jews, muslims, heretics, witches—in songs, stories, foods, vendor songs, literature, and art and today in graffiti, bumper stickers, exclamations, and banners of political uprisings. In the late 1960s, inaugurating the contemporary cycle of feminism, women of the world formed the hands gesture of the pubic V and remembered the primordial mother's values in their work for justice, equality, and respect for the earth and all its creatures.[27] In 2001, from different places, different fields of scholarship—and with different concerns—women and men scholars may be converging in a consensus that may already exist in the unarticulated knowledges of peoples of the earth. Noam Chomsky, authority in semiotics, holds that "the genetic endowment constitutes what we 'remember from an earlier existence.'"[28]

This book is one historian's attempt to bring together scientific documentation of african origins of the dark mother with evidence of cultural history for the hypothesis that the memory of the dark mother and her values have persisted for millennia, not only among women but among men—a memory that has acted as a subversive undertow to more than 2,000 years of the dominant violent civilization of the west.

Today her memory may be considered a metaphor of healing, as well as a metaphor of becoming. The mitochrondial energy in the DNA tht we inherit from our mothers is shaped in the form of two embracing serpents, or a double helix, which Cavalli-Sforza calls "symbol of the evolution of the universe...the unlimited possibilities of becoming."[29] The caduceus, helix symbol of healing and becoming, may be considered a symbol of this book.

Aware of the partiality of all knowledge, I have looked to sources in science and in cultural history for check and balance. Science and cultural history both affirm african origins and the continuing memory of the dark mother. In this old/new understanding, I include my own story—the deep education of a sicilian/american woman. In the 1960s, coinciding with completion of study for the doctorate in U. S. and European history, I was swept into that decade's passionate activism against racism and imperialism. In 1969, feeling I had been educated away from my roots, I went to Italy in search of my sicilian grandmothers. In the first stage of the journey I found italian feminists, whose groundedness implied they knew something that I did not know. Motivated to go beyond my training as a historian, wherein research used to be fastened solely to documents written by men supporting the dominant patriarchal culture, I embarked, along with a generation of women scholars, on the journey of helping to recover the unrecorded history of women.

My feminism is close to the womanism articulated by Alice Walker and other african-american women,[30] joining concern for women with concern for all the subordinated others whose stories have been left out of dominant histories This may be considered vernacular history; vernaculus, in latin, means slave.[31] For women historians, vernacular history means excavating the subordinated, or negated, cultures of women of the world. Antonio

Gramsci, major marxist theorist of Italy—and major contemporary theorist of the third world—emphasized the difference of beliefs of subaltern cultures (visible in folklore) from beliefs of the dominant culture. Gramsci's insight has helped me understand women's cultures, and to realize that my errand is to recover the deep histories of men as well as of women—people who, in addition to being exploited economically, had their cultures negated by white male elites, a term somewhat more precise than patriarchy.

Contemporary thealogian Karen Smith reminds us that women's civilization is submerged knowledge. It is "history we don't have, civilization that we don't remember, and traditions that did not get passed down to us."[32] This submerged knowledge is expressed by the body, according to Luce Irigaray,[33] and requires attention, as Simone Weil pointed out.[34] After publication in 1986 of my *Liberazione della donna. Feminism in Italy* in 1986, I wandered around Italy watching people act out deep beliefs in everyday religious and political rituals, deep beliefs, I discovered, that circle a dark mother.

In Italy she is called la dea madre, or god the mother. In the common epoch her memory and values were transmitted by comari, or godmothers, women who bonded with each other in her memory, helped one another birthing, caring for children, the sick, the elderly, the dying, while remembering and envisioning a better world. Nurturing all life, traditional peasant godmothers/grandmothers of Italy, and their sisters elsewhere, are similar to contemporary womanists and earth-bonded feminists. My grandmothers, comari of Sicily, and their sisters in other countries, nonviolently resisted violent patriarchy in everyday rituals, satirized injustice during carnevale, heartened one another in adversity, and inspired their men and children to work for a better life—for everyone.

In the late 1980s while observing everyday and festival rituals of Italy, I read the books of Marija Gimbutas. In Italy, archeological ruins of the many images of our ancient mother are often located underneath or near sanctuaries of black madonnas. In the common epoch these were places of religious heresy, persecution of witches, and sites of popular uprisings of dark others for justice. Images of black madonnas, and of other dark women divinities, I came to realize, may be considered signs of resistance to the dominant culture of church and state, as well as signs of the dark mother's values—justice with compassion, and equality.[35]

Search for my sicilian godmothers/grandmothers led me first to Sicily, then to Africa, then to west Asia where in 40,000 BCE african migrants created the "oldest sanctuary in the world." Later, this african sanctuary became the site of Mount Sinai, foundation place of judaism, christianity, and islam (see chapter two, this work). On migratory routes of paleolithic africans, then on paths of neolithic west asian farmers, then on trade routes of semitic canaanites, people looked to a dark woman divinity, to whom they built, in the common epoch, sancturaries of black madonnas(see my *Black Madonnas* as well as chapter four of this work).

Returning to my specific case of this very large story, in my ancestral regions on the african coast of western and northwestern Sicily, and in the southeastern iblean mountains named for the dark anatolian mother Cybele, people have historically risen up against injustice, from the Sicilian Vespers in the 13th century to the encampment of women of the world at Comiso in 1983, where they denounced Nato nuclear missiles and declared their vision of a radically democratic and green world.

Methodologically, I am both traditional and postmodern. The long and deep story of the dark mother of prehistory, whose memory has persisted underneath the dominant history of the historical epoch, may be studied, in my view, with traditional methods of researching and writing history; i.e., with empirical verification in specific place and time.[36] Yet studied with imagination about sources,[37] with the epistemological maturity for which postmodernism reaches, and with the wisdom that there are many ways of knowing.[38] Science and religion are both myths, said George Santayana, but myths are far from signifying nothing.[39] In sicilian culture we say stories rather than myths.

In this study, scientific findings and stories and rituals of popular cultural history have been related to my particular story, that of a mediterranean, specifically sicilian/american woman, whose ancestors, like the ancestors of every person on earth, originated in Africa. African migrations are the basic threads in my genetic tapestry, as they are in the genetic weave of all humans. My sicilian genetic tapestry is a ground pattern of african migrants, crossed by returning threads of west asian migrants and traders from Anatolia and semitic Canaan, with a warp of greek and roman invaders, more semitic strands of israelites in diaspora, a horizontal and circular weft of african/semitic moors expanding into Europe, and a woof of northern european adventurers and conquerors of Sicily from places later called Germany, Scandinavia, France, Spain, Austria, and northern Italy.

My present world view—that may have always been present in deep layers of my unconscious—surfaced in the 1960s during the african american civil rights movement and subsequent movements of ethnic and gender consciousness that converged with the tidal movements against racism and imperialism that characterized that decade.[40]

In the contemporary controversy over aryan versus african/semitic origins of world civilization, I respect, and largely agree with, Martin Bernal's documentation of african and levantine origins of high greek culture.[41] But I bring a woman's perspective to the subject, a view influenced by Simone Weil, who admired the greeks, but considered the *Iliad* a document of male violence. Whatever its glories, the high culture of Greece reflected the violence of indo-european/aryan speakers who invaded Macedonia and Dalmatia in the millennium before the common era, masculinized and distorted the image of the dark mother, tortured and overworked slaves, and subordinated women. Although the memory of the dark mother pulsed beneath the myths, rituals, art, and drama of high greek culture,[42] it was, despite the accolades of 19th and 20th century western theorists, characterized by violence and hierarchical subordination of people. As Martin Bernal has documented, the high culture of Greece became the aryan icon of european/american racists and imperialists of the late 19th century, and of nazis, white supremists, and people who transmit racism, often unknowingly, in our time.

Sicily is my base point of reference, not only because it is my ancestral place, but because ancients called this island crossroad of Africa, Asia and Europe, "the middle of the earth." Like other mediterranean islands, Sicily was early reached by paleolithic african migrants, then by neolithic migrants from Anatolia, later by west asian canaanite traders, and, in the common epoch, by moors from Africa. After 4000 BCE, indo-european aryan speakers, embodied later in dominant elites of Greece and Rome, introduced violence into Sicily, a violence that included slavery and other hierarchical oppression. In the common epoch, sicilians were subjected to greek, roman, byzantine, and then northern european rule, culminating in the miseria (miserable poverty) of the late 19th and early 20th centuries. The miseria propelled sicilians to find work in northern Europe and to immigrate to north and south America, where they experienced, along with other dark others of the world, racism, exploitation, and negation of their culture. (see chapter 8).

I have put african origins, godmothers, and our oldest mother's memory/promise into a story based on empirical data. At this juncture of world history, Noam Chomsky points out, a story may be a narrative reaching for a time when all of us look at ourselves, and others, differently. For Chomsky, scholar of semiotics, the potential for transformation exists in the core part of human language in mechanisms relating sound and meaning, "an innate grammar" not only "largely universal, but. virtually optimal."[43] Chomsky's view is similar to that of Gramsci who held that a sense of justice (buon senso) exists in all peoples, evident in stories, everyday and festival rituals, and in celebratory moments of politics. Chomsky's and Gramsci's views are close to Emmanuel Anati's jungian belief that mythology is a mirror of our collective memory, a memory that has maintained itself, "almost astonishingly," from prehistoric rock art to the renaissance art of Giotto, to the 20th century genius of Joan Miro and Marc Chagall.[44]

This book takes the form of the spiral view of history—before going forward, we must make a swing backward. I begin with the dark mother of Africa, Canaan, Sicily, and Malta, then focus on santa Lucia, black madonnas of Europe, my sicilian godmothers/grandmothers who, along with other dark others of Europe, looked to the dark mother. The story is placed in comparative perspective with the migration of my grandparents—with their belief in "bedda matri"—to the United States where they met offshoots of patriarchy—racism, social control of dark others, and education/inculcation for americanization. In counterpoint, I study the italian women's movement, and women's alliances with nonviolent men and students as a case of the continuing live memory of the values of the ancient mother. World possibility is suggested in the vibrant memory of the dark mother at the Beijing women's conference in 1995. and in contemporary signs of transformation.

For this study, I am grateful, above all, to my sicilian godmothers/ grandmothers who kept the memory and vision of the dark mother. And to my sicilian grandfathers who learned justice and equality in stories their mothers told them. Analogously I am indebted to womanist/feminist scholars and also to male theorists and scientists who implicitly hold our oldest mother's value of transformation. Among male theorists, perhaps my largest debt is to Antonio Gramsci, and other scholars with a dynamic view of history—among them the great neapolitan philosopher, Giambattista Vico. In *La Scienza Nuova* (1744) Vico said that the city of god is made by god, but humans make societies, that humans will make good societies insofar as they look to "common wisdom," or popular beliefs conveying the "poetic wisdom" of our oldest ancestors.

This book may be considered an attempt to retrieve this poetic wisdom—expressed in science, popular beliefs, and many other ways of knowing—for the generation anew of a just and green world.

Lucia Chiavola Birnbaum
Berkeley, California, 2001

Notes

1   See note on style.

2   The first part of this prologue is a shortened version of my invited paper for the XVYI International Valcamonica Symposium of Archeologists, "Prehistoric and tribal art. Deciphering the Image," Centro Camuno Studi Preistorici; Icomos International Committee on Rock Art, Darfo Boario Terme, Italia, September 21-26, 1999, a paper that formed the ground of chapters one and two of this book.

3   See writings of Judith Grahn, notably her Ph.D. dissertation, for the significance of the color ochre red; see writings of Elinor Gadon for significance of the pubic V.

4   Cheikh Anta Diop's works are those of a medical scientist of Africa who carried the memory. Drusilla Dunjee Houston, in her *Wonderful Ethiopians of the Ancient Cushite Empire*, first published in 1926, carried the memory of african origins of world civilization and buttressed the memory with wide research. (Baltimore,Maryland, Black Classic Press, 1985). A good deal of Houston's research was later confirmed by Cheikh Anta Diop in *Civilization or Barbarism. An Authentic Anthropology* (Presence Africaine, Paris, 1981, Brooklyn, N. Y., Lawrence Hill Books, 1991). Diop pointed out, before feminist scholars did so, that the oldest divinity we know was an african woman.

5   Luisah Teish, *Jambalaya. The Natural Woman's Book of Personal Charms and Practical Rituals* (San Francisco, HarperCollins, 1985); *Carnival of the Spirit. Seasonal Celebrations and Rites of Passage* (HarperSanFrancisco, 1994).

6   See footnote 3 above.

7   Emmanuel Anati, *Palestine before the Hebrews. A History from the Earliest Arrival of Man to the Conquest of Canaan* (New York, Alfred A. Knopf, 1963), 38.

8   Anati, *Il Museo Immaginario della Preistoria. L'arte Rupestre nel Mondo* (Milano, Editoriale Jaca Book SpA, 1995) 309.

9   Marija Gimbutas, *The Civilization of the Goddess*, ed., Joan Marler (HarperSanFrancisco, 1991). Marija Gimbutas, *The Language of the Goddess*, Foreword, Joseph Campbell (HarperSanFrancisco, 1980).

10   For a eurocentric male view, see Colin Renfrew's writings; e.g., "Archaeology, Genetics and Linguistic Diversity: Towards a New Synthesis," the

Charles M. and Martha Hitchcock Lectures, University of California, Berkeley, April 15, 1997.

11 See volumes and papers of the *Journal of African Civilizations,* Rutgers University, New Brunswick, New Jersey.

12 Ibid. 25, 30.

13 Monica Sjoo and Barbara Mor intuited african origins of the dark mother in *The Great Cosmic Mother. Rediscovering the Religion of the Earth* (HarperSanFrancisco, 1987, 1988.). Merlin Stone was early aware of the racism, as well as sexism, that surrounds the subject of the goddess; see *When God was a Woman* (New York, Harcourt Brace Jovanovich, 1978).

14 Cheikh Anta Diop, *Civilization or Barbarism. An Authentic Anthropology.* First published by Presence Africaine, Paris 1981; (Brooklyn, N Y., Lawrence Hill Books, 1991). 48.

15 Not entirely new. The scholarship of Bachhoven and other 19th century male scholars preceded contemporary scholarly work in women's spirituality. See Susan Gail Carter's Ph.D. dissertation on Amaterasu (CIIS, 2001) which has an excellent synthesis of this literature.

16 Louisa Calio, *Journey to the Heart Waters* (unpublished mss., 1999).71.

17 Theaologian, for many feminists, is the preferred spelling.

18 Lucia Chiavola Birnbaum, *Liberazione della donna. Feminism in Italy* (Middletown, Ct., Wesleyan University Press, 1986, 1988); *Black Madonnas. Feminism, religion, and politics in Italy* (Boston, Ma., Northeastern University Press, 1993; *Black Madonnas. Femminismo e Politica in Italia* (Bari, Italia, Palomar Editrice, 1997; iUniverse reprint edition, 2000*).*

19 See Randy Conner, et al. *Cassell's Encyclopedia of Queer Myth, Symbol, and Spirit. Gay, Lesbian, Bisexual, and Transgender Lore* (London, Cassell, 1997). Carolyn McVickar Edwards, *Sun Stories* (HarperSanFrancisco, 1995). *Hey Paesan! Writing by Lesbians and Gay Men of Italian Descent,* Edited by Giovanna (Janet) Capone, Denise Nico Leto, and Tommi Avicolli Mecca (Oakland, Ca., Three Guineas Press, 1999).

20 Stewart Brand, *The Clock of the Long Now. Time and Responsibility. The ideas behind the world's slowest computer* (New York, Basic Books, 1999).

21   L. Luca Cavalli-Sforza, et al. *History and Geography of Human Genes,* (Princeton University Press, 1994). Louise Levathes," A Geneticist Maps Ancient Migrations, " *New York Times, Science Times,* July 27, 1993.

22   Anati, *Arte Rupestre. Il linguaggio dei primordi.* Vol. XII, Edizione Italiana, 1994 (Edizioni del Centro Camuno di Studi Preistorici, Capo di Ponte (BS) Italia, pp. 23, 59.

23   Anati, *Il Museo Immaginario,* Loc. Cit. , 221.

24   Ibid, 217-18

25   Ibidem.

26   Carlo Ginzburg, *Ecstasies. Deciphering the Witches' Sabbath* (Originally published in Italy as *Storia Notturna,* 1989; New York, Penguin Books, 1991).

27   Lucia C. Birnbaum, *Liberazione della donna. Feminism in Italy* (Wesleyan University Press, 1986, 1988).Noam Chomsky, *Class Warfare. Interviews with David Barsamian* (Monroe, Maine, Common Courage Press, 1996). 2.

28   Noam Chomsky, *Class Warfare.*Loc.Cit., 2.

29   L. Luca Cavalli-Sforza, *History and Geography of Human Genes.* Loc. Cit.

30   Alice Walker, *In Search of our Mother's Gardens* (New York, Harcourt, Brace Jovanovich, 1983).

31   Karen Smith, "Neither Here nor There. The Epistemology of the In-Between," unpublished paper, 1996.

32   Ibidem.

33   A good introduction to Irigaray, is the *Irigaray Reader*, edited with an introduction by Margaret Whitford (Cambridge, Ma., Basil Blackwell Ltd., 1991).

34   See Lucia Chiavola Birnbaum, "Simone Weil and Transformation in Italy," Conference on Simone Weil, Graduate Theological Union, Berkeley, California, April 27, 1996.

35   See Birnbaum, *Black Madonnas,* Loc. Cit.

36   See Lucia Chiavola Birnbaum, "Marija Gimbutas and the Change of Paradigm," *From the Realm of the Ancestors. An Anthology in Honor of Marija Gimbutas* (Manchester, Ct., Knowledge, Ideas & Trends, Inc., 1997).

37   An excellent study that is very imaginative about sources is Elizabeth Wayland Barber, *Women's Work. The First 20,000 Years. Women, Cloth, and Society*

in Early Times (New York and London, W. W. Norton & Company, 1994.) I thank Yana Womack for giving me this book.

38   See Charlene Spretnak, *The Resurgence of the Real. Body, Nature, and Place in a Hypermodern World* (Reading, Ma. Addison Wesley Publishing Company, Inc. 1997).

39   George Santayana, *Scepticism and Animal Faith. An Introduction to a System of Philosophy.* In *Philosophy of Santayana,* edited by Irwin Edman (New York, Modern Library, 1942).

40   *See* Elisabeth Schussler Fiorenza, *Jesus. Miriam's Child. Sophia's Prophet. Issues in feminist Christology* (New York, Continuum, 1994)

41   Martin Bernal, *Black Athena. The AfroAsiatic Roots of Classical Civilization* (New Brunswick, New Jersey, Rutgers University Press). Volume I The Fabrication of Ancient Greece 1785-1985, 1987. Volume II The Archaeological and Documentary Evidence, 1991).

42   Robert Bellah proposed this musical metaphor in his essay, "The Five Religions of Modern Italy." In *Varieties of Civil Religion* (San Francisco, Harper & Row, 1980).

43   Noam Chomsky, *Class Warfare.* Loc. Cit. , 2 .

44   See chapter two, this work.

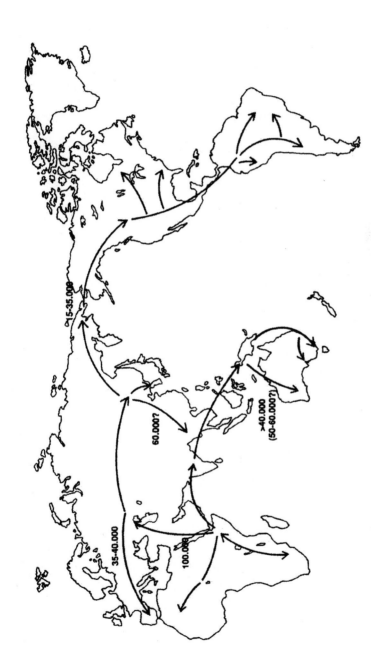

1. Map of human migrations in Africa after 100,000 BCE and after 60,000 BCE to every continent of the earth. From Luigi Luca Cavalli-Sforza, Francesco Cavalli-Sforza, The Great Human Diasporas. The History of Diversity and Evolution. Translated from the Italian by Sarah Thorne. Reading, Massachusetts, Addison Wesley Publishi

part one
african inheritance

chapter one

african origin of humans
african dark mother—oldest divinity
we know

African and african american scholarship on the african origins of civilization, as noted in the prologue, is the ground on which this study stands.[1] At the beginning of the third millennium, world scientists are in agreement on the african origin of modern humans—homo sapiens sapiens.[2] Although not adequately disseminated in popular understanding, there is almost no resistance in the scholarly world to acknowledging african origins of humans. Resistance to accepting a dark african woman as the oldest mother we know remains, however, in the scholarly world. In this chapter, and the next, we shall present the evidence of science for african origins of humans and african origins of the oldest divinity we know. Subsequent chapters will buttress the evidence of science for the origin of the black mother in all cultures —with the evidence of cultural history for persistence of her memory to the present.

L. Luca Cavalli-Sforza, major world geneticist, has summarized recent scientific findings. Specimens dated 3 and 4 million years ago, including Lucy, have been found in different locations in east Africa. Homo habilis has been found with certainty "only in Africa." Homo erectus expanded first from Africa, then from west and south Asia, then from Europe, then from east Asia. Three or four million years ago, african migrants walked into the west asian area of the Levant (contemporary Israel and Palestine), then into southeast Asia, Java, and eastern Asia.[3] Bones and stone tools recently found in the Longport Cave in central China offer evidence that humans migrated out of Africa into China "at least 1.9 million years ago."[4] Our species, homo sapiens sapiens, appeared in east and south Africa around 100,000 years ago, long before appearing elsewhere. Cavalli-Sforza concludes that modern humans, replacing earlier human types, originated in Africa, and that after 50,000 BCE, africans expanded into Asia, Europe, Australia, and North and South America.[5]

African inheritance, for Cavalli-Sforza, has bequeathed a legacy to all peoples of peaceful, festive, technologically inventive, and co-operative democracy. When modern humans appeared 100,000 years ago, they lived like their ancestors in small groups, without hierarchy or leaders, and with a social life grounded on reciprocal respect.[6] Contemporary african pygmies, who have retained characteristics of the paleolithic forebears of all humans, were co-operative then, and remain the most peaceful people Cavalli-Sforza has ever encountered.[7] In his reconstruction of human society of two to three million years ago, the geneticist describes small nomadic or semi-nomadic men who hunted, women who gathered fruit and vegetables, people who seasonally gathered together for festivals with dancing and rituals. As homo habilis, our african ancestors walked upright and formed stone instruments for hunting and preparing food. Stone tools dated 2,600,000 and 2,520,000 years ago have been found in Ethiopia's Gona River, tools that are "the oldest in the world by at least 120,000 years."[8]

Homo sapiens, our species, dates from 500,000-300,000 years ago, a species with individual differences but without difference between males and females. Lack of difference lasted a long time. In 40,000 BCE, africans migrated to Har Karkom in the Sinai and incised megalith figures shaped like humans without distinct gender characteristics. (See next chapter). The 26,000-18,000 BCE figure of the paleolithic mother found at Savignano in Italy has both female and male characteristics. Pregnant, her head is shaped like a phallus.[9] One difference between women and men is the mitochondria in the DNA, cellular structures that supply energy, inherited "solely through the mother's line."[10] Because of this DNA inheritance, Cavalli-Sforza holds that deep religious and political beliefs of offspring tend to resemble beliefs of the mother.[11]

DNA research demonstrates that homo sapiens sapiens emerged in Africa 100,000 years ago (overlapping and replacing neanderthals). After 50,000 BCE, african migrants walked or sailed to every continent of the world. DNA research also reveals that large migrations out of Africa were as recent as 20,000 years ago. From Africa, homo sapiens sapiens walked first to west Asia 40,000-50,000 years ago, then walked or sailed to western and eastern Europe, then to east Asia and Siberia, whence they crossed the ice over the Bering Strait, reaching the Americas between 30,000 and 15,000 years ago. (See map of african migrations)

Figurines of corpulent women with large breasts, called "Venuses" or goddesses, have been found along paths of african migrations into Italy, the spanish and french Pyrenees, the Dordogne area of France, and central and eastern Europe, notably in Austria, Germany, the czech and slovak republics, Bulgaria, and Romania. In the 1880s, at Monaco, near the present border of France and Italy, several of these figurines were found. Although most of have disappeared to antique hunters, seven figurines may be seen in the Musee des Antiquites Nationales at St. Germain-en-Laye outside Paris.

In October 1995 Wally and I visited a place of these figurines, Balzi Rossi in Italy (called Grimaldi Caves by the french), located between Menton in France and Ventimiglia in Italy. Along this italian/french mediterranean coast, I was startled by signs of the african mother. Bluffs are the color red ochre, grottoes are shaped like wombs. Shells on the beach have been identified as those of Senegal in Africa. At Balzi Rossi I imagined africans landing on beaches sheltered by the dramatic red ochre bluffs, entering the grottoes, and sculpting by firelight figurines of the dark mother.

Nude women, the figurines are one to six inches tall with large breasts and hips. Pregnancy of many of the figures suggests the dark mother's generation of life. Ample breasts convey nurturance. Imagination is set to flight by featureless faces and pendulous breasts. Some male theorists find "sexual parts often exaggerated." Sites of these figurines of the dark mother on paths of prehistoric african migrants along the mediterranean littoral of Europe often became, in the historic epoch, sanctuaries of black madonnas.

Scholars of the Frauen Museum in Wiesbaden, Germany were among the first (in our time) to acknowledge that other woman divinities existed besides the european images studied by lithuanian archeologist Marija Gimbutas. Oya Kala Dao, the 1996 exhibit of this women's museum, exhibited global icons of the dark mother—of Africa, Asia, Europe, North and South America, and Oceania.

African origin of modern humans has been confirmed by geneticists, archeologists, and paleontologists. Among geneticists, three different groups working on mitochondrial DNA confirm the origin of humanity in Africa. L. Luca Cavalli-Forza, geneticist, has also documented that africans demonstrate maximum genetic differences among themselves, and exhibit the greatest heterogeneity of any human group, on any continent. "The population that has had the longest time to differentiate itself shows the most diversity."[12] Evidence of genetics suggests that our african ancestors are older than dates confirmed by archeology.[13] The harmony of ancient mother-centered civilization is shown in that in paleolithic Africa there was no division between sacred and profane and no division of self and other—the mother and her nurture of all life were one. The concept of the other seems to have emerged in Europe with invasions of indo-european speakers after 4300 BCE.[14]

Emmanuel Anati, italian archologist, thinking on the origin of modern humans in central and south Africa, whence they migrated all over the world 60,000-50,000 BCE, implicitly credits africans, the first modern humans, with the origins of world civilization. Primordial africans held the huge curiosity from which all knowledge stems, as well as the ability to create art, to express themselves with an articulated language, and the capacity for abstraction, synthesis, and conceptualization…bases of religion, reasoning, and philosophy.

The matristic nature of this original world civilization is suggested in Anati's finding that the color red ochre was pervasive in african cave and cliff drawings 60,000-50,000 BCE when africans carried this sign of the dark mother with them when they migrated to all continents.[15] In South Africa, very near a cave drawing sketched in red ochre, a footstep in the sand dated 115,000 BCE has been described as very possibly that of a woman "in the lineage of our hypothetical common ancestor."[16]

Africa south of the Sahara, where modern humans emerged, is the region of the world with the world's richest rock art. Red ochre is the predominant color of the cave art in the region between Tassili n'Ajjer and Tadrart Acacus (about 300 walls painted with 2700 figures). Figures dancing, singing, playing musical instruments, engaging in initiation rituals, with body decoration and masks, characterize the art of the entire heterogeneous african continent, according to archeologist Umberto Sansoni. Ancient art of africans south of the Sahara suggests that they venerated their ancestors, considered animals and all life sacred, and that they lived without violence. Ancient african art abounding with fantastic creatures evokes contemporary surrealist art, notably that of Marc Chagall.[17]

African migration to all continents is confirmed in DNA evidence, in rock art, and in similarity of body type of prehistoric figurines of Africa, Old Europe, and Asia. Steatopygy is the awkward word for this body type, "as among the Hottentots, Bushmen, and certain other south African peoples."[18] Skeletons (e.g., of an old woman and a young man kneeling, found in Liguria in northern Italy) are described by anthropologists as having "Negroid features." Prehistoric african skeletons in the Bardo museum in Africa and sicilian skeletons in the Museo Paolo Orsi at Syracuse, Sicily are similar.[19]

African cave paintings of animals dated 30,000 BCE are sketched in red ochre, charcoal, and hematite. Stunning in their grace and beauty, art historians consider that the artistic level of these ancient cave paintings has never since been equaled. Specialists in rock art adjudge techniques of paleolithic art to be very sophisticated: the head of a bison "is drawn on the curve of a rock and is turned to obtain a double effect of perspective. Shading is used to give shape to the figures, some of them staggered, one behind the other, to obtain greater perspective."[20]

Among evidence in Sicily of african migrants, is the 10,000 BCE painting in the Grotta dell'Addaura outside Palermo of men and animals in a ritual scene, considered the oldest cave scene of humans in Europe.[21] On the italian peninsula, paleolithic mother figurines, notably the "Venus" of Savignano, 26,000-18,000 BCE,[22] resemble other representations of the dark mother found along later african migration paths into Europe, at Laussel Dordogne, France (22,000-18,000 BCE); Lespugue Haut-Garonne, France (20,000-18,000 BCE); Willendorf, Austria (20,000-18,000 BCE); Dolni Vestonice, Czechoslovakia (20,000 BCE); and Petersfels, Germany, (14,000 BCE). These figurines of the dark mother mark african migration paths into Europe—first Sicily, then Italy, France, Austria, the former Czechoslovakia, and Germany. Hair of the figurine of Willendorf, Austria is arranged in cornrows, african style still used by african american women. Later african migrations are suggested in figurines of full-bodied neolithic mothers, including the Lady of Pazardzik in Central Bulgaria (4500 BCE), and the pregnant woman with a phallic head of Cernavoda, Romania (5000 BCE).

Independently, L Luca Cavalli-Sforza, geneticist, and Emmanuel Anati, archeologist, have confirmed Marija Gimbutas' finding that the civilization of Old Europe before 4000 BCE was harmonious, that beliefs evident in cave and cliff art circled a woman as the progenitor of life and metaphor of the fecundity of the earth, and that prehistoric peoples lived co-operatively without wars, fortresses, or slavery.[23] According to Gimbutas' thesis, (confirmed by L. Luca Cavalli-Sforza), after 4000 BCE violent warriors from the eurasian steppes overtook this peaceful mother-centered civilization. These indo-european speakers, called kurgans after their burial mounds, are also known as aryans.[24]

Scribes of dominant cultures, who have posited aryan, or indo-european, origin of western civilization, have ignored the probability that before the ice thawed, the peninsula of Asia that the greeks called Europe was probably contiguous in places with Africa, thereby facilitating primordial african migration into the region later called Europe. There is also evidence that africans sailed west to the new world. Ivan Van Sertima, in this hypothesis, has pointed to african figures in the olmec civilization of Mexico.[25] Westward migrations from eastern Asia to Europe have been continuous from prehistory to the present, accounting for the genetic composition (by continent) of contemporary europeans—65% asian and 35% african.[26]

Evidence of the african origin of world civilization mounts daily. In November 1999, african origin of the alphabet, hitherto credited to canaanites of west Asia, has been located in the desert west of the Nile. "Carved in the cliffs of soft stone, the writing, in a Semitic script with Egyptian influences, has been dated to between 1900 and 1800 B.C., two or three centuries earlier than previously recognized uses of a nascent alphabet. The first experiments with alphabet thus appeared to be the work of Semitic people living deep in Egypt, not in their homelands in the Syria-Palestine region, as had been thought."[27] This finding also converges with scholarship (discussed in chapter two) documenting complex (back and forth) migrations from Africa to west Asia and return migrations from west Asia to Africa.

The polycentric, or multiregionalist, thesis, that acknowledged african genesis but held that peoples developed differently in different areas of the earth, was early discounted by Cavalli-Sforza, who considers the evidence to be scant for polycentric or multiregional hypotheses. He points to Africa's peoples as the most diverse of the world.[28] At the beginning of the third millennium, both the neanderthal and polycentric theses (critical for theories of european origin) have been decisively refuted by world scientists. A requiem has also been sounded on the theory of multiregionalism—used in the past to defend the notion of a white race. In 2001 scientists hold that modern man evolved only once—in Africa. From Africa, ancestors of modern humans migrated all over the world, without mixing with older branches of humanity.

Rebecca Cann, professor of molecular anthropology of the University of Hawaii, wonders why the idea of separate races has held such power. Why did some scientists, as well as other scholars, resist DNA evidence attesting to african origins of all humanity? The DNA theory—which confirms inheritance through the mother—Cann concluded, was not palatable to some male scientists.[29]

In 2000, Cavalli-Sforza's *Genes, Peoples, and Language,*[30] affirms his belief in interdisciplinary research and acknowledges his passion to make known that scientific data has established that the main differences among humans are between individuals, not between populations, "or so-called 'races.'" Whatever differences exist, he argues, may be attributed to climate. Cavalli-Sforza also offers an answer to the question—if there was an african Eve, was there an african Adam?

Yes, the geneticist states, there was an african Adam, adding enigmatically, "but processes of paternal and maternal transmission took place independently." According to recent genetics research on the male Y-chromosome, which supplements work on the DNA, our primordial ancestors whom the public likes to call Adam and Eve both lived in Africa, although not necessarily in the same region. Both Eve and Adam were born about 144,000 years ago. A surprising finding emerged from research on the male Y-chromosome—in prehistory, women, conventionally regarded as sedentary, traveled greater distances than did men.

The new human tree, rooted in the male Y-chromosome as well as in DNA inheritance from the mother, corroborates earlier findings of genetics. First expansion from Africa was from east Africa to Asia, probably via Suez and the Red Sea. African migrations into west Asia continued along the south coast of Asia. Northeast Asia was probably reached from southeast and central Asia. From southeast Asia, expansion continued farther south to nearby New Guinea and Australia. Expansion into Europe was relatively late, beginning about 40,000 years ago, coming from east, west, and central Africa.[31]

It has taken a couple of decades for the matter of DNA inheritance through the mother to be acknowledged. Massive resistance existed among male scientists who frowned on discussion of the spiritual implications of goddess figurines. Now that due deference has been given to the Y-male chromosome, substantiating that there was an Adam as well as many Eves, male scientists, hitherto hostile to spiritual theorizing based on the DNA transmitted through the mother, are now discussing spiritual implications of the male Y-chromosome.

Edward O. Wilson, in an interview with the *Wall Street Journal,* vouchsafed that a new basis for spiritual values might be found, not "in the usual religious sources, " but in what he calls "the inspiring story of human origins and history." We need, states Wilson, "to create a new epic based on the origins of humanity....Homo sapiens have had one hell of a history! And I am speaking both of deep history...evolutionary, genetic history...and then, added on to that and interfacing with it, the cultural history recorded for the past 1,000 years or so."[32] Another male scientist, meditating on recent work on the male Y-chromosome, was moved to declare, "We are all Africans at the Y chromosome level and we are really all brothers."[33] Although the conclusion of scientists that "we are really all brothers" is good news, Wilson did not mention that everyone has an african black mother.

For an african american woman ethnographer, Necia Desiree Harkless, all of this is not news—our african origins, african migrations to all continents, and ancient and contemporary beliefs in the dark mother. These truths, states Harkless, are not yet appreciated by dominant world cultures, but they "will undoubtedly have a great impact on the twenty-first century."[34]

O

An image of the bird-headed african snake goddess in the orant position (arms upraised in celebration) dated 4,000 BCE, has been called an image of our creatrix. Angeleen Campra's doctoral study of Sophia has taught me that generatrix is the more appropriate term. The image is held in the Department of Egyptian Antiquities of the British Museum. Preceding this anthromorphic image were her signs—the color ochre red and the pubic V. Her characteristics are those of a bird and a snake, yet she is a woman, With legs firmly planted in the earth, her arms celebrate the universe, and her breasts offer nurturance to all life. Why hasn't she been acknowledged?

Slave traders, slaveholders, and imperialists (european, arab, and north american) enslaved Africa's peoples. African resources were stolen, african treasures sacked, icons and other art objects were looted and taken away. African traditions were appropriated, destroyed, distorted, or suppressed. What remains in Africa today is what could not be stolen: the memory of the dark mother in rock engravings, cave paintings, other art, and rituals.

Along with her early signs connoting generation of all life, african prehistoric art associates the dark mother with the earth's fruitfulness; she is depicted with corn showering down between cow's horns. Women are often depicted dancing. Men are painted running with antelopes, elephants, rhinoceroses, lions, and giraffes. In regions of the Hoggar, Tadrart Acacus, and above all in the Tassili, "we have some twelve thousand paintings done between the fifth and first millennia, which include the most beautiful renderings of the human form that prehistory can show."[35]

In the neolithic era, a black-topped red polished ware appeared in Nubia and elsewhere. "These vessels (nearly all open bowls) have a dark red exterior and a shiny black interior, the black extending also to the outside for half inch to an inch below the rim. The red was achieved by painting the surface with red ochre before firing, while the black seems to have been imparted by placing the vessel, directly after firing, rim downward, in a mass of densely smoking material such as leaves or straws."[36] This technique, characteristic of the pottery of northeastern Africa, was subsequently known as far away as India.[37]

During the millennium before Jesus, continuing into the first five hundred years thereafter, the major divinity of the mediterranean world appears to have been Isis of Africa, dark mother of many names. Great mother of the mediterranean, Isis inherited a long matristic tradition of Africa whose signs were the color red ochre and the pubic V, as well as spirals and circles, and human identification with animals. Scholarship since the 1960s has recovered what the ancients knew: Isis was an african deity, whose origins were in Nubia, or upper Egypt. Nubia, at the confluence of the Blue and White Niles, was an african region whose civilization flourished for "more than five hundred years before the building of the great pyramids of Egypt."[38]

In her sanctuary at Philae in Africa, Isis was black. Metaphor of the dark mother of humanity and precursor of black, as well as church-whitened, madonnas of christian Europe,[39] her civilization at Meroe, Nubia from 100 BCE to 400 CE conveys her values. Region of inner Africa best known to the ancients, it was called Ethiopia, a name given in antiquity to "all parts of Africa occupied by dark-skinned peoples." Egyptian artists utilized a "red-brown paint for the skin color of Egyptian men, yellow for Egyptian women, and a dark brown or black for all Nubians." Greeks and romans called Ethiopia (the area south of Egypt) the "Land of the Burnt faces, " and called the Sudan "Land of the Blacks."[40] Ethiopia today comprises Nubia.[41] Although nubians resemble other peoples of the Sudan, they are unique in speaking an ancient group of languages unrelated to the arabic of their neighbors.[42] Egypt built some of its massive monuments in Nubia, notably the great rock temples of Abu Simbel, but Nubia gave the dark mother Isis to Egypt, and the rest of the world.[43]

The little island of Philae in Nubia was known as "Holy Island," as well as "Interior of Heaven," and "City of Isis."[44] In the 1960s, William Y. Adams, leading nubiologist, anthropologist, archaeologist, and UNESCO expert, supervised the salvaging of Nile artifacts and treasures during the construction of the Aswan dam. Adams considers veneration of Isis to be "one of history's most important ideological transformations." Within the microcosm of Nile lands, worship of Isis became "the first truly international and supra-national religion, no longer claimed as the proprietary cult of any one ruler but sanctioned by and conferring its blessings upon several. Philae became a holy city and place of pilgrimage alike for all classes and all nationalities: Meroites, Egyptians, Greeks, Romans, and desert nomads."[45] Worship "of the age-old fertility goddess of Egypt," for Adams, anticipated the role of "Christianity and Islam on the larger stage of the Middle Ages."[46]

The city of Meroe, site of the kushite royal court, was the center of an empire "that included not only much of Nubia, but also regions far south of modern-day Khartoum. Meroitic culture was strongly connected to central African traditions although it made use of Egyptian styles, to which it added graeco-roman elements."[47] Study of nubian archeology and history has established the centrality of the dark mother Isis, who is considered to have exemplified african matrilineal traditions. "It was only through the royal women that Nubian rulers inherited the throne. All kings and queens had to be born to a queen, usually the ruler's sister."[48] The seamless fit between religion and daily life in Africa is suggested by the fact that an african woman, as priestess of the dark mother, was "Mistress of Heaven," as well as "Mistress of the House."[49]

Eyes of Isis inside tombs of egyptian pharaohs looked to eternity; e.g., that of Khnumnakht (100-100 BCE), whose sarcophagus is now in New York's Metropolian Museum of Art. Her eyes can be seen on the many amulets worn to this day by mediterranean peoples to ward off the "evil eye." The ubiquity of the belief in the "evil eye" may convey the wide-spread popular appeal of the dark mother, as well as patriarchal anxiety before the mother's riveting gaze.[50]

Veneration of Isis, according to R. E. Witt, spread from her center in Nubia to Afghanistan, the Black Sea, and Portugal, to northern England.[51] By the first century of the common era, one of her largest temples outside Africa was located in Rome, while others were located at Ostia and Pompeii. At Philae in Nubia, Isis is invoked: "Hail Queen, mother of god." At Ostia, outside Rome, Italy, she was celebrated on the 5th of March, when sailors returned to the sea, naming their boats and ships for her. Women of Rome, after immersing themselves in the icy Tiber, proceeded on their knees all along the river edge to the Pantheon, today a gathering place for feminists.

The image of Isis most popular at the height of the roman empire appears to have been that of Isis nursing her child, Horus. Besides queen of the sea, Isis was considered queen of heaven and of earth, and was easily transmuted into the christian holy mother. Legions of the roman empire, whose ranks were drawn from subordinated dark peoples of three continents, carried images of african Isis, as well as images of Isis melded together with west asian divinities Cybele, Inanna, and Astarte all over the known world, from Africa to Asia, to Rome, France, England, to the Danube[52]. At Benevento, where a great iseo flourished in the roman epoch, her followers were later called witches.[53]

In October 1999, when Wally and I visited the sanctuary of Isis at Philae, I remembered Lucius Apuleius' description. Roman citizen of Athens who studied at Carthage and lived in the interior of Morocco, Lucius said he was awakened by "all the perfumes of Arabia," when Isis appeared and said, "I am Nature, the universal Mother, mistress of all the elements, primordial child of time, sovereign of all things spiritual, queen of the dead, queen also of the immortals, the single manifestation of all gods and goddesses that are."

Worshipped by many names throughout Africa, Asia, and greek and roman empires, she was known as Isis, Hathor, Ma'at, Artemis, Demeter-Persephone, Hera, Mother of Corn, Juno, and Hecate. She was Lilith of west Asia and Kali of India. Hymns invoked her as "the one who rises and dispels darkness," solar ruler who "smites her enemy," whose radiance "fills the earth with gold-dust."[54]

The memory of the ancient african mother is recalled today in the poetry of Luisah Teish, african american poet and writer who traces her heritage to Egypt, which she calls the "mystical cradle of civilization" and finds Isis in yoruba goddess Yemonja, mother goddess who "nurtures us through the cycles of Life." She also finds Isis in yoruba's Oshun, goddess of love, art, and sensuality who "represents the Erotic in Nature." Africa, for Teish, is a continent where "deities walk among human beings and dance is worship." Acknowledging african diasporas, Teish finds reverence for the earth in african ibo beliefs and in native american "need to walk in balance." Teish' poems praise yoruba Yemonja as "mother of the night, the great dark depth, the bringer of light" who is related to Isis and Hathor. She considers the implications of the many manifestations of the dark mother: "The Horned Cow, the many-teated Sow, the queen bee, the Mothertree, the Pregnant Womb, the Grain-seed broom, the candle's wick, the matrix, and woman, you are my daughter."[55]

The civilization of the dark mother of Africa is glimpsed at Meroe in Nubia, region of upper Egypt in the area called Ethiopia. Egypt, despite eurocentric misconceptions aligning the country with the "Orient" or the "Near East,"[56] is an african country shaped by the Nile, river that carries african peoples and products back and forth along a north-south axis, particularly between Egypt and Nubia. In the ancient civilization of nubian Meroe, matrilineal succession was the custom, yet genders co-existed peacefully. Some queen mothers ruled alone, many ruled with husbands or sons. In mother-centered cultures of Africa, religions also co-existed peaceably. At Meroe, the religion of Isis honored the religion of the lion-headed god called Apedemek as well as that of Amun. Priests and priestesses of each religion shared in the political and economic administration of Meroe.

An egalitarian civilization that nurtured all life, Meroe was a noted center of learning and commerce that spread its prosperity to all peoples. Every day, in the temple called Table of the Sun dedicated to goddesses and gods, africans offered food and other life-sustaining goods. "Those in need could come at any time and take freely of the offerings."[57] This ancient african tradition, persisting over millennia, is recalled today in San Francisco in the vibrant community services of Rev. Cecil Williams of Glide Memorial Church.

The Table of the Sun at Meroe was the precursor of roman temples to Cerere (Ceres), grain goddess of Rome, where the poor would come for free wheat. This ultimately african celebration of wheat is kept to this day in Italy in mid-August at the christian festival of the assumption of the virgin into heaven. On August 15, 200,when we were in Sicily, we went to her festival at Gangi, in the mountains of northwest Sicily when many hundreds of emigrant workers come with their family on this date every year. We brought home a triple cluster of wheat from this festival, that celebrates pagan wheat goddesses, and put it on the front door of our Berkeley home.

In Rome, the temple of wheat goddess Ceres became the church of Santa Maria di Cosmedin, a church with a black madonna. In the early historic epoch, a sculpture that connotes roman male appropriation of Isis was placed at the entrance to this church. The legend of this sculpture (called Bocca della verità, or Mouth of truth) has it that the mouth of truth will bite the hand of anyone who tells a lie. Contemporary italian feminists, enacting the dark mother's legacy of truth and justice, have placed replicas of the Bocca della verità in theaters where people can deposit written denunciations of corrupt mafia chiefs and political officials.

Italian evidence of veneration of the african dark mother may be found in icons of Isis in the national museum at Naples, and icons at Pompeii,

Benevento, Palestrina, Aquileia, Verona, and in Rome. Much of the evidence of the widespread veneration of african Isis in the roman epoch was destroyed by the volcanic eruption that laid waste to Pompeii.[58] In 1997 the Isis exhibit at Milan documented the vast arc of veneration of Isis in late antiquity and early christianity, an arc that extended from Africa to Europe, to the Ukraine, to India.

After christianity was established in 323 CE, church fathers, aiming to obliterate pagan beliefs, destroyed Meroe in 450 CE. What was it they found so threatening in this african civilization that identified so strongly with nature, particularly the Nile? "Every year the land arose from the watery flood richer and more full of life; every year the migratory birds swooped down into the marshes for food and rest. A great order, ancient and ever renewing, sustained Egypt while nations rose and fell all around it...Nature worked patiently, bore richly, and sustained continually. The human order which grew out of that great original natural magic was as unique as its setting."[59]

This grounding in a constant and sustaining earth may help us understand why egyptians attained an extraordinary level of artistic, architectural, and moral excellence. "The 'gods' and 'goddesses' of Egypt literally sprang from the soil and the water of the river, and literally were one with the air and the creatures which flew through it, all interweaving into the phenomenon of the country itself." Everything, and every creature, was imbued with the force of life: "The hieroglyphic word for beetle means 'to be.' The beetle and sun are both analogs of the same force, not symbols." For the earth-bonded person, in Africa, Sicily, and elsewhere, "The name of the thing and the thing itself are the same."[60]

Earth-bonded theology is not ponderous. In one egyptian creation story, the creator Amun runs around honking after laying an egg. Africans, who regard their deities familiarly, call Amun the "Great Cackler." Similarly, africans attributed animal characteristics to humans, and human characteristics to animals, identifying divinity with animal and human forms.[61] Sometimes the goddess was a cow named Hathor, other times she was a woman with a Hathor headdress. Horus, son of Isis, could be a hawk, sometimes a man with a hawk's head, or a child in the arms of his mother.[62] Harmony between humans and animals characterized ancient Africa, as did harmony between men and women, a contentment visible in many depictions of embracing couples. Seeing life as a spiral, africans believed new life came from death.

Isis melded with Ma'at, african goddess whose name connotes mother,[63] and with Sekhmet, whose name means "powerful one." Ma'at had a feather on her head that signified justice. Many representations of Isis (as well as of Ma'at) have feathers. Feathers, an egyptian guide advised us, connote equality, since they are the same, back and front. When a person died, his or her heart, the seat of intelligence, would be weighed on a scale balanced by the feather of Ma'at. If the heart was not as light as the feather, the soul would be lost to Apet, the devourer.

Ma'at, or mother, embodied truth, ethics, justice, and righteous behavior.[64] Sekhmet, the fierce aspect of the african dark mother, was a woman with a lion's head. Hundreds of statues of Sekhmet were found in the temple of Mut in Karnak. Like Isis, Sekhmet originally carried a sun disk on her head and an ankh, signifying life, in her hand. The ankh is said to prefigure the christian cross, although the christian symbol has no female oval.[65]

African Isis melded with anatolian Cybele, sumerian Inanna, canaanite Astarte, and roman Diana. Isis'distinguishing images were a throne, a boat, sails, and the annual flooding of the Nile. Often depicted with outstretched wings, Isis harks back to the paleolithic bird and snake goddess of Africa. Attesting to african migrations' carrying african beliefs to all continents, a contemporary native american figurine is that of a venerated woman with wings. A 20th century sicilian artist depicted comari, women who bonded together in memory of the mother, sheltered by protective wings of Isis.

In antiquity, at Byblos in west Asia, african Isis was identified with the canaanite goddess Astarte. With hellenization, Isis became the great mother; her consort Osiris, or "the great black," became Zeus, Pluto, and Dionysus. The enduring truth of Isis, whose civilization centered in nubian Meroe, may be that she embodied veneration of all life…trees are sacred, so are birds, crocodiles, the dung beetle, the hooded cobra, and all living creatures.

R.E. Witt, historian, following the transformation of a "purely African faith into a world religion," points out that african veneration of Isis became greek, then graeco-roman"[66] as greek and roman empires swept through Africa, Europe, and Asia. After 332 BCE, when Alexander of Macedonia conquered Egypt, Alexandria in Africa became the capitol of an empire that stretched from the Nile to the Danube, city where africans, asians, europeans, jews, and greeks mingled, where Osiris became Aesculapius, or Serapis, healing god of Greece and Rome, and Isis, blending with anatolian Cybele, canaanite Astarte, and graeco-roman goddesses, became great mother of the Mediterranean.[67]

All over the known world in the first centuries of the common era, slaves and noble women venerated african Isis as a divinity who "prevailed through the force of love, pity, compassion, and her personal concern for sorrows."[68] Before christianity did so, the religion of Isis promised life after death. Isis centers have been found throughout the roman empire; in Gaul, Portugal, Spain, Britain, Germany, and Italy, particularly in places that later became sanctuaries of black madonnas (See chapter 4).

In Italy, Isis was a mother divinity associated with healing; the 6th century BCE temple to Isis at Pompeii is located next to a temple of Aesculapius, or Serapis.[69] A significant characteristic of Isis, one later associated with the christian madonna, was that she was a compassionate mother. In the christian epoch her son Horus was represented as a christ figure. Isis is often depicted with a laurel wreath and two prominent ears, symbolizing that she listened with both ears to the prayers of all those who came to her, an image that can be found to this day in italian folklore.

Water, always associated with Isis, held a sacred quality: holy water, holy rivers, and holy sea. The serpent, identified with Isis; was always sacred. Hathor, was associated with regeneration. The cow, another image of Isis, became sacred in India. Music, associated with Isis, was conveyed by the image of Isis carrying a sistrum, rattle still heard in african music today. Isis and wheat, in the roman epoch, became Ceres and wheat. In the christian epoch Isis became santa Lucia, whose images always carry a sheaf of wheat. The olive tree, associated with Isis, has today become symbol of nonviolent transformation. Italy's contemporary nonviolent left political coalition is named L'Ulivo, or the olive tree.[70]

Mistress of religion in Egypt, Isis was god the mother, yet in Isis there was no division between feminine and masculine. She was beloved by women and men, young and old, and all social classes. Her statue at Philae, created between the second and first centuries before Jesus, carries the sistrum in one hand and the ankh in the other. In her 600 BCE image in the Museum of Cairo, Isis is figured as a black nursing mother, who bears a startling resemblance to christian images of the nursing madonna.

Veneration of Isis, her spouse Osiris, and son Horus persisted in all the pharaonic dynasties, a 3,000 year old history when belief in Isis spread from Meroe and Alexandria to "the whole Mediterranean basin."[71] In Italy and other latin countries where the holy family is a focus of devotion, the trinity of Isis and her husband and child became the popular christian trinity of Maria, Joseph, and Jesus, popular trinity that differs from the motherless trinity—father, son, and holy ghost—of canonical christianity.

At african Memphis, hymns praised Isis as a civilizing, universal divinity who had ended cannibalism, instituted good laws, and given birth to agriculture, arts and letters, moral principle, good customs, and justice. Mistress of medicine, healer of human maladies, sovereign of earth and seas, protectress from navigational perils and war, Isis was "Dea della salvezza per eccellenza...veglia anche sulla morte," divinity of salvation par excellence, who also watches over the dead.[72]

The signal relevance of the dark mother Isis to our own time may be that she signifies nonviolent transformation. The cosmology and psychology of this value of nonviolence may be realized if we understand that in Isis, who gave "light to the sun," there was no division of female from male, and no separation of one female from another. Her sister Ma'at, with whom she melded, was goddess of truth. Isis and Ma'at epitomized order in nature, a principle carried forward by Pythagoras and his followers in the greek period, and by scientists thereafter. In the african civilization of Isis, human beings and social justice were joined. Each human was judged at death by Ma'at's feather of justice, and by the negative confession: "I have not committed iniquity.... I have not oppressed the poor.... I have not defaulted.... I have not caused the slave to be ill-treated.... I have not murdered.... I have not made any to weep.... I have not falsified the beam of the balance."[73] Values of the isiac negative confession suggest why, in the 20th century, Simone Weil held that hebrew scriptures were indebted to egyptian sacred writings.[74]

Isis was appropriated by Greece and Rome in cults of Hera, Demeter, Fortuna, Ceres, and Juno, and by christianity in cults of saints—notably Lucia (see chapter five). Roman emperors and christian fathers destroyed her temples, but the legacy of the african dark mother, despite attempted obliteration and suppression, has persisted in art. The memory may be glimpsed in Picasso's *Les Demoiselles d'Avignon*, african in appearance, who bear a startling resemblance to Isis and to the many black madonnas in this region of France (See chapter four).[75]

For Jean Leclant, egyptologist at the Academy of France, "Isis, mother of Horus, triumphant, but at the same time broken-hearted, prefigures the Madonna col Bambino of the christian religion."[76] Black madonnas of Europe, and other dark female divinities of the world, may be the most tangible evidence we have of the deep and persistent memory of the african dark mother. Her continuing legacy is marked by passionate identification with the oppressed and with values of justice with compassion, equality, and transformation. In the christian epoch, Isis' temple at Pompeii was succeeded by many sanctuaries of black madonnas. At Pomigliano dell'Arco, rituals venerating the black madonna are fervent. At Montevergine, suggesting how her icons carry the history of the subaltern, the black madonna is called black slave mother. At Foggia, where peasant communists would come in pilgrimage to her, the black image is called l'Immacolata.[77] Black madonnas may be found throughout Italy, as documented in my book, *Black Madonnas,* and throughout the world, as illustrations in this book suggest.

In Sicily, on first migration paths from Africa, the memory of Isis is everywhere. Dozens of icons of Isis along with Bastet, her cat familiar, may be seen in sicilian museums. At carnival time, throughout the christian epoch to the present, figures of Isis and her cat express the laughter of subaltern peoples at church and state.

In Africa in the fifth century of the common era, nubians and their neighbors took up arms to prevent forced dedication to christianity of temples of Isis at Philae. Yet by the middle of the sixth century, byzantine emperors had imposed a patriarchal version of christianity as state religion on Nubia. When, less than a century later, islamic invaders took Egypt, nubians resisted but finally negotiated a treaty in which they kept christianity and political sovereignty. In the 15th century when Nubia fell to arab nomads, islam became the state religion. Yet, in Africa, underneath patriarchal religions of christianity and islam, the memory persists to this day of the ancient dark mother.[78]

Glimpsed in daily and festival rituals, the memory may be closer to bodily resonance than to cognitive remembrance. The memory has persisted in Africa in contemporary rituals, as well as in rituals in all lands reached by african migrants, which is to say all continents of the world. Victor Turner, in fieldwork among the ndembu, a mother-centered culture of northwest Zambia, describes a girls' puberty ritual when a young woman is separated from her mother and her childhood dies. The ritual is enacted under a milk tree that exudes milky white latex. Echoes of this ritual of the separation of mother and daughter may be found in many of the world's myths, notably the myth of Demetra and Proserpina. For the ndembu, the milk tree is said to be, not symbolize, milk, lactation, breasts, and nubility. It is also the place "where the ancestress slept," where the novice's grandmother, mother, and all ndembu women, were initiated into womanhood, and where the tribe began. For the ndembu, the milk tree is the principle of matrilineage, mother-centeredness, and is the whole ndembu nation.

The memory of the dark mother also persists in contemporary african popular beliefs. For the yoruba of Africa, the spiral, sign of the mother, determines life. Everything is constantly moving in a spiraling motion. "The whole life span of a man or a woman is a journey. That is our belief....All movements are journeys. We are progressing, we are moving."[79] In this movement, yoruba women have a strong sense of their own power, enabling them to accommodate to male insecurities. For example, two wives wrap the hair of a transvestite priest of Agemo in female style.[80] Yoruba women are economically independent, and become dramatically so when they reach menopause, or when they become grandmothers, at which time they declare independence from domestic work

The civilization of Isis has bequeathed to contemporary africans, and to other earth-bonded peoples, a "high degree of tolerance towards the gods and the religious practices of those they encountered." It has been common practice in Africa simply to incorporate the gods of others into their own pantheon "with an all-inclusiveness that saw all deities as one more manifestation of the same overarching principle."[81]

O

What are the implications of the ancient african dark mother for contemporary feminist theology? Today, western feminist theologians are venturing near to what has been the suppressed subject of the african dark mother. Delores Williams, african american womanist theologian, considers Hagar, dark mother of Ishmael sent into the desert by Abraham and Sarah, to be protected by god, and the most significant biblical figure for african american women. For Williams, patriarchy is an inadequate concept because "it is silent about white men and white women working together to maintain white supremacy and white privilege."[82] Williams' womanist theology is informed by "concern for poor black women, children and men immersed in a fierce struggle for physical, spiritual and emotional survival and for positive quality of life formation...."[83] In Williams' theology, Hagar is the figure who embodies the mothering, nurturing, caring, enduring, resisting capacities that form the center of african american women's spirituality.[84]

Ada Maria Isasi-Diaz, latina, has written a mujerista theology that bypasses the term feminist, which she considers to have white middle class connotations. A cuban in exile in the United States, Isasi-Diaz is concerned about racism and ethnic prejudice; her mujerista perspective emphasizes everyday life, love of neighbor, and justice.

A sicilian/american woman, I resonate with africana and latina theologians who stress the importance of everyday religious beliefs and rituals in challenging injustice.[85] Married to a jew (our sons consider themselves jews), I relate to feminist redactions of judaism, particularly that of Asphodel P. Long, british feminist who was brought up an orthodox jew. Long regards her work as a midrash, or commentary, on Hochma and on Asherah, "divine principles in the Hebrew religion and in later Judaism."[86] Drawn to the "divine female figure of Wisdom, called Hochma in Hebrew and Sophia in Greek, who pervades Hebrew and Christian scriptures,"[87] she departs from conventional judaism wherein the figure of Wisdom is identified with the torah. She also differs from christianity wherein the female figure called Wisdom "became part of the male Jesus and thence the Church, while for many other Christians she became an aspect of the Virgin Mary."[88]

Long points to the frequency with which representatives of jewish orthodoxy railed against popular practices, considering this evidence that everyday jewish beliefs differed from official jewish doctrines. "What is called the popular religion continued to be widespread, no matter how stringent the persecution against its participants."[89] Official judaism demonized the "Hebrew goddess," as Raphael Patai calls her, but she was never, apparently, obliterated in jewish popular culture.[90] An extraordinary number of african and west asian dark mother images have been excavated in Israel.[91]

Christian theologian, Elisabeth Schussler Fiorenza, who uncovers biblical texts to find the hidden woman of hebrew and christian scriptures, considers that "By naming Jesus as the child of Miriam and the prophet of Divine Sophia, I seek to create a 'women' defined feminist theoretical space that makes it possible to dislodge christological discourses from their malestream frame of reference."[92] Sophia's children, according to Fiorenza, included John the Baptist as well as Jesus; both were "emissaries of Divine Wisdom," and both were killed.

Critical of conservative political forces that use religion as a cover for their own economic interests, as well as of right wing religious movements around the world who reject progressive social measures and human rights for women, Schussler Fiorenza regards her role as that of a "trouble-maker." Reflecting on the patriarchal dogma that women must be submissive, Fiorenza points out that subordination of women originated, not in christianity, but in the vaunted greek city state where one could exercise democracy only if one were "free born, propertied, educated and a male head of household, excluding all others."[93] Catholicism and protestantism, for Schussler Fiorenza, are equally patriarchal, but the protestant reformation, by eliminating women religious figures, deepened the patriarchalization of theology.[94] Although an iconoclast, Fiorenza does not venture into the controversial area of religion before judaism and christianity. She refers to, but does not discuss, the theological implications of a "black divine woman" found in egyptian wisdom literature.[95]

This study may be regarded as part of the enterprise in which Delores Williams, Ada Isasi-Diaz, Asphodel Long, and Elisabeth Schussler Fiorenza are engaged. With considerable respect for everyday judaism, christianity, islam, and buddhism, it seems to me that the next step toward religious understanding, and a just world, is to bring the dark mother of prehistory and popular history to consciousness and to public knowledge. We need to bring her to consciousness in light of genetic and archeological evidence that verifies that all of us descend from an african dark mother, that we are all peoples of colors of many tribes, many climates, and many diasporas. Knowledge of african origins may help dispel bigotries grounded on ignorance which may be our largest obstacle to social justice. In our violent time, we need to bring the dark mother to consciousness because she connotes justice with compassion.

Acknowledging the dark african mother who preceded patriarchal world religions does not, to this sicilian/american woman, seem all that iconoclastic.[96] It may be a matter of how we think. Erik Hornung, egyptologist of the University at Basel, refers to the complementarity of egyptian logic, which resembles complementarity in physics. "For the Egyptians two times two is always four, never anything else. But the sky is a number of things— - cow, baldachin, water, woman— it is the goddess Nut and the goddess Hathor, and in syncretism a deity a is at the same time another, not-a."[97] For Hornung, "the nature of a god becomes accessible though a 'multiplicity of approaches,' [and] only when these are taken together can the whole be comprehended."[98] Sicilians, as Justin Vitiello reminds us, know this intuitively.[99] So do artists, craftsmen, poets, and peasants of the world. In the 1970's, when I began to research my italian godmothers/grandmothers, I came across a tile with a blue-black star with thirty-two points in a blue green sea. The tile was named Iside, italian for Isis.

Necia Desiree Harkless, ethnographer of Nubia, Meroe, Kush, and Nigeria, and authority on the sacred art of north Africa, may have caught the a central meaning of our african dark mother in her poem, *Evolution*

Ageless I stepped out of the sky
Touched down into the sea
Saw my image/ In the reflection of the Sun....
Built temples and streets emblazoned
With my totem from Tyre to Timbuctoo
Ageless I spun back into the sky
Touched the moon dust and proclaimed
We are One![100]

Notes

1   A good bibliography of african history may be found in Philip Curtin, Steven Feierman, Leonard Thompson, and Jan Vansina, *African History. From earliest times to independence.* 2nd edition. (London and New York, Longman, 1995). Cheikh Anta Diop's masterpiece is *Civilization or Barbarism. An Authentic Anthropology* (Paris, Presence Africaine, 1981; Brooklyn, N. Y., Lawrence Hill Books, 1991).

2   See for example the large agreement among papers presented by scholars from Italy, Germany, Spain, Sweden, Austria, U.S.A., France, Greece, Namibia, and Morocco at "Arte preistorica e tribale. Decifrare le immagini," the XVII Valcamonica Symposium, September 21 to 26 1999 Darfo Boario Terme, Italia, My paper for the symposium, "Converging Interpretations of Prehistoric Signs for Woman," formed the basis of the first two chapters of this book. African origin of world civilization remains a controversial topic for many europeans, and more americans. The taboo was visible at the Milan conference "Le radici prime dell'Europa. Stratificazione, processi diffusivi, scontri e incontri di culture," Banca Popolare di Milano, October 27,28, 1999. Organizers of this conference on the roots of Europe did not invite one african, or african-american, scholar to participate.

3   L. Luca Cavalli-Sforza, *History and Geography of Human Genes* (Princeton, N.J., Princeton University Press, 1993). See also Louise Levathes, "A Geneticist Maps Ancient Migrations," *New York Times, Science Times*, July 27, 1993.

4   John Noble Wilford, "Bones in China Casting New Light on Human Ancestors," *The New York Times,* November 16, 1995.

5   *History and Geography,* Loc. Cit. Chapter 2. Genetic History of World Populations, 60-64.

6   Luca e Francesco Cavalli-Sforza, *Chi Siamo. La storia della diversità umana* (Milano, Arnoldo Mondadori, 1993), 38.

7   Ibid., Chapter II.

8   "Archaeology," *Encyclopedia Britannica Year Book*, 1997.

9   Lucia Chiavola Birnbaum, *Black Madonnas. Feminism, religion, and politics in Italy* (Boston, Northeastern University Press, 1993; iUniverse edition, 2000), 8.

10   Louise Levathes, "A Geneticist Maps..." Loc. Cit..

11   Conversation with author, 1994.

12   Cavalli-Sforza, *Chi Siamo*, Loc. Cit., 107.

13   Ibid., 104-5

14   See also Morris Berman, *Coming to our senses. Body and spirit in the hidden history of the west* (New York, Simon and Schuster, 1989).

15   Emmanuel Anati, *Il Museo Immaginario della Preistoria. L'arte Rupestre nel Mundo* (Milano, Editoriale Jaca Book SpA, 1995), 217-218.

16   "Tracking the First of Our Kind," *National Geographic*, September 1997, 95. Paul G. Bahn and Jean Vertut, *Journey though the Ice Age* (Berkeley and Los Angeles, University of California Press, 1988, 1997).

17   See Umberto Sansoni, *Le Piu' Antiche pitture del Sahara. L'Arte delle Teste Rotonde*. Prefazione di Emmanuel Anati (Milano, Jaca Book, spa, 1994).

18   *Webster's Encyclopedic Unabridged Dictionary of the English Language* (New York, Gramercy Books, 1989).

19   See Lucia Chiavola Birnbaum, "The Long History of Sicilians," Loc. Cit.

20   "Dawn of Art: A New View," *The New York Times*, June 8, 1995.

21   See L. Luca Cavalli-Sforza, *History*, Loc. Cit. Also Birnbaum, *Black Madonnas*. Loc. Cit.

22   A good analysis of paleolithic goddesses can be found in Anne Baring and Jules Cashford, *The Myth of the Goddess. Evolution of an Image* (Arkana Penguin, London, 1991, 1993). See Chapter 1, "In the Beginning: The Paleolithic Mother Goddess." The authors do not acknowledge african origin of paleolithic goddesses of Old Europe.

23   See Marija Gimbutas, *The Civilization of the Goddess*, ed., Joan Marler (HarperSanFrancisco, 1991). Also, *The Language of the Goddess* (HarperSan Francisco, 1989). Elinor W. Gadon, *The Once and Future Goddess. A symbol for our time* (HarperSanFrancisco, 1989). Gimbutas made an enormous contribution to feminist cultural history, but she did not acknowledge african origins of the goddess. Her work on invasions of aryan speakers has been

corroborated by Luca Cavalli-Sforza, Ph.D., "Genetic Evidence Supporting Marija Gimbutas' Work on the Origins of Indo-European People," *From the Realm of the Ancestors. An Anthology in Honor of Marija Gimbutas* (Manchester, Ct., Knowledge, Ideas & Trends, Inc., 1997. See also, Emmanuel Anati, *Il Museo Immaginario della Preistoria. L'arte rupestre nel mondo* (Milano, Editoriale Jaca Book, SpA, 1995), 13, 186 - 235, passim.

24   For a good analysis of the aryan conquest and replacement of earlier mother-centered cultures with sky gods, slavery, and subordination of women, see Riane Eisler, *Sacred Pleasure. Sex, myth, and the politics of the body. New paths to power and love* (HarperSanFrancisco, 1995), 88 ff. The standard study is J. P. Mallory, *In Search of the Indo-Europeans. Language, Archaeology and Myth* (London, Thames and Hudson, 1989).

25   See Ivan Van Sertima, *They Came Before Columbus. The African Presence in Ancient* America (New York, Random House, 1976). Also, Cheikh Anta Diop, *Civilization or Barbarism. An Authentic Anthropology* (Presence africaine, Paris, 1981); *The African Origin of Civilization Myth or Reality.* Edited and translated by Mercer Cook (Chicago, Ill, Lawrence Hill Books, 1974). Also, Basil Davidson, *African Civilization Revisited. From Antiquity to Modern Times* (Trenton, N. J., Africa World Press, Inc.,1991).

26   See Cavalli-Sforza, *Human Diasporas* (Addison-Wesley, 1995). Levathes, "A Geneticist Maps Ancient Migrations, " Loc Cit.

27   John Noble Wilford, "Finds in Egypt Date Alphabet in Earlier Era," *The New York Times,* Nov. 1, 1999.

28   L. Luca Cavalli Sforza, *Chi Siamo.* Loc Cit. 103.

29   See "La Riscossa dell'Eva Africana," *il manifesto*, giovedi, 30 marzo 2000. Gianfranco Biondi e Olga Rickards. Also, same issue, Rebecca Cann, "la madre della nostra madre," *Paleologia,* Loc. Cit. See also,"The Human Family Tree: 10 Adams and 18 Eves. Tracing Human History through Genetic Mutations,"*Science Times, The New York Times,* Tuesday, May 2, 2000. The Y-chromosome, male counterpart of the DNA (inherited solely through the mother), has been incorporated into a human family tree by Dr. Douglas C. Wallace and colleagues of Emory University, School of Medicine in Atlanta.

30   Chapter 3, "Of Adam and Eve," Luigi Luca Cavalli-Sforza, *Genes, Peoples, and Languages,* Loc. Cit

31   Ibid., 90-91.

32   Ibid., See also, "Human Family Tree: 10 Adams and 18 Eves" Loc. Cit.

33   Ibid.

34   Necia Harkless Harkless, *Poems & Heart Images* (Lexington, Kentucky, Heart to Heart Associates, 1995). Passim.

35   Burchard Brentjes, *African Rock Art,* Tr. Anthony Dent (New York, Clarkson N. Potter, Inc. Publisher, 1965), . 71.

36   William Y. Adams, "Ceramics," *Africa in Antiquity,* Loc. Cit., 127. The priority of africans in making tools was underlined in the recent discovery of a 2.3 million year old "tool factory" in Kenya. See "Ancient tool 'factory' linked to pre-humans," *The Vancouver Sun,* May 6, 1999.

37   Ibid.

38   See "Foreword," by Michael Botwinick, *Africa in Antiquity. The Arts of Ancient Nubia and the Sudan* (New York, The Brooklyn Museum, 1978). See Jocelyn Gohary, *Guide to the Nubian Monuments on Lake Nasser* (The American University in Cairo Press, 1998). See page 14 for Meroe, where women held high status. On our 1999 visit to Nubia in Upper Egypt, we noted that in the small temple to the queen at Abu Simbel, she is of equal stature with the king. She wears the Hathor head dress of cow horns surmounted by a sun disk with the two plumes (connoting equality), and holds the sistrum against her breast.

39   See Lucia Chiavola Birnbaum, *Black Madonnas.,* Loc. Cit.

40   Ibid. 13.

41   William Y. Adams, "Geography and Population of the Nile Valley," *Africa in Antiquity,* Loc. Cit. 17.

42   Ibid. 20.

43   See "Goddesses," in *Mistress of the House. Mistress of Heaven. Women in Ancient Egypt,* ed., Anne K. Capel and Glenn Markoe (New York, Hudson Hills Press in association with Cincinnati Art Museum, 1996). 121 ff.

44   See John H. Taylor, *Egypt and Nubia* (London, The British Museum Press, 1991).

45   William Y. Adams, *Nubia,* Loc. Cit., 338.

46   Ibid.

47   Ibid. 23.

48   Ibid. 25.

49   Mistress of the House. *Mistress of Heaven.* Loc. Cit. 9

50   See Lawrence DiStasi, *Mal'Occhio. The Underside of Vision* (Berkeley, Ca., North Point Press, 1981.

51   R. E. Witt, *Isis in the Ancient World. Aspects of Greek and Roman Life* (Ithaca, New York, Cornell University Press, 1971;Baltimore, Md., Johns Hopkins University Press paperback, 1997). For the higher respect given to women in ancient Egypt than to women in the high culture of Greece, see Gay Robins, *Women in Ancient Egypt* (Cambridge, Ma., Harvard University Press, 1993).

52   *The British Museum Book of Ancient Egypt,* edited by Stephen Quirke and Jeffrey Spencer (London, British Museum Press, 1992). 196.

53   "Guardate bene Iside sembra una Madonna," *La Curiosità, la Repubblica,* 29 agosto 2000.

54   Lucius Apuleius, *The Golden Ass.* A new translation by Robert Graves, (New York, Farrar, Straus & Giroux, 1951). 264-266.

55   See Luisah Teish, *Carnival of the Spirit. Season Celebrations and Rites of Passage* (HarperSanFrancisco, 1994), Introduction, 22. Also, Drewal Thompson, *Yoruba Ritual. Performers, Play, Agency* (Bloomington, Indiana, Indiana University Press, 1992) 22.

56   See Edward W. Said, *Orientalism.* (New York, Vintage Books, 1979).

57   D. Jean Collins, "The Message of Meroe," *Gnosis Magazine,* Spring 1990. No. 15.

58   Stefania Adamo Muscettola, "La decorazione architettonica e l'arredo," Soprintendenza Archeologica per le Province di Napoli e Caserta, *Alla ricerca di Iside. Analisi, studi e restauri dell'Iseo pompeiano nel Museo di Napoli* (Napoli, Museo Archeologico Nazionale di Napoli, 1992).

59   Michael Crisp, "The Spirit of Egypt," *Gnosis Magazine,* Spring 1990. No. 15.

60   Ibid.

61   See "Votive Figurines," *Egyptian Art in Munich,* edited by Sylvia Schoske (Munchen, Staatliche Sammlung Agyptischer Kunst Muchen, 1993), 4

62   Ibid.

63 "Figure of the goddess Mut," *Egyptian Art in Munich* (Loc. Cit.) 52.

64 Ibid.

65 "Standing statue of Sakhmet,"Ibid., Loc. Cit. 38.

66 E. E. Witt, *Isis in the Graeco-Roman world. Aspects of Greek and Roman life.* Loc. Cit. Also, *Alla ricerca di Iside. Analisi, studi e restauri dell'Iseo pompeiano nel Museo di Napoli* (Roma, Arti S.p.A., 1992).

67 Witt, *Isis,* p. 69. Although Witt echoes some eurocentric notions ("Our western World's Graeco-Roman and Christian civilization has emerged and taken shape out of the cultural melting pot of the Near East."), he presents a great deal of evidence for the theme of this book that Africa was the origin of modern humans whose demic migrations left a significant african legacy to world civilization; e.g., "From Memphis and Alexandria the cult of Isis and her Temple Associates shed an incalculable influence on other rival faiths, including even Christianity." (preface).

Witt, a lecturer in Classics at Queen Mary College, University of London, where he specializes in greek and roman religion, has written an indispensable book, first published in 1971, for the education of contemporary classicists and others who denounce "afro-centrism." A Witt sampling: "Egypt for its inhabitants was the Black Land." (14). "Throughout the 4,000 years of Egyptian history every Pharoah was the incarnation of the youthful Horus, and therefore was the son of Isis, the Goddess Mother who had suckled and reared him." (15). "Herodotus, [who] had earlier stayed in Egypt and had written about its religion ...concluded that its gods had been appropriated by the cities of Greece." (16). "Later antiquity could think of Isis as the Egyptian soil which the Nile commingles with and fructifies." (19). "Already in the Ptolemaic age she was known at Philae as Isis of the Innumerable Names. Now, however, she was identified with all the purely anthropomorphic goddesses of the Graeco-Roman Pantheon...Demeter and her daughter Persephone...Pallas Athena...Aphrodite and Venus...Hera...Artemis...Wisdom (Sophia)...." (20). "In Italy itself the Egyptian faith was a dominant force. At Pompeii, as the archaeological evidence reveals...Isis played a major role. In the capitol, temples were built in her honor...obelisks were set up, and emperors bowed to her name. Harbours of Isis were to be found on the Arabian Gulf and the Black Sea. Inscriptions show that she found faithful followers in Gaul and Spain, in Pannonia and Germany. She held sway from Arabia and Asia Minor in the east to Portugal and Britain in the west and shrines were hallowed to her in cities large and small...Beneventum, the Piraeus, London." (21). "The friend of slaves and sinners, of the artisans and the downtrodden, at the same time she heard the prayers of the wealthy...." (23). "The cult of Isis had its cradle in north-east Africa, in Egypt and Ethiopia." (23).

"To understand ancient Egyptian religion at all, and especially the religion of Isis, we must recognize the sacredness of life in all its forms for the whole Nile civilization." (25) "...the cult of animals doubtless followed after the worship of sacred tree...." (26). "Animals were generally symbols of divinity." (28). "...the ankh...a case of an Isiac symbol prefiguring a characteristically Christian token, the cross." (32). "Throughout the long history of Egyptian religion Isis and her brother-husband remained complementary deities." (36). "...Byblos in Phoenicia...where Egyptian antiquities have been unearthed was a point of economic and religious contact between Phoenicia and the Nile country. It was there that Osiris was assimilated to Adonis (Thammuz) and Isis herself into Astarte (Istar, Ashtaroth)." (43) "...rites of Dionysus and Demeter bore the closest resemblance to those of Osiris and Isis." (67). "...in the Cyclades Isis was blended with Artemis..." (68). "But Isis on Delos is even more than an Egyptian turned Greek. For besides her identification with Aphrodite, Tyche, Nike, Hygieia...and Artemis, she is also invoked as Astarte of Phoenicia, as the Mother of the gods, and as the Great Mother." (68-69). "The obelisks formerly belonging to the Iseum Campestre are now in the Squares called Pantheon, Dogali, Minerva, and Navona [in Rome]." (87). Among the holy servants of Isis, "The Synod of the Wearers of Black...paid particular devotion to Isis as 'the black-robed queen." (97). "Isis and her companion gods from Egypt gained a foothold in Italian cities by a readiness to take a comparatively low rank...friend of the masses...her home hard by the business and trading center dear to the common man." (136-137)

"Herodotus states that the first people to institute festivals, processions, and religious presentations were the Egyptians...'and the Greeks have got their knowledge from them.'" (165). "Isis was an insidiously dangerous foe for Christian theologians because she was believed to give her worshippers their daily bread." (180). "The ritual of the Christian Church owes a considerable and unacknowledged debt to the Egyptian religion that preceded it in the Graeco-

Roman world." (184). "In the theology and art of Gnosticism Horus and Christ could easily be blended." (218). "In the middle of the first century AD Isiacism, far from being dead, was in the ascendant." (259).

"The evidence is unimpeachable that the places where Paul preached culti-vated the faith of Isis." (261). "Augustine...remarks that no idolatry is more pro-found and more superstitious than that of Egypt." (262). "...agape is a cult name for Isis, who in Egyptian tradition as old as the Pyramid Texts personifies tender-ness, compassion and divine love." (266) "Clearly the Pauline view of Isiacism was penetratingly critical. Paul's world was a patriarchy, his religion was Christological and monotheistic, and God was found in fashion as a man. Isis was female, Isis was the champion of idolatry, and Isis was the lover of the Nile menagerie. And yet the Pauline and the Isiac faith had at least one common char-acteristic. Each swept aside racial and social distinctions. 'There is neither Greek nor Jew.... Barbarian, Scythian, bond nor free: but Christ is all, and in all.' Change Christ to Isis...and the words are still true." (268). "Giordano Bruno...was convinced that the wisdom and magic-born religion of ancient Egypt excelled the fanatical theology that burnt dissident thinkers as heretics....the unfrocked monk, perished on 1 February 1600 for his intransi-gent denial that Christianity was unique." (269)

68   *Egyptian Art in Munich*, Loc. Cit., 60.

69   Superintendenza Archeologica per le Province di Napoli e Caserta, *Alla ricerca di Iside. Analisi,* Loc. Cit., 7.

70   Ibid., 16

71   "Iside. Mito Mistero Magia," *Archeologia Viva*, marzo-april 3 1997.

72   Ibid., 43.

73   Quoted in Asphodel P. Long, *In a Chariot Drawn by Lions. The Search for the Female in Deity* (Freedom, Ca., Crossing Press, 1993), 85. See also David Kinsley, *Hindu Goddesses. Visions of the Divine Feminine in the Hindu Religious Tradition* (Berkeley, Los Angeles, London, University of California Press, 1968).

74   For Weil, see chapter two, this work.

75   See Ladislas Segy, *African Sculpture Speaks.* 4th edition, enlarged (New York, Da Capo Press, Inc., a subsidiary of Plenum Publishing Corporation, 1969, 1975), 7.

76   "Iside in Mostra a Milano. Un'inedita rassegna a Palazzo Reale," *Archeologia Viva*, marzo-april 1997. In the hostile protestant environment of the United States, it is remarkable that memory of Isis can be found at all; one significant source for the memory in the United States is Hilda Doolittle's (H.D.) *Helen in Egypt*. I am indebted to Clare Fischer for presenting this theme to our women's group.

77   See Birnbaum, *Black Madonnas.*, Loc. Cit.

78   *The British Museum Book of Ancient Egypt*, Loc. Cit. For Egyptian interchange with sub-Saharan Nubia, see 39-4l, 202-19.

79   See Mercy Amba Oduyoye, *Daughters of Anowa. African Women & Patriarchy* (Maryknoll, N. Y., Orbis Books, 1995). 32.

80   Thompson, Loc. Cit. See 72, 130.

81   See Anna Joyce, "Dark Mother as Symbol of Resistance in Haiti. A Historical Overview," term paper for class, Dark Mother, California Institute of Integral Studies, Spring, 2000.

82   Delores S. Williams, *Sisters in the Wilderness. The Challenge of Womanist God-Talk* (Maryknoll, New York, Orbis Books, 1994). See 185 ff.

83   Ibid. 196.

84   Ibid. 235.

85   Ada Maria Isasi-Diaz, *Mujerista Theology. A Theology for the Twenty-first Century* (Orbis Books, 1996).

86   Asphodel Long, *In a Chariot Drawn by Lions. The Search for the Female in Deity* (Freedom, Ca., The Crossing Press, 1993). 15

87   Ibid. 14, 15,

88   Ibid. 16

89   Ibid. 131

90   Ibid. chapter 9.

91   Amihai Mazar, *Archaeology of the Land of the Bible. 1,000-586 B.C.E.* Center for Judaic-Christian Studies (New York, et al., Doubleday, 1992). See 77-78, passim.

92   Elisabeth Schussler Fiorenza, *Jesus. Miriam's Child. Sophia's Prophet. Critical Issues in Feminist Christology* (New York, Continuum, 1994). 3,8.

93   Ibid.

94   Ibid. 168.

95   Ibid. 162.

96   Luigi L. Cavalli-Sforza, Paolo Menozzi, and Alberto Piazza, "Demic Expansions and Human Evolution," *Science,* 29 January 1993, Volume 259, 639-646.

97   Erik Hornung, *Conception of God in Ancient Egypt. The One and the Many.* Translated from the German by John Baines (Ithaca, New York, Cornell University Press, 171). 241.

98   Ibid. 252.

99   See Justin Vitiello, *Poetics and Literature of the Sicilian Diaspora. Studies in Oral History and Story-Telling* (San Francisco, Mellen Research University Press, 1993).

100   Necia Desiree Harkless, *Poems and Heart Images*, Loc. Cit., "Evolution."

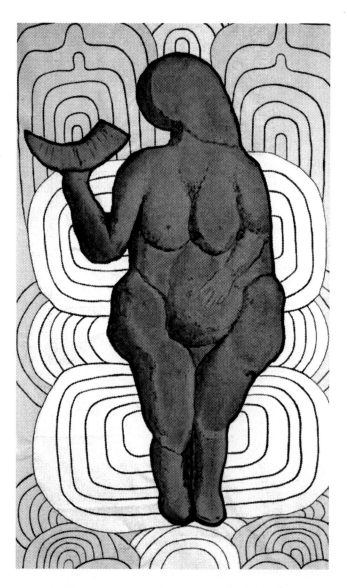

2. Venus of Laussel, France. 25,000 BCE
Banner by Lydia Ruhle

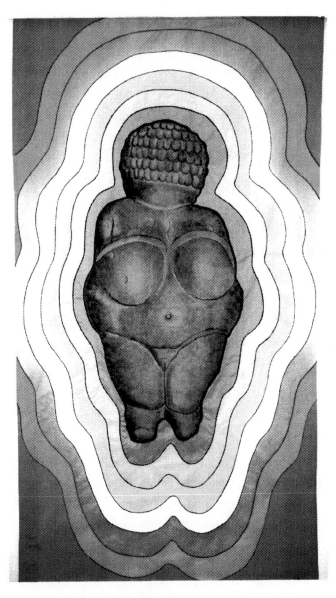

3. Venus of Willendorf, Austria. 25,000 BCE
Banner by Lydia Ruhle

4. Siberian dark mother 20,000 BCE

Banner by Lydia Ruhle

5. Pubic figures, 10,000 BCE, Cava del Genovese

Egadi Islands, Sicily

Photograph by Wallace Birnbaum

6. Isis and Horus
Bazaar, Cairo, Egypt
Photograph by Wallace Birnbaum

7. Ashanti dark mother
Photograph by Wallace Birnbaum

chapter two

migrations from Africa
Har Karkom in the Sinai peninsula—
Sicily and Malta in the
Mediterranean—Canaan in west Asia

This chapter explores three cases of african migrations to all continents after 50,000 BCE, cases meant to stimulate readers to track their own origins and diasporas. The first case is Har Karkom in the Sinai peninsula of west Asia, where in 40,000 BCE african migrants created the "oldest sanctuary in the world," a case with large import for the origin of world religions.

The second case refers to Sicily and Malta, mediterranean islands that reveal the complexity of african migrations. For example, africans reached Sicily at a date probably earlier than 50,000 BCE when they migrated everywhere. African in inheritance, sicilians migrated to Malta ca. 5200 BCE. According to the accepted view, descendants of these sicilian migrants created after 3800 BCE the impressive megalith civilization of Malta, a civilization centered on a sacred woman. The accepted view does not acknowledge that Africa was the continent of origin of sicilians, as well as of everyone else, including people of Malta, whose archipelago is only a few kilometers from Africa.

The third case is that of canaanites, called phoenicians by the greeks. Canaanites were descendants of africans who migrated to west Asia, perhaps as early as 70,000 BCE. In the millennium and a half before Jesus, canaanites founded a maritime empire based in the Levant of west Asia, and after 800 BCE, based on the north coast of Africa at Carthage. In their sailings and entrepots, canaanites carried images of the dark mother throughout the ancient world. Although militarily defeated by israelites, canaanites were major players in the drama suggested in this book, wherein the memory and values of the african dark mother persisted in the common epoch in everyday cultures of judaism, christianity, and islam.

Africa and west Asia: Har Karkom

In October 1996 Emmanuel Anati, chief of the italian archeological expedition to Har Karkom, invited Wally and me into the Center for Prehistoric Studies at Capo di Ponte, Italy. Har Karkom, he said, is located on Mount Sinai, but religious activity existed there before the time of Moses.

In his 1963 study of prehistory to the israelite conquest of Canaan, as mentioned in the prologue, Anati concluded that the oldest religion we know is centered on a woman. In subsequent writings, Anati has associated the origin of religion with the creation of visual art, development of an articulated language, and emergence of religious archetypes in the creation myths of the world's peoples. The common theme of creation stories of the world, Anati points out, is a verdant and peaceful place of origin. Hebrew and christian scriptures refer to this place as the garden of Eden. For Anati, the garden of Eden probably refers to the valley of the Rift in central and south Africa where modern humans first appeared 100,000 years ago, whence they migrated into the rest of Africa, then into the Sinai, and, after 50,000 BCE, into the rest of the world (see map of african migrations). The valley of the Rift, before it dried up into the Sahara desert, was a verdant savanna with fruitful plants and animals of every species, a peaceful place that did, indeed, resemble a garden of Eden.

Before the invention of writing, our "greatest and most significant historical archive," for Anati, is rock art painted or incised on caves and cliffs.[1] The richest prehistoric rock art we know is located in sub-saharan Africa where our species began and where first migrations commenced—from Kenya, Tanzania, Natal, Zambia, Zimbabwe, Mozambique, Namibia, Botswana and Lesotho. Ochre red, sign of the dark mother in rock art, may, states Anati, "be the most ancient evidence of artistic creation in the world."[2] Rock paintings in central and south Africa, and thereafter in art wherever africans migrated, are characterized by a predominance of the color red or purple[3] as well as spirals, straight or wavy lines, petals, and concentric circles—signs, according to Marija Gimbutas, Judith Grahn, and other feminist scholars—of the goddess.[4]

In the 1980s, the "oldest sanctuary in the world" was uncovered by Anati's archeological expedition to Har Karkom, where an open air museum dated 40,000 BCE conveys the sense of a sacred place with beautifully aligned altars, megaliths, and a cliff art record of peoples who have lived there. Biblicists have been concerned that archeological findings at Har Karkom might throw the veracity of biblical writings into question. This 40,000 BCE mountain that Anati calls the Mountain of God has evidence of african culture. In the bronze age, the site became "a sacred mountain of immense importance" whose altars, paths, megaliths, and pebble patterns became known as Mount Sinai,[5] founding place of judaism, christianity, and islam.

After 70,000 BCE, africans used the "natural bridge" of the Sinai peninsula to walk to west Asia, where, at Har Karkom, they used flint stone tools "of African type of upper and middle paleolithic epochs"[6] to incise the upright and smoothed megaliths that resemble the human body. Similar to modern art, incisions on the megaliths suggest an eye, a mouth, or nostrils. Seventy-seven of these megaliths shaped like humans (sometimes oval, sometimes rectangular) and often situated inside a circle of rocks, may be the oldest grouping of megaliths in the world. Megaliths of Har Karkom precede (by eons of time) megalith structures of Malta, Great Britain, and elsewhere.

Har Karkom suggests an ancient place of veneration with evidence of ancient fires, round or oval platforms surmounted by altars, pebble drawings, and paths leading to rock formations in the cliffs.[7]

The cliff art of Har Karkom shows bonds with Africa, particularly for the periods 50,000-38,000 and 38,000-30,000 BCE. Migrating africans in groups of ten to thirty constructed tents, shaped and incised rocks[8] and drew pictures on the cliffs. The change from the african sacred mountain to the Mount Sinai of judaism, christianity, and islam is marked by bronze age rock drawings of the ten commandments, a rod and a serpent, and an altar surrounded by twelve megaliths.

The setting of Har Karkom, for Anati, "takes one's breath away...." Two peaks vividly resemble a woman's breasts. In the panorama of the surrounding desert, the path of human-shaped megaliths leads from a sanctuary into the rock cliffs. Creation of the sanctuary required great human power; moving a megalith into place required the strength of four or five people. "Behind these acts was already the spirit of the human as artist who several millennia later produced cavern art."[9] Har Karkom, for the archeologist, evokes wonder—wonder before nature, wonder before the human body, wonder before human relations with animals, and wonder before the relation of humans and nature. Anati's interpretation of the african origin of this earliest sanctuary in the world resonates with contemporary audiences: in 1997 his film "Har Karkom: Mountain of God?" won first prize at the international archeological film festival at Rovereto, Italy.[10]

"Complementary" is the word Anati uses to describe the ancient african society suggested in cliff art of Har Karkom. The cliff art records that the community looked to a complementary calendar of sun and moon, and that complementarity characterized relations between women and men. Complementarity is also suggested in the relation between mountain and plain, between light and shadow, between day and night, between the dark of the grotto and the light of the external world—an "existential" relationship between the present and the past, and fluid boundaries between what is sacred, what is profane, what is religion, and what is art.

In 1995, Anati concluded that the cliff art of Har Karkom is the "oldest art that we know."[11]

The prehistoric african megalithic culture at Har Karkom appears to overturn the theory that megaliths are attributable to the celts who settled in Portugal, Brittany, France, and Great Britain about 10,000 BCE.[12] In recent years, the celtic diffusion theory of the origin of megaliths was replaced by the hypothesis of autonomous development. In light of DNA evidence of prehistoric migration out of Africa into west Asia, the 40,000 BCE sanctuary of Har Karkom probably constitutes the first megalith grouping in the world. Other megalith formations, in France, England, Scotland, Ireland, Italy, northern Germany, Spain, Sardinia, Malta, as well as in Tibet, north Asia, and south India, are plausibly connected to prehistoric african migrations throughout the world. The 40,000 BCE african megaliths at Har Karkom in the Sinai are much older than megaliths of Malta (after 3800 BCE) than megaliths of Stonehenge (2300 BCE), and than temples of Crete (2000 BCE).

Whatever their origin, megaliths exert a distinct pull. Easter Sunday 1995, Wally and I, with british friends Patty and Lianne Jarrett, walked among the megaliths of Avebury in southeast England, discovering with divining sticks distributed by an english women's group that megaliths have magnetic power. Valerie Kack-Brice's dissertation demonstrates that megaliths in Brittany, and elsewhere in France, tap into memories of the ancient mother. In the christian epoch, megaliths in France were associated with saint Anne, grandmother of Jesus and mother of Mary. In the renaissance, saint Anne was painted by Masaccio as black.[13]

Africa, Sicily and Malta

Sicily and Malta, considered mediterranean islands of Europe, are located close to the continent of Africa; the islands were even closer in paleolithic times. Sicily was probably contiguous with Africa before the thawing at the end of the last ice age. As to Malta, recent findings indicate that humans from Africa reached the maltese archipelago "in the last phases of Ice Age during what is known as the pleistocene period, between 15,000 and 18,000 years ago."[14] In 5200 BCE sicilians sailed the short distance from the west and south coasts of their island to Gozo, small island off the coast of Malta.[15]

The subject of origins of sicilian and maltese civilizations has been marked by worry that world civilization might be traced to Africa. The worry circles the eurocentric notion that "the dawn of civilization [is] a European, that is a western event," although geologically, as shown by a recent study of Malta, the maltese archipelago is an integral part of the world of Africa and Sicily.[16] This chapter suggests placing Malta in the context of african and sicilian history. Sicily, case in point of this book, is closely examined in the next chapter, and throughout the study, in the context of african as well as european history.

Before racist worries clouded the subject, it was self-evident to Diodorus Siculus, historian who lived two decades before Jesus, that civilization began in Africa, and that the major divinity of the known world was Isis, dark mother of Africa. Siculus confirmed african origins of world civilization in the science of geology and in popular beliefs. Today, african origins of world civilization have been confirmed in genetics, rock art, and, as this book demonstrates, in everyday beliefs of subordinated cultures of Europe and the rest of the world.

Africans, and their descendants, according to Cavalli-Sforza's theory of demic migrations, carried their beliefs wherever they migrated. Cristina Biaggi, in her authoritative study of Malta, considers the twenty-four megalith temples scattered throughout Malta and Gozo to be "mute witness to an immense expression of faith that pervaded the population and dominated the life of Malta between 3800 and 2500 B.C.E."[17] Her analysis of the similarity between maltese megaliths and those of the British Isles loans additional evidence, in my view, to the hypothesis that african migrations account for megaliths throughout the world.[18]

In Malta, more than 40 statues of a sacred woman have been unearthed. The most famous is the sleeping lady in the Hal Saflieni hypogeum (3300-2500 BCE) who resembles paleolithic figurines of the dark mother found along earlier african migration paths throughout Europe and Asia. Art associated with the dark mother of Africa is replicated in Malta in the color ochre red, and in spirals symbolizing birth, growth, death, and renewal. The tree of life in the 10,000 BCE rock painting at Addaura outside Palermo, Sicily, is also found in maltese art.[19]

Stones of maltese structures sometimes weigh more than 20 tons, so heavy they had to be put in place with rollers. The people who exerted the mighty effort to build the temples grew emmer wheat (ancient type of wheat that grows in Italy and the Middle East) and lentils, hunted red deer, used pots similar to those made in Sicily, probably wove garments from the hair of sheep and goats, and built complex monuments. The Hal Saflieni hypogeum, a three-story maze of more than thirty interlocking chambers, with niches, semicircular chapels, and altars, is considered the largest megalith monument of the Mediterranean. Dated 3300-2500 BCE, the hypogeum was discovered in 1902 when workmen came across a cistern with running water along with 7,000 human skeletons covered with red ochre. An image of the tree of life was found in the oracle room of the hypogeum, where rituals are thought to have celebrated the spiral of seasons embodied in a female divinity. Like african (and asian) art, maltese art features red disks and concentric circles that may have symbolized the dark mother and the solar heat necessary for life.[20]

In 1998 Jennifer Berezan sang in the hypogeum "in a chamber hued out of the rock...the sound was the purest and richest acoustics I've ever experienced.... I felt moved beyond words and...immense gratitude....The power of the hypogeum to heal and transform felt very alive....I experienced the energy there as a profound kindness that opened my heart and flooded me with a sense of being held, loved, forgiven, and empowered. I left with a joyful heart and a feeling of deep longing for what I know we have lost in this modern culture."[21] On February 6,

2000, Jennifer brought this experience to a large concert audience in Oakland, California, singing "Returning to the Mother of Us All."

For many scholars, prehistoric veneration of the dark mother is visible in the rock temples and female statues of Malta, as well as in the neolithic pots that some theorists consider symbolic of woman and transformation. In the christian epoch, in Malta, as elsewhere, the memory of the dark mother was transmuted into veneration of the madonna, particularly in her black images. Willow La Monte, resident scholar in Malta, notes that legendary events associated with the madonna, for example, when she was believed to have saved Malta from the Turks, or to have sent a relief ship during a world war two bombardment, have become popular "national holidays with noisy celebrations in churches throughout the islands."[22]

Beneath the dominant patriarchal christian culture of Malta, a subterranean culture with a belief in the dark mother is visible. On Gozo, behind the altar of the church of Our Lady of Loreto at Ghajnsielem, there is an image of a very black madonna and child. At Guardamangia, at the back of Our Lady of Loreto church, there is a seated black madonna. Willow La Monte notes that there is a whitened madonna in front and at the back, the black madonna of Guardamangia. Not far from the whitened madonna in front is a sign of the prehistoric dark mother—"an amazingly large vulva shape" across the agate front of the lectern.[23]

Another black madonna may be seen outside Malta's international airport. With the whimsy frequently found in folklore, the black madonna is popularly considered protectress of aviation, recalling the legend that angels flew the casa of the black madonna of Loreto from the holy land to Italy. Other maltese dark images of the madonna recall the island's muslim past, e.g., "the quite beautiful Madonna Tas-Samra," whose name is arabic for brown or brunette.[24] The name of this maltese black madonna supports my hypothesis that the memory of the prehistoric dark mother is visible in the popular cultures of religions of the world, in this case, in the popular art of Islam.

Marija Gimbutas, Cristina Biaggi, Veronica Veen, Willow LaMonte, and other scholars, consider maltese rock temples and statues evidence of the civilization of the goddess.[25] In what may be a gender difference in perception, some male archeologists dispute this.[26] Attempting to adjudicate the controversy, Anthony Bonanno advises, "the most one can aspire to achieve is to construct paradigms and archetypes (Anati 1986) or models which will withstand the test of time and of more tangible and empirical evidence (Renfrew 1986)."[27] Reaching for balance, Bonanno points to the proximity of the maltese archipelago to Africa, the sicilian emigration to Gozo, the Ghar Dalam cave where sicilian migrants settled and left evidence of religious rituals, and the earliest maltese temple (Gigantija at Gozo) whose form is that of a gigantic mother. If art is evidence of religious feeling, the latter can be sensed in the high level attained by builders of maltese temples, e.g., the corbelled walls and spirals in the hypogeum's oracle room. Deep religious feeling is also conveyed in Malta's imposing sculptures of women.[28]

Violence arrived in Malta after 2500 BCE about the same time aryan speakers invaded Greece, south Italy, and Sicily. Invaders of Malta vanquished a peaceful people who buried their dead in the earth, in contrast to aryan invaders who used bronze weapons and cremated their dead. After aryan invasions, histories of Malta and Sicily are similar—a pattern of invasion and imposition of patriarchal beliefs. Yet, after 1100 BCE, canaanites came to Malta as well as to other places in the mediterranean with icons of Isis, Astarte, and Tanit, tapping earlier african beliefs in the dark mother.[29]

Romans defeated african/canaanite/carthaginians in Africa, Sicily, and Malta. Thereafter byzantine emperors of the eastern church imposed patriarchal papal christianity. In the 15th century, spanish invaders brought the inquisition to Malta and Sicily, leaving an imprint of inquisitorial christianity that can be felt to this day:. Contemporary maltese officials advise visiting scholars of the prehistoric dark mother not to use words like "goddess" when making public presentations. Malta's dominant violent patriarchal culture was evident to us in our visit in 1996—in militaristic appointments of catholic churches and in statues of women as figures of shame. Yet underneath the patriarchal culture of Malta, the memory of the dark mother—an amalgam of african Isis, anatolian Cybele, canaanite Astarte, carthaginian Tanit, and black madonnas—persists. Her values, justice, equality, and transformation, are evident in the contemporary political left of Malta.

Cultural affinities of Malta and Africa are explored in *Goddessing,* international journal of scholars founded by Willow LaMonte. In a 1995 issue, Asphodel Long discussed beliefs she had come upon in her research in west Africa, notably the belief in the goddess of the earth as the goddess of justice. "...if you treat the Earth well, She'll be good to you and if you treat the earth badly you won't find your harvest come out." This belief, she pointed out, is similar to one associated with the goddess Ma'at in Egypt and with goddesses of the Ashanti, and of Benin, Ghana and Nigeria. Long cited Eva Meyerwitz, european jew who fled nazi Germany to live in Africa, who concluded that west asian religious beliefs, notably those of Canaan, were very similar to those of west Africa.[30]

Willow LaMonte has analyzed similarities between Akua'maa, dark mother divinity of Guinea who protected "abundant and safe childbearing," canaanite Astarte, and Tanit, dark mother of Canaan and Carthage who protected childbirth and children. The ankh, pervasive in Africa and Malta, is the symbol of woman and life carried by Isis.[31] A womb oval over a vertical cross, the ankh is identical to the symbol of Tanit. Over the centuries the ankh has remained popular in Malta and in Africa. In the 1960s the ankh surfaced in the United States, worn by women in that decade's passionate movements for justice.

Gozo, island museum of the prehistory of Sicily and Malta, remains matrifocal and matrilineal to this day. The creation legend of the temple of Gigantija (3300-3000 BCE) in Gozo recounts that a giant woman, Gigantia, considered foremother of the maltese, floated in the sea with a girl and a boy before coming ashore at Gozo. The legend, Veronica Veen, dutch cultural anthropologist, points out, remembers a verdant land whence the first maltese came. This seems to me a case of the persistence of the memory of a verdant land in the world's creation legends; in this case, the verdant land refers proximately to Sicily, and ultimately to the savannah of central Africa where modern humans began and whence they migrated to all continents of the world.

Marlene Saliba, maltese scholar and poet, points out that in maltese popular perception there is no sharp break between veneration of the primordial mother and worship of the christian mother of god. Marlene remembers the creation legend of Malta in her poem, "The Giantess of Gozo."

> Under the light of a full moon,
> in the wake of Spring,
> the Giantess remembers
> how once long, long ago
> in such an identical stillness of night
> she, with a baby at her breast
> stone upon stone
> gave birth and shape to these magical Gozitan Temples...
> She remembers how her kin
> used to live of old, content.
> Days without fear and pain, without wars;
> enjoying the fruit and lush crops of the land.
> A productive wonderful time
> when the stars seemed nearer the human heart
> and the meaning of all life;
> when music and the sounds of nature were one....[32]

For sicilians who migrated to Gozo and then to the maltese mainland, "the goddess was the origin of everything," states Veronica Veen. "Men and women lived together in generally small communities in a spirit of sharing and cooperation." Prior to aryan invasions, co-operation, sharing, and equality were the way of life. "There were no wars. Communities were matrilineal and matrilocal."[33] Communities were small, numbering between 40 and 100. This may be "too roseate" a picture of neolithic Sicily and Gozo, says Veen. Still, she says, if we had a little of the neolithic way of life, "we would live in a nicer world now."[34]

Comfortable on the sea as well as on land, sicilians and gozitans traded for black obsidian, the black pumice rock (used in food perparation) found on the Lipari islands off the northeastern coast of Sicily, near the black madonna of Tindari. The trade in black volcanic rock and black obsidian in Sicily, Malta, and Anatolia, was considered holy because associated with the dark mother.

The pot of Skorba, unearthed near the earliest mother figurine found in Malta is shaped like a bird goddess. Pottery of Gozo resembles that of Africa and Sicily, incised with lozenges, zigzags, dots along lines, and little circles, eyes, chevrons, and rain-dashes, symbols that Marija Gimbutas associated with the female divinity. Most of this pottery is grey or black, with a preponderance of shiny, polished black vessels. Black, according to Veen, "must have been, like the darkness of the cave, the colour of the regenerative powers of the earth, which were supposed to revive the dead."[35] Zigzags may have symbolized water streaming through fertile fields. New moons and vulvas, in african culture, are symbols of becoming. The lozenge with dot, and the eye of the dark mother, may also be considered symbols of becoming and renewal. The pot of Skorba has moon handles and is dated 4400-4200 BCE.[36] The pot, for Veen, preserves and transforms food, as the dark mother preserved and transformed life.

Today at Gozo, the civilization of the dark mother can be felt in the studio of a young sculptor, Joe Xuereb, whose stone pieces, full of curves and rounds, as well as his pendants of Tanit figures, are receiving international recognition. We commissioned a sculpture of lovers whose intertwined bodies evoke the gender complementarity Emmanuel Anati considers characteristic of ancient mother-centered human societies. Joe Xuereb has entitled this sculpture of embracing lovers, "Tenderness."

Africa, Asia, and Canaan

The greeks called them phoenicians; they called themselves canaanites. In the two millennia prior to the common era, canaanites in trade and settlements so thoroughly blended african and asian images of the dark mother that contemporary art historians find it difficult to distinguish between what is african and what is west asian. In the cult of high greek culture that thrived in the late 19th century imperial thrust of europeans (a cult perpetuated to this day by eurocentric scholars), there has been a tendency to credit the greeks for anything notable in late antiquity. This perspective has not only negated african origins and beliefs, it has blurred the significance of west asian canaanites as carriers of african beliefs, notably the belief in the dark mother.

Canaanites came out of west Asia, route of early african migrations, and site of 40,000 BCE megaliths and art of Har Karkom, as well as iconography of Sumer. Once migrants from central and south Africa reached west Asia, they could have traveled anywhere in the world, but we know very little about their itineraries throughout Asia, except that DNA data indicates that homo sapiens sapiens migrating out of Africa into west Asia did take routes throughout Asia as early as 60,000-70,000 years ago.[37] The large breasts and hips of the mother figure of Chagar Bazar closely resemble mother figurines found along african migrant paths into Europe.[38] Ancient sumerians, who produced the first written historical documents, referred to themselves as black or dark-headed people.[39]

Symbols of west Asia suggest african origins. For example, the "cult stand" of Taanach (1000 BCE) features african symbols. "From bottom to top: naked goddess flanked by two lions; two sphinxes, two lions and two gazelles flanking a sacred tree; and an animal supporting a winged sun disc, with sphinxes on the sides."[40] African routes into Asia are also suggested in the image of the mother divinity of Catal Hoyuk (7,000 BCE), who resembles earlier dark mother figurines dated 26,000 BCE found along african paths in Italy and France. African migration routes in Europe and Asia are confirmed in the similarity of 26,000 BCE mother figures found along the south coast of France and Italy, in Anatolia in the 8th century BCE, and later in Sicily and Malta.

The first written document we have is that of Enheduanna (2300 BCE), of Sumer. High priestess serving moon god Nanna and moon goddess Inanna, Enheduanna may have expressed the strong reaction to violent aryan invasion of a woman living in the harmonious civilization of the dark mother.[41] Suggesting the continuing interchange of Africa with west Asia, Enheduanna lived in a kingdom that united west Asia and Africa, northern and southern Mesopotamia, as well as Turkey, Iran and Egypt. The power of the dark mother of Africa and west Asia may be sensed in Enheduanna's poetry. Betty Meador describes her as priestess, poet, dream interpreter, and religious leader,[42] who sang of Inanna as "Lady of the largest heart" who expressed a "holy woman's rage."[43]

Canaanites consolidated their culture in the region of west Asia today called Palestine, whose ties with Africa were very close.[44] Although they built "mighty Canaanite City States" in the second millennium before the common era, the history of the canaanites in ancient Palestine has largely been ignored or silenced by biblical scholars of Israel. After world war two, mainstream historians emphasized ancient Israel as "the taproot of Western civilization, the pinnacle of achievement,"[45] while canaanite religion (referred to as a "fertility religion") was said to have been surpassed and supplanted. "Thus Israelite history supersedes and in effect silences Canaanite, i.e., indigenous Palestinian history."[46] Although archeologists acknowledge the high level of canaanite culture, they portray woman-centered canaanite religion as inferior to male-centered judeo-christianity identified with western civilization.[47]

The history of canaanites and israelites is interconnected, and controversial. "Israelites all came from a local Canaanite underclass," according to theologian Norman Gottwald.[48] The name Israel does not appear in inscriptions. It is very difficult to "distinguish sharply between what may have been an Israelite and a Canaanite settlement. But it was in this area that Israel later appears...."[49] "Their beginning point was Canaan, and they went back to Canaan."[50] One significant pivot in this controversy may be that when Israel emerged, Canaan was "part of the Egyptian empire" of Africa.[51]

After 1100 BCE, canaanites established ports and settlements around the Mediterranean, notably in Sicily and Malta. The religious center of this peaceful maritime empire was the dark mother Astarte with her consort Ba'al. According to the bible, israelites, who venerated Jahweh, defeated canaanites who worshipped Astarte. Yet reverence of Astarte, in her many images, appears to have persisted in the popular culture of judaism. As Asphodel Long noted, "defeated peoples often kept earlier beliefs underneath the victor's new names, ideas, and languages,"[52] a theme explored later in this book.

Archeology offers evidence of the persistence of the memory of the dark mother in the "Land of the Bible." Amihai Mazar, of the center for Judaic-Christian Studies in Jerusalem, in an Anchor Bible Reference Library volume, documents the ubiquity of women divinity figures in the land of the bible. In the temple at Nahariyah, for example, a mold was found that reproduced images of the "naked, horned goddess" Astarte.[53]

The significance of Palestine, which Mazar calls "basically Canaanite, that is to say, West Semitic in origin," was that it was a "bridge between Egypt and northern Syria,"[54] a bridge that connected Africa and west Asia. "Clay figurines made by pressing clay into molds were common canaanite art objects. In general, they represent the naked fertility goddess, and like the biblical teraphim (Genesis 31: 19-35, I Samuel 19: 13-16) they were probably used by women. The naked goddess is usually standing, holding snakes or lotus flowers; in most cases her hair is styled with the typically Egyptian 'Hathor locks.'"[55]

In northwest Sicily, land of my maternal ancestors, canaanites founded settlements at Palermo, Solunto and nearby Himera. In southeast Sicily, land of my paternal ancestors, canaanites traded at Syracuse and Ragusa Ibla, and established emporia at Modica and elsewhere. In west Sicily along an african maritime route, a major canaanite settlement was established at Mozia, island off Trapani. On our visit to Mozia a few years ago we discovered that stories are still told about nymphs whom local people associate with la dea Tanit.[56] In our summer 2000 study tour in Sicily, we were assaulted by the continuing effort of established authorities to denigrate canaanites and to deny the existence of the dark mother divinity. The head of the tourism office at Marsala showed us the beautiful youth of Mozia, a canaanite stronghold until destroyed by greeks. The official insisted that the acclaimed sculpture was greek, not canaanite. When I asked him about the many images of canaanite goddesses in the museum at Mozia, he belittled them as "door knockers."

From their base in Carthage, canaanites sailed the Mediterranean with images of the african dark mother Isis and images of their own horned Astarte blended with carthaginian Tanit. They decorated their shrines to Astarte with the color purple, a variant of the red ochre that africans used to signify the dark mother as generatrix of life. Africans earlier, and canaanites later, appeared to have identified the woman divinity with megaliths. In popular cultures, megaliths are considered sacred stones "in which the divinity was believed to reside."[57]

Purple dye, derived from a mollusk valuable for dye; has been described as "the color of congealed blood, blackish at first glance but gleaming when held up to the light."[58] The latin word for purple is purpureus, "very, very holy." The name Canaan means land of purple dye,[59] just as canaanite/phoenicians refer to themselves as people of purple dye.[60] The word purple interchanged with the word scarlet: Jesus' robe, in the gospel of Mark, is described as scarlet.[61] Ancient altars of Canaan and Israel were covered in purple. In the middle ages, when the valence of the dark mother was co-opted by medieval monarchs, the color purple was associated with royalty. Today on good Friday, catholics drape church statues in purple.[62] Alice Walker, in her Pulitzer prize winning novel, associated women's spirituality with the color purple.

Ultimate precursors of canaanites of west Asia were africans. Immediate precursors were people of the vibrant levantine civilization of Ebla (2500-1600 BCE). Ebla maintained close ties with Africa, as well as with peoples and cultures of the asian interior. The name Ebla may refer to Cybele, suggesting that anatolian Cybele melded with canaanite Astarte in the Levant.[63] Eblaites spoke a semitic language. "Semitic," an often misused word, refers to languages spoken by a wide range of peoples who lived, and continue to live, in the west asian Levant, as well as in Malta and Africa: canaanites, amorites, ugarites, byblians, ammonites, edomites, moabites, hebrews, palestinians, arabians, syrians, iraqi, aramaic and ethiopian peoples, et al.[64] The semitic family includes about seventy different languages of west Asia and Africa, some still spoken today.[65]

Sarepta, another west asian archeological site, offers more information about canaanites who founded this city in 1600 BCE, prior to gaining ascendancy all along the levantine coast from Ugarit to Byblos, Beirut, Sidon, Sarepta, Tyre, Haifa, Joppa, and Jerusalem.[66] At Sarepta, close bonds of canaanites with the african civilization of Isis are evident in artifacts of Horus, images of Bastet, amulets of cat-headed human figurines, and clay thrones flanked by sphinxes. Artifacts include a seated pregnant woman who evokes Isis and Cybele. The nonviolence of canaanite civilization is apparent at Sarepta...there are no weapons.[67]

By the 7th century BCE, when the canaanite settlement at Carthage was founded, veneration of the carthaginian dark mother Tanit had melded with that of west asian "Ashtart."[68] Israelites, by this time, whatever their reputed canaanite origins, vocalized the name of the canaanite dark mother Ashtart with vowels of the hebrew word for "shame," Ashtoreth.[69] Enemies of canaanites assigned fearful associations, including child sacrifice, to the carthaginian dark mother Tanit. Contemporary archeologists and anthropologists, noting that Tanit was a mother divinity who protected childbirth and nurture of infants, conclude that the constant linking of Tanit with tophets, which israelites, as well as greeks and romans, called places of child sacrifice (a denigration that has been repeated ever since), was probably a libel of canaanites by their enemies. Contemporary scholars consider tophets to be children's cemeteries.[70] In October 1996 when we visited the tophet on Mozia, we saw a burial ground for children adjoining an adult cemetery. In 2000 at Mozia, when we asked the tour official if we could see the tophet, he said there was "nothing" to see. Canaanites may have been libeled, or obliterated, because they represented the threat that nonviolent people always present to violent dominant cultures. Later denigration of canaanites may have been related to racism. Late 19th century european racists associated Carthage with "degeneracy." Why degeneracy? In this halcyon period of european imperialism in Africa, racists considered it "degenerate" that canaanites lived productively and in peace with africans in the north african city.[71]

Canaanite artistic ability and craftsmanship have also been slandered, a palpable libel if one views the extraordinary figure of the youth of Mozia, and the craftsmanship of the reconstructed canaanite ship of Mozia. The bible attests to canaanite workmanship and canaanite nonviolence; e.g., "expert sailors, skilled workmen in stone, wood, and metal....above all, men of commerce and trade,"[72] whose places were characterized by a conspicuous absence of objects usually employed in warfare, no spear points, no dagger blades, et al.[73]

Ashtart of west Asia and Tanit of Africa melded in mediterranean cultures. Ashtart, the better known of the two, was primarily "patroness of love and fertility." Tanit, whose name appears on hundreds of stelae wherever canaanites touched port or settled, blessed conception, successful childbirth, and nurture of children from infancy through their early years.[74] In canaanite popular religion Ashtart became "Ishtar and Ishar (the just one)." The harmony of canaanite civilization is conveyed in sculptures of men and women embracing.[75]

Probably learning from africans,[76] canaanites followed them as master navigators of the ancient world,[77] founding settlements in the Mediterranean where they preferred "to adapt existing prehistoric sacred places to their particular needs."[78] More precisely, canaanites brought icons of Isis and Astarte who blended well with local women divinities (whose origins. were also, in all probability, ultimately african). Canaanites directed a large maritime commercial empire from Carthage (today's Tunisia), which they established in 814 BCE. By 824 BCE they had created a network of commercial maritime routes throughout the Mediterranean[79] whose entrepots and settlements were blessed both by Isis, dark mother of Africa, and by Astarte, dark mother of west Asia. Their melding is suggested in the inscription on a tablet, dated two hundred years before the common era—"the awesome deity Isis, the deity Astart."[80]

Historians have not yet acknowledged the large significance of canaanites in world civilization. Etruscans of Italy, whose origins baffle scholars and whose liberated women intrigue contemporary feminists, may become more understandable if we consider the hypothesis of etruscan contact with levantine and african canaanites. Canaanite and etruscan statues of men and women demonstrate the gender equality and contentment that seem to have characterized africans in prehistory and canaanites in late antiquity.[81]

O

Recognizing the ultimately african origins of world religions challenges the patriarchal belief that the oldest divinity was male, as well as the feminist belief that the prehistoric female divinity originated with the west asian agricultural revolution. African signs of the dark mother, notably the color red and the pubic V, were dispersed with african migrations to all continents after 50,000 BCE. West asian images of "fertility goddesses" have been found at Mureybit, 8000-7600 BCE. Not until "ca. 7000 BCE,

[was] the female deity...joined by a male, who remained less important, however."[82]

The dark mother was african in origin. Although her images took different forms in different regions[83] the images shared certain characteristics. Horns and piercing eyes were common to images of the dark mother of Africa, west Asia, Sicily, and Malta. Hundreds of figurines of horned women dated 2500 BCE have been found in the land of Canaan in west Asia. At Tell Brak, more than 300 figures with arresting eyes have been found in the Eye Temple. Carved mostly of alabaster, figurines are of individuals, or of couples; sometimes the figurine is that of a mother holding a child.[84] In the folklore of the historic epoch, the anxious patriarchal belief in the "evil eye" of the dark mother was countered by the popular belief that the mother's eye can protect from the evil eye. All mediterranean cultures share the belief in the evil eye (mal'occhio in italian), which is popularly countered by amulets of the protective eye of the dark mother.[85]

Canaanites, major carriers of the belief in the african dark mother, confirm cultural ties of Africa and west Asia, of Palestine and Anatolia, and of west and east Asia.[86] The city-based culture of Ebla, precursor of Canaan, existed at the same time as societies of Sumer and Akkad.[87] The official cult of the agricultural city-state of Ebla was associated with sacrifices, in contrast to the popular cult that venerated a woman divinity. Later, women divinities of Ebla had consorts, notably the deities Baal or El.[88] Ebla derived most of its wealth from sheep, textiles, and control of trade routes (especially for metals) to and from the anatolian plateau,[89] and with the far east. Carbonized cloves found in an eblaite house indicate that canaanites probably traded with east Asia three thousand years before the common era; cloves were not known to the west before roman times.[90]

What about women of Canaan? Canaanite women as well as men held the elevated vocation of scribe.[91] Yet the term "handmaid," often used by the dominant culture of Ebla, suggests that by this time (2500-1600 BCE), women played a subordinate role to men.[92] By the date of the founding of Ebla, aryan invasions had brought hierarchy, subordination of women, and other violence into west Asia. The impact of violent aryan invasions is indicated in that after 2300 BCE, canaanite Astarte, in one manifestation, became Ishtar, goddess of war.[93] The story of Inanna's descent into the underworld may tell the story of the rape and conquest by aryan speakers of the dark mother's nonviolent civilization.[94] Yet, here, as in other places where aryans invaded, the older religion of the dark mother was not completely destroyed. In a temple dedicated to Ninkarrak, goddess of healing, 6,637 beads were found. Beads of lapis, carnelian, agate, and chalcedony were given to people in need of protection from bad omens.[95]

Even after violent aryan invasions, exemplifying the hypothesis that subaltern cultures continued to carry the memory of the dark mother, women of Canaan seem not to have been subordinated.[96] At Mari, male and female divinities appear to have been equal; a jar was inscribed, "I bless you to Jahweh and his 'Ashera.'" In canaanite/ugaritic culture, Ashera was the consort of the male god El. As Raphael Patai has analyzed[97] and Asphodel Long and Elinor Gadon have documented ("under the veneer of official Yahwism, popular beliefs in the goddess were probably held both by 'Canaanites' in Israel and by 'reprobate' Israelites.'").[98] Dennis Pardee, who has studied popular ugaritic beliefs,[99] points to one difference of popular religion from official hebrew religion. Popular religious beliefs circling the dark mother tended to be descriptions of what had taken place and what is to take place, in contrast to the universal prescriptions of official hebrew texts, whose god was Jahweh.[100]

Wherever canaanites sailed, settled, and traded, they brought the color purple, (notably in textiles dyed purple), clay face masks, small glass amulets, and figurines of Astarte/Tanit with her arms raised in a gesture of blessing (similar to orant posture of the african goddess of 4,000 BCE in the British Museum).[101] Clay face masks, particularly a grinning one in the Whitaker museum at Mozia, are similar to clown faces in the christian epoch, and similar to images in italian vernacular architecture satirizing figures of power, stimulating me to think that canaanite legacy of resistance to injustice was taken wherever canaanites reached, from west Asia to Africa to Europe to east Asia, a legacy of resistance to injustice that ultimately remembers the just civilization of the dark mother of Africa.

Canaanite influence in Sicily was pervasive. In addition to canaanite settlements in my ancestral regions of Palermo and Ragusa Ibla, there were settlements at Mozia and Erice on the west side of the island, at Caltagirone in the center, and at Megara and Siracusa on the east coast. To these places, canaanites brought icons of Isis from Africa and of Astarte from her sanctuary at Byblos in west Asia. Astarte characteristically held a flower in each hand. Later she was called Ziz, perhaps a dialect rendering of Isis, with whom she blended. The memory of Isis and Astarte persisted in palermitan folklore in the popular story-song Ziza. At the Whitaker museum on Mozia we saw many images of Astarte melded with carthaginian Tanit.

Isis and Astarte are everywhere in sicilian museums. Along with Bastet, her cat familiar, Isis holds the sun with lunar horns on her head. Astarte has horns on her head.and a characteristic pose of offering her breasts in nurturance, an image found in early african art. In the patriarchal epoch, the finger gesture of horns (perhaps remembering Astarte or Isis) became an insult to a male, conveying that a man had been cuckolded by his woman, who retained the dark mother's power over her own sexuality.

Images of Cybele, dark mother of Anatolia brought to Sicily by neolithic migrant farmers and early traders, are visible today in Sicily, notably at Palazzola acreide, where we saw her image cut into the rock in our 2001 tour. Cybele in Sicily (and elsewhere) is characteristically depicted in a seated posture, sometimes flanked by lions and nursing two infants (see her image found in eastern Sicily at Megara Hyblaea).

In the folklore of Italy, the canaanite dark mother is remembered in the festa dei morti, day of the dead in November, month of Astarte/Estar. In Israel, Italy, and elsewhere, Astarte is remembered as queen Esther who presides over purim, carnival festival of the jews.[102] Astarte/Esther became the name of the christian holy day of easter, a clue, perhaps, to the enigmatic "easter laughter" of popular cultures of the Mediterranean. (See chapter 7).

Western historians identifying with aryan greek civilization have downplayed the slavery, subordination of women, and violence that accompanied artistic and other achievements of high greek culture.[103] In the contemporary controversy over african/semitic, or aryan, origins of western civilization, the main point may not yet have been engaged—harmonious cultures of the dark mother of africans and their descendants, west asian canaanites, were vanquished by aryan greeks and romans, who did, indeed, inaugurate violent western civilization.

Racist anxiety hovering over canaanite connection with Africa, sexist worry about canaanite veneration of a woman divinity, as well as contemporary Israeli political troubles with Palestine, may all have something to do with the denigration, or negation, of canaanite achievements. Yet study of the culture of the canaanites, accurately viewed as an offshoot of african civilization, may help us see the suppressed potential of western civilization. Among canaanite achievements, the invention of the alphabet (in Africa, not in the Levant, as we have recently learned) extended learning beyond elites to everyone.

The central acrophonic principle of the phoenician alphabet, linguists point out, is "for the lady" Ba'lat who is identified with the goddess Hathor, sister of Isis, of Egypt.[104] The naked canaanite divinity Astarte melded with the african divinity Hathor who wears many gold pendants. Her hair is set in the Hathor style, yet, like Astarte, she often holds a flower in each hand. Like Isis, she often holds snakes. Sometimes she stands on a lion or a crescent moon. Scholars are unable to say whether these figurines are west asian or egyptian/african. Sometimes she is the african goddess Qudsho, sometimes she is Astarte/Anat.[105] Perhaps the reason scholars cannot differentiate between images of women divinities of Africa and west Asia is that they are one, with different names, yet referring ultimately to the dark mother of Africa.[106]

Melding of images of the dark mother is evident at Dura-Europos on the Euphrates near the Persian Gulf, founded by canaanites in 300 BCE, where several images of the dark mother were venerated: Astarte (called Artemis by the Greeks), local goddesses Atargatis and Azzanathkona, and a mother divinity seated on a throne flanked by lions, a figure that evokes Isis, Cybele, and Astarte, of Africa, Anatolia, and Canaan.

In the 700 years before the common era, when Carthage was the north african capitol of the canaanite maritime empire, belief in the dark mother pervaded the known world. From Africa, canaanite ships sailed to entrepots concentrated along the southern coast of Spain, including Gibraltar, thereby controlling the straits as well as inland mines. In Sardinia, canaanites established way stations at Tharos, Nora, Bithia, and Sulcis en route to spanish mines. Trading along the north coast of Africa, they turned down onto the atlantic coast, and are said to have circumnavigated the african continent. In south Italy and Etruria, canaanites left evidence of their presence. A golden inscription (in phoenician as well as etruscan) may be seen today in the Museo Archeologico of Villa Giulia in Rome. Based in Carthage, Africa, canaanite trade may have stimulated the growth of the maritime wealth of Magna Graecia and Etruria, and may be the key to what art historians call the "orientalizing" of etruscan culture.

Carthage, at one time the richest metropolis of the ancient world, with 700,000 inhabitants, according to the historian Strabo,[107] was a multicultural city of Africa where african and west asian cultures melded; e.g., a carthaginian mask of the sixth century BCE is that of a man with a bronze ring in his right ear, a silver ring in his nose, and asian eyes. The mask was found in a cache of many egyptian amulets and sphinxes.[108]

After the period of canaanite expansion, greeks, between the eighth and sixth century BCE, began to colonize Sicily at Himera on the north coast and at Selinunte in the western part of the island. Greeks and canaanite/phoenicians (by this time called carthaginians) vied for supremacy in the Mediterranean. Carthaginians conquered Selinunte and Agrigento on the southwest coast of Sicily, and annexed Gela and

Camarina in southeast Sicily. When Dionisus, greek tyrant of Syracuse, in the 4th century BCE destroyed Mozia, canaanite/phoenician holdings in west Sicily passed to Lilyboeum (named for Lybia in Africa) where ships from Africa took port. Lilyboeum was later called Marsala by the arabs (Mars Allah, port of Allah). African and canaanite presence in western Sicily may still be felt today in the easter mysteries centered on the black madonna of Trapani.[109]

African Isis, canaanite Astarte (joined with carthaginian Tanit), and anatolian Cybele fused in canaanite trade and continued to fuse in the period of greek colonization.[110] The goddess of Grammichele in southeast Sicily (5th century BCE) near my ancestral Ragusa, has hair fashioned in african corn rows, asian almond eyes, and an enigmatic expression. Greeks, appropriating the valence of african Isis, called her Demeter.[111] Blending is apparent in roman statues of Astarte depicted as Cybele seated between two lions with a sceptre in her hand alongside her consort Hadad enthroned between two bulls. Under the romans, Cybele became Ibla, and Astarte, melding with sumerian Inanna, became Diana.

Although greeks in the peace treaty with Sicily of 405 BCE recognized carthaginian possession of the west part of the island and the autonomy of east Sicily, strife continued. At Imera on the north coast of Sicily, greeks defeated carthaginians in 409 BCE, a defeat vindicated by african Hannibal, descendant of canaanites, who crushed greek and sicul troops near Agrigento. With elephants, Hannibal crossed the Pyrenees, the Alps, and the Apennines, and vanquished the romans at Trasimeno—before roman Scipio defeated Carthage in 204 BCE.

Canaanites, who venerated the dark mother, may be said to have left a legacy of resistance to injustice, as discussed above. They also bequeathed a legacy of radical democracy, a theme underlined by Sabatino Moscati, late italian historian whose life work was the study of canaanites. Moscati pointed out that canaanite holdings in Sicily were autonomous polities; at Erice, for example, a local popular assembly and senate governed the canaanite city.

Direct african influence in Sicily is apparent in the name Isis in the Regina Grotto near Palermo. A seated mother divinity flanked by sphinxes was found at the carthaginian settlement at Solunto. The sign of Tanit and a disk with a healing caduceus were found at Mozia and at Lilibeo.[112]

Violent romans (descendants of aryan italics), like violent greeks (descendants of aryan hellenes), regarded peaceful canaanite/phoenician/carthaginians who venerated the dark mother, as a threat. Proclaiming, Cartago delenda est, romans destroyed the african city in 146 BCE, spreading salt on the land so that no humans could live there. Yet humans continued to live in Carthage, and canaanite/carthaginian influence has persisted in everyday and festival rituals all over the Mediterranean. When the roman empire fell, african peasants spoke a punic language and called themselves canaanite; some africans still do so today.

Belief in the dark mother survived roman defeat of Carthage. Romans attempted to obliterate Astarte by assigning dreadful traits to her, particularly in her representation as Tanit, but nurturant characteristics of the canaanite dark mother remained in many statues of Astarte melded with Isis. African ancestry of the dark mother was transmitted in the roman image of a black Diana with many breasts nurturing animals and humans, an image that may be considered an immediate precursor of black madonnas of the christian epoch. Images of black Diana may be seen today in the Museo Nazionale at Naples and in the Capitoline Museums in Rome.[113]

Fusing of divinities of Africa and west Asia, and Greece is suggested in a statuette of Isis (50-100 CE), found at Byblos in the Levant. Her crown is a double feather with cow horns (Hathor), two slanted grain sheaves (Isis), and a sun disk (Horus).

O

Symbols of the african dark mother have persisted throughout the history of Sicily—the pubic triangle, breasts, eyes, snakes, the circle, the circle bounded by a snake, snakes as lunar horns embracing a circle, and the spiral connoting life and history. Her memory has been embedded in sicilian folklore where the color black is associated with good, in sicilian museums that hold dozens of images of Isis and her cat Bastet, and in carnival satire of clerical and secular authority. Blending of african images of the dark mother with west asian images is visible in Sicily. The memory of the sumerian goddess Inanna, is recalled in the dialect word for grandmother, nanna, and the sicilian word for lullaby, ninna nanna. Inanna has also persisted in the name of the madonna's mother, Anne, whom Masaccio painted as the dark mother standing behind her whitened daughter Maria. Cybele persisted in sibyls who carried her name, in Ibla of Ragusa Ibla, and in the name of the iblean mountains where Ibla's neolithic sanctuaries were located. [114]

The memory of the dark mother may be considered the bass music of the story of humanity from prehistory to the present. The bass music remembering the dark mother, it is my hypothesis, has continued to resonate up to the present in popular cultures underneath imposed, or adopted, religions of judaism, christianity, and islam. This bass music is evoked in Kay Kaufman Schelemay's study of contemporary Ethiopia.[115] For centuries, christian missionaries tried in vain to convert the falasha of Ethiopia. Yet in the 1860s, perhaps remembering canaanites in Africa, the falasha converted to judaism. Beta Israel rituals of the falasha are close to ancient african beliefs in Isis, wherein god is considered "crown of the poor" and "strength of the weak,"[116] a meaning today associated with european and other black madonnas. (See chapter four, this book).

Despite greek and roman invasions, christianization, and european imperial conquests, the memory of the ancient dark mother has remained in popular african beliefs. Isis' sistrum, popular musical instrument of Africa from prehistory to the present, is believed to exorcise evil spirits. Ethiopians, whether they subscribe to judaism, christianity, or islam, believe that the sistrum exorcises evil spirits. Similarly, the zar cult is a basic african belief. "Individuals of all religious groups, Christian, Moslem, Falasha, and followers of autochthonous traditions, observe special rites of the zar cult to exorcise these spirits that can inhabit an individual and cause sickness or misfortune."[117]

African belief in the dark mother is accompanied by respect for different religious forms. In Ethiopia at Benin Sefer, "at the top of the hill was the synagogue; at the bottom, a mosque. Five times a day the sounds of the muezzin chanting prayers from the minaret...in counterpoint, on Sundays and holidays...the bells of the many Ethiopian Orthodox churches...."[118]

O

Shared memories of peoples of the earth are visible in similar creation stories. In his study of the exodus from Egypt,[119] Emmanuel Anati has found that the "common denominator" of the world's creation myths "takes us back to the initial migration of homo sapiens who left his place of origin in Africa, to explore...the world."[120] Over the millennia, the memory of the exodus of our ancestors from the verdant savanna of Africa became the myth of the garden of Eden. The myth became the creation story of the nation of Israel, but the pattern of exodus and reaching the promised land, for Anati, can be found in the creation stories of all peoples.

The story of exodus from Egypt, wandering in the desert, journeying to the foot of a sacred mountain, and mingling with other tribes before reaching the "Promised Land,"[121] resonated in the speeches of Reverend Martin Luther King, Jr. during the african american civil rights movement of the 1960s. The story remains central to the ongoing struggle of african americans, and of others, for justice, equality, and transformation.

Notes

1   Emmanuel Anati, *Il Museo Immaginario* (Loc. Cit.), ll. Anati has inspired local people of the Valcamonica in Italy to think about prehistory. Vera Zappia has researched prehistoric foods prepared by grandmothers of this area, foods which transmit very ancient memories. She found that focaccia di nocciola has a long history going back to the neolithic age, as does polenta. Also ancient are gnocchi, lumache (snails), frittata (omelette), fagiolini (green beans), mushrooms, wines, and biscotti. See Vera Zappia, *Il passato e Noi. Le Ricette della Nonna Camuna* (Breno, Pro Loco di Angolo Terme, 1994).

2   *Il Museo*, 217-218.

3   Ibid, 222.

4   Ibid, 221-223.

5   Emmanuel Anati, Luigi Cottinelli, Federico Mailland, "Il santuario piu' antico del mondo," *Archeologia Viva,* marzo/aprile 1996, 29.

6   Ibidem.

7   Ibid., 28.

8   Ibidem.

9   Ibid., 34.

10   C. Beretta e P. Pruneti, "Da Har Karkom a Rovereto," *Archeologia Viva,* marzo-aprile 1997.

11   Ibidem.

12   Emiliana Petrioli, *Miti e Megaliti. Monumenti di pietra nella civiltà dei Celti* (Video, supplemento della rivista *Archeologia Viva,* 26/10/72).

13   Valerie Kack Brice, *Dolmens and St. Anne in Brittany,* Ph.D. Dissertation, California Institute of Integral Studies, San Francisco, 1999.

14   I am indebted to Yana Womack and Willow LaMonte for sending me the article: "Cave Drawings which trace the sojourn of early man," *Malta Independent,* 29 December 1996.

15   Themistocles Zammit, *The Prehistoric Temples of Malta and Gozo* (Updated edition by Karl Mayrhofer, 1995). See Francesco Fedele, "Malta: Origini e sviluppo del popolamento preistorico," *Missione a Malta. Ricerche e studi sulla preistoria dell'arcipelago maltese nel contesto meditorraneo,* a cura di

Ariela Fradkin Anati, Emmanuel Anati (Milano, Jaca Book spa, Centro Camuno di Studi Preistorici, Capo di Ponte (Bs), Italia , 1988), 59.

16   See Harald Haarmann, *Early Civilization and Literacy in Europe. An Inquiry into Cultural Continuity in the Mediterranean World* (Berlin, New York, Mouton de Gruyter 1996). See also Colin Renfrew, *Before Civilization. The Radiocarbon Revolution and Prehistoric Europe* (New York, Alfred A. Knopf, 1974).

17   Cristina Biaggi, Ph.D., *Habitations of the Great Goddess* (Manchester, Conn., Knowledge, Ideas & Trends, 1994), 4.

18   Ibid.

19   Ibid., 45.

20   Emiliana Petrioli, "Hal Saflieni," *Archeologia Viva*, maggio-giugno 1989.

21   Communication to author January 15, 1999.

22   Willow La Monte, communication to author, November, 1996. I am deeply indebted to Willow for sharing her knowledge of Malta, and for taking us on a personal tour of the island in October 1996.

23   Ibid.

24   See Willow La Monte, "Black Madonna Sampler," *Goddessing*, Spring, 1997.

25   See Marija Gimbutas, *The Language of the Goddess* (HarperSanFrancisco,1989), passim. And Elinor Gadon, *The Once & Future Goddess*. Loc. Cit. (HarperSanFrancisco, 1989), Chapter 5.

26   See essays of Fondazjoni Patrimonju Malti in association with the National Museum of Archaeology. Also Anthony Pace, ed., *Maltese Prehistoric Art 5000 - 2500 BC.* (Malta, Patrimonju Publishing Limited, 1996).

27   Anthony Bonanno, "The Artist in Prehistoric Religious Ritual: Servant or Master?," in Anthony Pace, ed., *Maltese Prehistoric Art 5000-2500 BC,* Loc. Cit.

28   Anthony Bonanno, *Malta. An Archaeological Paradise.* 5th edition (Valletta, M. J. Publications, Ltd., 1995).

29   See Sabatino Moscati, "Some Reflections on Malta in the Phoenician World," *Journal of Mediterranean Studies*, 1993. Vol. 3, No. 2: 286-290.

30   Willow LaMonte, "Asphodel Long," *Goddessing Network News,* Winter '95/96.

31   Willow LaMonte, "Akua'maa," *Goddessing Regenerated* ,Summer's End/Autumn 1996.

32   Marlene Saliba, *Time-Faring. Poems.*(Malta, Formatek Ltd., 1994).

33   Veronica Veen and Adrian van der Blom, *The First Maltese. Origins, character and symbols of the Ghar Dalam culture* (Haarlem, Holland, a fia publication, 1992), 10.

34   Ibid., 11.

35   Ibid., 45.

36   Ibid., 55.

37   See Cavalli- Sforza, et al. *History and Geography of Human Genes* (Princeton, N. J., Princeton University Press, 1994), 195.

38   See Julian Reade, *Mesopotamia. British Museum* (Cambridge Harvard University Press, 1991), 17. Ashmolean Museum, The Ancient Near East (Oxford, 1994).

39   Anne Baring and Jules Cashford, *The Myth of the Goddess. Evolution of an Image* (London, Penguin Arkana, 1991), 181.

40   Ibid., 380.

41   See Betty De Shong Meador, "Inanna: Lady of Largest Heart, Women's Sacred Texts: Ancient Expressions of Feminine Spirituality." Lecture to the C. G. Jung Institute of San Francisco, April 12, 1995.

42   Ibidem.

43   Ibidem.

44   See Sabatino Moscati, *Ancient Semitic Civilizations* (New York, Capricorn Books, 1957). Chapter Five.

45   Keith W. Whitelam, *The Invention of Ancient Israel. The Silencing of Palestinian history* (London and New York, Routledge, 1996), 1.

46   Ibid., 42.

47   Ibid., 57.

48   Norman K. Gottwald, *The Hebrew Bible in its Social World and in Ours* (Atlanta, Georgia, Scholars Press, 1993). Chapter 7, "Israel's Emergence in Canaan, an Interview with Norman Gottwald," 92-93.

49   Ibid., 94-95.

50   Ibid., 101.

51   Ibid., 100

52   Asphodel Long, *In a Chariot Drawn by Lions. The Search for the Female in Deity* (Freedom, Ca., Crossing Press, 1993), 45.

53   Amihai Mazar, *Archaeology of the Land of the Bible, 10,000-586 B.C.E.* (New York, et al, Doubleday, 1990, 1992), 52, 78, 79, 137, 220.

54   Ibid., 237.

55   Ibid., 273-274.

56   See Tommaso Spadaro, "I cigni," *I racconti di Motya* (Marsala, La Medusa Editrice, 1989).

57   Moscati, *Ancient Semitic Civilizations*, 115-ll6.

58   Ibid., 126

59   See Judy Grahn, *Blood, Bread, and Roses. How Menstruation Created the World* (Boston, Beacon Press, 1993).

60   Ibid., 266.

61   Barbara G. Walker, *The Woman's Encyclopedia of Myths and Secrets* (HarperSanFrancisco, 1983), 829-830.

62   For Good Friday ritual of people acting as jews at San Fratello, Sicily see Chapter 7, this work.

63   Ibid., 31

64   *Ebla to Damascus. Art and Archeology of Ancient Syria,* ed., Harvey Weiss (Seattle and London, Smithsonian Institution in association with University of Washington Press, 1985), 38-39.

65   Ibid., 36.

66   See James B. Pritchard, *Recovering Sarepta, A Phoenician City* (Princeton, New Jersey, Princeton University Press, 1978). See 4-5. See also Claude Baurain, Corinne Bonnet, *Les Pheniciens. Marins des trois continents* (Paris, Armand Colin Editeur, Paris, 1992). The definitive study of the phoenicians is *I Fenici,* Direzione scientifica di Sabatino Moscati (Milano, Bompiani, 1988).

67   Pritchard, Loc. Cit., Passim.

68   Ibid., 107.

69   Ibid., 25.

70   Ibidem

71   Ibid., 140-141, 144, 148.

72   Ibid., 27.

73   Ibid., 93.

74   Ibid., 148.

75   *Ebla to Damascus*, Loc. Cit., 145. See Alfonso Archik, "the Royal Archives of Ebla. " Also "Seated Couple," # 65.

76   L. Luca Cavalli-Sforza, et al., *The History and Geography of Human Genes* (Princeton University Press, 1994). See Ivan Van Sertima, *They Came Before Columbus. The African Presence in Ancient America* (New York, Random House, 1976). for the thesis that africans sailing west early reached south and central America.

77   See Cavalli-Sforza, *History,* "Africa." Loc. Cit.

78   Sabatino Moscati, "Some Reflections on Malta in the Phoenician World," *Journal of Mediterranean Studies*, 1993. Vol 3., No. 2, 286-290.

79   Archeologia Viva Video, *I Fenici e il Mare* (Firenze, Giunti Gruppo Editoriale, 1991).

80   R. A. Oden, Jr., *Studies in Lucian's Syria Dea* (Missoula, Montana, Scholars Press for Harvard Semitic Museum, 1977), 5, 47, 51, 54-55, 38, 40, 76, 77, 79-80, 89, 91, 94, 97-98, 101, 103, 105, 124, 142, 155. See also P. R. S. Moorey, *The Ancient Near East* (Oxford, Ashmolean Museum, 1994).

81   *La donna etrusca* (Roma, Edizioni ebe, 1987), p. 7. For etruscan women dancing completely nude, 13. For women at banquet with men, 14-15. For the etruscan Mater Matuta (holding a child), 82., for a canaanite face on a necklace, 109.

82   *Ebla to Damascus*, 65.

83   Ibid., 155.

84   Ibid 118.

85   See Lawrence DiStasi, *Mal'occhio. The Underside of Vision.* (Berkeley, Calif., North Point Press, 1981).

86   *Ebla to Damascus*, Loc. Cit., 138-139.

87   Ibid., 139, 145-146; 222.

88   Ibid., 113.

89   Ibid., 145-146.

90   Ibid,. 222.

91   Ibid., 198

92   Ibid., 199.

93   See Figure 21, Baring and Cashford, Loc. Cit., 204.

94   Sylvia Brinton Perera, *Descent to the Goddess. A Way of Initiation for Women* (Toronto, Canada, Inner City Books, 1981).

95   Ibid, 221.

96   Ibid., 246.

97   See Raphael Patai, *The Hebrew Goddess.* Third enlarged edition (Detroit, Wayne State University Press, 1990). For african presence in eastern Asia, see Runoko Rashidi, co-edited by Ivan Van Sertima, *African Presence in Early Asia* (New Brunswick and London, Transaction Publishers, 1985, 1995). Beads, associated with veneration of the dark mother in antiquity, became a pervasive symbol of justice in the 1960s; Dick Gregory, african american moral critic of the 60s, told me that his mail was inundated with beads.

98   See Elinor Gadon, "The Hebrew Goddess and Monotheism" in *The Once and Future Goddess.* Loc. Cit.

99   *From Ebla to Damascus,* 257.

100   Ibid., 258.

101   Ibid., 264.

102   See Chapter 7, this work.

103   *Ebla to Damascus,* 265.

104   Ibid., 272.

105   Ibid., 264.

106   Ibid., 288. See Donald B. Redford, *Egypt,Canaan, and Israel in Ancient Times* (Princeton, N. J. , Princeton University Press, 1992).

107   Judith Lange, "1000 anni di Tunisia," *Archeologia Viva,* Luglio/Agosto 1989.

108   Abdelmajid Ennabli, "Cartagine. Civiltà risorta," *Archeologia Viva,* luglio/agosto 1995.

109   See Lucia C. Birnbaum, "African Heritage of Italian, Other European Americans, and All Peoples of the Earth," in Ishmael Reed, ed., *Multicultural America. Cultural Wars, Cultural Peace. Essays on Post Black-White America* (Viking Penguin, 1996).

110   See Jane Ellen Harrison, *Prolegomena to the study of Greek Religion* (London, Merlin Press, 1962, 1980) for the "more primitive stratum" behind greek rituals, 1-31.

111 *The Archaeological Museum of Syracuse Paolo Orsi.* Text by Giuseppe Voza, Photographs by Mimmo Jodice (Siracuse, Ediprint, 1987).

112 Sabatino Moscati, *Italia Punica*, Loc. Cit. 9, 40, 41, 48,156, 173, 181. See also Sabatino Moscati, *La bottega del mercante. Artigianato e commercio fenicio lungo le sponde del Mediterraneo* (Torino, Società Editrice Internazionale, 1996), a work Moscati completed near the end of his life that demonstrates the similarities of canaanite art of west Asia (at Tiro, Sidone, Nimrud, and Cyprus) to the art of Africa, and the similarities of canaanite stele and jewelry in Sicily, Sardinia, and Spain. See also Moscati, *Il tramonto di Cartagine. Scoperte archeologiche in Sardegna e nell'area mediterranea* (Torino, Società Editrice Internazionale, 1993).

113 See the black Diana in the Museo Nazionale in Naples and the black Diana in the Capitoline Museums in Rome. For tophets, not as places of child sacrifice, but as children's cemeteries, see Archeologia Viva Video, *I Fenici,* Loc. Cit., 2.

114 From *Ebla to Damascus,* Loc. Cit., 218.

115 Kay Kaufman Shelemay, *A Song of Longing. An Ethiopian Journey* (Urbana and Chicago, University of Illinois Press, 1994). 30.

116 Ibid., 47.

117 In 1997 a highly educated neapolitan advised me that he does not carry business cards because he shares the popular italian belief that a business card may provoke the mal'occhio (envy).

118 Shelemay, *A Song* , 62.

119 Emmanuel Anati, *Esodo tra mito e storia. Archeologia, esegesi e geografia storica* (Capo di Ponte (BS) Italia, Edizione del Centro Camuno di Studi Preistorici, 1998).

120 In *Esodo,* Anati has correlated archeological findings and findings of other disciplines to date the biblical story of the exodus from Egypt to Mount Sinai: to the 350 years between 2345 and 2181 BCE.

121 Ibid., Loc. Cit., "Conclusioni," 251-255.

8. Woman dancer of central Arabia
5300 BCE

Archives of Emmanuel Anati,
Centro Camuno di Studi Preistorici, Italy
Sculpture reproduction by D. Longo

9. Hebrew priestess Qadeshah

Painting by Max Dashu

10. Black madonna of Malta with african spiritmarks

Painting by Monica Sjoo

chapter three

dark mother of Sicily—Ibla Nera. sibyls and black madonna of Chiaramonte Gulfi

"Written history will always remain polemical, in fact a hermeneutic problem. The real focus now must be based on personal experience and not the explosion of compounded human events....We shall not be entangled by arguments among racists....By shifting our focus on the global to the personal arena, we actually give life a new meaning and provide a better recipe for the so-called global history."
—Nicolas Otieno, *A Flight into the Unknown*

The prehistory of Sicily, my ancestral island, encourages a fresh interpretation of all places considered european. Sicilian prehistory, in my view, may best be understood in the context of ancient and continuing migrations from Africa into Sicily (and into the rest of the world), and in the context of belief in the dark mother carried by african migrants into islands of the Mediterranean and to all continents of the earth after 50,000 BCE. As discussed earlier, Diodorus Siculus, historian of late antiquity, and sicilian

81

historians up to the present, have documented their histories with scientific findings and with popular beliefs. Both science and everyday beliefs have documented ancient, and persisting, sicilian beliefs that Africa is the matrix of world civilization, and that the center of african civilization was the dark mother.

Although the likelihood of a prehistoric land bridge between Africa and Sicily has not yet been confirmed, we do know that Sicily is closer today to Tunisia in Africa than it is to Rome or Naples in Italy. Sebastiano Tusa, sicilian archeologist, advises that in the ice age Sicily was much nearer to Africa than it is today.[1] As discussed earlier, from prehistory until the roman era, the west coast of Sicily up to Palermo was an african maritime route. On this route, off Trapani at Levanzo in the Egadi islands, in the Grotta del Genovese, there are pubic symbols of the dark mother

According to Gimbutas' hypothesis, which has been confirmed in genetics data, after 4,000 BCE, throughout the region of present-day Europe, aryan-speaking invaders from the eurasian steppes, who worshipped a male sky god, assaulted the civilization of the dark mother. Ensuing waves of destruction evoked frantic behavior of priests and priestesses of the dark mother. Lamentations of sibyls, female prophetesses who remembered the dark mother and her values, mourned the attack on their harmonious world, and made dire predictions. In the christian epoch, black madonnas, in Sicily, and elsewhere, may be considered images recalling the african dark mother. In this chapter, we examine sibyls of late antiquity and the black madonna, (now whitened), of Chiaramonte Gulfi.

O

Herodotus, greek historian who visited Egypt in 450 BCE, credited egyptians with discovering the solar year, which divided the year into twelve parts. Egyptians told Herodotus that it was they who had first brought into use "the names of the twelve gods, which the greeks took over from them." Egyptians, according to the historian, were the first to carve figures in stone, to design images of gods and goddesses, and the first to build altars, and temples.[2]

Diodorus Siculus, in his history of Egypt to conquest by persians in 525 BCE, said that "the Ethiopians [i.e., the black peoples]…were the first of all men."[3] For Basil Davidson, contemporary africanist scholar, Diodorus' history is significant because he drew on many sources that have been lost, and had a unique ledge for viewing mediterranean civilization. Diodorus' family was greek, he lived under the romans in Sicily,[4] and he wrote a history of Egypt while living in Africa. His chronology has been criticized, but his observations on egyptian "government, law, society, geography, religion, and natural history" remain invaluable.[5] Diodorus observed, more than two millennia ago, what Martin Bernal and others today confirm: "Egyptians usually complain that the greeks steal credit for all the most famous gods and heroes of Egypt, and even for their african colonies."[6] Egyptian colonies, according to Diodorus, extended as far as India.[7]

The belief in Isis, african dark mother, a belief which spread throughout the known world, according to Diodorus, derived from "her manifestations through healing."[8] She was venerated because she was believed to be "the source of great and numerous blessings for all mankind." African women held honored status because of Isis and her lawful rule after Osiris died. This honored status was demonstrated in the african custom that "the queen enjoys greater authority and honor than does the king; while among the common people the wife is likewise master of the husband, since in the marriage contract the man promises to obey his wife in all things."[9]

Human life, in Diodorus' account, began in spontaneous generation in the "fertile alluvial mud of the Nile,"[10] a view close to that of contemporary scientists who have documented in the DNA and in rock art that our species first emerged in central and south Africa. Recording common beliefs of his time, Diodorus also stated that after a great flood, "the rebirth of life obviously began in Egypt."[11] "Awestruck and wondering," egyptians turned their eyes to the heavens and concluded, "two gods, the sun and the moon, were primeval and eternal; and they called the former Osiris, the latter Isis."[12]

The name Isis, for Diodorus, signified "ancient," bestowed for her "ancient and immortal" origin. Isis was depicted with "horns on her head, both from the moon's horned appearance when in its crescent, and because the horned cow is sacred to her among the Egyptians."[13] The hieroglyph for Isis, according to Edward Murphy, editor of Diodorus' writings, represents seat, or throne, helping us understand the isiac origins of the many enthroned goddesses of antiquity, and the many enthroned black (and white) madonnas, or "majesties," of medieval Europe.[14]

Egyptians conceived of the earth "as a sort of womb for all life," denoting it as the "mother," said Diodorus, a concept that the greeks appropriated in designating "the earth as Demeter, or earth mother."[15] Helping us understand african paleolithic and neolithic depiction of divinities in animal form, Diodorus said that people in antiquity believed that the gods visited the inhabited world, "revealing themselves to men in the form of sacred animals."[16] He is also helpful for understanding the african origin of the association of wheat with the dark mother: "After Isis had discovered the value of the wheat and barley which happened to be growing among the other grasses about the country…and Osiris had perfected their cultivation, all men were content to "change their fare," desisting from cannibalism. Egyptians in Diodorus' time praised Isis by carrying wheat and barley sheaves, just as sicilians later depicted santa Lucia carrying wheat. Italian folklore rituals, from antiquity to the present, remember the african dark mother with wheat. The national dish of Italy is pasta.

The belief in justice, for Diodorus, derived from Isis having "established laws which encourage men to deal justly with each other and to refrain from unlawful violence and outrage through fear of punishment."[17] After Osiris' death, Isis accepted the love of no other man, continuing for the rest of her life "to reign in perfect justice and to excel all monarchs in kindness to her subjects." To her nubian sanctuary at Philae, where she was depicted as black, pilgrims brought offerings of milk—until church fathers destroyed the sanctuary in the 5th century CE.[18]

Anticipating contemporary DNA research, Diodorus held that west Asians were african in origin. "Jews lying between Syria and Arabia," were "expatriates from Egypt." Traditional jewish circumcision of male children was an age-old custom, according to Diodorus, "imported from Egypt."[19] Like Herodotus, he credited egyptians with the origin of astronomy and other sciences.[20]

Historians since the late 19th century who have focused on the high culture of Greece as aryan have not acknowledged Diodorus' history, perhaps because his observations were not flattering to high greek culture; e.g., it was the greeks, said Diodorus, who introduced many cruel customs into Egypt, including exposure of unwanted infants.[21]

In the late 19th century, Raffaele Solarino, sicilian physician and historian, dampened european enthusiasm for aryan greeks. Bringing a sicilian view to the matter of myths, he differed from greek understanding of myth which inflects doubt by contrasting myth with reality, In contrast, Solarino held, "Myths can not live for a single day without a historical substratum."[22] In his history of Ragusa, he recorded the ancient mediterranean belief that africans were the first sicilians and confirmed sicilian veneration of the dark mother, pointing to wooden sanctuaries built to Ibla Nera (black Ibla) in Sicily in the millennium and a half before the common era.

In the period european theorists were crediting aryan greeks for the origin of western civilization, Solarino amassed geological and archeological evidence to confirm the popular belief that mediterranean civilization originated in Africa.[23] He examined the spirals and circles inscribed on prehistoric artifacts in sicilian communities, and stated what sicilian experts today verify—early inhabitants of Sicily lived in circular villages surrounded by moats.[24] Analyzing the popular belief that in death humans return to the mother, Solarino pointed to the african origins of paleolithic burial of humans who were laid to rest in a fetal position in uterine-shaped grottoes.[25] Noting what womanists, feminists, and others today remember, Solarino said that before greek, roman, and christian civilizations there was no separation of the spirit, or the soul, from the body. This african holistic belief, which is counter to christian canonical doctrine, has persisted throughout the christian epoch in subordinated cultures of the world.[26] More than a hundred years ago, before the contemporary controversy over whether the origin of greek high civilization was aryan or african and levantine, Solarino considered it demonstrably obvious that the high civilization of Greece stemmed from Africa and west Asia.[27]

Solarino said that Ibla Nera, called black by classical roman writers as well as by sicilians, was the diminutive affectionate contraction of the name of the west asian divinity Cybele, whose images were probably brought to Sicily by migrating anatolian farmers after 10,000 BCE.[28] Subsequently, west asian traders blended Cybele with semitic Astarte, and with african Isis. Greeks changed the sicilian name, Ibla Nera, to Ibla Hera,[29] erasing the blackness of the african mother and denigrating her moral power by naming her Hera, subordinated wife of Zeus, father god who ruled the patriarchal greek pantheon.

Ibla Nera may have been called black not to single out her black skin, because as Cavalli-Sforza points out, up until 5,000 years ago all migrants out of Africa to all continents were dark.[30] Before invasions of light skinned aryan speakers after 4,000 BCE, all mediterranean peoples and their deities were probably dark. To the ancients, black probably did not refer to skin color but to the black volcanic rock of Mount Etna, on whose flanks sicilians built Ibla's sanctuaries. Ibla Nera in Sicily and Cybele in Anatolia were both identified with an active volcano and with the trade in volcanic black rock, or obsidian, a trade, as mentioned earlier, that they considered holy. In Anatolia, which means land of the mother, Cybele was called Mother Goddess of Obsidian. The association of black rock with the dark mother persisted: when romans thought to co-opt popular veneration of Cybele, they sent for a black rock. The black kaaba stone of islam and black madonnas of christianity are icons of the subaltern cultures of both of these religions.

In the late 20th century, Giuseppe Leggio, local historian of Ragusa, linked Ibla Nera's temples with the arrival, at some date after 10,000 BCE, of the sicani, a datum that coincides with Herodotus' finding that africans were the first to build temples. Temples built by sicani of Africa in Sicily were of wood and have left no traces. Earlier temples in Sicily challenges conventional understanding that temples of Malta (3800 BCE) were the first built in the Mediterranean.

According to sicilian stories, sicani were africans who migrated first to west Asia, then walked through Europe to the Pyrenees, and then backtracked through present day France and Italy before settling in western Sicily. These stories about the sicani are confirmed today in genetics research of african migration routes. Like Diodorus Siculus, Leggio relied on popular beliefs as well as science to document his history, saying that the african origin of sicilians was evident not only in folk stories about the sicani, but in the similarity of sicilian and algerian skeletons.[31]

The memory of the african dark mother is also conveyed in west asian migrations into Sicily after 15,000 BCE in three known temple sanctuaries to Ibla Nera in the iblean mountains. All three sanctuaries of Ibla Nera faced toward Africa. Her major sanctuary was located in the volcanic center of the island, at Paterno'. Another was located near Ragusa and Chiaramonte Gulfi, place of a black madonna in southeastern Sicily. On the east coast of the island, a sanctuary to Ibla Nera was situated at Megara Hyblaea, in whose icon, dated ca. 600 BCE, she is a seated mother suckling two babes. It may be relevant that this statue of a dark woman divinity is close to Acireale, where a contemporary scurrilous carnevale lampoons patriarchal church and state, and features images of Isis and of her cat.[32]

In paleolithic times, african migrants in Sicily lived in grottoes and caves; in neolithic times, west asian migrants lived in tents grouped together in a circle grounded on rocks, roots, and mud. Womb-like grottoes dug into rock cliffs, earlier used for habitation, later became ritual or burial sites. In Sicily prehistoric civilization of the dark mother is marked by spirals incised on artifacts at Castellucio and in spirals in the necropolis near Noto. In the Stentinello culture, named for the village near Syracuse where they were first identified, neolithic ceramics of Sicily were characteristically large polychrome vases decorated with red, brown, and yellow cords, colors associated with the dark mother of Africa.[33] Invasions of aryan speakers into Sicily after 1900 BCE are documented in the introduction of offensive and defensive weapons into the island's earlier harmonious mother-centered culture. Shields and daggers have been discovered in necropoli near Syracuse, Pantalica, and Montagna di Caltagirone. Aryan origins of the shields and daggers are suggested in their resemblance to greek weapons from Mycenae.

Solarino's 1885 appraisal of early sicilian peoples is revealing. He did not care for aryan greeks, nor for the aryan branch of the italics, the siculi, who arrived in Sicily in 1900 BCE. Aryan siculi and aryan hellenes were both violent. He did like the semitic canaanites of west Asia, who may have arrived in Sicily as early as the 1400 BCE, and founded trading settlements at Palermo, Mozia, Ragusa, and Modica around 800 BCE. Canaanites, in contrast to greeks, said Solarino, did not have the "mania of conquest." They worked hard, maintained good relations with Africa, and sailed great distances searching for tin and amber. Canaanites, whom the greeks called phoenicians, explored Africa's west coast, and traveled as far north as the Scilley islands off british Cornwall.[34]

To Modica, canaanite trading center in the iblean mountains, sicilians brought domestic animals, wool, leather, cereal, wine, and oil, which were then transported by caravan to ships bound for Carthage, Africa. At Carthage, canaanite traders picked up metals, textiles, spices, as well as african and west asian icons of the dark mother, and brought them back to Sicily.

Canaanites came peacefully to trade in Sicily; greeks and romans came and enslaved sicilians. During the punic wars when greeks and romans needed help to fight canaanite/carthaginians, sicilians did not respond. Sicilian dislike for violent greeks is evident in sculptures by native craftsmen now housed in the Ashmolean Museum in Great Britain. Sicilian dislike for violent romans, who exploited the island as the granary for the empire, became intense after what sicilians called roman "barbarities" during the punic wars. After destroying carthaginian Camarina outside Ragusa Ibla, romans, according to sicilian sources, raped, plundered, and "profaned" native temples.[35]

In Magna Graecia, or south Italy and Sicily, art historians have identified many sicilian images of the dark mother as greek. "Greek," as contemporary scholars point out, was a category in antiquity that referred to cultures of Africa, west Asia, south Italy, Sicily, and Sardinia, as well as to Greece. The collection of "Ancient Greek Terracottas" in Britain's Ashmolean museum, which I studied in the spring of 1995, is a case in point. Most of the "greek terracottas" were created in south Italy and Sicily. African and west asian influence is quite apparent. See "Standing woman" of Taranto whose face resembles Sekhmet, lion-faced goddess of Egypt; "Fragmentary female" of Taranto whose hair is fashioned in african cornrows; woman of Gela, a west asian Astarte figure; and "winged" couple of Taranto evoking Isis and an african/west asian lover. Sicilian artisans who created these sculptures reveal resentful attitudes toward greek culture—an image of Athena at Taranto looks, not like militaristic greek Athena, but a sulky, defiant woman. The image of the african slave boy of Taranto conveys empathy. Ashmolean terracottas may be regarded as evidence, at the beginning of the common era, of sicilian resistance to greek and roman invaders who demeaned the dark mother and tried to destroy her values.

Other art in Sicily and south Italy reveals the melding of african and west asian images of the dark mother. A 100 BCE representation of the mistress of the beasts has wings of african Isis and lions of west asian Cybele.[36] After 598 BCE, when greeks took african and canaanite Camarina, african and west asian icons were replaced by greek images.

Greek images cut the african dark mother Isis into separate mother and daughter figures and subordinated both to male gods.[37]

Constricted by imperial and violent romans, sicilian slaves rebelled. At Enna, in the center of Sicily, a syrian slave named Euno invoked the dark mother, formed an army, and fought off the romans for forty years.[38] Enna is the setting of the graeco-roman legend that recounts Hades' abduction of Proserpina and her mother Demetra's search for her daughter all over the iblean mountains. The myth may tell what actually happened: the rape of the civilization of the african dark mother by aryan/indo-europeans. The christian adaptation of the myth of the mother looking for her daughter became the ritual of the statue of the madonna being carried from church to church on holy Saturday looking for her son.

O

As greek and roman violence assaulted the earlier nonviolent civilization of the dark mother in Sicily, Africa, and the rest of the ancient world, male priests of the dark mother. and female priestesses—sibyls named for Cybele—expressed despair and anxiety. Will Roscoe has studied the desperate behavior of male priests of the mediterranean great mother—african Isis blended with anatolian Cybele, and levantine Astarte. These priests, who spread throughout the greek and roman world, lived in collectives, begged alms, and expressed wild veneration of the dark mother in a frenzy of self-mutilation, self flagellation, blood letting, and ecstatic dancing. Male priests, like female sibyls, made ominous prophecies.[39]

In the first centuries of the new millennium, in far-flung cities of the roman empire, priests of the dark mother whitened their faces, perhaps in mourning, a tradition clowns continued in the historic epoch. In long robes, yellow slippers, bleached and curled hair, rings and necklaces, some with knives, priests would ask for a coin for the great mother. Called galli, these priests of the great mother became others, neither women nor men.

Not a small sect, "similar patterns of religious gender transgression can be found in most Old World civilizations, from the Mediterranean all the way to Southeast Asia…."[40] They survive to this day among the hijra in Bombay, described in 1994 as a "cross-dressing cult of the mother goddess" numbering 50,000. Like rituals of the ancient galli, rituals of the hijra, are characterized by music, bawdy behavior, and frenzied dancing.

Precursors of the galli, according to Roscoe, were third millennium BCE cross dressing servants of Inanna, or of Ishtar in Mesopotamia. They played flutes, drums, and cymbals, and had intercourse with men, a custom thought to bring good fortune. It was believed that the great mother could change men into women, a psychological process that may have been the "castration" described by ancient writers, or the "male temple prostitution" condemned in biblical writings. Augustine and other church fathers condemned homosexual sex as lewdness, but homosexuality persisted, and has been celebrated in carnivals, and gay pride demonstrations, throughout the christian epoch.

In greek patriarchal expropriation, veneration of the dark mother was transferred to Dionysus, god of fertility, wine, and drama, and son of the father god Zeus. Yet veneration of the dark mother persisted in sphinxes, sirens, and sibyls. Greek appropriation and popular resistance is visible at Hera Lacinia's sanctuary at Capo Colonna in Crotone where the icon of the greek goddess is flanked by winged sirens. The continuum of the african dark mother of antiquity into the christian epoch is suggested in the winged siren and seated sphinx of Crotone, which became the black madonna of Capo Colonna, who is fervently venerated to this day.[41]

Romans refined expropriation with co-optation. Aware of the large popular enthusiasm for the dark mother, roman officials arranged for a black meteorite to be brought to Rome to honor Cybele in games called ludi to celebrate the "great mother of the gods." Expropriation and co-optation may have been necessary because the value of justice associated with the dark mother inspired cultural and political resistance to injustice, and uprisings against authorities.

In early years of the common era, the african religion of Isis and her son Horus, whose west asian images were Cybele and Attis, merged with the christian mother Mary and her son Jesus, Sibyls who remembered the dark mother were precursors of black madonnas and of peasant women called comari, or godmothers, who transmitted (as we shall see in subsequent chapters) the memory and the values of the dark mother throughout the historic age.

Greeks imposed the name Artemis on canaanite Astarte, and merged Artemis with the delphic sibyl. [42] The delphic sibyl, another case of appropriation, was said, by officials, to owe her power of divination to Apollo. Depicted as a crone dressed as a young girl, the sibyl of Delphi was said to consider Apollo her brother.[43] The dark mother, in christian scriptures, was disguised as Sophia, or Wisdom, or obliterated.

The disappearance of the dark mother evoked an atmosphere of crisis and anxiety, that infused sibylline prophecy in late antiquity and early christendom. After 70 CE when romans destroyed the jewish temple at Jerusalem, jews in diaspora came to Italy, where many acculturated to dominant graeco/roman culture. Acculturation was accompanied by apocalyptic fears.[44] The jewish prophetess in Book 3 of Oracula Sibyllina remembered jewish history before Abraham, describing herself as daughter-in-law of Noah.[45] The tiburtine sibyl of Rome, writing in greek as a christian, foretold the end of the world when the capitol of christendom was moved to Constantinople.

The sibyl, like the dark mother, was known by many names and was identified with the known world of antiquity: Asia, Europe, and Africa. The asian sibyl was called "Sambethe, the Chaldaean or Jewish Sibyl." Like Oracula Sibyllina, she was also associated with the time before Abraham and Moses, depicted as sailing with Noah on the ark. The erythraen sibyl was identified with Babylon. The hellespontic sibyl was located in west Asia at Troy, which aryan greeks destroyed in 1100 BCE. The delphic sibyl was associated with greek Artemis and with roman Diana of Ephesus.

In late antiquity and the early common era, sibyls mourned aryan destruction of the civilization of the dark mother, covering the known world with their lamentations—libyan sibyl of Africa, delphic sibyl of Greece, cimmerian sibyl of Italy, erythraean sibyl (Cassandra) of Babylon, sibyl of Samos, Greece, cumean sibyl of Magna Graecia (south Italy and Sicily), hellespontic sibyl of Troy, phrygian sibyl of Asia, canaanite sibyl in Sicily, and the tiburtine sibyl of Rome.[46] Eurocentric historians would later refer only to sibyls[47] of Ephesus in Asia, Samos in Greece, and Cumae near Naples in Italy, omitting the african sibyl of Libya, [48] an omission that may mark the beginning of historical obliteration of the african origins of world civilization.[49]

The folk story about Italy's cimmerian sibyl recounted that she migrated from Asia to Cumae near Sorrento, that she pined away believing she would never see her native land again. Only her voice remained. This popular belief persisted to the 20th century when italian/american migrants expressed nostalgia for their motherland in the popular song, *Torna a Sorrento*, conveying longing for south Italy, and, perhaps, a deeper longing for the civilization of the dark mother longer ago in Africa and in Italy. My father, who emigrated from Sicily to the United States, wept when he listened to *Torna a Sorrento*.

Caves, trees, and water associated with the dark mother were likewise associated with sibyls. Sibylline prophecies were given in caves, sibylline responses were sometimes drawn as lots written on the bark of trees, and ritual bathing was associated with receiving sibylline prophecy. Cumae, first greek settlement in Magna Graecia, place of the cimmerian sibyl, may have recalled african origin in her name, Melancraera, or Black Head. The sibyl of Cumae lived in a cavern dug into a mount in the region near Naples (and Sorrento) where sanniti, who worshiped the dark mother Mefite, fought greeks and romans heroically before they were vanquished. In this region in the christian epoch, region, belief in the dark mother has persisted to this day in many sanctuaries, and fervent pilgrimages to black madonnas.[50]

Artifacts of Cumae reveal roman mutilation. Patriarchal Jove and his subordinated wife Juno were superimposed on the sibyl of Cumae. Greek and roman expropriation of the dark mother and her wisdom is visible in the greek myth that Zeus swallowed the mother Metis, and Athena was born from the father's forehead. Yet the memory of the dark mother persisted. In the cavern of the cumean sibyl, in an underground crypt where greek and roman images of gods and goddesses were found, archeologists came across an african tree of life and an ankh of Isis.

In the period of greek and roman expropriation and co-optation of veneration of the dark mother, the despairing sought out the sibyl. Virgil, the roman poet, described the site of the cumaean sibyl. "The side of the cliff of Cumae is cut out into a vast cavern, into which a hundred approaches lead, a hundred mouths, from which as many voices pour, the answers of the Sibyl."[51] In late antiquity and the early common era, the sibyl of Cumae prophesied, "I see wars, grisly wars and the Tiber foaming with much blood."[52]

The spread of sibyls and their dire prophecies from west Asia and Africa to the entire graeco-roman world[53] worried authorities. Officials of augustan Rome, anxious about sibylline denunciations of the corruption of imperial power and prophecies of the imminent fall of Rome, forbade private ownership and burned sibylline books. Inaccessible to the people, a few sibylline books were locked in official archives. When violent suppression did not work, authorities resorted to co-optation, apparent in Augustine's City of God, misogynist treatise that became the foundation of canonical christianity. The church father said he found in sibylline writings "no worship of false or fictitious deities."[54] Sibyls, said Augustine, predicted the coming of christianity.[55]

Art may convey the story of sibyls more accurately. On the facade of the casa enclosing the black madonna of Loreto in Italy, sibyls precede hebrew and christian prophets. On the ceiling of the sistine chapel, Michelangelo painted five sibyls alongside seven jewish prophets. On the floor of the cathedral of Siena, the continuity of sibyls and black madonnas is conveyed in the proximity of images of the libyan sibyl of Africa and a black madonna of Europe.[56]

Sibyls and black madonnas, both popularly venerated, have been swallowed by the church. But clerical discomfort is evident. When I asked the sacristan in the duomo of Siena where I could find the black libyan sibyl and the black madonna said to be on the floor of the cathedral, he responded that they were not black, but "sporche" (dirty), a word with pejorative sexual overtones.

When in 1997 we visited a church famed for its fresco of sibyls in the Sibylline mountains of Italy, we discovered that the fresco had been moved to a back room. A popular story about this sanctuary to the madonna dell'Ambro (madonna of amber) links her to canaanite search for the ancient translucent fossil resin used in jewelry in antiquity. Today amber jewelry is popular among feminists of Italy, the United States, and elsewhere; it is said to "spiritualize the intelligence." The phrase implies that remembering the ancient dark mother of Africa, whose values were justice with compassion, equality, and transformation, as well as the dark mother of Canaan, whose political legacy is resistance to injustice, may, indeed, spiritualize the intelligence.

Joyce Lussu, contemporary italian feminist communist, describes sibyls as all our mothers and all our daughters "who keep the memory of the prehistoric peaceful civilization and envision a future of communitarian democracy wherein people share ethical and social responsibilities in a society in close rapport with nature."[57]

In 1997 in Italy we discovered that these values are still alive in the Sibylline Mountains. We came upon an ecological farm, La Campana, located near Montefiore dell'Aso, a cooperative of professional men and women who in the 1970s fled Milan (vortex of italian capitalism) to live close to the earth doing meaningful work. The little community has maintained itself as a communal group for three decades. Residents of La Campana live in personally restored farmhouses in a community where everyone combines professional pursuits with manual labor. The founder, and moral center, of the commune is an elderly woman. Men and women of the communitarian democracy have adopted an african child who has been brought up as a daughter by the whole community. When we visited La Campana, there was a festa for the daughter who was shortly to leave for college.

A scholar studying sibyls concluded that the tradition was handed down from mother to daughter, that all sibyls derive from an original mother prophetess, to whom subsequent sibyls were related as daughters; e.g., the cumean sibyl was the daughter of the tiburtine sibyl.[58] The tiburtine sibyl, associated with the document *Dream of nine suns*, places the history of humanity in nine ages, beginning with the establishment of christianity in the 4th century. This dream book recounts journeys of the sibyl in Africa, Egypt, Ethiopia, Asia, Macedonia, Cilicia, Galatia, Babylonia, Lydia, and prophesizes a messianic king, an antichrist, and a day of judgment.[59] In the oracle of the tiburtine sibyl, the sibyl is a queen who reigned in Galilee, Ethiopia, Libya, Persia, and Rome.[60] How the sibylline tradition was co-opted by secular authorities may be seen in medieval editions of the oracle of the tiburtine sibyl, connecting sibyls with queens of the holy roman empire.

Italian and other feminists concerned about violence to the earth and all life are today recovering the sibylline tradition.[61] In the 20th century the woman closest to the sibylline tradition may have been Simone Weil, (see chapter eleven) who, like earlier sibyls, remembered the civilization of the dark mother. Shaken by the deepening violence of the 20th century, Simone Weil fasted herself to death in 1943.

O

Christianity, after an open-ended first three centuries that might have institutionalized the egalitarianism of Jesus, did not do so; patriarchal christianity became the religion of the roman empire after 323 CE.[62] In 431 CE at Ephesus, Anatolia, on an african migration path where canaanite Astarte, greek Artemis, and roman Diana had been venerated, a church council recognized Mary as the mother of god. But the mother remained unacknowledged in christian doctrine, whose trinity remains father, son, and holy ghost. Ghost she may have been to church fathers, but the memory of the dark mother has remained alive in legends about sibyls, icons of black madonnas, art, and in everyday and festival rituals of peasant cultures of judaism, christianity, and islam, as we shall see in subsequent chapters.

In Sicily the memory of the dark mother may be found in stories about the black madonna of Chiaramonte Gulfi, where my ancestral paternal great grandparents lived. The town is situated outside Ragusa Ibla, home of my immediate paternal grandparents before they came to the United States in the early 20th century. Chiaramonte Gulfi, on the path of pre-historic african migrants, became a place of veneration of Ibla Nera at some point around the 1400 BCE, when migrants and traders from west Asia founded the town. They called the town Akrillae, for Acre in west Asia, where canaanites had venerated the dark mother Astarte.[63] In the first centuries of christianity, in this town at the foot of the Monti Iblei where black Ibla had been venerated, a devotion arose to a black madonna who was believed to protect the poor, a devotion that has continued to this day.

In the annual procession, men pull the statue of the black madonna with a rope for four kilometers, women walk barefoot, and migrant workers come home from afar to kiss the icon of the dark mother and the earth.[64] The region of Akrillae/Chiaramonte Gulfi is located on an agricultural plain of the Monti Iblei where vines, almonds, carob, and fichi d'India are grown. It is famed for its beautiful women, fine air, pecorino cheese spiced with saffron, black pepper, sausage, artists, scientists, writers, and its miracle-working black madonna.

The origin in the christian epoch of the black madonna of Chiaramonte Gulfi is dated to the period of strife between iconoclasts and iconodules in Byzantium, although the deeper origin that renders the ground sacred may be related to its location on the path of paleolithic african migrants and to its neolithic sanctuary to black Ibla. In the early christian epoch, according to legend, santa Lucia of Syracuse came to Akrillae. She stayed in a grotto in the Monti Iblei now called the Grotta di santa Lucia, where a little church was built for her. Like a nurturant breast of the earth, one of the peaks of the Monti Iblei, named for the dark mother, is called santa Lucia.[65]

In this region where Ibla Nera was revered in antiquity and a black madonna today is adored, popular catholic beliefs are strikingly different from doctrinal catholicism. Chiesa San Salvatore does not refer to Jesus as the christ, but to Jesus as saint saviour. The church of san Giovanni Battista, as does folklore in Sicily (and Malta), honors the precursor and prophet, John the Baptist, equally with Jesus, suggesting, perhaps, that it is the prophetic tradition (linked to sibyls) that underlies the popular christianity of this region. The church of santa Teresa d'Avila honors the nun of a jewish conversa family (see chapter six this work) who kept her ultimate beliefs in silence. The church of santa Maria di Gesu' is dedicated to saint Mary of Jesus. The church of santa Sofia points to the dark mother embodied in the wisdom literature of egyptian, hebrew, and christian scriptures.[66] Grottoes and springs, here as elsewhere, remember the sacred waters of Isis.

The legend about the black madonna of Chiaramonte Gulfi recounts that during the 8th century controversy in Byzantium over icons, merchants, intent on saving images of madonnas from destruction by iconoclasts, put two statues on a ship without sails and without a helmsman. The ship came ashore at Camarina in Sicily, outside my ancestral Ragusa Ibla. Statues of mother and son were put in two carts without drivers, whose oxen carried the mother to the place she wanted her sanctuary built, in the iblean mountains at Chiaramonte Gulfi.

In the popular catholicism of Sicily, in contrast to doctrinal catholicism, mother Maria and her son Salvatore are both venerated as saints. In this region where black Ibla was venerated in the period before christianity,

Mary's son is called saint saviour, or Salvatore, and given the diminutive affectionate form, Turiddu, a name sicilian mothers give to beloved sons. Turiddu was the name my nanna Lucia gave to her son, my father, and the middle name Wally and I gave to our middle son, Marc Turiddu, who has always followed his own path. In sicilian folklore, mother and son live in different places. According to the story, the cart with Maria stopped at Akrillae on the sicilian plain named for Acre, the west asian town where canaanite Astarte was venerated. A christian church was built for the dark mother at Akrillae. Oxen carried the son's statue farther up into the mountains, where a christian church was built for him as well.

In the 4th century CE a christian community arose at Akrillae. Catacombs of southeast Italy (I have visited some of them) are more numerous than those of Rome. Later, the town was taken by african moors, who named it Gulfi. After 1060, scandinavians who had settled in France in the 9th century, invaded Sicily and took the town. Normans here, as elsewhere in Sicily, tried to impose canonical christianity and its medieval concomitants—anti-semitism and feudalism—on the people. Yet the memory of the dark mother persisted, sometimes circuitously. The french family, Chiaramonte, who came with the normans in the 11th century, replaced the name Akrillae with their own name, Chiaramonte, a name that refers to Clermont in France, place of two significant black madonnas (see chapter four).

The association of the dark mother with justice may be glimpsed in the history of Chiaramonte Gulfi. In 1282-3, the Sicilian Vespers, an uprising against french angevin invaders, began at Palermo and spread around the island. The angevin french, who continued the norman attempt to impose canonical christianity on sicilians, bloodily put the uprising down. In the 19th century, Chiaramonte Gulfi again became the site of revolutionary uprisings, again suppressed. Before world war one, poverty sent many chiaramontese, and other sicilians, to find work in the United States, or in Africa. After the second world war, chiaramontese departed to find work in Austria, the Americas, northern Italy, Switzerland, and west Germany.

In their diasporas, the people of Chiaramonte Gulfi brought the memory of the dark mother with them. Today black madonnas are worshipped in migrant worker quarters of cities of central Europe where foreign workers from south Italy and Sicily, as well as from Africa and southeast Asia, find a common bond in images of a black madonna. (See chapter four, this work).

In the 19th century, my sicilian relatives called the black madonna of Chiaramonte Gulfi la mammà. In my childhood in Kansas City, sicilian/americans always called their mother, la mammà. A legend of Chiaramonte Gulfi recounts that the icon of their black madonna did not come from Constantinople at all, but from misera Palestina. Perhaps this was a half-remembrance of the canaanites who brought their dark mother Astarte with them when they came to Chiaramonte Gulfi in 1400 BCE before they founded a trading settlement here in 800 BCE.[67] Inside the popular legend that the dark mother was rescued from Constantinople in the 9th century CE may be an inner story: the dark mother was rescued from the capitol city identified first with patriarchal greeks, then with greek orthodox christians, who tried to co-opt or suppress the memory of the dark mother.

Black madonnas who carried the memory of the primordial dark mother into the christian epoch were, and remain, deeply loved. In 1839, major folklorist of the iblean mountains, Salvator Amabile Guastella, wrote a poem, *Maria dei Gulfi*, invoking her as "the breath of another age" to whom "your children...the poor and the desperate, look."[68] Traditionally, in the iblean mountains of Sicily, she was called "Mamma Maria."[69] The most popular song, almost the anthem, of migrants from south Italy and Sicily to the United States in the early 20th century was *O Marie!*

When we first visited her sanctuary at Chiaramonte Gulfi some years ago, I was dismayed to find that the madonna, whom I had read was black, had been sculpted of undarkable white carrara marble. Who whitened her? Beginning with the normans, authorities saw to it that the thaumaturgic image was kept under church control aligned with secular authority. Today's white marble statue is dated between the 15th and 16th centuries CE, period of the spanish inquisition and domination of Sicily (1412 to 1713), an era of cruel persecution of moors, jews, heretics, and women (see chapter seven), punctuated by popular uprisings that were crushed. In what may have been a token of resistance to spanish defeat of moors, and resistance to spanish inquisitors who made victims walk through town with shirts painted with infernal flames before they were beheaded, people of Chiaramonte Gulfi have kept the moorish part of the town's name, Gulfi.[70]

Inquisition persecution in this iblean region was particularly directed at women who flouted patriarchal sexual prohibitions. Rosa di Cunta, discovered having a liaison, was undressed and publicly flogged.[71] (See chapters six and seven). The long arm of inquisition persecution reached nuns; one of them, inscribed in the order Santa Maria di Gesù, was jailed and exiled for "false and malicious testimony against the faith."[72]

In the context of the persisting memory of the prehistoric dark mother, and historic persecution of subordinated peoples who looked to her, the madonna of Chiaramonte Gulfi has remained a symbol of resistance. Although whitened by the church, she is popularly considered black. Under spanish persecution followed by austrian domination, she was considered a beacon of justice. On February 3, 1848, despite the presence of austrian troops, citizens of Chiaramonte Gulfi raised the french tricolor in insurrection, rang the bell of the madonna's church, and carried her image through the town.[73] In the 1890s when socialist fervor swept Sicily, people looked to Madonnuzza for sustenance.

Not a transcendental figure, little girls represent her in processions, men "accompany" her on pilgrimages, and women identify with her. In a description of a 19th century pilgrimage, "Men leaped, danced, ran, shouted...musicians played, and people shouted Viva Maria!" Fireworks crackled and mothers lifted their children to see Matri Nostra! or "our mother,"[74] a phrase in distinct counterpoint to the Pater Noster of the church.

In the christian epoch, when religious heresy and political resistance were associated with black madonnas,[75] cultural resistance often slid into political insurrection. During the Sicilian Vespers, every frenchman who could not say ceci, dialect word for chick peas, was put to the sword. Ceci, or chick peas, germinating legumes originally from Africa and Asia,[76] popularly signify regeneration and the dark mother. Roasted ceci are eaten today at all sicilian pilgrimages and festivals. When news of the Sicilian Vespers reached Paris, french authorities sent punitive expeditions to every sicilian town that had participated in the uprising. Citizens of Chiaramonte resisted for two months ("Better dead than subjected to the French!"). Betrayed by a false peace overture, the french came in and killed all the town's inhabitants.

A perennial legend of Chiaramonte Gulfi recounts that there are "hidden treasures and enchantments" in the Grotta di Paraspola near the sanctuary of the black madonna. In one story, a little nun dressed in black can be seen walking near this grotto. Nuns, like black madonnas, remain inside catholic churches, yet the blackness of black madonnas, like the traditional black habit of nuns, and the traditional black dress of sicilian peasant women, may signify the continuing memory of the dark mother, and implicit resistance to patriarchal christianity. Today implicit resistance to patriarchal marriage may be at hand in the contemporary popularity in the United States of black and ochre red for bridesmaids' gowns.

In a Chiaramonte Gulfi story about the grotto near the black madonna's sanctuary, the central figure is a jew. In popular perception (of sicilians and others) jews connote the epoch before christianity. In the christian epoch, oppressed sicilian peasants identified with persecuted jews (see chapter seven). The legend about the treasure in the grotto near the sanctuary of the black madonna recounts that the treasure has not been found because it is "enchanted." Another story tells that once in winter at the stroke of midnight a priest riding his mule saw a light in the grotto. He went inside, and to his great astonishment, saw a market displaying beautiful fruit. Not a soul was there, but he left a coin for an orange. When he arrived home, he discovered that it was a golden orange, symbol of transformation.[77]

Another popular story of Chiaramonte Gulfi suggests how subordinated peoples keep their own history in tales that differ from official history. The protagonists of this story are african carthaginians who fought greeks and romans in Sicily. Imilcone of Carthage, descendant of Hannibal, brought twenty five thousand foot soldiers, three thousand horsemen, and twelve elephants to Sicily. After he reconquered Agrigento, Imilcone rested at Akrillae, later the site of the black madonna of Chiaramonte Gulfi.[78]

The iblean mountains, named for the dark mother, protectively encircle the region around Chiaramonte Gulfi. Here the dark mother's values (justice with compassion, equality, and transformation) have been transmitted from mother to child for more than two thousand years. This vernacular history confirms the theme of gramscian scholars, notably Alistair Davidson, that a core of values, a buon senso has been conveyed in popular wisdom down through the ages. Buon senso, visible in the folklore of subaltern peoples of the world, offers the hope that a just world will emerge from the people at the bottom of society who, despite negation of their culture, have retained this communal good sense, or senso commune from prehistory to the present.[79]

In 1983, this buon senso was visible at Comiso, town near Chiaramonte Gulfi, when women of the world came together to protest NATO nuclear missiles, On women's day, March 8, international and italian women carried bed sheets printed with declarations of opposition to hierarchy, militarism, exploitation, sexual violence, ecological disaster, destructive force, and delegation of life decisions. Remembering the values of the primordial dark mother, embodied here in the whitened black madonna of Chiaramonte Gulfi, women declared the values of a better world: self-determination, denuclearization, liberated work, human spaces, clean seas, creative force, and responsibility for life[80].

Notes

1   Sebastiano Tusa, "Prima Sicilia," *Archeologia Viva,* Maggio/Giugno 1967),

2   Basil Davidson, *African Civilization Revisited. From Antiquity to Modern Times* (Trenton, Africa World Press, Inc., 1991, 1993). 60.

3   Alistair Davidson, "Gramsci and the Pacific Rim," paper presented to Italian Research and Study Group, Center for Western European Studies, University of California at Berkeley, March ll, 1998, 61.

4   Ibidem.

5   Edwin Murphy, *The Antiquities of Egypt.* A translation with notes of Book I of the *Library of History of Diodorus Siculus* (New Brunswick, and London, Transaction Publishers, 1990). xi.

6   Murphy, 29.

7   Ibid. 17, 19.

8   Murphy, 31.

9   Ibid., 33.

10   Ibid., 10, note ll.

11   Ibid., 13.

12   Ibid., 14.

13   Ibid., 14-15.

14   Ibid., 15. See chapter 4, this work.

15   Ibid., 16.

16   Ibid., 17.

17   Ibid., 19.

18   Ibid., 27, n. 45.

19   Ibid., 35.

20   Ibid., 88.

21   Ibid., 101.

22   Dr. Raffaele Solarino, *La Contea di Modica. Ricerche Storiche.* First published 1885. (Ragusa, Libreria Paolino, 1982), Vol. 1, 45.

23   See Martin Bernal, *Black Athena. The Afroasiatic Roots of Classical Civilization* (New Brunswick, Rutgers University Press, 1991), Vol. 1.

24   Solarino, *La Contea,* Loc Cit; 52.

25   Ibid., 56.

26 Ibid,, 72.

27 See Cheikh Anta Diop, *Civilization or Barbarism*. Loc. Cit.

28 Ibid., 27, n. 45.

29 Bernal, *Black Athena,*. 75.

30 See first chapter, this work.

31 Giuseppe Leggio, *Ibla Erea* (Ragusa, Tip. Leggio e DiQuattro, 1978). 14 ff.

32 Solarino, *La Contea* , Loc. Cit., 83.

33 Ibidem

34 Ibid., 120.

35 Ibid., 187-88.

36 C. E. Vafopoulou-Richardson, *Ancient Greek Terracottas* (Oxford, Ashmolean Museum, 1991).

37 See Giovanni Di Stefano, "Gli Elimi e il Dio Arpocrate," *Archeologia Viva*, May-June 1994. Cf. R.E.Witt, *Isis in the Graeco-Roman World*, Loc. Cit., 15ff.

38 Leggio, *Ibla Erea*, Loc. Cit., 203.

39 Will Roscoe, "Other Genders: Problems and Possibilities for Feminist Theory." Scholars Seminar,Institute for Research on Women and Gender, Stanford University, Stanford, February 19, 1992.

40 "Dal santuario di Hera Lacinia," *Archeologia Viva*, May-June 1996.

41 I thank Maria Cimino and Yvonne Kohler for helping me understand popular beliefs in Sicily, with particular thanks to Maria for the booklet, *La Madonna Colonna di Crotone. Storia e pietà mariana dalle origini ai giorni nostri.* A cura di Don Bernardino Mongelluzzi. (n.d. Graffiche Cusato Edizioni, Capocolonna, Italy).

42 "Dal santuario di Hera Lacinia," Loc. Cit.., 10, 12.

43 Ibid., 12, 14.

44 H. W. Parke, *Sibyls and Sibylline Prophecy in Classical Antiquity*, edited by B. C. McGing (London and New York, Routledge, 1988), 6, 7.

45 Ibidem.

46 Ibid., 30, 31, 35.

47 Ibid., 64.

48   The image was recovered for the jacket of the first U. S. edition of my *Black Madonnas.*

49   Ibid., 78.

50   See Birnbaum, *Black Madonnas,* Loc. Cit.

51   Quoted in Parke, *Sibyls,* Loc. Cit., 80.

52   Ibid., 79.

53   Ibid., 125.

54   Quoted in Parke, *Sibyls,* Loc. Cit., 170. See also Peter Burke, *The Renaissance* (Atlantic Highlands, Humanities Press International, Inc., 1989).

55   Parke, *Sibyls,* Loc. Cit., 170.

56   See cover of Birnbaum, *Black Madonnas.* Loc. Cit. See Robin Lane Fox, *Pagans and Christians* (HarperSanFrancisco,1986), 202, 203, 681. Also, Ross Shepard Kraemer, *Her Share of the Blessings. Women's Religions among Pagans, Jews,. and Christians in the Greco-Roman World* (New York and Oxford, Oxford University Press, 1992). See Elaine H. Pagels, *The Johannine Gospel in Gnostic Exegesis: Heracleon's Commentary on John* (Nashville & New York, Abingdon Press, 1943).

57   Birnbaum, *Black Madonnas,* Loc. cit., 162.

58   Jeanne Baroin, Josian Haffen, *La Prophetie de la Sibylle Tiburtine* (Paris, Annales litteraires de l'Universite' de Besancon. Les Belles Lettres, 1987).. 17.

59   Ibid., 24, 30-31,

60   Ibidem.

61   See Birnbaum, *Liberazione della donna,* Loc. Cit., Part II.

62   See Elaine Pagels, *The Gnostic Gospels* and *The Origin of Satan* (New York, Random House, 1995). For the condition of women and slaves in this period, see Philippe Aries and Georges Duby, General Editors. *A History of Private Life.* Vol I, *From Pagan Rome to Byzantium.* Paul Veyne, editor. Arthur Goldhammer, Translator (The Belknap Press of Harvard University Press, Cambridge, Ma. And London, England (1987). Particularly 39, 53, 55, 160, 170, and 217: "Pagan religion oppressed no one." Fabrizio Mancinelli, *Le Catacombe Romane e l'origine del Cristianesimo.* Introduzione di Umberto M. Fasola (Firenze, Scala, 1981). See Ramsay Macmullen, *Christianity & Paganism in the Fourth to Eighth Centuries* (New Haven and London, Yale University Press,

1997) for the persistence of earlier beliefs underneath the official christianity of the roman empire. Macmullen also points out the diminished stature of women in christianity in comparison with their status in "traditional cults" (8)—notably the murder of Hypatia at the beginning of the fifth century, when the patriarch Cyril allowed a mob to kill her (15). Part of the history of persecution of pagans in Africa by official christianity has been obliterated because sources were destroyed by invading Vandals of Spain and France. (23). Long before the open persecution of non-christians in the period of the inquisition, roman emperors could favor their christian co-religionists in appointments, in commanding all citizens to attend christian churches, et al. In the first three centuries, christianity, won over about a tenth of the population, then "many times that number in the next three generations." (72). By the beginning of the fifth century, half the population still held prechristian beliefs. (72). "Diana worship lived on in Spain, celtic Italy, and Gaul." (74). Crosses to keep out illness and other misfortune were displayed on doorposts just as the ankh, sign of life, had earlier. (143). It was not a question of pagan and christian beliefs at odds with one another, but a good deal of intermixing. (144). In art the intermixing of pagan and christian symbols was to have a long life. (148).

63   Giovanni Ragusa, *Chiaramonte Gulfi nella storia di Sicilia (dalle origini ai nostri giorni)* (Modica, Franco Ruta Editore, 1986).

64   *Venuta da Lontano, L'antico culto della madonna di Gulfi. Storia e tradizione.* A cura di Giuseppe Cultrera, Francesco cultrera, Gaetano Guastella (Ragusa, Utopia Edizioni della S.C. Ulisse a r.l., 1990). "Presentazione."

65   Ragusa, *Chiaramonte Gulfi.* Loc. Cit.See Carmelo Conti, *Il vento a corde dagli iblei. Autori del novecento* (Ragusa, Criscione Tecnoplast. Graficarta s.r.l., 1987). Per conto della Edizione Greco s.a.s. Catania. R. Poidomani, *Carrube e cavalieri,* (Ragusa Thomson, 1970). Poidomani, a cousin on my paternal grandmother's side, wrote novels based on peasant life in the iblean mountains.

66   See Elisabeth Schussler Fiorenza, *In Memory of Her.*Loc. Cit.

67   Ragusa, *Chiaramonte,* Loc. Cit., 15.

68   Ibid., 28.

69   Ibid., 60.

70   Ibidem.

71   Ibid., 67.

72   Ibidem.

73   Ibid,. 89.

74   Ibid., 154.

75   See Birnbaum, *Black Madonnas.*, Loc. Cit.

76   DeAgostin, *Grande Dizionario della Lingua Italiana,* (Firenze, Remo Sandron, new edition 1990).

77   Ragusa, *Chiaramonte*, Loc. cit., 173-174.

78   Ibid., 179-180. See Leonard Cottrell, *Hannibal. Enemy of Rome* (New York, Da Capo Press, 1992).

79   Alistair Davidson, "Gramsci and the Pacific Rim," Italian Research and Study group, Center for Western European Studies, University of California, Berkeley, March ll, 1998.

80   See Birnbaum, *Liberazione della donna*, Loc. Cit.,. 248. See chapter 12, this work

11. Dark mother of Megara Hyblaea, 600 BCE, Sicily
Permission granted from Museo archeologico Paolo Orsi, Syracuse, Sicily

12. Canaanite youth "with attitude"
Mozia, Sicily
Photograph by Jodi MacMillan DeMartile

13. Sicilian Demeter, Enna, Sicily
Banner by Lydia Ruhle

14. Black madonna of Adonai,Sicily
Photograph by Jodi MacMillan DeMartile

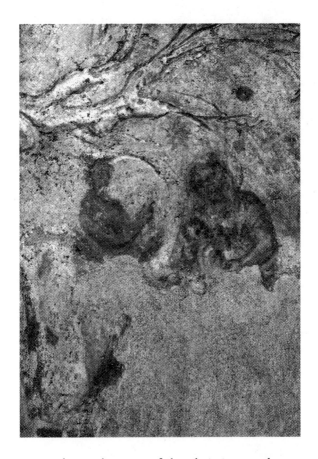

15, Ochre red image of the christian madonna
Priscilla Catacombs, Rome, Italy
Photograph by Wallace Birnbaum

16. San Benedetto il Moro, sanctuary of santa Rosalia
Palermo, Sicily

Photograph by Jodi MacMillan DeMartile

part two

*black madonnas,
saints and peasant women
as godmothers*

chapter four

black madonnas on the white continent of Europe

"I unequivocally believe that She is the new symbol of hope and unity for the new millennium."

—Stephanie Romeo

Images of black madonnas may be our most palpable evidence of the persisting memory of the primordial dark mother of Africa on the continent of Europe, continent, historically associated with the notion of a white race. After researching images of black madonnas of Italy for a previous book, I discovered that France had many more than did Italy, that there were black madonnas in Spain, Switzerland, Austria, former Czechoslovakia, Bulgaria, Germany, Poland, lands of former Soviet Russia, former Yugoslavia and elsewhere in Europe—as well as images of black madonnas and other dark women divinities throughout the world. Images, we are coming to realize, are "legitimate systems of signs with which we are provided in order to describe the world."[1]

On our summer 2000 study tour of Sicily, we came across the oldest black madonna I know, Madonna dell'Adonai, at Brucoli, Sicily. Mary Beth Moser found her in Ean Begg's gazette of black madonnas, we walked down a dirt path, and were then dismayed to learn that the little church was closed for restoration. Chickie Farella convinced the workmen that it was very important that we see the black madonna. And the door opened.

Brucoli by the sea, outside Syracuse, is on an ancient african migration path. In the millennium before the common epoch, it became a canaanite settlement, then a place where canaanites with a mother-centered world and greeks and romans with patriarchal cosmologies fought in the iblean mountains for Sicily. In the grotto at Brucoli in the sicilian region of Gesira, africans left the color black on the dark mother, canaanites and israelites gave the hebrew word for god to the Madonna dell'Adonai, and we are left to meditate on the african, canaanite, israelite, and christian origins of western civilization in this little church said to have the oldest image of the madonna in christendom.

In the quiet church, we found the sermon the rector of the sanctuary, R. Palmiro Prisutto, had delivered in french to pilgrims to the black madonna of Adonai on her feast day, the fifth of August, a few days before we came upon her. The sermon pointed out that the sanctuary, called sainte Marie, Mere de Adonai, or saint Mary, mother of Adonai, is "the oldest sanctuary to Mary in Sicily and probably of the christian world."

The grotto, visible only from the sea, is hidden by vegetation. At the end is the dark mother painted, at a date unknown, on the grotto wall. The grotto may span the eon from prehistoric african migrants, neolithic migrants from west Asia, to canaanite traders in the millennium before Jesus, greek settlers after the 8th century BCE, and jews and christians fleeing roman persecution in the lst century CE.

In the 3rd century CE, a christian church was erected over the grotto. After, christianity was established, the grotto church was abandoned. At the end of the 17th century, a cow herder came upon its ruins. News of the image of the black madonna spread and it became a place of pilgrimage. During the earthquake of 1693 the little church was the only one in Sicily to escape damage. In the 18th century it became a benedictine hermitage, a self-sustaining monastic order of lay inhabitants who kept vows of poverty, chastity, and obedience.

The image in the grotto is called Marie Sanctissima Mater Adonai, holy Mary, mother of Adonai. In his sermon the rector noted that the name Adonai is the hebrew name for the lord. "To many the title seems strange, and difficult to accept given the date of the image...a hebraic title in a graeco-roman building?" Mary, mother of the lord with a hebrew name evokes the period before establishment of christianity when there was little difference between persecuted jews and persecuted christians. This oldest black madonna in christendom, connotes, for me, the african mother of everyone, a dark mother who has had many images, who has figured in different popular beliefs and rituals of the world, whose echoes are still audible in popular cultures of judaism, christianity, islam, and who brings to our questions the immense silence of all black madonnas.

O

In this chapter I shall bring together what I know about black madonnas of Europe, leaving the illustrations to convey the heterogeneity and ubiquity of black madonnas and other black women divinities who may be found all over the earth.

The subject of black madonnas has stimulated a great deal of grassroots and academic research. Tours lead people to the many black madonnas of France, I wrote a book on black madonnas of Italy and have led study tours to sites of the dark mother of prehistory and of black madonnas in Sicily and plan a similar study tour to Spain. In light of contemporary problems, one research priority, in my view, is the prehistoric dark mother and black madonnas of eastern Europe. Recently

Charlene Spretnak brought to her class on Mary at California Institute of Integral Studies an image of the black madonna in Croatia, to whom her grandmother prayed

In eastern Europe, the black madonna of Czestochowa is the most well known dark woman divinity. Judy Matthews visited the black madonna of Czestochowa at the Jasna Gora Monastery in 1998. "The guide said that she's actually brown, not black (interesting, yes?) and it's because she was a Palestinian (not Jewish, not Israeli, but a Palestinian) woman, so she'd naturally be olive-skinned. It was quite an amazing experience seeing the icon surrounded by believers; they blow trumpets when they unveil her and the energy is very intense. After the icon was broken during a robbery in the 15th century, the restorers left several slashes on her cheek as a reminder. My intuitive response when I saw them was that unconsciously they had given her the wounds of Christ…the Mother cult is so strong in Poland."[2]

In Istanbul in 1998 when Wally and I saw the mother figure Hagia Sofia in Istanbul, I realized that icons of the byzantine dark mother need more research, not well-known aristocratic images of the mother, but simpler images embodying popular beliefs. With the arrival of christianity, beliefs older than christianity were conveyed in images of artists of Egypt, Syria, Mesopotamia, and Anatolia. These and later images from this part of the world have been called "byzantine" by art historians.

There are many byzantine black madonnas in Italy. In Rome, for example, Madonna del Conforto in S. Maria Nova dated the 5th or 6th century CE; l'Icona dell'Hodigitria dated 8th century CE in the Pantheon, a favorite meeting place of italian feminists. In Puglia, byzantine dark madonnas are everywhere. The very dark mother in Carpignano Salentino dated the 10th century symbolizes the significant amalgam in the salentine peninsula of ancient beliefs and contemporary radical politics.[3]

Friends send discoveries. Joan Levinson came across a black madonna in Paris in the church of St. Julien le Pauvre, an image that supports my thesis that black madonnas often signify the resistance of others in christian Europe. Arabic writing borders the painting of the black madonna in this church, where students of the University of Paris held assemblies from the 13th century until 1524, when their riotous meetings were banned. In 1968, french students in the quarter of St. Julien le Pauvre joined students across the world demonstrating against the U. S. invasion of Vietnam.

Phylis Martinelli gave me a painting sent by her son in Spain. A contemporary rendering in red of the black madonna of Montserrat, the art work recalls the original ochre red of the dark mother. Neal and Linda Birnbaum saw a black madonna at Bourges-en-Bresse in a region of France where there are many images of the dark mother. And many heresies, notably the cathar heresy, as well as heresies circling Mary Magdalen.

Perhaps because the meaning of black madonnas is only partially accessible to consciousness, people are often startled to realize they have always known that a madonna was black, but had not consciously noted that she was. Renate Holub remembered that the madonna to whom her mother prayed, in Oggersheim, Germany, was black. Tony Fasel, on a trip to his hometown, Fribourg, Switzerland, suddenly realized recently that the icon of the madonna he knew in his youth in the Fribourg church adjoining the franciscan Couvent des Cordeliers, was black.

Sometimes people find black madonnas in journeys to find their roots. Xequina Maria Berber, researching her cultural inheritance, wrote a thesis on dark vanilla colored madonnas of Mexico. Emily Gruen White sent me a picture of the black madonna of Svata Hora (Holy Mountain) in former Czechoslovakia near Pribram, where her catholic grandmother lived. Louise Paré, researching the history of her ancestral Ukraine, came across babas, giant stone grandmother figures (originally painted red) pulled out of a river where they had been thrown in the 9th century. Later, she found many black madonnas in russian lands, notably in Moscow on Red Square. In November 1999 Louise wrote how startled she was to discover that the large black icon of mother and child at the southeastern end of Red Square "overshadowed the much smaller icon of God the Father above the entrance." She watched people touch the earth after making the sign of the cross.

On entering the church, Louise became disoriented. Like most americans, her ideas about russian religious beliefs were formed by U.S. cold war rhetoric. Inside the church, she gasped, "There before me was the largest icon of the Black Madonna I had ever seen...no altars and no crucifix." She felt her energy shift: "Here I was: in Moscow, in Red Square, a few yards from Lenin's tomb, standing before this icon of the Black Madonna. My mind echoed the negative rhetoric about the evil empire at the same time I felt in my heart the pain and beauty of so much suffering and transformation that was held in this place." When she watched a ukrainian mother show a younger woman how to do the ritual honoring the black madonna, she thought about her own mother, and how the belief in the dark motherhas been transmitted over the centuries, and continued to be transmitted, even under soviet communism.

Solace Wales Sheets discovered a hidden black madonna at Sommocolonia in Tuscany where, during world war two, african americans, in the segregated platoon of "Buffalo soldiers," valiantly fought against the nazis. Solace has worked to dedicate a transnational monument to peace on the hill in Sommocolonia where christmas week 1944, the african american platoon fought heroically and Lt. James Fox sacrificed his life. In 1998, Fox was belatedly given the U. S. Congressional Medal of Honor. The black madonna of Sommocolonia, hidden by the people during the nazi occupation, was kept in the little church adjoining the historic hill—until the day in 2000 when the historical monument was dedicated, when it mysteriously disappeared.

Sometimes the color of the black madonna shifts. In a tiny village in Calabria, Tina Stromsted found the "madonna so present here...in red, blue, purple and white depending...sometimes light and sometimes dark...." Memories prompt questions. Myrna Smith remembered that the Jesus of her childhood in the Philippines was black. Curious, she thought, because in the Philippines catholic authorities paint his mother white.

Jennifer Colby recalled a black madonna in the lutheran church of her childhood in east Oakland, California, whose parishioners were mostly african american. Later, studying liberation theology of Latin America, she found images of the dark mother all along the cordillera "that runs like a spine through South America, through Argentina, Chile and up into Peru...continuing through to Mexico and the Sierras of California." Mountains, for Jennifer, and other people from time immemorial, "are a woman," sometimes "red and volcanic...sometimes brown...." Sometimes black, Jean Demas has researched land rights and Pele, dark goddess of Hawaii, whose lava tresses streaming down her volcanic mountain, are very black.

When associated with a search for roots, the dark mother pulls across continents. Miri Haruach, african american, wrote a doctoral dissertation on the womanist relevance of the queen of Sheba, whose queendom extended from Africa to Asia. Gia Amella, italian/american, went to Alta Villa Milizia outside Palermo, where ex-votos in the church basement depict the black madonna floating above the figure she is healing. Like milagros, thought Gia, of Mexico.

The memory seems accessible to artists. In the 1960s Heidi Schwabacher painted angels with black faces; in 1996 she wrote that she does not know why she painted the angels black. Several years ago Joan Clair painted a madonna that she realizes now, from symbols in the painting, is an african dark mother. She has recurrent dreams of a black madonna whom clerical authorities are painting white.

An international phenomenon, in Beijing, China at the 1995 world conference of women, the dark mother of Asia was everywhere in images of Kuan Yin, dark goddess of compassion. American women were impassioned to take figurines of the buddhist woman divinity back to the United States. In a bazaar area of the conference, I came upon a young chinese woman painting an asian woman divinity, a very black mother and child, all ovals and spirals.

In Turkey, I was surprised to learn that in this islamic country there is an annual pilgrimage to the black madonna of Ephesus, whom we saw when we were there in 1998. Not so surprising, I later reflected, the shrine is located on an ancient migration path of africans; later it became a sanctuary to the canaanite dark mother Astarte, whom the greeks called Artemis and the romans, Diana.

In the 1960s in Berkeley, California, where the dark mother was a metaphor of the african american civil rights movement and of student uprisings against racism and imperialism, a bumper sticker declared, "God is black…and is she pissed!" Today in Berkeley, bellwether city of cultural and political radicalism of the United States, the dark mother lives in the images of Robert Lentz. The July 1997 issue of *Street Spirit, Justice News & Homeless Blues,* featured a Lentz painting of a black madonna, Protectress of the Oppressed.[4] Another Lentz image of the dark mother is Madre de los Desaparecidos, mother of the "disappeared" of Latin American countries whose dictators have "disappeared" dissidents. White handprints in the corner of this painting reminded me of handprints in prehistoric african caves; today the hand signifies the oppressed.

In Anne Bouie's office in Oakland, California, she pointed to an image of the black madonna of Le Puy. Her many visits to this black madonna in France, said the african american woman, have sustained her in her work helping U. S. teachers confront unconscious racism.[5] Anne Bouie has sustained me in the often-bruising encounters with hostility that my writings on the dark mother sometimes provoke. A project countering racism created by women of color is named Maat Dompim, for Maat, african mother goddess of balance, and for Dompim, the bush, where the voice of the dark mother, say her followers, can be heard.

Margrit Schmid, who has found many black madonnas in mountain fastnesses of Switzerland, sent a card in 1997 from "the darkest place," ex-Yugoslavia, where the famed madonna of Medugorje is white, yet the most passionate new pilgrimage is to a black madonna located in a very old place, in Croatia. In a 1998 fax, Margrit said that on a beautiful winter day in January she peered through a tiny window of a closed chapel at St. Katharinenthal, at the border of the Rhine near Schaffhausen, Switzerland, and saw a black madonna.

Elinor Gadon's essay on Lilith of the Levant and Kali of India stimulated me to meditate on the shared values of dark woman divinities of different cultures.[6] A postcard from India from Michele Radford described the similarity of rituals associated with Kali and rituals associated with black madonnas of Europe. Kali, "lit up with neon lights," is carried at night through the streets to the river for a ritual bath. "Loud instruments are played by people walking in the streets next to the figure…like the madonna in Europe."

In her counseling work using art therapy, Cristina Van Camp Zecca, of California and Italy, finds a recurrent figure of a dark woman in the sand play of troubled children. For Janine Canan, poet and physician, the dark mother as Kali connotes the breaking that precedes transformation. "You who bring grief/ who destroy beauty/ who abandon lovers/ who betray human hope—stronger and more violent than Death/ You force me open, Great One/ My heart is too small—I'm shattering…." China Galland, in her 1998 book, *The Bond Between Women. A Journey to Fierce Compassion*,[7] tells stories of women moving from anger at injustice to compassion, and from compassion to action. For China Galland, and others, the dark woman divinity sustains the work of repair and healing the world.[8]

My study of black madonnas has become a labyrinth wherein I have often been been surprised, and now remain awed by the vastness of research that needs to be done. I have just come across a scientific finding that the dark mother of the olmec world of Mexico is dated 3,000 years ago,[9] long before conquistadores brought the black virgin from Guadalupe in Spain to the new world, where she became the "goddess of the Americas." Marlene Barlow of Costa Rica advised me that there are many, many black madonnas in Central and South America. Elaine Soto who has painted several of them, reminds us that latin american migrants in the United States look to black madonnas. See her "la Virgen del Barrio," of Spanish Harlem in New York City.

The black madonna in Cuba offers many insights. "Breaking a tradition that forced black believers to adore white icons, images of the Black Virgin have evolved in Latin America with the blending of Catholicism and African cults."[10] An example of how popular beliefs and art often anticipate scientific findings, the Virgin of Regla, patron saint of Havana, is a doll with jet black face and hands, dressed in light blue fabric with silver embroidery. Her skin and clothing connect her with Jemanja, yoruba god of the ocean of west african tradition. The black mother carries a white child, expressing the popular belief that "genetically, whites come from blacks," a popular belief now confirmed by genetics research.[11] The black madonna may be powerful throughout all of Latin America because she surprises and moves people who do not care for patriarchal papal catholicism. For many, the black madonna in Latin America signifies the recognition that all peoples are one.[12] In Africa, where ancient and christian figures of the dark mother commingle, the black madonna of Soweto is on the site of 20th century bloody resistance to apartheid.

Black women divinities can be found in all continents of the earth, coinciding with the scientific datum that africans migrated to all continents after 50,000 BCE. Black madonnas of Europe, located on prehistoric african migration routes in the historic epoch, became places of cultural and political resistance in heresies challenging canonical christianity, and defying unjust rulers in popular uprisings.

Slaves taken from Africa to the new world kept the memory of the dark mother in everyday and carnival rituals, dramatically in Jamaica and Brazil, but all over central and south America. In the Americas, images of black madonnas often brought by european conquistadores melded with native american women divinities, and have become centers of liberation struggles for social justice. The Virgen of Guadalupe, patron saint of the Americas, sustains mexican/american farm workers and zapatistas of Chiapas.

Elaine Soto captures the meaning of black madonnas in words and paintings. For her confirmation in catholicism when she was ten, her mother chose Monserrate for her name, a name Elaine did not like until she learned it referred to a beautiful black madonna of Puerto Rico. A jungian psychologist today, she thinks on the inplication of black madonnas—bkack is the initial stage of alchemical transformation. Understanding darkness, for Soto, will help us confront racism and help in our work of transforming ourselves and the world. Her radiant paintings of black madonnas, exhibited in 1999 at the Union Theological Seminary in New York, are helping to accelerate this transformation by understanding the african roots, sometimes via Europe, of black madonnas in the new world. See illustrations in this book of Soto's paintings, particularly La Guadalupe of Mexico and the Americas, La Monserrate of Latin America, Carito of Cuba, El Pozo of Puerto Rico, Shango of Brazil, Erzulie of Haiti, and La Virgen del Barrio of Spanish Harlem in New York.[13]

African american women, perhaps more than any other group, need to recover their own stories of black women divinities. The National Shrine of the Immaculate Conception in Washington, D. C., a sanctuary with a black madonna, coordinated the May 9, 1998 pilgrimage to "Our Mother of Africa," open to all peoples. "The Madonna and Child are situated in a small room facing a bronze bas-relief that chronicles the struggle of black people taken as slaves from Africa and brought aboard ships to the New World." The new chapel was built "mostly by Catholics of African-American descent," who consider the black madonna a symbol of "racial harmony."

Sometimes one can reach the meaning of black madonnas via art. After Stephanie Romeo created an african figure of indeterminate gender (the indeterminate gender of the original african dark mother), she realized that black madonnas point to healing and justice in the third millennium.

O

A very large subject whose implications keep proliferating, this chapter focuses on black madonnas on the white continent of Europe. Anyone tracking her/his diaspora from Africa to all continents will find a plenitude of other dark women divinities.

My 1993 study of black madonnas of Italy[14] focused on images and icons in Sicily at Trapani, Alta Villa Milizia, Tindari, Chiaramonte Gulfi, and on the italian mainland at Palmi, Seminara, Naples, Avellino, Montevergine, Foggia, Bari, Siponto, Bologna, Florence, Siena, and Oropa, on paths of paleolithic migrations of africans walking or navigating the short distance between Africa to Sicily and Italy. Migrants from north and west Africa also walked or sailed to Spain, crossing at Gibraltar, and proceeding on foot into the Pyrenees where many black madonnas remain hidden today, thence into France where many images of the dark mother can be found in the Auvergne, the Dordogne, the Massif Central, and Provence.

From France, prehistoric african migrants walked into Switzerland, where the major black madonna of german-speaking peoples may be found at Einsiedeln. Hundreds of other images of the dark mother were hidden in Switzerland during 16th century religious wars of the reformation and counter-reformation, hidden to save them from destruction by protestants and from whitening by catholic clergy. Paths of primordial africans in central and eastern Europe are marked by the famous black madonna of Czestochowa in Poland and the many dark madonnas called byzantine of eastern Europe. After publication of my 1993 study of black madonnas of Italy, I have come across more italian images[15] and have learned that the image often migrated with europeans to the new world; e.g., the black madonna in the sanctuary of Chivasso in Turin was taken to Latin America by a catholic missionary in the 17th century.[16]

The subject widens in implication and continually gives me pause. When the italian edition of my *Black Madonnas* won the Premio internazionale di saggistica Salvatore Valitutti in Italy in October 1998, I flew to Naples, where Giambattista Vico wrote *La Nuova Scienza,* a book I had not thought about since graduate school. As I was driven to award ceremonies along the serpentine route to the little village of Bellosguardo, I realized that there may be a disconnect, and a lapse of time, between what one knows intellectually and what one understands deeply in the body.

Along the way we crossed where Carlo Levi wrote the classic, *Christ Stopped at Eboli,* wherein he described black madonnas of this region as pagan women divinities coming out of the earth. All of a sudden I understood (in an example of delayed understanding) what Vico meant when he said that in order to build a good society, we need to recover the poetic wisdom of our ancestors.

Access to this wisdom is sometimes cognitive, more often than not it is delayed until bodily understood. Sometimes one has an indirect glimmering. I had been to Loreto, national sanctuary of the black madonna in Italy, several times, but when I examined the list of pilgrims to this "major marian sanctuary of the catholic church," my previous assumptions as an intellectual historian became shaky. Rene Descartes, conventionally regarded as the philosopher of masculinist rationalism, brought thanks in 1624 to the black madonna of Loreto for "having illuminated his philosophic method." Galileo Galilei, founder of the scientific method, visited the dark mother in 1618 and again in 1624. So did Robert Montesquieu, enlightenment philosopher considered to have been concerned to eradicate "superstition." Michel Montaigne, french philosopher of "scepticism," visited the dark mother in 1680.

Thinking about these visitors to the black madonna of Loreto, it seems to me that black madonnas imply a theory of knowledge based on scientific method and scepticism, both grounded on ultimate belief in the harmonious universe of the dark mother. Black madonnas also suggest an epistemology of realism (the ultimate object of faith is really there). The world view embodied in black madonnas has inspired great art, musical masterpieces, and classical works of literature. Caravaggio, powerful realist painter of Italy visited the black madonna of Loreto, as did great musical composers Wolfgang Mozart and Johannes Brahms, and Miguel Cervantes, author of Don Quixote, major classic of Spain.[17] The visitor list to the black madonna of Loreto leads me to meditate on the unverbalized beliefs in the dark mother of earlier philosophers, artists, musical composers, and writers—beliefs that may not be accessible to our fractured 20th century western world view.

This chapter focuses on black madonnas of Spain, France, Italy, Switzerland, Germany, and lands of Russia. In Spain she is called mare de deu, in France vierge noire, and in Italy la madonna nera—mother of god, black virgin, and black madonna. She has international, national, local, and hidden sanctuaries. At her international and national sanctuary in Loreto, Italy, twelve masses in english are available to visitors from the United States, the United Kingdom, the Philippines, and Japan (a guided tour in japanese is also offered). Twelve masses in spanish, and nineteen in portuguese, accommodate not only iberian but central and south american pilgrims. International and national pilgrimages to black madonnas at Loreto in Italy, Czestochowa in Poland, Einsiedeln in Switzerland, and Montserrat in Spain, draw multitudes.

In the fall of 1996 we watched buses from all over Europe climb the craggy mountains to the black madonna of Montserrat in Spain and watched swedes spill out of a bus and dance in celebration.[18] The international Messaggio della Santa Casa of Loreto, a continuing gazette of loretan images all over the world, noted in its July/August 1996 issue that women in pilgrimage at Primosten, Croatia in former Yugoslavia, carried a painting of the black madonna. This pilgrimage conveyed a primary meaning of the dark mother—she nurtures all life. These pilgrims in ex-Yugoslavia protested ethnic hatreds that kill.[19]

I have tried to categorize black madonnas by country, but black madonnas, and saints associated with them, are not easily contained within national boundaries. The black madonna of Montserrat Spain, and saint Teresa, whom I call saint of dark others, refer to the prehistory and history of Africa and of west Asia, as well as to the prehistory and history of Spain, whose modern empire stretched across Europe and the new world for three hundred years. Not containable in ethnic categories, the image of the black madonna of Montserrat outside Barcelona, Spain, for example, is described by an art historian as "a Gothic princess of striking beauty and tenderness."[20] Gothic she may be, but she is ebony black and popularly called "la Moreneta," the little black woman. The title of the book about her in the Montserrat museum remembers the woman in the *Song of Songs.* Nigra sum. I am black.

Dark madonnas cross epochs of time as well as continents. Santa Maria del Carmine of Spain is a dark madonna associated with santa Teresa, patron saint of Spain, who is also venerated in Italy, France, and the Americas. Teresa reformed the carmelites, order rooted in ancient Mount Carmel in Galilee near the present border of Africa and west Asia. The dark image of Santa Maria del Carmine in the Brancacci Chapel in Florence, Italy is called Madonna del Popolo, a striking dark mother of the people whose visage is african and semitic. In Rome, the Madonna del Popolo in S. Maria Maggiore has been whitened.

In Spain, black madonnas may be found at Cadiz, major entry point from Africa, at Avila where Teresa was born, and at Guadalupe whose icon was brought to Mexico by conquistadores. Black madonnas of Spain recall a long prehistory of migrating africans, a history evoked in the basque country of the Pyrenees, an enclave not touched by invading aryan speakers. Basques have a preponderance of Rh-negative blood type.[21] The Basque language is "a true isolate in Europe...not related to any other extant language [it] does not belong to the Indo-European family."[22]

The black madonna of basque Mondragon, recalling the african dark mother of prehistory, points to a cooperative world future. Mondragon does not connote "my lady," medieval salutation to the christian madonna, but "my dragon," prehistoric african and asian symbol of the dark mother. People of Mondragon have created the world's most successful cooperatives, whom international socialists consider models of decentralized socialism.[23]

The black madonna of Montserrat in Spain is situated among dramatic rock formations that seem to push up from the center of the earth. She is everywhere in Spain, with images in the monastery of Clarisse in Madrid as well as at Ador, Algezares, l'Alcud de Carlet, Sant'Andreu de Llavaneres, Artes, Begis, Brafim, La Codonera, Chelva, Llardecans, Lloverola, Lloret de Mar, Lloret de Vista Alegre, Monfort del Cid, Moia, Mutxzamel, L'Olleria, Pina de Montalgrao, Santo Pola, Renau, Sogorb, Ulldecona, Ulldemolins, et al., places so small they can not be found in most atlases. A constantly renewing phenomenon, in the 20th century the 400 year old hermitage at Tarragona was converted into a sanctuary of the "mare de deu de Loreto."

Rebecca Vincent's 1994 essay for my class on black madonnas tracked black madonnas of Spain to prehistoric goddesses of Africa; e.g., to Caelistus who held power over the stars, the sun, moon, weather, and life, who melded with egyptian Isis and carthaginian Tanit. Caelistus also melded with anatolian Cybele, reminding us that Spain is a dramatic case of the complex layers of african migrations into Europe. Paleolithic migrants came to Spain from Africa. Neolithic farmers and traders came to Spain from Anatolia and west Asia. Canaanite traders, in the millenium and a half before Jesus, founded entrepots and settlements all along the south and east coasts of Spain, bringing more african and west asian images, which melded with african images of the dark mother brought by earlier migrants.

Memories of the african and canaanite/carthaginian dark mother persisted in Spain into the common era, flourishing in the everyday cultures of israelite jews in diaspora and of expanding moors from Africa. Andalusia, spanish region closest to Africa, has the highest concentration of Tanit figures of Carthage. Bloody christian wars in Spain to vanquish the moors, and christian persecution of jews, heretics and women, are the historic backdrop for the very passionate easter week rituals in Spain, notably at Seville, rituals with images of the dark mother.[24]

Despite killing and suppression, a subterranean memory of the values of the dark mother has remained visible throughout the centuries in the autonomous lives of remarkable women of Spain. Some women remained in the church as nuns or saints, notably Teresa, whose story is explored in chapter seven. The memory of the dark mother may be glimpsed in popular spanish beliefs wherein women are believed to have special powers. In cultures of others of christian Spain—sephardic jews, moors, and gypsies—women are thought to have "menstrual magic," enabling them to kill flowers and foliage, wound animals, and to ignite and extinguish fires. Some women are believed to have gracia: the power to find lost animals, determine if someone lost is safe, to protect and to heal, themes found in moorish, sephardic jewish, and gypsy cultures of Africa, west Asia, and Europe.

Black madonnas of Spain are powerful figures whose legends recount that she would command a sanctuary to be built and if her will were not carried out, she would punish. Like Kali of east Asia, spanish black madonnas are venerated without glossing over the dark mother's destructive, as well as regenerative, powers. The ferocity as well as the beneficence of the dark mother is recognized in most popular cultures. Rose Romano, italian/american poet, recalls that the madonna of her neapolitan/american childhood was not a "wimpy" madonna. In the sicilian/american culture in which I grew up, the most forceful expletive males could summon, my brother Louis reminds me, was "Madonn!"

The realistic view of the dark mother in Spain has produced stunning art: e.g., Dama de Elche, who closely resembles carthaginian Tanit, bonds fecundity and regeneration with death. Recesses in the shoulders of the Dama de Elche hold ashes of the deceased. The Sagrada Familia church of Antonio Gaudi in Barcelona—considered the church that exemplifies the authentic values of the Mediterranean—was commissioned to be built in the spirit of the black madonna of Loreto. Gaudi worked on la Sagrada Familia until he died, leaving an unfinished church with dragons, seashells, snails, and the broken tiles of many cultures.[25]

Trans-national lineaments of black madonnas are suggested at Saintes Maries de la Mer on the south coast of France, where gypsies travel from afar in an annual pilgrimage on May 24. Hundreds of people crowd into the small underground crypt of the church midst flickering candles, and reach out to touch her,[26] a scene movingly described by China Galland in *Longing for Darkness. Tara and the Black Madonna.*[27]

The church has tried to absorb black madonnas, but heretical popular beliefs around the dark mother elude clerical clutch. Marie Boucher has pointed out that the black madonna of the sanctuary and pilgrimage of Saintes Maries de la Mer is called santa Sara by the church, but gypsies call her Sara-Kali. Outwardly deferring to the church, gypsies keep their own beliefs in the dark mother in an oral and secret tradition. "The name given by the Gypsies to Sara, 'la Kali,' in both romani and hindi means 'the Black woman' and 'the Gypsy woman.'"[28] Gypsies are believed to have originated in India, to have migrated to Persia, Armenia, the Levant, Anatolia, the Balkans, Romania, Hungary, and Macedonia before arriving in western Europe. Others went to Egypt, crossed north Africa and the straits of Gibraltar to reach Spain, where many gypsies still live in caves or tents.[29] Like prehistoric and contemporary africans, hindus, and other earth-bonded peoples, gypsies consider everything alive to be sacred.[30]

The meaning of matriarchy as it existed in prehistory may, perhaps, be understood by studying the social structure of gypsy life and other isolated matriarchal cultures.[31] When a gypsy man marries, he marries into the wife's family; children speak the mother's, not the father's, dialect. Scarcely exercising power *over* anyone, women in prehistoric and contemporary matriarchies were/are accorded family power similar to the power accorded to healers, a power deriving from "a strong affinity with the Earth and its mysteries...."[32]

Journeys of gypsies from Asia to Africa to Europe suggest the continuing blending of peoples and images of the dark mother from prehistory to the present. Peoples of India immerse Kali in the holy river Ganges;

gypsies immerse Sara-Kali in the Mediterranean sea. Mer, french word for the sea, Marie Boucher points out, is almost identical to the french word for mother, mere.[33] The pilgrimage site of the black madonna of Saintes Maries de la Mer is located in a region of early african migration paths, where, millennia later, canaanites brought images of Astarte, Isis, and Cybele and established an entrepot, in this region of France where christians built many sanctuaries of black madonnas.[34]

Gypsy culture helps us understand veneration of black madonnas and other black divinities by people considered other by dominant cultures. Gypsies put on (like one puts on a protective cloak) the religion of the dominant culture wherever they happen to be, but keep their deep beliefs to themselves. In external affiliation, gypsies may be catholic, orthodox catholic, hindu, muslim, whatever, but their actual beliefs are kept in a secret oral tradition glimpsed in rituals surrounding the black madonna— a black woman who seems to be the earth, all the waters of the earth, all creatures, and themselves[35] A few years ago, Wally and I were participant observers in the pilgrimage to saintes Maries de la Mer. Priests sang to santa Sara, male gypsies on horseback "guarded" the black mother, and thunder and lightning split the sky as a passionate crowd of pilgrims took Sara-Kali into the sea. The next day, a more subdued church procession honored Sara-Kali's two white half-sisters.

"The saintes Maries who are celebrated at the pilgrimages at Stes. Maries de-la-mer are Mary Salome', Mother of the Apostles James and John, and Mary Jacobe', sister of the Virgin Mary, who, according to the most commonly told Catholic version of the legend, were fleeing persecution. Every account of the story specifically mentions that the holy Marys were accompanied in their perilous journey by their Black maid servant Sara, who was considered an important member of the company."[36] Marie Boucher has found at least eight versions of the story of the two processions. One very heretical version recounts that Jesus and Mary Magdalen married, and that their daughter is the black madonna of saintes Maries de la Mer.[37]

Mary Magdalen and black madonnas are intertwined in popular understanding; both are subversive of canonical church doctrine. Mary Magdalen was the first to see the risen Jesus; the apostles did not believe her because she was a woman. Although church fathers branded her a fallen woman, Mary Magdalen may be the most beloved saint of France. She is popularly connected to black madonnas, sometimes directly, sometimes subtly; e.g., the figure of the whitened madonna, in the church of Sainte-Marie-Madeleine at Aix-en-Provence in France, has a black hand.

Folk stories recount that Mary Magdalen arrived in Provence by boat, that she spent her last days at St. Baum. Margaret Starbird has pursued this legend in *The Woman with the Alabaster Jar. Mary Magdalene & the Holy Grail*,[38] finding many similarities between black madonnas and the other Mary. The town of Vezelay in France, for example, has relics of Mary Magdalen as well as a sanctuary of a black madonna. After the 11th century, Vezelay became the fourth largest pilgrimage center of christendom, after Rome, Jerusalem, and Campostela in Spain. At Vezelay, protestant huguenots and french revolutionaries destroyed images of the black madonna as well as images of Mary Magdalen.

In France, as elsewhere, archeology confirms the continuum of the ancient dark mother with black madonnas of the christian epoch. A temple of african Isis was found underneath the cathedral of the black madonna at Le Puy; ruins of a temple to anatolian Cybele were found near the black madonna of Lyon; artifacts of canaanite black Astarte have been found near the black madonna of Marseilles, et al.

Popular heresies carried the memory of the dark mother into the middle ages. Heresies of the cathars of southwestern France, on a path of prehistoric african migrations, so threatened the church that the pope declared a domestic crusade against them. Anti-catholic agitation during the protestant reformation in France led to the destruction of many images of black madonnas. Yet pervasive popular beliefs may account for the preservation of black madonnas in France who are more openly black than in Italy, seat of the papacy, where many images have been whitened.

Black icons of the virgin are more powerful than white ones, states Marie Durand-Lefebvre in her study of black madonnas of France, perhaps because black images evoke many kinds of emotions. The small "African" in his mother's arms "sometimes looks closer to delivering an anathema than a blessing."[39] In her search for origins of black madonnas, Durand-Lefebvre notes that the portrait of the madonna that saint Luke painted from life in Jerusalem was that of a woman of Judea who sojourned in Egypt, who, she states, "would have been dark."[40] The shulamite woman in the *Song of Songs* declared she *was* black. Durand-Lefebvre agrees: "Following the genealogy of Christ...Marie would be the descendant of David and would therefore be susceptible to belong to the Ethiopian race,"[41] a conclusion confirmed by contemporary genetics, and attested to by the interchange of africans and west asians in prehistoric and later times.

In France we have found vierges noires at Chartres, Nimes, Toulouse, Tours, Le Puy, Orleans, Rocamadour, Nancy, Metz, Clermont-Ferrand, Lyon, Paris, Avignon, as well as at saintes Maries de la Mer, Notre Dame du Chateau d'Anjony, Notre Dame de Marsat, and Notre Dame des Neiges at Aurillac. There are many, many more. French scholars, in careful analysis, note that protestant England has no indigenous images of black madonnas (there are a few copies of european catholic images), that Austria, Czechoslovakia, and Belgium[42] have copies of black madonnas of Montserrat of Spain and of Loreto of Italy. Why is it, asks Sophie Cassagnes-Brouquet,[43] that the mother of Jesus, is almost the only religious figure represented in the color black?[44]

Of the handful of other religious figures depicted as black, perhaps the most significant is saint Anne, mother of Mary, and grandmother of Jesus, who is painted black in the 13th century window of Chartres. In France, particularly in Brittany, saint Anne is given the reverence Mary receives elsewhere, a subject Valerie Kack-Brice has researched, discovering that prehistoric dolmens of France are identified with saint Anne[45]. During the renaissance, saint Anne was painted by Masaccio as a dark mother standing *behind* her daughter Mary. In Florence in 1424 the artist was inscribed in the order Compagnia di San Luca dedicated to Luke, the saint who painted Maria from life. In Masaccio's painting, dark saint Anne seems to be a rendition of Isis of Africa melded with Inanna of Sumer. The image of her daughter Maria is the whitened verion of the church.

Marie Durand-Lefebvre, exploring legends and stories of black madonnas, said she was led to Africa and the "Orient" (that curious word that up until recently included Egypt). Classical graeco-roman writers, she notes, described Isis, Cybele, Diana, Hera and Dionysus as black;[46] european icons of black madonnas were often made of black basalt imported from Egypt. A black madonna found in Holland has been traced to Syria.[47] Crusaders did not mention the color of mother images in the holy lands, according to Durand-Lefebvre, because "they may all have been black."[48] Exploring the connection between the ancient dark mother and sibyls, she found that a sibyl often became a benefactress saint.[49] Analyzing the similarity between christian pilgrimages to black madonnas and islamic pilgrimages to the black rock at Mecca, Lefebvre noted that black madonnas of christianity and the black rock of islam are popularly considered intermediaries between humans and god.[50]

Intuiting the continuum, Isis of Africa-canaanite/carthaginian Tanit of Africa-black madonnas, a pattern analyzed in earlier chapters of this work, Durand-Lefebvre noted that Notre Dame d'Afrique noire preceded the black madonna of Lyon.[51] Osiris is painted black in *Livres des Mort*; black divinities are found in the tomb of Tut Ankh Amon; Hathor-Nut was black.[52] Supporting Martin Bernal's thesis of the african origin of greek high culture, Durand-Lefebvre finds that there was, indeed, a black Athena.[53] Confirming Jung's intuition, and my research, she considers Isis the major model for black madonnas of Europe.[54] Her analysis of the color black converges with conclusions of feminist scholars that in doctrinal judaism, christianity, and islam, black is the color of error, the night, negation of light, impurity; and evil, yet in popular cultures of judaism, christianity, and islam, black refers to the earth and to the mother of all creation.[55] Supporting Judith Grahn's thesis that since paleolithic times the ochre red of childbirth and menstrual blood has been a sign of the goddess, the color red can be found, somewhere, in almost all representations of black madonnas of France.[56]

Cassagnes-Brouquet's study notes that in a census of 1550, before destruction of images during the protestant reformation, there were 190 black madonnas in France. A recent survey counted 205, most of them copies of old ones that were destroyed. An accurate number is difficult to ascertain because in France, as elsewhere, many are hidden and many are stolen. But the number of black madonnas in France seems to be increasing, not decreasing. Regions of France with the most black madonnas are the Auvergne, the Massif Central, the western Pyrenees, Provence, and the valley of the Rhone,[57] places where primordial africans migrated, and where roman legions, drawn from subordinated classes of Africa, Asia, and Europe, venerated images of the dark mother.[58]

Megaliths, sacred in ancient times and in vernacular history, are associated with black madonnas, particularly in Brittany and the Auvergne in France, in Italy, as well as in Africa, and perhaps everywhere africans migrated. In Puy-de-Dome, where there are many black madonnas, women press an ear against the dark stones to listen to subterranean voices. Sick people are brought to megaliths shaped like dolmens (two or more megaliths with a flat rock across them) in the belief dolmens have healing power; funeral corteges pause at dolmens to put souls of the dead at rest.

Healing powers of the dolmen on which the cathedral at Le Puy is built are related to the healing powers of the black madonna inside the cathedral. At Albepierre in the Cantal, newly-weds dance around a menhir (a megalith standing alone or with others). At Aurillac, where we looked in 1996 for the black madonna of the snows, a menhir is thought to be a place of fairies, as is Saint Flour, place in France of one of the very few figures of a black Jesus without his mother.[59]

Sharon Anthony's study of Jeanne d'Arc reveals that the black madonna to whom Jeanne prayed was Notre Dame des Miracles, that the black madonna to whom her mother prayed, when Jeanne was in jail at Rouen, was the powerful image of Le Puy. The subject of black madonnas can be approached by genetics, archeology, mythology, anthropology, and study of popular beliefs and rituals, but as Sharon Anthony realized in her journey searching for black madonnas of France,[60] and as I have, the dark mother ultimately eludes rational analysis.

Joseph Campbell, prescient thinker of the 1960s, spent months meditating on the black madonna of Chartres (at that time situated behind the altar) before embarking on a career to confirm the validity of myths. Was Vincent Van Gogh consciously aware of the statue of the black madonna, who signifies death and regeneration, at Alyscamps, a cemetery that he repeatedly painted? Simone Weil organized against injustice when she taught at Le Puy, whose chthonic vierge noire is renowned. People of the town, perhaps half aware that Weil's passion was related to the ancient dark mother's values of justice and equality, called Simone Weil la vierge rouge (see chapter eleven), color of the original sign of the dark mother. Did Henry Adams know in the late 19th century when he wrote a paean to the madonna, that there had been a black madonna at Mont St. Michel?[61] A protestant whose search for the mother drew him to gothic cathedrals, did Henry Adams know that there was a black madonna at Chartres?[62]

Jacques Huynen, who has written a perceptive study of the enigma of black virgins of France,[63] was drawn to the vierge de Marsat, as I was when we visited the image in 1996. He calls her "splendide lumiere de la nuit"…splendid light of the night. In a historically appropriate metaphor, Huynen calls the black virgin of Marsat "a sphinx who poses troubling questions to her viewers."[64] Almost all black madonnas of France, Huynen found, are near dolmens or menhirs. He attributes megalithic dolmens and menhirs to druids and celts, a view that was superseded by the belief that megalithic dolmens are indigenous, and that is now challenged by the view that megaliths are related to paleolithic african migrations (see chapter two).

The meaning of Notre Dame de Bonne Deliverance, black madonna outside Paris at Neuilly, was delivered to me across continents. The week before the October 1991 firestorm that destroyed our home, as well as hundreds of others in Berkeley, Alison Klermont, of my Berkeley women's group, mailed me an image of a black madonna on a postcard that was given to her wordlessly by a girl in the metro. Before we fled our burning home, Wally saved my manuscript on black madonnas, and I swept up Alison's postcard with the image of the black madonna of Neuilly. We now live in a radiant mediterranean home built on the ashes of the old, a constant reminder that the dark mother signifies regeneration as well as destruction. The name of the black madonna of Neuilly is Bonne Deliverance.

African origins of black madonnas may be clearer in France than they are elsewhere. The south of France was on the path of paleolithic african migrations and sailings; Marseilles, major port of entry of africans, later of canaanites, is near the Grimaldi Caves (Balzi Rossi) where the large cache of 26,000 BCE figurines of the dark mother was found.[65] In the millennium before the common era, canaanites established an entrepot at Marseilles where they brought their own Astarte, as well as images of Isis of Africa and of Cybele of Anatolia.[66] Revolutionary implications of black madonnas are felt at Marseilles, where *La Marseillaise*, anthem of the french revolution, was born, and where, a few years ago, we participated in a powerful workers procession on May 1st, day of the international festival of workers of the world, in the month that celebrates the mother.

Openness about the color of black madonnas in France contrasts with evasiveness about the color black in Italy, where the church has lightened or whitened many of them. In France she is popularly called La Noire (the black woman). High french culture is another matter. An incident involving the office of antiquities of the Louvre has helped me understand how high culture has negated cultures of others. When I wrote to the museum for permission to include a reproduction of an image of Isis in my book on black madonnas of Italy, the official sent the permission, but prefaced it with a pontifical statement that I was in error—Isis was neither african nor black.

Healing powers of black madonnas are suggested by her image in a volcanic region at Lourdes, France, a major healing site of the world. Healing black madonnas are associated with wooded areas, water (the sea, a lake, a river, a fountain), grottoes and caves, and with the subterranean, often volcanic, chthonic earth. Healing is central to the christian message, yet the black madonna "was considered a stranger to the Christian tradition,"[67] states Cassagnes-Brouquet. Church fathers of catholicism early excised the dark mother from the bible, omitted her from the trinity, and when all else failed, tried to appropriate, and to whiten, the popular image. Protestants destroyed her images: there are almost no significant women figures in protestant church history. Negation and co-optation have been more successful in Italy, seat of the papacy, than in anti-clerical France, where icons of black madonnas remain powerful, and unsettling.

In the middle ages, enthroned black madonnas of France and Spain recalled Isis of Africa suckling Osiris, and seated Cybele of Anatolia giving birth. In the middle ages, sanctuaries of black madonnas of France became way stations for the major pilgrimage to saint Jacques de Campostella in northwest Spain. In France, churches with black madonnas were often built *before* the great wave of church building to the madonna in the 12th century: Chartres was built in 1013; Le Puy before 1093. Enlightenment rationalist denigration of "superstition" helped stoke violence against black madonnas during the french revolution. Crying "death to the Egyptian!" french revolutionaries burned her in effigy.[68] Yet popular veneration of the dark mother survived the revolution; peasants in contemporary processions in french villages carry heavy statues of black madonnas on their shoulders.

Some black madonnas of France vividly suggest african origins; e.g., La Vierge Noire de Saint Gervazy in Puy de Dome, is clearly an african figure. Sometimes, the images convey african and west asian provenance, e.g., Notre Dame de Meymac, called "the Egyptian," has an "oriental" turban. Dramatically african are La Negrette in Espalion, Aveyron and La Vierge de Sous-Terre de Chartres. La vierge noire of Chateau D'Anjony reminded me of an african slave woman of the United States. A major symbol of the primordial dark mother is evoked in the piercing eyes of french black madonnas (e.g. Notre Dame du Marsat in Puy de Dome). Eyes of the very black Notre Dame de la Bonne Mort at Clermont-Ferrand bless a good death.

Like Isis, black madonnas of France are majestic figures. See Notre-Dame de Vauclair and the regal black figure of Notre Dame de Saint-Gervazy (Puy de Dome). Some seem to come out of the earth (Notre Dame du Chauteau (Cantal). Notre-Dame de Rocamadour is a lean and tall dark mother resembling lean and tall Isis, as well as contemporary african sculpture. Notre Dame de Beaune, with no pretension to pulchritude, is a powerful black presence. Most infants held by black madonnas of France are not infants, but miniature adults who seem to signify that the black mother holds all humans in her hands. In France, black madonnas tend to be formidable rather than tender; e.g., the black madonna of Sainte Foy de Conques. Most black madonnas of France are not maidens, but older women with sagging breasts and stomach. La Negrette (Chapelle de l'hopital d'Espalion, Aveyron) conveys the ravages of more than two thousand years of violence inflicted on the dark mother and on dark peoples. Black madonnas of Clermont-Ferrand suggest her appropriation by high culture, yet she continued to be venerated in the popular cultures of others; one image is situated in the cathedral and another image, reminding us that her base is in the popular culture of others, is located in a volcanic area in a "sacred wood." This was the quarter of the city inhabited by canaanites before the common era, then inhabited by israelite jews in diaspora, then by persecuted early christians.[69] Vierge

Noire du Port of Clermont-Ferrand, is not located at a sea port; the name may refer to a port of another realm .

One of the most formidable images of black madonnas I have come across is the black madonna of Bourisp found by Karen and Guy Benveniste in the french Pyrenees. The stark visage of the black madonna in the painting (the original icon has been stolen), seems moorish to Guy. He persuaded the priest to xerox the story of the black madonna of Bourisp, a story that suggests how the church has attempted to use black madonnas to teach church doctrine, yet older meaning keeps overtaking patriarchal messages.

If read with the "hermeneutics of suspicion" (recommended by Elisabeth Schussler Fiorenza for church writings), one can gather a good deal from the story. Handed down orally, the story recounts that the old church in Bourisp was dedicated to saint Orens. Born at Huesca in Spain, son of the governor of Catalonia, saint Orens gave up his wealth for a life of spiritual contemplation, receiving a revelation around 400 CE that he should destroy the pagan statue to Apollo near the church.

The story then changes course, and recounts the local legend about the origin of the church: a black madonna in a cart drawn by oxen took her to the place she wanted her church built (a recurrent theme in stories about black madonnas). The story tells of the many miracles wrought by the black madonna, miracles that often have overtones of justice. For example, a young peasant woman was about to be married when the lord of the manor demanded his patriarchal right to sleep with the bride of a peasant on the eve of the wedding, a loutish custom common to the feudal nobility of Europe. Whereupon a miracle, involving an ox and a black rock, occurred. The monstrous lord was killed, and the peasant couple lived happily ever after. The story, starting out as an edifying account of church victory over paganism, took a side journey into a local story about the apparition of a black madonna, and ended, inadvertently, with a blow to patriarchal denigration of women. The miracle has overtones of popular christianity and popular islam, involving a black madonna and a black rock .

Justice and equality, values conveyed by black madonnas, were subversive in the european high middle ages when the church fixed the hierarchical form of church and state as a pyramid with an enthroned christ at the top, the virgin and the twelve apostles below Jesus, and then saints like Francis of Assisi, Anthony of Padua, Benedict of Aniane, and Isidore of Seville. Copied by secular authority, the apex of the pyramid was the king, then noblemen, then knights and clergy, with peasants at the bottom.

Yet medieval pilgrimages suggested another social structure. Wayfarers from central and eastern Europe walking in pilgrimage to saint James, Santiago de Campostela in Spain, stopped at sanctuaries of black madonnas. Although predominantly male, the pilgrims were bonded to the mother. In the legend of saint James, or Santiago, he was comforted by Nuestra Senora del Pilar in Zaragoza, today the most famous marian shrine of Spain.[70] In the 20th century Ernest Hemingway remembered Pilar in *For Whom the Bell Tolls.*

For Russia, an excellent study of customs and rituals that transmit the memory of the dark mother has been written by Joanna Hubbs. Reconstructing the many facets of the dark mother of Russia, especially her connection with the earth, Hubbs analyzes the persistent memory that has come to be identified with the metaphor, mother Russia. In contrast to Mary of the church, lovely and forever young who rules from the sky, the significant woman figure of russian popular culture is Paraskeva-Piatnitsa, "elderly and unsightly goddess," who ruled on earth and was associated with the fertility of fields and humans. Called the "Dirty One," in contrast to Mary who was called "Most Pure," for Hubbs, "Paraskeva was a pagan deity beloved of the people who had obliged the church to adopt her."[71] She is venerated in the Balkans, in Greece, and in russian lands. The russian "Dirty One" in contrast to "Most Pure" has had resonance elsewhere. My sicilian/american mother, whose favorite dress color was black, said she loved her grandchildren the most when they became dirty playing in the earth.

In the Balkans, Greece, and russian lands, Paraskeva is identified with saint Phoeina who was martyred under Nero, and with the greek saint Anastasia. Paraskeva's name means Friday, the day that *precedes* sabbath days of judaism and christianity. Friday, sacred to western slavs, was dedicated to Venus by the french and italians. Fridays were identified with Paraskevas, twelve goddesses who, like the planets, controlled human destiny. The popular belief was that honoring twelve sacred Fridays throughout the year protected people against fire, sickness, flood, and other catastrophes. Friday, until the 18th century, rather than Sunday was the weekly holiday in Russia. In contemporary United States today, Friday night is celebratory for jews, college students, yuppies, and others.

In russian lands, Paraskeva-Pianitsa is the central figure of popular culture, in contrast to patriarchal images of orthodox christianity. Tall and thin with long flowing hair, she is not the old grandmother with kerchief-covered head, nor the young girl in braids. In implicit resistance to church doctrine of twelve male apostles, Paraskeva has twelve handmaidens. Her icons are found in trees, by springs, and on hills. Wooden images of Paraskeva explicitly identify her with the prehistoric tree of life.

Representations of Paraskeva are often located in places where she symbolizes subversion of secular authority. Red Square in Moscow, for example, historically had a spot believed to be sacred to Paraskeva. During the soviet period when religion was outlawed, women came, under peril, to pray here on Fridays. Today, two images of the black madonna, as mentioned earlier, may be found on Red Square.

In the Paraskeva tradition, women were not to spin on Fridays; if people defied the dark mother's wish that there be no spinning, images of eyes watched, striking fear. "By dishonoring Friday and disobeying the saint, a woman betrayed the cult which stressed feminine hegemony over all life."[72] On Fridays, Paraskeva was believed to suffer Jesus' pain, considered analogous to the torturing of flax being spun. In traditional Russia, Fridays were consecrated to love-making and to healing. Milk and eggs produced on Friday were believed to protect against fire.[73] Old women in russian lands enforced the laws of Paraskeva, just as nonne in Italy saw to it that rituals of carnevale kept to tradition, and babas in jewish american culture enforced kosher laws in the kitchen. As "Mother Moist Earth," Paraskeva is similar to black madonnas; both are associated with the fertile earth.

Scholars of russian studies, for reasons that invite speculation, have not made the connection between the primordial african black mother and byzantine dark madonnas. African american scholars, notably Danita Redd, *have* made the connection, finding a close resemblance of byzantine dark madonnas to african Isis.[74] In lands of former Soviet Russia, the memory of the dark mother is arising today from centuries of suppression under orthodox christianity and decades of soviet rule opposed to religion. Despite official suppression, the memory persisted, visible in images of many black madonnas, most of them whitened, but some kept black (e.g., black madonna of Kazan). Artists and poets transmitted the memory across the centuries in Russia. Vladimir Soloviev in the eleventh century painted the dark Madonna of Tenderness to whom he dedicated a poem, "God is with us." God, in this case, is a dark mother. The poem affirms that *she* is with us, not in the blue beyond the world, nor in documents of somnolent centuries, but in all our tumults and unquietnesses, "a joyous mystery within us."[75]

In Germany and Switzerland, centers of hostility to women during the protestant reformation, the submerged memory of the dark mother is today rising to consciousness. Despite protestant destruction, some images of black madonnas remained in Germany, as did hundreds hidden in Switzerland during the wars of religion. The memory is visible in a volume, *Maria of Nazareth—Unsere Schwester?* (Mary of Nazareth—Our sister?), wherein feminist catholic women of Germany consider black madonnas of Einsiedeln, Switzerland, Montserrat, Spain, and Czestochowa, Poland to be in continuum with Isis of Africa and black Diana of Ephesus in west Asia. In this 1983 study, catholic women theologians associated black madonnas with saint Anne, and with the symbol of the red apple. Anne recalls Inanna, dark mother of west Asia, Maria's mother and Jesus' grandmother. The red apple, early symbol of life, was turned by church fathers, in the story of Adam and Eve in the Garden of Eden, into a symbol of sin.

In Germany the most significant pilgrimage to the black madonna is located at Altötting,[76] which we visited in 1999. Local people had only a vague impression that the sanctuary existed, but international buses brought pilgrims to participate in the procession of penitents carrying crosses around the octagon-shaped sanctuary. Other black madonnas in Germany may be found at Oggersheim, Nuremberg, and Trier, where Karl Marx was born (interestingly, his children called him Moor). Trier is the site of one of the most subversive carnivals of Europe. The relationship of Karl Marx to black madonnas is highly provocative. See his June 21, 1856 letter to his wife, whom he likens to a black madonna.

In Switzerland, Jutta Voss' work in feminist religious studies tracks the changing meaning of menstrual blood. Sacred in the civilization of the dark mother of prehistory, menstrual blood was branded impure in the epoch of patriarchal christianity. For Voss, a necessary step for women in the recovery of their integrity is to bring the ancient meaning of symbols (before they were mutilated by patriarchy) to consciousness. This, she states, is necessary to heal the relationship of humans to nature and its "cosmic rhythms."[77]

In Germany today, the most systematic, and perhaps most significant, research on the dark mother may be that conducted by Heide Gottner-Abendroth, who has uncovered radically democratic implications, persisting in subaltern cultures, of veneration of the dark mother. Brought up a lutheran, she taught philosophy at the University of Munich before she founded Hagia, Academy for Research in Matriarchy and Matriarchal Arts, in Winzer, Germany.

Heide removes patriarchal distortion from the word matriarchy. "When matriarchal spirituality speaks of the 'Goddess,' it does not mean an omnipotent, omniscient supreme Mother in Heaven, a counterpart to God the Father. On the contrary. This concept signifies nothing more, and nothing less, than the inherent spiritual capacity in every individual, which harmoniously expresses itself together with the totality of the intellectual, emotional, and physical capacities of the person. The Goddess does not exist independent of those capacities; she is something like the unifying thread, the vitality, the energy of life. In this sense, the Goddess is present in every person and in all creatures and elements that possess or impart the vital energy."[78]

In the best tradition of german scholarship, Abendroth is researching and writing a multi-volume history and analysis of matriarchy grounded on research she has undertaken in Ireland, England, Scotland, France, Germany, Switzerland, Iceland, Malta, Crete, Syria, Egypt, China, Mexico and New Mexico. Uninterested in matriarchal spirituality removed from the world, Abendroth brings the findings and insights of ethnography, anthropology, and first-hand field research to her study.

She wants to do for Africa, Asia, and North and South America what Marija Gimbutas did for Old Europe, hoping that her research of matriarchy will lead to the transformation of violent hierarchical patriarchy into peaceful radically egalitarian democracy, The economic implication of matriarchy, for Abendroth, is reciprocity, equality, and mutuality. The social implication of matriarchy is matrilineality, or inheritance through the mother's line, in a clan social structure wherein everyone helps one another. The gender implication of matriarchy is that significant roles of males are those of brothers and sons, rather than of fathers and husbands. The political implication of matriarchy is a polity built on kinship, with decisions made by consensus. Culturally the implication is that the earth is a great mother; the world and all creatures are divine and part of the great mother.

In matriarchal society, according to Abendroth, there is respect for the old, nurture of children, no separation of holiday and everyday, and since every creature is believed to be reborn, there is no fear of death. A messenger of hope, as well as an impressive scholar, Abendroth tells her audiences that the age of matriarchy in prehistory was very, very long, that the age of patriarchy has covered a very short period of time, and that hierarchical and violent patriarchy may be considered a short accident in the ongoing story of matriarchy.[79]

In Switzerland, the memory of the dark mother is becoming conscious among protestant, as well as catholic, feminist theologians. A 1996-7 lecture series on black madonnas, *Schwarze Madonna*, at Gwatt-Zentrum am Thunersee, organized by Angela Romer, feminist reformed minister, traced precursors of the black madonna of Einsiedeln, Switzerland to the paleolithic goddess of Willendorf, Austria, to the mesopotamian divinity Inanna, and to greek goddesses of the Cyclades. Black madonnas of France were highlighted, notably Notre-Dame de la Bonne-Mort of Clermont-Ferrand and the black madonna Sous-Terre at Chartres. I was invited to speak on black madonnas of Italy. Another woman from the United States sent a painting, *Die Alte*, portraying old women as dark, wild, and wise.[80]

Margrit Schmid, lecturer in the *Schwarze Madonna* series, spoke. She has found scores of black madonnas in isolated swiss mountain villages where they were hidden during wars between catholics and protestants during the reformation and counter-reformation. She has also found several black madonnas in border areas of Switzerland, where people sought safety from persecution during the wars of religion. Today Margrit Schmid has found many black madonnas in foreign workers quarters in european cities, where workers from Italy, Turkey, and the Tamil region of India, uprooted from their homelands, exploited, and persecuted, look to icons of the dark mother. This seems a telling datum to me confirming the survival of the memory of the dark mother in subaltern cultures of the earth, crossing national and continental boundaries.[81]

Worried about the Gwatt series on black madonnas, a pastor of the reformed church in Switzerland asked the synod, leading body of the reformed church, to investigate, saying that the programs leaned toward an "esoteric and alternative spirituality," not in conformity with reformed teaching. In a hearing to "clarify the matter," 200 people gathered, women strongly supported the black madonnas series, and vindicated Angela Romer, reformed minister who initiated the program. Articulating the connection of black madonnas with feminist consciousness, Angela said, "This is not about a cult.… This is about our own energies, awareness, and acknowledgment of our own power."[82]

An unfinished subject, like Gaudi's unfinished church, black madonnas continually crop up, unexpectedly, to give me pause. In 1997 on book tour in Italy for the italian edition of my study of black madonnas, a woman in the audience came up to me with an image of the dark mother sent by her daughter in Los Angeles in the U.S. who had learned I was to speak in Bologna, Italy. Deborah Rose went to France in search of black madonnas; afterward, she wrote, "the last thing I expected was to re-enter Catholicism, the religion of my childhood." She found that "devotions of the catholic faithful were keeping alive a reverence for the mother that I suspected was much older than that to the Christian Mary." Her twenty five years of work in holistic health care have made her "a firm believer in body memories and cellular consciousness. On an individual, and I believe on a collective level, the body remembers the past. And the oldest memory is of darkness as the source and the beginning. The dark mother is the original mother."[83]

Necia Desiree Harkless, african american ethnographer, remembered that during world war one, her father, a U. S. soldier, visited the chapel of Notre-Dame de Myans in the french Alps. In 1994 when Harkless traveled to this sanctuary, she found that this madonna is called "Our Lady, Black, the Ethiopian." Over the entry door to the sanctuary is the biblical message, "Then saith He to the disciple, 'Behold thy mother.'" John: 27. In her poem, "The Trauma of Designated Color," Harkless asks, "What is

Black? Is it being alienated. Is it being exploited? Is it a color? a frame of mind, a genetic trait...." "Is it really the absence of white or all the colors mixed on an artist's palette.... Or is it the masks at the Ball of Life...."[84]

Notes

1   Erik Hornung, *Conceptions of God in Ancient Egypt. The One and the Many.* Translated from the German by John Baines (Ithaca, N. Y. Cornell University Press, 1971, 1982. Cornell Paperback 1996, 258.

2   Letter to author, December 8, 1998.

3   Grazio Gianfreda, *Iconografia di Otranto tra oriente e occidente* (Lecce, Tiemme, 1994). Danita Redd, african american scholar, early pointed to the connection between Isis of Africa and black madonnas, particularly of eastern Europe. See her chapter, "Black Madonnas of Europe: Diffusion of the African Isis," *African Presence in Early Europe,* ed., Ivan Van Sertima (New Brunswick and London, Transaction Publishers, 1985, 1993).

4   See Robert Lentz, *Bridge Building Images.* July 1997 issue of *Street Spirit,*.l.

5   Communications and observations of author.

6   Elinor Gadon, "Revisioning the Female Demon. Lilith and her Indian sisters: those other goddesses," *ReVision,* 1997. See Tracy Pintchman, *The Rise of the Goddess in the Hindu Tradition* (Albany, State University Press of New York, 1994). See also Janine Canan, "Oh Kali," *Changing Woman* (forthcoming).

7   Riverhead Books. A member of Penguin Putnam Inc., 1998.

8   See China Galland, *Longing for Darkness. Tara and the Black Madonna, a Ten Year Journey* (New York, Penguin/Penguin, l990).

9   Romoloi Santon, "Eredità olmeca," *Archeologia Viva,* novembre-dicembre 1996.

10   Ana Castillo, ed., *Goddess of the Americas. Writings on the Virgin of Guadalupe* (New York, Riverhead Books, 1996). "The Black Virgin," *Art in America,* March 1988, 56-7.

11   Ibidem.

12   Ibidem.

13   Elaine Soto, Ph.D. *Black Madonnas* catalog. (New York, 1999).

14   Lucia Chiavola Birnbaum, *Black Madonnas. Feminism, religion & politics in Italy* (Boston, Northeastern University Press, 1993, Bari, Italia, Palomar Editrice, l997, San Jose, Lincoln, New York, Shanghai, iUniverse, 2000). Ean Begg, *The Cult of the Black Virgin* (London, Arkana Penguin. 1985),an excellent

gazette of black madonnas of Europe, has inspired many researchers. See updated and expanded 1996 version. China Galland, *Longing for Darkness*, Loc. Cit., is an important story of a search for black madonnas, a book that is inspirational in therapy groups.

15   *Il Messagio della Santa Casa. Mensile del Santuario di Loreto*, keeps a gazette of black madonnas. See February, 1999 issue; P. Giuseppe Santarelli, "Iconografia Lauretana," which discusses several black madonnas of Italy that I had not known about when I wrote the book, e.g., those of Crema, Torreto di Gagliole, Cembra, Montefiorino, and Mortara. An evocative example is the "Madonna Asiatica" of Cembra (Trento) who has a dark red face and does not hold a baby.

16   "La Vergine Lauretana 'pellegrina' in America Latina nel Seicento," *Il Messaggio della Santa Casa*, Dicembre 1997.

17   "Testimonianza storiche dell'internazionalità del santuario di Loreto…." *Il messaggio della santa casa*, N.5 maggio 1997.

18   See *All Montserrat* (Pisa, Editorial Escude de Oro, S.A.,n.d.). Also Anselm M. Albareda, *Historia de Montserrat* (Barcelona, l'abadia de Montserrat, 1988).

19   The painting is in a church at Tersatto built in 1292.

20   *Nigra sum. Iconografia de Santa Maria de Montserrat*. (Montserrat, Publicacions de l'Abadia, 1995) 237.

21   J. Bertranpetit and L. L. Cavalli-Sforza, "A genetic reconstruction of the history of the population of the Iberian Peninsula," *Ann. Hum. Genet.* (1991), 55, 51-67. Great Britain, 51.

22   Ibid., 58.

23   See chapter one, this work.

24   See Timothy Mitchell, *Passional Culture. Emotion, Religion, and Society in Southern Spain* (Philadelphia, University of Pennsylvania Press, 1990). Cf. Birnbaum, Chapter nine, "multicultural liberation theology of easter in the streets," *Black Madonnas. Feminism, religion & politics in Italy* (Boston, Northeastern University Press, 1993. iUniverse 2000).

25   See Rainer Zerbst, *Antonio Gaudi, 1852-1926. A Life Devoted to Architecture* (Koln, Benedikt Taschen Verlag GmbH, 1993).

26   China Galland, *Longing for Darkness*,Loc. Cit.

27   Ibidem.

28   Marie Boucher, "The Enigmatic Sara: Matron Saint of the Gypsies & Ancient Divinity," *Goddessing, Winter Moisturing/Spring Forthing*, 1998).

29   Marie Boucher, "The Enigmatic Sara: Matron Saint of the Gypsies. Ancient Divinity & Black Madonna," unpublished paper, 1994.

30   Ibid., 5.

31   A subject being researched today by Heide Gottner-Abendroth; see her *The Goddess and Her Heros*, Tr., Lilian Friedberg (Stow, Ma., Anthony Publishing Company, 1995).

32   Boucher, "The Enigmatic Sara," *Goddessing*, Loc. Cit.

33   Ibid., 15.

34   Ibid., 20.

35   Ibid., 121.

36   Ibid., passim.

37   Ibidem.

38   Margaret Starbird, *The Woman with the Alabastar Jar—Mary Magdalene & the Holy Grail* (Santa Fe, New Mexico, Bear & Company Publishing, 1993).

39   Marie Durand-Lefebvre, *Etude sur l'origine des Vierges Noires* (Paris, G. Durassie & Cie, Imprimeurs, 1937). 7-8.

40   Ibid., 10-11.

41   Ibid., 124.

42   An image of a black madonna in Prague was brought to me by Susan Groag Bell, colleague at the Institute for Research on Women and Gender of Stanford University. The image of the black madonna was located on the outside of a building that during the communist regime faced communist headquarters of Prague. Elinor Gadon advises that today it is called house of the Black Madonna. Elsa Polansky visited Prague in 2001 and took the photo reproduced in this book.

43   Sophie Cassagnes-Brouquet, avec la collaboration de Jean-Pierre Cassagnes, *Vierges Noires. regard et fascination* (Editions du Rouergue, Passage des Macons, 1990).

44   There are a few images of a black Jesus without his mother in Sicily, in Genoa, at St. Flour in France, and in 1999, in peasant demonstrations of Chiapas, Mexico.

45   Valerie Kack-Brice, *Silent Goddesses: A Study of Elder Breton Women and Saint Anne*, Ph.D. dissertation, California Institute of Integral Studies, June 1999.

46   Cassagnes-Brouquet, 129.

47   Ibid., 134.

48   Ibid., 136.

49   Ibid., 137.

50   Ibidem.

51   Ibid., 143.

52   Ibid., 151.

53   Ibid., 154.

54   Ibid., 165.

55   Ibid., 166

56   Judy Grahn, *Blood, Bread, and Roses*, Loc. Cit.

57   Cassagnes-Brouquet, 24.

58   Ibidem.

59   Hogues Berton, *Sorcellerie en Auvergne. Sorciers, Guerisseurs, Medicines magiques et traditionnelles* (Cournon d'Auvergne, Editions de Boree, 1995). 165-198.

60   Sharon Anthony, *The Courage to Burn: Following Jeanne d'Arc and the Black Madonnas.* Unpublished manuscript. For Jeanne d'Arc's mother praying to the black madonna of Le Puy when her daughter was imprisoned in Rouen (17). The black madonna of Notre Dame des Miracles, to whom Jeanne d'Arc prayed, was also known as the Black Egyptian (18).

61   Ibid., 17, 18.

62   Destroyed by French revolutionaries. See Henry Adams, *Mont-Saint-Michel and Chartres* (Boston and New York, Houghton Mifflin Company, 1904).

63   Jacques Huynen, *l'enigme des vierges noires* (Chartres, Editions Jean-Michel Garnier, 1972, 1994), 9.

64   Ibid., 144.

65   See chapter one, this work.

66   See chapter two, this work.

67   Cassagnes-Brouquet, 62.

68   Ibid.

69   Michelin Guide de Tourisme, *Auvergne Burbonnais* (Clermont-Ferrand, France, 1988).

70   See William Melzer, *The Pilgrim's Guide to Santiago de Campostela* (New York, Italica Press, 1993). 69-70.

71   Joanna Hubbs, *Mother Russia. The Feminine Myth in Russian Culture* (Bloomington and Indianapolis, Indiana University Press, 1988, 1993). 117.

72   Hubbs, *Mother Russia*, , 120.

73   Ibid., 120-121.

74   See Danita Redd, "Black Madonnas of Europe: Diffusing of the African Isis," in Ivan Van Sertima, *African Presence in Early Europe* (New Brunswick and London, Transaction Publishers, 1985). Sixth printing 1993. For Isis in the abbey of Saint-Germain-des-Pres in Paris, see *Guide de Paris mysterieux* (Paris, Editions Tchou, 1985). 86, 87.

75   "Dio e' con noi, Madonna della Tenerezza di Vladimir"secolo XI), *Il Messaggio della Santa Casa*, Dicembre 1997.

76   Heide Gottner-Abendroth, *Matriarchal Mythology in Former Times and Today.* Translated by the author with Lise Weil (Freedom, California, The Crossing Press, 1987).

77   Jutta Voss *La Luna Nera. Il potere femminile e la simbologia del ciclo femminile.* Italian translation, Amelia Muscetta (1996, Como, Red edizione). Original edition (Zurigo, Kreus Verlag, 1988).

78   Heide Gottner-Abendroth, *The Dancing Goddess. Principles of a Matriarchal Aesthetic.* Tr., Maureen T. Krause (Boston, Beacon Press, 1991. Verlag Frauenoffensive, 1982). 217. See also Heide Gottner-Abendroth, *The Goddess and Her Heros.* Tr., Lillian Friedberg (Stow, Massachusetts, Anthony Publishing Company, 1995).

79   Heide Gottner Abendroth, "Women's Matriarchal Cultures in Prehistory, " presentation, New College, San Francisco, California, March 27. 1998.

80   "Schwarze Madonna,". Mai 1996 bis November 1997. Leitung: Angela Romer. Gwatt-Zentrum am Thunersee. Kirchliche Bildungsarbeit.

81   Multicultural Europe is a contemporary project of Dr. Renate Holub and colleagues in interdisciplinary studies at the University of California at Berkeley.

82   "Die Angst des Pfarrers vor dem Weiblichen," *Kanton Bern*, 28 August 1996.

83   Deborah Rose, *Goddessing*, 1998.

84   Necia Desiree Harkless, *Heart to Heart. Poems and Heart Images* (Lexington, Kentucky, Heart to Heart and Associates, 1995), "Notre-Dame de Myans," and "The Trauma of Designated Color."

17. Black Diana of Ephesus

Photograph by Wallace Birnbaum

18. Aya Sophia
Istanbul, Turkey
Banner by Lydia Ruyle

19. La Monserrate
Spain
Painting by Elaine Soto

20. Pilar-Toto
Spain
Painting by Elaine Soto

21. Black madonna of Chartres, France
Banner by Lydia Ruhle

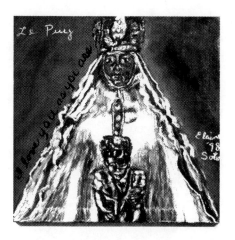

22. Black madonna of Le Puy, France

Painting by Elaine Soto

23. Black madonna of Altötting Germany

Banner by Lydia Ruhle

24. Sara Kali
Saintes Maries de la Mer, France
Painting by Elaine Soto

25. Postmodern icon. House of the Black Madonna.
Prague, Czech Republic

Photograph by Elsa Polansky

chapter five

santa Lucia, dark mother's wisdom and nurturance as saint of light. dark and light in sicilian culture

"Darkness preceded light and She is Mother"
—Inscription on the altar of the cathedral, Salerno Italy[1]

This chapter explores the role of saints in the story of the dark mother. As the illustration suggests, Magdalen has an important role in this story. Although male clerics tried to obliterate her by branding her a fallen woman, she has remained beloved in popular beliefs as the first person to see the risen Jesus. Lucia's story is a variant on this theme. In church co-optation santa Lucia is identified with light, but popularly she is celebrated on the longest night of the year, December 13th. Popular understanding of Lucia is close to the african view of the dark mother: "mother of the night, the great dark depth, the bringer of light."[2]

Lucia's city was Syracuse in Sicily, ancient port on the Ionian sea, where primordial migrants from Africa walked or sailed, where neolithic west asians migrated from Anatolia, and where canaanites came to trade in the century and a half before Jesus. Before the common era, aryan greeks colonized Sicily in the 8th century, followed by aryan romans in the 3rd century. Syracuse, earlier african, west asian, and mother-centered, became a wealthy maritime port where aryan greeks and then aryan romans, imposed a violent patriarchal culture that demeaned the dark mother, and splintered mother and daughter into separate, subordinated, divinities.[3]

The effect of violent aryan invaders was manifest in greek and roman men's abusive treatment of animals, women, and slaves, in animal sacrifice, and in frenzied popular revelry. Greek temples of Sicily glow at dusk, but the beauty is haunted by the memory of slaves lashed to build them. Dionysius, greek tyrant of Syracuse, whipped enslaved sicilians to build 20-foot thick walls to stave off african carthaginians defending their holdings in Sicily. Like 20th century nazis who considered themselves aryans, put africans at the bottom of a racial hierarchy, and killed millions of jews, gypsies, and others, aryan rulers of ancient Greece and Rome were violently hostile to african and semitic carthaginians. In the roman senate, the constant declamation was "Carthage must be destroyed!" Until it was.

Lucia's story should be understood in this historical context. After carthaginians were defeated by romans, Sicily in the era of Lucia may be glimpsed in mosaics of Piazza Armerina. Under the overlordship of wealthy roman landowners, sicilian society was divided into the wealthy who luxuriated in villas while brutalizing slaves captured in war, and pressing other sicilians into poverty. Created by african artisans, mosaics of Piazza Armerina resemble mosaics in the Bardo Museum of Tunis. The patriarchal god Neptune chases and rapes nymphs, slaves massage roman masters. Cruel roman circus sports, pitting humans against animals, are depicted in the Salone del Circo. In 135 BCE in this showplace of imperial Rome at Piazza Armerina, slaves rose up against oppression. Invoking the dark mother, slaves fought off romans for decades. Others resisted culturally. A mosaic in the gymnasium of the imperial villa depicts young women exercising almost nude, an example of women privately doing what they want, although publicly forced to obey constrictive patriarchal customs.

After 70 CE, the canaanite semitic strand in Sicily was widened by israelite jews in diaspora. In grottoes near Syracuse, jews and early christians hid from roman persecution under Diocletian. Over a grotto at Brucoli where refugees painted a dark mother. (see chapter 4), a christian church was erected a few years before Lucia was born in 284 CE to a patrician christian family at Ortigia, in old Syracuse.

Lucia's father, of roman lineage, wanted the child to have the name of a venerable roman matron; the mother, of greek inheritance, wanted a hellenic name. They compromised on Lucia, name meaning light given to christians—filii lucis estis—you are children of light.[4] As a girl, Lucia read the *Song of Songs*, (that unique passage in hebrew scriptures that describes the civilization of the dark mother)[5] and stories of christian saints, particularly the story of Agata of Catania, whose breasts were cut off, in martyrdom, said the church, to her christian faith.

A young man wanted to marry Lucia. Her mother fell ill; mother and daughter went to Catania to pray to saint Agata. On her return, Lucia was drawn to the message of Jesus who told his followers that they who do not marry are like angels of god in heaven, that they should renounce all they possess, take up the cross, and follow him.[6] Vowing virginity and fidelity to Jesus, Lucia rejected her suitor. Today Lucia is venerated as an early virgin martyr of the church. Church fathers narrowed the meaning of virginity to sexual chastity, but ancient women, and contemporary feminists, consider a virgin an inviolate woman who makes her own choices, sexual, and otherwise.[7]

The church story of Lucia can be found in a book published when my nanna Lucia was a girl: "a luminous woman, a virgin faithful to her Spouse, a loveable saint. A model of Christianity heroically lived…courage…martyrdom…." Using its version of the story of Lucia to teach christianity's victory over paganism, the church listed a triumphal series of events. Lucia, unwilling to renounce christianity and her virginity, suffered martyrdom under the romans in 310 CE; shortly thereafter Diocletian was driven from the throne, and in 323 CE christianity became the religion of the roman empire.[8] The story I learned as a girl in catholic religious instruction was that during roman persecution of christians a soldier attempted to rape Lucia. She saved her virginity by plucking out her eyes and giving them to him. The church image of the saint for whom I am named was Lucia offering her eyes on a plate to her rapist, thereby blinding her vision.

Lucia's body, like that of Jesus, was buried in a cave. The body remained there during incursions of vandals and goths until byzantines took the body to Constantinople. After crusaders took that city, Lucia's body was brought to Venice, where it lies today in the church of saints Geremia and Lucia. Major saint of south Italy and Sicily, Lucia is also celebrated in Rome where several churches carry her name, notably S. Lucia alle Botteghe Oscure in the medieval shop area of jews that was the seat of the italian communist party in the 20th century. Santa Lucia, sung by venetian gondoliers, neapolitans, and Luciano Pavarotti, is celebrated in festivals at Syracuse, Palermo, Vittoria, Ragusa, Chiaramonte Gulfi, Messina, Catania, and elsewhere

Although the church used its story of Lucia to teach the triumph of the church over paganism, of light over darkness, and of purity over impurity, popular stories about the saint ascribed wisdom and nurturance to her, both ultimately referring to Isis. Separating wisdom from nurturance, the greeks appropriated wisdom and assigned it to Athena. The gnostics assigned it to Sophia, and the romans assigned it to Minerva. The nurturance tradition, originating in Isis, was carried forth by canaanites in Astarte, and by sicilians in Demetra, the wheat goddess. Lucia may be considered a christian rendition that distorts the whole woman personified by Isis. The cathedral in Syracuse with a chapel dedicated to Lucia is built on a canaanite temple to Astarte—which became a greek temple to Athena, and then a roman temple to Minerva.

Lucia may also be considered a popular assimilation into christianity of a major myth of the western world, the story of Demetra and her daughter Proserpina. Sicilians, like peasants the world over, are epistemological realists:[9] the ultimate object of perception really exists. In this perspective, instead of myths there are stories. If a story is believed, sicilians consider it true. One story sicilians consider true is that of Demetra and Proserpina. Demetra means mother, and her daughter Proserpina's name means first.[10] At the Lago di Pergusa at Enna in the navel of Sicily, Proserpina, (dark in the popular imagination) was abducted by Hades. Her mother Demetra roamed the Monti Iblei with a torch searching for her daughter, withering grain and flowers, until she found her, when the dark wheat ripened and red poppies bloomed. As they do every springtime.

Lucia may also be considered a popular saint who resembles Mary, mother of Jesus. Today in Sicily, celebrations of santa Lucia and santa Maria both feature fireworks and singing.[11] Lucia, like Maria and her mother Anne, is popularly considered a santone, or great saint—a great saint who transmits earlier pagan traditions. Today, on August 15, when the church celebrates the madonna's assumption into heaven, sicilians at Gangi, for example, celebrate the roman wheat goddess, Cerere.

Lucia also conflates the story of mother and daughter, She is popularly honored in December at the time of the winter solstice, festival of the dark mother, and in May, spring festival of her daughter Maria. At the winter solstice (December 13 in the julian calendar) Lucia brings gifts to all children, not discriminating between those who have been naughty and those who have been nice. In her May festival at Syracuse, in which we have participated, the silver figure of Lucia carries a sheaf of wheat, associating her with african Isis, graeco-roman Demetra, and with roman wheat goddess Cerere.

Heretical and pagan connotations have clung to Lucia. In France, Lucia is venerated in places of heresy; e.g., at Albi in the cathar region. In Spain, she is remembered at Toledo, where moors, jews, and christians lived peacefully together until christian church and state scapegoated moors and jews. In Germany, at Dusseldorf, Lucia is represented as a pagan maiden goddess, as she is in Russia, with hair spilling onto her shoulders, a hairstyle that became popular in the 60s and 70s in the United States, Italy, and elsewhere. Before the protestant reformation, England held a festival for saint Lucy; today the english still remember her at the time of the winter solstice. Algeria in Africa built churches to her; Christopher Columbus named the island for her that he reached on her day, December 13. Dante, in the *Divine Comedy*, associated Lucia with his love, Beatrice. Belgium, Holland, and Switzerland named churches for her.

Swedes on December 13th tell the story that once Lucia appeared in a halo of light bringing food to starving peasants. In the popular swedish festival of Lucia, a girl with a diadem of candles followed by children in white tunics, silver stars, and candles, bring gifts to homes and hospitals. Today, in Petaluma, California, the festival of Lucia draws several hundred of swedes for four hours of food, music, and dance.

Croatian/americans soak wheat and plant it on Lucia's day, December 13th. On christmas eve, bowls of wheat are placed on the table where everyone gathers. A prayer is read that health and happiness, symbolized by grain and grapes at christmas time, should prevail throughout the year. Everyone carries wheat and a candle through rooms of the home in a blessing ritual recalling those who have died.[12]

Sicilian folklorist Giuseppe Pitrè noted the popular association of Lucia with wheat and feeding the hungry. On December 13, sicilians touch neither bread nor pasta but eat cuccia (couscous), north african whole wheat kernel cooked with honey, wine, and ricotta. Once, the story goes, when people of Syracuse were famished, Lucia sent them a ship full of wheat. Like the jews who fled in exodus without time to bake bread and ate unleavened matzoh, hungry sicilians ate the unmilled grain sent by Lucia. Sicilians call whole grain bread, pane integrale, a term that may remember inviolate Lucia. Bread, popularly associated with african Isis, later with graeco-roman wheat goddesses Demetra and Cerere, was associated in the christian epoch with santa Lucia, and with the belief that bread connotes good. In sicilian culture, the optimal compliment one can give someone is, "She/he is as good as bread."

Patrizia Tavormina, african/canadian writer and actress who now uses the african/sicilian name Nzula Angelina Ciatu, wrote me that she considers Lucia a "feminist harbinger." Nzula celebrates Lucia every December 13 "by cooking cuccia, whole wheat kernel boiled, sweetened with sugar or honey." Nzula met a woman who had had two visions of santa Lucia, in which she was a "dark-skinned woman with long coarse black kinky hair," in contrast to church images, "pale-skinned and blondish," of Lucia.

Lucia, always depicted with a sheaf of grain in Sicily, is associated not only with the nurturant values of african Isis, but also with the communal african ritual at Meroe, in Nubia, of distributing grain to the poor. Like the african dark mother, Lucia connotes regeneration; on her December day in Sicily she is celebrated with nuts and legumes, foods connoting regeneration. On santa Lucia day, at Comiso in the Monti Iblei, children throw nuts to the people from the roof of the cathedral.

In popular understanding of sicilians, Isis, Demetra, and Cerere—african and roman wheat goddesses who preceded christianity —as well as christian saints Anne, Maria, and Lucia—are considered "great saints."[13] At Palazzolo Acreide, where Cybele is sculpted onto a rock cliff, Lucia's festa dispels the winter darkness with fireworks. The easy transition in sicilian popular culture from pagan goddess to christian saint is visible in this town where Cybele, asian pagan dark mother, is also called a santone, or great saint.

Conveying what actually happened when the church appropriated pagan goddesses as christian saints, the theme of popular stories is that Lucia's eyes (symbolizing the vision of the dark mother) were torn out. Analogously, Agata's breasts, symbolizing the nurturance of the dark mother, were cut off. Caravaggio realistically painted the story of Lucia, depicting a church figure supervising two burly workmen digging Lucia's grave, while women weep.[14] Lucia's popular meaning is caught at Canicattini Bagni, paleolithic site in Sicily, where Lucia is sought for eye maladies connected with loss of wisdom. In italian popular culture, loss of wisdom means loss of hindsight, or memory of the past, and loss of vision, or faith in the future.[15]

Light and dark in sicilian history

Just as the church tried to replace the african dark mother, who connoted life, death, and rebirth, with santa Lucia as chaste maiden saint of light, church and secular authorities tried to lighten images of the christian madonna, whose earliest images were dark.[16] The church had to contend with popular beliefs in the miracle-working powers of images of the dark mother, as well as the subversive cultural and political implications of the dark images. In popular themes underlying political traditions of the left in Italy, the black of anarchism is understood as fidelity of subordinated peoples to the truth of the earth.[17] The association of black madonnas with subordinated peoples is evident in the name italians give to the black madonna of Montevergine, whom they call la schiavona, great black slave mother.

Normans, pale scandinavian adventurers who took Sicily for the pope in 1060, are glorified by western historians, but contemporary italian historians view them as mercenaries. In the 9th century, normans settled in France, before expanding, taking Sicily in 1060 and Britain in 1066. They had been hired by the pope to take south Italy and Sicily away from the moors of Africa, whose stay had been benign for the people. The norman invasion, an arrangement with the papacy to remove "infidels" and impose canonical doctrine on the people, meant the return of large landowners, incitement to hatred of moors and jews, and the hierarchical social and economic system of feudalism. The political effect of feudalism was to keep poor people under control of large landowners, while enriching holdings of the church aligned with the light-skinned nobility. Culturally, the norman invasion of south Italy and Sicily meant keeping the sacred under the control of the catholic church and maintaining the hegemony of the church aligned with the nobility by labeling beliefs of the under classes "profane" or "infidel."[18]

Normans stratified sicilian society in the pattern it was to hold, almost without modification, until the 20th century: the nobility allied with catholic clergy at the top, keeping artisans (who constituted a nascent bourgeoisie) at bay, and oppressing peasants at the bottom.[19] Carlo Cipolla, leading economic historian of Italy, responded to late 20th century demagogic pronouncements of the Northern League, who urged secession of the rich north from the poor south of Italy. The economic gap between the north and the south, said Cipolla, began with the norman invasion, when the french feudal system of Normandy was transplanted to south Italy and Sicily "just at the moment in which feudalism was being challenged in the rest of Italy with the rise of mercantile cities." Normans institutionalized a feudal system that concentrated power in the hands of a few large landholders, a system that perpetuated the poverty of south Italy and islands for the next nine centuries.[20]

Normans also brought frenchmen and lombards of north Italy to Sicily. The lombard connection in Sicily was visible in my maternal grandmother's maiden name, Lombardo (see chapter eight). Invasions of lighter skinned northerners, accompanied by rape and other coupling, whitened darker skinned sicilians. Images of madonnas were lightened, perhaps to strengthen the hegemony of church and state governed by light-skinned male elites. After the 9th century, the catholic church, identifying white with canonical purity and black with impurity, paganism, heresy, subversion and the other, tried to extirpate the other—conquering moors, persecuting and expelling jews, then, in the early modern period, persecuting jewish conversos. Earlier, heretics had been tolerated and heretical women ignored so long as they stayed in subordinated roles. But in the modern era, white male elites considered heretics, especially women heretics threatening, and persecuted and killed them. (See chapter seven).

In the 12th century, the economy of Sicily was fixed under Frederick II, holy roman emperor seated at Palermo, for subsequent centuries:

exporting agricultural products, importing textiles and clothing from Lombardy and Liguria, iron and steel from northern Europe, an economy that perpetuated the colonial subordination of Sicily under foreign rulers.

All foreign rulers, beginning with greeks and romans, have tried to impose their beliefs on sicilians. After the 15th century, the spanish installed the engine of the inquisition to terrorize people into conformity to church doctrine and obedience to the state. In this terror, women were controlled by a severe double standard of sexuality, wherein it was the woman, not the man, who was punished for being raped.

In histories of Sicily written by chroniclers of the ruling classes, normans—ancestors of 17th century english settlers in New England in the land that became the United States—are praised as benign and tolerant. History that glorifies the normans, stated italian historian George Pistarino at a recent historical conference in south Italy, negates "una storia persistente...di lungo periodo," a long history of subordinated peoples whose ways of living and "spiritual connection" persists over long periods of time, notwithstanding change of rulers. For Pistarino, this is a story of the perennial relationship of humans with the sustaining earth, and the perennial fatigue of overworked common people.[21]

Rather than glorify the norman monarchy and its works of art, for example, the mosaics of Monreale that were created by moorish artisans,[22] said Pistarino, historians should concentrate on uprisings like the Sicilian Vespers, a popular insurrection against invaders,[23] focus on those senza storia, (people whose history has not been recorded), and concentrate on the history of everyday life, the material culture, and the history of classes. This means looking at european and islamic history not as separate, but as part of a larger history that includes the "slavic world...the Mongols and Tartars...the Turks."[24]I would add to Pistarino's perspective that an accurate view of european history recognizes african origin of europeans, notes the distortion of african beliefs by european white male elites, and acknowledges the popular beliefs that kept the memory alive of the african dark mother, and her values.

This change of view will require a geographical perspective that differs from conventional teaching. In a recent study of medieval Sicily, Glauco Maria Cantarella considers Africa the center of the medieval world, the middle ages as the period when moors of Africa expanded toward Europe, and Sicily as "part of the Arab world of North Africa."[25] In this optic, normans were "Europeans who imposed themselves [in Sicily] in an Arab and African frontier country."[26]

It depends on what perspective the historian takes, that of the rulers or the ruled. Sicilians were (are) not likely to identify with greek, roman, byzantine, or other foreign rulers. Loyalty may be feigned. When the holy roman empire was ruled by the french at Palermo, ecclesiastic and noble courtiers spoke french at the court, as did moors, arabs, and jews who, under pressure of persecution or death, probably feigned christianity.[27]

When the dominant authority is officially christian and you are not, but you must, under threat of death, defer in public to the dominant religion, it was obviously preferable to attend a church with a black madonna, rather than a church with a whitened one whose connotations were obedience to church and state. As discussed earlier, images of black madonnas, are often located in regions of subordinated peoples and sites of historical resistance.

For rulers, black madonnas are a constant reminder of the possibility of popular subversion. Historically, officials of dominant church and state must have chafed, until they could whiten images of the dark mother. The black madonna of Chiaramonte Gulfi remained black until spaniards arrived with the inquisition in the 15th century and ordered the black madonna sculpted in white marble. The black madonna of Alta Villa Milizia outside Palermo became less and less black over time as a succession of northern europeans ruled the sicilian capitol.

The black madonna of Tindari, whose inscription, "I am black and beautiful," of the *Song of Songs* of hebrew scriptures, has remained black, although the church inserted a racist "but" before the word "beautiful." At Erice and at Trapani, african/canaanite/moorish strongholds on the western african shore of Sicily, the madonna of Custonaci has remained black.

Authorities may whiten an image of a black madonna, but my research indicates that even when whitened, she remains, in popular perception, a black madonna. [28] In the first centuries of the common era, church and state appropriated the valence of the dark mother of Africa, hoping to attach it to church and state by whitening images of the madonna and associating Lucia with light. Yet the question imposes itself: who is being remembered when people sing *"Santa Lucia?"*

Notes

1   I am indebted to Josephine DeMartile for bringing this inscription to my attention.

2   See chapter two, this work.

3   Jane Ellen Harrison. *Prolegomena to the study of the Greek Religion* (London, Merlin Press, 1962, 1980), 257-321. Giuseppe Iacono, *Folclore religioso nella Contea di Modica*. Prefazione di Antonino Buttita. (Ragusa, CTG-Criscione Tecnoplast Graficarta srl, 1989). (Milano, Cografa S.r.l.-Usmate, n.d.)

4   Pasquale Fuiani, *Santa Lucia. Profili della vita e del culto della vergine e martire siracusana* (Siracusa, Flaccavento, 1994. Originally published 1886). See also,"Saint Lucy, Virgin," in Jacobus de Voragine, *The Golden Legend. Readings on the Saints.* Tr., William Granger Ryan, Vol I. (Princeton, N. J., Princeton University Press, 1993). Peter Brown, *the cult of the saints. Its Rise and Function in Latin Christianity* (Chicago, University of Chicago Press, 1981).

5   See Iacono, *Folclore religioso. Loc Cit.*

6   Fuiani, *Santa Lucia,*15.

7   See Ann Kay McNamara, *Sisters in Arms: Catholic Nuns Through Two Millennia* (Boston, Harvard University Press, 1996).

8   Jacobus de Voragine, *The Golden legend. Readings on the Saints.* Tr., William Granger Ryan, Vol. I, 27-29.

9   See Charlene Spretnak, *The Resurgence of the Real. Body, Nature, and Place in a Hypermodern World* (Reading, Ma., et al., Addison-Wesley Publishing Company, Inc. 1997).

10   My sicilian/american mother would exasperate me by saying that if she considered something true, it was true.

11   Pamela Berger's path-breaking work, *The Goddess Obscured. Transformation of the Grain Protectress from Goddess to Saint* (Boston, Beacon Press, 1986) does not mention Lucia, although Lucia is a vivid example of a saint who took on the characteristics of the grain goddess Isis, later called Demetra. Berger's book remains indispensable, however, particularly for northern Europe, in helping us understand how prechristian symbols were transmuted into christian art and folklore.See also Willow LaMonte, "Sicilian Goddess Chronicles: July 31 – August 3, 1995." *The Beltane Papers. A Journal of Women's Mysteries,*

Issue 19. Willow describes the ground on which the Cathedral of Syracuse is built. This church to santa Lucia is "a very well-preserved 5th-century BCE Greek Temple of Athena…Earlier a temple to Artemis had been on the site, and before that a sanctuary to an earlier pre-Greek Goddess…. The side street of the cathedral is called Via Minerva, and although it was very cool to see streets named after Goddesses, I wished it were possible to know the names of those earlier deities. Inside was just unbelievable!! The Doric columns are massive, unadorned, their presence strongly resonating a deep, deep power, quite beautiful and handsome, but not at all 'pretty.' The sheer size and power of the columns overwhelms…you can really, truly feel the ancient temple in the immediate present. Now, I don't really cotton to Athena at all; for me, She's the ultimate patriarch's Goddess, but I've always admired the strong and empowered way She's depicted (love those outfits, love those shoulders!). And, I must admit, I had to appreciate this temple as a reflection of that strength embodied. This temple's got Power Shoulders!"

12   I thank my sister Joie Mellenbruch for sending me this information about croatian/american rituals in Kansas City, Kansas.

13   Sabino Greco, *Miti e leggende di Sicilia* (Palermo, Dario Flaccovio Editore, 1993),59.

14   The painting is in the Chiesa di S. Lucia al Sepolcro, in Syracuse, Sicily.

15   See *Con Lucia a Cristo* (Siracusa, Tipolitografia Cav. Domenico Marchese & Figli, 1994).

16   See Birnbaum, *Black Madonnas*. Loc Cit.

17   Dominant elites can manipulate and invert the meaning of colors and symbols. Fascists co-opted the color black, using black for values antithetical to those of the dark mother. Nazis co-opted the symbol of the labyrinth, turning it into the swastika. See chapter nine, this work, for how white male elites in the United States have manipulated the word "democracy."

18   See Peter Brown, *The Rise of Western Christendom. Triumph and diversity AD 200-1000* (Oxford, U.K., Blackwell Publishers Ltd, 1996, 1997)Brown suggests that prechristian mentalities of peasant Europe did not die until the 19th century (101).

19   Vincenzo D'Alessandro, *Terra, nobili e borghesi nella Sicilia medievale* (Palermo, Sellerio Editore, 1994), 19-20; 22-23, 45, 56-57 (Philadelphia,

University of Pennylvania Press, 1991). See also Salvatore Tramontana, *L'effimero nella Sicilia* (Palermo, Sellerio editore, 1984, 1988). Barbara M. Kreutz, *Before the Normans. Southern Italy in the Ninth & Tenth Centuries* (Philadelphia, Pa., 1991).

20   Carlo M. Cipolla, "The South Italian Question: It's the Fault of the Normans," *Il Sole*, May l, 1996.

21   Centro di studi normanno-svevi. Università degli Studi di Bari, *Terra e uomini nel Mezzogiorno normanno-svevo. Atti delle settime giornate normanno-sveve*, Bari, 15-17 ottobre 1985. A cura di Giosue' Musca. 294.

22   Masterpieces of moorish artists in the period of norman ascendancy are cathedrals of Palermo, as well as the cloisters of Monreale outside the city. See *La Cathedrale de Monreale* (Milano, Co.Graf, Editrice, n.d.)

23   See chapter 4, this work.

24   *Terra e uomini,*. Loc. cit., 296-296.

25   Glauco Maria Cantarella, *La Sicilia e i Normanni. Le fonti del mito* (Bologna, Patron Editore, 1989). ll.

26   Ibid., 17.

27   Ibid., 64.

28   See Birnbaum, *Black Madonnas,* Loc. Cit.

26. Mary Magdalen
Photograph by Sharon Anthony

27. Santa Lucia

Photo design by Wallace Birnbaum

chapter six

godmothers—le comari dei Monti Iblei[1]
peasant women and the dark mother

> *"...spirituality understood as dignity, liberty...as faith in life and hope in the future, as love...for the earth...form a richness whose deep roots [are found} in the dialect, customs, the incredible longevity of the oral tradition, the persistence of memory...with moral, social, and metaphysical implications."*
>
> —south italian scholar

Peasant and other women of Sicily who called themselves comari, or god-mothers, embodied the dark mother and her values of justice with compassion (or nurturance), equality, and transformation. For millennia they transmitted her memory and values in stories and rituals resisting violent patriarchy. The godmother legacy is visible today in Italy not only among peasant mothers and feminist daughters, but also among sons, lovers, and husbands, offering the possibility of a coalition of women and men for an "uncruel revolution."[2]

To reconstruct the traditional world of peasant women godmothers, I have explored rituals of the Monti Iblei, region of Sicily where Ibla Nera was venerated in prehistory and where my grandmothers/godmothers venerated the black madonna of Chiaramonte Gulfi in the christian epoch. (See chapter three). In the late 20th century, women of the world gathered here, at Comiso, to witness against violence and proclaim a new world.

The culture of godmothers in Italy has many african echoes; e.g., kinship of humans and animals. The word for godmother, comare, may refer to a fox, a hen, or to a neighbor woman. Kinship, in peasant Italy as well as in Africa, crossed religious boundaries; e.g., a peasant woman might ask a christian friar to help her interpret the hebrew cabala. In Italy as in Africa, pagans and christians are viewed in continuum (see previous chapter). In contrast to church demonization of pagans, italian popular christianity often views pagan divinities as christian saints; e.g., santa Venere (saint Venus). The song of pagan sirens—especially Scilla and Cariddi of south Italy and Sicily—whatever one's religious affiliation—is heard by everyone.[3]

In the early common era in the popular culture of the Monti Iblei, people appeared to have continued to live in the harmony of prehistory, wherein humans and animals, pagans, jews, christians, moors, and heretics lived together peaceably. Church doctrine separated humans from animals, but peasants extended christianity to animals; a peasant woman would exclaim when a fish was caught for christmas eve dinner, "O Dio! He was going in search of Gesù Bambino." The exclamation not only transgressed church doctrine in extending christianity to animals, it revealed a major popular heretical belief—Jesus was not considered the christ, but his mother's baby, Gesù Bambino.[4] Continuity of the values of prehistory into the historical epoch is expressed in Salvo Monica's 1958 sculpture, *"Le comari"*, two peasant women bonding, protected by what appear to be wings of Isis.

Women conveyed the values of the dark mother in stories they told and lullabies they sang to their boy as well as girl children. Food carried the memory. In italian pilgrimages and popular festivals everybody eats nuts and legumes (e.g., calia, roasted chick peas) conveying regeneration.

Torrone (nougat candy with nuts) suggests that the memory is not only regenerative, it is sweet.

In Italy, as in Africa, the memory of the primordial dark mother who nurtured *all* her children is visible in the easy interplay among religions in the popular culture. There was a peasant tendency to distill all religions to an essential message: there is no love greater than that of a mother for her children; we are all her children.[5] Blending hebrew scriptures and christian parables, sicilian peasants would ask, "What did Isaiah teach? That we are made one for the other."[6]

To understand the world of my grandmothers, I have chosen to explore rituals of carnevale. When my nanna Lucia and nannu Luigi were young, Salvatore A. Guastella's *L'Antico Carnevale della Contea di Modica. Schizzi di Costumi Popolari* was published. The book contains a trove of carnival beliefs and customs, as they existed for millennia in my paternal grandparents' region of Sicily, a cultural heritage that my grandparents, father, and aunts and uncles brought with them to Kansas City, Missouri.

Festivals, scholars have pointed out, are moments when deep beliefs are expressed; during celebratory times, there may be a spontaneous eruption from the unconscious. Carnival was the one time of the year european peasants, despite constrictions of patriarchy, and the reformation and counter-reformation, could express deep beliefs that were covered over the rest of the year with outward deference to church, society, and state.[7]

Researching how peasants celebrated carnival before the inquisition terrorized people into hiding their beliefs, Salvatore Gazelle discovered that for more than a millennium, Thursday of carnival week was the day of the comari. One could celebrate church holidays of christmas and easter with whomever, but Thursday of the comari was to be celebrated with one's own. Thursdays have remained special in Italy, often the day during easter week of the procession of the black madonna.[8]

At some point during the protestant reformation, catholic inquisition and catholic counter-reformation (from the 15th to the 18th centuries, with continuing influence thereafter), when catholic and protestant clergy identified women with the devil, the catholic church changed carnival Thursday of le comari to carnival Wednesday of the devil. Whereupon, peasants, put their beliefs under protective cover of christian doctrine, and changed the meaning of Wednesday of the devil, calling it Wednesday of lu zuppiddu, diminutive affectionate name for the crippled devil. Peasants, outwardly deferred to church doctrine in identifying the devil with women, but they changed the nature of the devil. Not Lucifer, malevolent devil of christian theology, the people's devil was a very human and crippled figure who wore a red mask (color of life associated with the primordial dark mother), who did not want to hear about melancholy, loved wine and feasting, admired bold young women, witty humor, and enjoyed voluptuous dancing. The peasants' devil had horns and a tail but lu zuppiddu, like satyrs, was not diabolic.

Peasant interpretation of the devil as a benign, lame figure who loved life was carried to the sicilian/american culture of Kansas City of my childhood where diavolo, diavoluni, diavola—affectionate names for the devil—were often used to express admiration of a person's mischievousness. Santo diavolo (saint devil), one of my mother's favorite expletives, conveys how far popular beliefs careened away from church doctrine that embodied evil in the devil, women, and dark others. This helps us understand why, in sicilian popular culture, people tend not to demonize, but to identify with, the other.

Godmothers remembered in everyday and festival rituals the dark mother's nurturance of everybody. As late as 1776, Thursday of le comari was celebrated in the contea (county) of Modica by distributing macaroni to the poor, a variant of the ancient african ritual of distributing wheat to the hungry at Meroe in Nubia, discussed earlier. From Africa the belief was transmuted into graeco-roman rituals of Demeter/Demetra, into roman rituals of Cerere, and into christian rituals of santa Lucia.[9]

Before the counter reformation, the continuum of pagan with christian beliefs was manifested on the feast day of le comari, when gifts of the pig—the pig was the totem of wheat goddess Demetra—were distributed.

Comari visited friends, relatives, and poor people leaving pork chops, pig's liver, pig's ears, pig's snouts, pig's feet, all favorite foods of my ragusano father, and of many african americans today. Protectively covering pagan beliefs with christian ritual, le comari would also bring gifts of the pig to newly baptized infants.

During the counter reformation, when the church changed Thursday of le comari to Wednesday of the devil, Thursday of the comari became Fat Thursday. Then it became Fat Tuesday, or Martedì Grasso of contemporary carnival in latin countries. The memory of the dark mother continued to be transmitted, but allusively; e.g., Fat Thursday was called fat because pig lard was the chief ingredient of a minestrone made especially for the day. This minestrone, lu lardaloro, remembered the pig of the dark mother with a soup in which lard was mixed with legumes and herbs. Recalling the harmonious civilization of the dark mother, the soup was believed to have healing qualities to calm and resolve family vendettas.

Family vendettas in the patriarchal epoch could be long-lived and virulent. If a pig, part of a wedding dowry, subsequently died, litigation often ensued; sometimes a sicilian husband would send his wife back to her parents. I remember a long vendetta of my sicilian/american aunts circling around who had broken whose mirror many years ago. Another vendetta concerned a gravesite in the family cemetery plot; "stolen" for a husband, said my mother, perhaps remembering ancient matrilineal civilization.[10]

Inquisition attempts to suppress the memory of the dark mother were accompanied by attempts to subordinate once autonomous women. The decline in women's status in the modern era is evident in the custom of the wedding dowry. A dowry of a woman of Chiaramonte Gulfi, in the ancestral region of my paternal grandmothers, listed what goods Vita Pavonc brought in marriage to Salvatore Morando in 1812; the list reveals a dominant patriarchal culture with a continuing memory of the ancient dark mother:

• Money payment due every santo natale until death. (By 1812, after more than three centuries of the inquisition, the day of the mother's holy birthing had been masculinized and demeaned to an annual money payment, due on christmas, that the wife's family had to pay the husband).

- Farm with vines and olive trees. (Vines, in greek masculinist appropriation, were associated with Dionysus, son of Zeus. Yet the memory of the olive tree, dear to the dark mother, and later to the madonna, has persisted. In the late 1990s, in what appears to be a surfacing of the memory of the dark mother, L'Ulivo, or the olive tree, is the name of the contemporary coalition of the nonviolent left in Italy).

- Tithe to the church of S. Filippo (revealing the money connection of patriarchal marriage to the church).

The rest of the items of the dowry defined women's work in patriarchal sicilian culture. From childhood until she married, the prospective wife embroidered the biancheria (white linens) of her marriage and deathbed, as well as linens of the family table. The items she brought to the marriage emphasized women's responsibility for her family's sustenance and well being. Only a few items of the dowry were for her personal use:

- Six embroidered napkins
- Six towels for making bread
- Four pairs of sheets and unfinished pillow cases
- Four pillows and four embroidered/cut work pillow cases
- Six towels, two for daily use, four with embroidery/cut work for festivals
- Six face towels with embroidery/cut work
- Six hand-woven and embroidery/cut work tablecloths
- Furniture cover with a fringe
- Silver rolling pin
- Great chest made of walnut wood to keep the family linens

- Heirloom frying pan
- Candlesticks
- Large pot
- Buffet table
- Six chairs "from Ragusa"
- Mantilla (revealing the influence of spanish patriarchal culture in Sicily)
- Gold earrings
- Festival outfit and an everyday outfit of clothes[11]

Sicilian women's embroidery and cut work symbolized women's subordinate status under patriarchy, yet doing needlework provided space for creativity as well as time of their own when women could escape family noise, imagine, pray, meditate, and remember. Feminist historians studying women's weaving and embroidery have discerned figures in the handiwork that kept the memory of the dark mother alive in jewish, christian, and islamic cultures. Women wove symbols of the dark mother into their embroidery/cut work and carpets; men painted her symbols on tiles. Today in Sicily women's needlework has become commercialized; in some places women embroider linens to be sold to mainland boutiques from childhood until they lose their eyesight.

In the United States in the 20th century, sicilian/american girls were taught to embroider and sew, tasks that conveyed lessons of women's work and submissive destiny. When I was fourteen, nanna Lucia, in one of her pronouncements, said that I should not have any notions, just because I did well in school, that I was going to college. I was to plan to go to sewing school to be trained for a sewing job in a factory to augment the family income. The local sewing school, Jane Hayes Gates, was a protestant institution for training italian, jewish, and polish immigrant girls for the textile industry. My sicilian/american mother, fiercely nurturant of her children, defied her mother-in-law, earning the money during world war two sewing soldier uniforms in a textile factory to supplement my scholarship so that I could go to college.

In Italy, the legacy of Fat Thursday of the comari—when women nurtured anyone who needed care—remained alive in the culture as women's work in the patriarchy, and after 1968, as concerns of feminists—care of children, the aging, the sick, the poor, and the marginalized. In the traditional festa of the comari, women brought gifts of sustenance to family, friends, and the needy—pasta, flour, a piece of cheese, lard, and firewood. Comari, planning to visit an old widower, would put provisions into a basket: pasta made with egg, a little piece of pork, four fingers of wine, and cardooni, sicilian green similar to chard. After making the old man's bed, sweeping the floor, washing the cooking pot, and putting oil in the lamp,[12] they would go on to the next person who needed care.

Food, the staff of life celebrated in italian culture, remembers the life-giving qualities of the dark mother. Before the miseria of the late 19th century, carnival was a celebration of pasta, remembering the ancient association of wheat with the dark mother. In the streets, in baskets on roofs, and in windows, sicilian women praised the dark mother with displays of homemade pasta. Street stalls offered goat and lamb, rabbit and hare, pig's liver, flasks of wine, and the traditional sicilian liqueur, rosolio, which my ragusane aunts in Kansas City made for visitors. Padroni gave gifts to lessers on natale and pasqua (christmas and easter), and always on Fat Tuesday of carnevale. Noble families sent servants from house to house with flour, cheese, ricotta, or meat. In the working classes, gifts were appropriate to one's mestiere (vocation): a porcaro gave truffles, a cheese maker cheese, a gardener cardooni, farmers gave asparagus, and women gave eggs and hens, a custom feminists would satirize in the 1970s with cartoons depicting women as brood hens full of eggs.[13]

For poorer sorts in the contea, carnival was a brief respite from the hard work of the rest of the year. Braccianti (farm workers) labored hard and were paid little, often in kind; e.g., wheat, oil, cheese. Women in peasant families helped in the fields at harvest time, and made bread at home every

Saturday, two thirds of the loaves going into the husband's bag to sell in town. In between other tasks, women did embroidery/cut work for their daughters' dowries. After her daughter married, the mother did embroidery/cut work on linens to sell in town, later to mainland shops, as discussed above. When the miseria deepened in the 1890s, a peasant woman might become wet nurse, as did my nanna Lucia, for infants of the nobility in the local castle.

During the miseria, peasant men who worked in the fields often had only bread for their mid-day meal, sometimes accompanied by half an onion or three or four olives—all three foods associated with the dark mother. In the first years of the 20th century, when my father was a boy in Ragusa Ibla, he worked in the fields eating bread and an onion at mid-day to save up money to go to the opera, his lifelong passion. Family dinner for peasants was often a soup made with fava beans, legume believed to have regenerative qualities; in the christian overlay of this pagan belief, peasants would say that for each fava eaten, one sin would be forgiven.

Bread, for sicilian and other peasants, was the basic food, although peasants could not always afford it. In winter in Sicily, women and children ate carobs, in springtime wild greens, and in autumn fichi d'India (prickly pears). In this meager peasant diet, wine was reserved for harvest time, and macaroni made with egg was special. But carnevale was a festa when sons and husbands, who may have had to travel far to find work, would return home; the family would enjoy pasta cu sugo, everyone lifted wine glasses in brindisi (toasts), everyone teased with sensual themes, and everyone sang until midnight.[14]

After 1487, when the office was instituted, the persecutorial hand of the spanish inquisition was felt for more than three centuries in regions of my sicilian maternal and paternal grandparents. In this period when the modern nation state was formed, catholic and protestant states were strengthened by persecuting others. Moors were first branded infidel, then conquered by hired normans. Jews in 1492 were banished from the spanish realm (south Italy and Sicily) with the aim of religious cleansing.

Christianized under threat of death, or expulsion, jews were then persecuted in the 16th and 17th centuries for "judaizing." In this same
period, women all over Europe, often lesbians and/or healers, were
branded as witches, tortured, and put to the stake.

In the inquisition handbook, *Malleus maleficarum*, women were said to
be secretly in league with the devil, a belief underlying church and civil
law and custom that justified subordination, control, and persecution of
women. Both catholic and protestant states enforced a double standard of
sexuality against women, a double standard apparent in a case in my
ancestral contea di Modica wherein the law was that if the son of the
landowner seduced a peasant girl, it was she who was punished. In one
case of seduction in the contea, Rosa was taken to a prison for women,
where her hair and eyebrows were shaved. Stripped naked to the waist (a
patriarchal inversion of african and canaanite mother goddesses who
offered their breasts in nurturance), she was mounted on a crippled don-
key. Preceded by a trumpet and tambourines, the woman as a figure of
shame and fear was made to pass before the people of Chiaramonte Gulfi.
Not considering this punishment enough, Rosa was lashed until she
reached the home of the landowner father of the rapist, where she fainted.
In the castle that night the baron celebrated with church authorities. The
son fled; what happened to Rosa is unknown.[15]

Yet women resisted. In everyday and carnivale rituals, often under protective cover of women's work, they satirized church and state and
expressed values of the dark mother. During carnevale in the contea di
Modica, women would sit in the sun in a circle while they denounced
injustice. Denunciations of injustice were called frutti, or the bounty of
the dark mother. During the counter reformation, criticism of the clergy
was not permitted except for limited criticism on Domenica grassa of carnival week. On Fat Sunday, nuns, church organists, sacristans, and, by the
end of the 19th century, priests, were mocked. On Fat Sunday, suppressed
emotions of people in the church would rise to the surface, e.g., jealousies

of nuns who compared family gifts, inter-monastery rivalries over a shared saint, etc.[16]

The carnival ritual of women sitting in a circle in the public square mending stockings while insulting representatives of church and state was openly subversive. Women would tell scurrilous riddles, mock men's sexual prowess, and aim barbs at conventional chaste matrons ("who in youth did not have the reputation of a Penelope").[17] Denouncing hypocrisy and injustice in church and state, peasant women talked openly about sexual activities of priests, and named perpetrators of injustices. In the late 20th century, echoes of this were visible in italian feminist calls for justice often couched in anti-clerical and ribald phrases.[18] "Son of a bishop!" (figlio d'un vescovo!) is a favorite italian feminist expletive aimed at an overbearing male.

Dreams, for ancients and peasants, were considered divine. Dreams, particularly on carnival Monday, day of the moon, when workers paraded with music, often carried subversive messages. So did dreams on Tuesday, day of the poor. A dream of the color black during carnival was considered a good omen, as it was in everyday stories, riddles, and witticisms. Vanniaturi, vendors of fruits and vegetables sang popular beliefs—black grapes were good, white grapes meant misfortune. (See chapter eight, this work, for heretical vendor songs). In dreams, a black egg signified fecundity, a white egg signified tears. A dream of a black fig (connoting vulva) meant compassion, a dream of a white fig meant disgrace. A dream of a black dog (Diana's?) coming into a church was a sign of providence; a white dog coming into the church was a sign of a theft. Theft constantly crops up in popular stories about the church; peasants regarded church whitening of black madonnas as theft. Popular interpretation of the color black as good was dramatically contrary to church interpretation of black as the color of evil and the devil.[19]

The dark mother was remembered in carnival pageants that satirized worldly rulers. Spanish captains, girded by the inquisition of church and state, were described as looking "as if they could swallow the earth."[20] In a pageant at Modica, a dark old woman with a long black veil knitted a garment of black wool, while running about furiously. Called "la vecchia delle fusa," the old woman purred like a cat, perhaps recalling Bast, Isis'cat. The old woman in black, according to popular belief, knew the whereabouts of enchanted treasure.[21]

Mocking the church during carnival sometimes became tumultuous; revelers, festooned with animal horns, faces painted with smoke and red earth, jumped, howled, ran around madly, and would take over the church.[22] A popular carnival pageant in the contea as well as other places in Italy[23] satirized church marriage; a mismatched old couple would be united in marriage by the church while the carnival audience sang ribald ditties and banged kitchen pans in satire of institutionalized love, an echo, perhaps, of the uninstitutionalized love of prehistory and of the medieval love poetry of troubadours celebrating love outside of patriarchal marriage.

Carnival humor teaches the ethic of justice of the civilization of the dark mother, the justice implicit in the round of the seasons. Summer is always followed by autumn is always followed by winter is always followed by spring....One carnival skit enacted revolutionary justice, "He who laughs on Friday, cries on Saturday."[24] Another, "What is up, must come down." These revolutionary themes of carnival were taught to her children by my sicilian/american mother. A contemporary african american ditty has a similar theme: "What goes around comes around," prompting me to think that italian and african folk wisdom about justice ultimately relates to the ethic of justice of ancient african culture (See chapter one).

Not a sober ethic of justice, in Sicily and other peasant cultures, justice is celebrated with sensual themes, leavening justice with compassion. Clerics, even under the eye of inquisitors, were sometimes drawn into the merry-making. Friars of San Dominico, principal monastery of Modica, liked to celebrate the mysteries of the pagan dea Libitina (goddess of caprice) at carnival time, inviting friends to honor her by dancing, jesting, teasing in an atmosphere that Guastella described as "voluptuous."[25]

Carnival may be considered a ritual of subordinated people subverting constituted religious and secular authority. Gentlemen in the contea di Modica put on decorous historical presentations; peasants declaimed "fiercely aggressive" satirical poetry targeting clergy and nobility on Domenica grassa, while workers expressed defiance with music on Monday. The graeco-roman legend of the kidnap and rape of Proserpina, and the mother Demetra's grief (a story that may enact the aryan kidnap and rape of matristic civilization) was celebrated by all classes, a dramatic example of the persistence, even after aryan invasions, of the memory of the civilization of the dark mother. The best carnival pageants, said Guastella, were those of Ragusa, city which "everyone knows was probably Hybla Heraea,"[26] graeco-roman name for Ragusa that replaced Ibla Nera.

Workers' carnival pageants enacted sicilian life as it existed for millennia, impassioned, and "pagana nell'essenza," (pagan in essence) said Guastella.[27] The shift from matristic prehistory, when symbols of the vulva were pervasive in rock art, to patriarchy when sensuality was celebrated with symbols of masculine genitalia, was evident in carnival symbols in the patriarchal epoch—flasks, gigantic bunches of grapes, and large coconuts. Class conscious as well as ribald, peasant satire during carnival was directed at landowners, gentlemen, and the prominenti: political, professional, and social leaders, including doctors and notaries.

Poetic license during carnival permitted poets to "tell the thing as it clearly is and without subterfuge."[28] An unnamed 16th century sicilian poet was said to tell "the thing as it clearly is." The phrase, "tell it like it is," floated to the surface during the african american civil rights movement of the 1960s in the United States.[29] The 16th century sicilian poet who told it "like it is" was described as fiercely mordant, of rare honesty and acute intelligence, small in stature, with a bald head, mobile features, luminous eyes, and "black as an Ethiopian."[30]

Subterranean memories and beliefs expressed during carnival were also visible in pilgrimages to black madonnas. In Italy these pilgrimages customarily begin the Monday *after* easter. After the church told its story on

Sunday, people enacted older, and deeper beliefs after easter, culminating on May lst, day that became the festival of workers of the world. At Palazzolo Acreide, named for the ancient city of Acre where the canaanite dark mother was venerated, the traditional pilgrimage to the dark byzantine madonna Odigitria featured pilgrims wearing carnival masks and costumes, a ritual that supports my hypothesis that the black madonna is a mask of the ancient dark mother. During this traditional pilgrimage to a black madonna, everyone, including the clergy, wore masks during carnival revelry that lasted all night.

At Palazzolo Acreide, the traditional pilgrimage to the dark madonna featured a group of women covered with black silk capes, faces hidden except for one eye, who sang, danced, and carried torches (remembering Demetra looking for her daughter with a torch?). Women in black broke up processions of male confraternities, who, during the era of the counter-reformation, tried to make popular feste conform to church doctrine. At dawn the procession of the icon of the dark madonna and revelers would reach the edge of town, where an image of the dark mother Cybele is sculpted on the mountain.

Roistering during the pilgrimage to the black madonna at Palazzolo Acreide would climax with bells, songs, and shouts of joy. Guastella marveled that church authorities would permit this riotous religious pilgrimage but concluded that local clergy recognized that this was an antichissima popular festa, so ancient that the church could not, and should not, intervene.[31] When the church did intervene, peasants sometimes foiled clerical efforts to stamp out popular beliefs by changing genders. Or was this a return to the multivalent sexuality of the ancient dark mother often sculpted with a phallus for a head and pregnant?

During the counter-reformation, males expressed the memory of the dark mother in cross-dressing carnival rituals. On martedì grasso, from morning until after midnight, male artisans in black gowns, black wool caps, and smoke-blackened faces, walked in solemn procession. In the late 19th century, as socialist radicalism mounted to confront the miseria of

196 • *dark mother*

Sicily, male peasants in black gowns adopted women's carnival ritual of denouncing injustice, sitting in a circle on a busy street while they satirized authorities of church and city.

The contemporary italian left, concerned about the disappearance of oral traditions conveying themes of justice and resistance to injustice, encourages the preservation of folklore. Recovery in Sicily has been facilitated by collections of late 19th century folklorists. Most regions of Italy since the 1960s have been concerned to preserve folklore as part of the endeavor to build a new and just society. Tuscany is a case in point. Center of partisan resistance to the nazis during world war two, since then the region has, along with Emilia, been considered a model of local communism in Italy. Sometimes called "communism with ragu," concern for justice and equality is leavened with good italian food.[32] In Tuscany the night in April 1996 that the left won the national Italian election, victory was celebrated in peasant carnival style: men triumphantly carried a large round of cheese around the piazza. Identifying the political victory of the left with the black madonna, the former mayor, a communist, vowed that on the morrow he would go on foot to give thanks to the lucan (san Luca) dark madonna of Bologna.

Tuscan and sicilian folklore share many themes. A study of popular beliefs of the region of Lucca uncovered stories about witches and the belief in the mal'occhio, or evil eye, a belief associated with the piercing eyes of the dark mother that persists to this day all around the Mediterranean in Africa, Asia, and Europe.[33] Tuscan stories about the mad people of Gello are similar to sicilian stories about Giufà, the name muslims in Sicily gave to the son in the christian trinity wherein Giufà is a clown fool who does his mother's errands. These popular stories about a mother who sends her clown fool son to do her errands may be regarded as a carnivalesque telling of the christian story by subordinated dark others, replacing the patriarchal doctrine that the father sent his son to do his will on earth,[34]. with stories that the mother sent her clown fool son to subvert patriarchy.

Ribald jokes about padroni and priests abound in Tuscany as well as in Sicily. Sensual themes are often covered by allusions to fruits and vegetables. Anticlericalism is rife in both regions: priests are portrayed as greedy minions who barter spiritual absolution like fish vendors negotiating the price of a trout. Peasants in Tuscany, Sicily, and elsewhere,[35] are irreverent to the canon and to clerics, and speak very familiarly to the dark mother and her son. Irreverence extends to jokes about the sexual peccadillos of priests, humorous tales of husbands and wives cuckolding one another, and witty (and complicit) stories about homosexuality. Criticism of the christian canon and clergy is light in spirit, but italian popular satire can become mordant when referring to the hypocrisy of invoking the gospel while refusing food to the hungry. Which is to say, carnival and other forms of satire in the vernacular culture of Italy, and elsewhere, carry the central message of justice and equality of prehistory into the historic epoch, and adopts humor to send barbs at religious, social, and patriotic hypocrisy.

Notes

1   This chapter, in different form, as "Peasant women's resistance. Le comari dei Monti Iblei," was published in *ReVision, A Journal of Consciouess and Transformation, Winter 1997.*

2   The legacy of the dark mother to the male left of Italy is discussed in chapter eleven, this book.

3   See Carmelo Conti, *Il vento a corde dagli iblei. Autori del novecento* (Catania, Edizione Greca, 1987). 23, 28, 31.

4   Ibid., 35.

5   Ibid., "A sogghira c'a nora 'n fanu mai farina bona…" 142 ff A mother in law and daughter in law grinding wheat together never make good flour.

6   Ibid., 61.

7   For more discussion of carnevale in Italy, see Birnbaum, *Black Madonnas.* Loc. Cit. For carnaval in south America, see Claudio Edinger, *Carnaval* (United Kingdom, Dewi Lewis Publishing, 1996. Arnaldo Jabor says of carnival in Brazil, that this is "African Orientalness" (introduction). The spirit of carnival in the United States today is perhaps best captured in gay pride demonstrations.

8   See Birnbaum, *Black Madonnas (Loc. Cit.)* and Birnbaum, *Liberazione della donna (Loc. Cit.)* for full bibliographies of the italian women's peasant tradition. The writings of Giuseppe Pitre' are an indispensable source of sicilian folklore; e.g., Giuseppe Pitre', *Fiabe, Novelle e Racconti. Popolari Siciliani.* Volume Quarto (reprinted Catania, Gruppo Editoriale. Brancato-Clio-Biesse-Nuo va Bietti, 1993). See also Mario Grasso, *Lingua delle Madri. Voce e pensiero dei siciliani nel tempo* (Catania, Prova d'Autore, 1994). A good background study for this chapter is David I. Kerzer and Richard P. Saller, *The Family in Italy from Antiquity to the Present* (New Haven and London, Yale University Press, 1991).

9   See chapters onc and five, this work.

10   See Joie C. Mellenbruch, *Momma Katie*, work in progress.

11   Serafino Amabile Guastella, *L'Antico Carnevale nella Contea di Modica. Schizzi di Costumi Popolari.* Seconda Edizione (Ragusa, Piccitto & Antoci Editori, 1887). 23-25. See also S. A. Guastella, *Le Domande Carnescialesche e gli scioglilingua del circondario di Modica.* (Ragusa, Piccitto & Antoci Editori, 1888).

Gino Carbonaro, *La donna nei proverbi. Tradizioni popolari siciliane* (Ragusa, Thomson Editore, 1981, 1982). For the wedding dowry, see Gino Carbonaro. *Customs and Habits of the Sicilian Peasants.* Edited and translated by Rosalie N. Norris. Translated from: *Costumi e Usanze dei Contadini di Sicilia,* Salvatore Salomone-Marino, 1897, Edited by Aurelio Rigoli 1968 (Rutherford, Madison, Teaneck, Fairleigh Dickinson University Press, 1981).

12   Guastella. *L'Antico carnevale,* 32-34.

13   See Birnbaum, *Liberazione della donna. Feminism in Italy* (Middletown, Ct., Wesleyan University Press, 1986, 1988). 247.

14   See Guastella, *L'Antico carnevale,* 37-38 for the meager earnings of peasants.

15   Ibid., 48-52.

16   Ibid., 26-28.

17   Ibid., 59 ff.

18   See Birnbaum, *Liberazione della donna. Feminism in Italy. Loc. Cit.,* 1986, 1988.)

19   Guastella, *L'Antico carnevale,* 68 ff.

20   Ibid., 73.

21   Ibid., 82.

22   Ibid., 83.

23   See L. Birnbaum, *Black Madonnas, Loc.* Cit, .chapters 5 and 6.

24   Guastella, *L'Antico carnevale,* 87.

25   Ibid., 97.

26   Ibid., 101.

27   Ibid., 103.

28   Ibid., 105.

29   In the 1960s, another sign of the surfacing of ancient memories was the expletive "motherfucker," pervasive in radical circles of the U.S; perhaps a half remembrance of the dark mother whose consort was often a son.

30   Ibid., 107.

31   Ibid., 125.

32   *Siciliani, a* journal that demonstrates the shift of the center of the italian left from the center of Italy to the south and the islands, is also significant in showing how the struggle against the mafia in Italy has brought together an

anti-fascist, anti-racist, anti-violence coalition of women and men. *Sikania,* another sicilian journal, reminds its readers that aboriginal sicilians were the sikani, who had migrated from Africa.

33   Oscar Guidi, *Gli. Le streghe. Antiche credenze nei racconti popolare della Garfagnana* (Lucca, Maria Pacine Fassi, editor, 1990).

34   Discussed in Birnbaum, *Black Madonnas* Loc. Cit.

35   Maria Luigia Rossi, *L'Aneddoto di tradizione orale nel comune di Subbiano. Novelle, barzellette, bazzecole* (Firenze, L. S. Olschki Editore, 1986). 55-64. See also Birnbaum, *Black madonnas*, Loc. Cit. chapter 4.

28. Comari Laboratorio
Siracuse, Sicily
Photograph by Pat Bennett

chapter seven

dark others—jews, moors, heretics, women dark mother and commonality of persecution.[1]
Teresa—saint of dark others

"The right to remember.... When it is truly alive, memory doesn't contemplate history, it invites us to make it."[2]
— Edouardo Galeano, *Upside Down*

This chapter explores commonalities among those persecuted as other by dominant white male elites of Europe, a persecution that began before the common era with greek and roman subordination of the dark mother, abuse of women and slaves, and defeat of african semitic carthaginians—a persecution of others that continued with the establishment of christianity. In the late middle ages and early modern era, persecution and killing of dark others—who looked to a dark mother—intensified. European states, in alliance with the church, conquered african moors, then persecuted and killed jews, women, and heretics.[3]

In 1970, in what may have been an irony of history, the vatican commemorated santa Teresa, of a jewish conversa family, as the first woman doctor (theologian) of the church. Teresa taught her nuns "mental prayer," an excellent way of keeping heretical beliefs of marginalized others out of the persecutorial clutch of church inquisitors. This chapter concludes with a note about spanish conquistadores/missionaries in the new world who killed and imposed catholic beliefs on native americans who held earth-bonded beliefs. As we shall learn in the next chapter, puritans, english invaders of the north american continent, identified dark others with sin, and killed native americans, enslaved africans, and hanged dissenting women.

O

The history of hebrew speakers in Italy stretches back to the millennium before the common era when canaanites of west Asia founded trading posts and settlements in Africa and all around the Mediterranean, notably in Sicily, Malta, Sardinia, Spain, France, and Italy. Italians implicitly recognize this long history in their word for jews, ebrei, or hebrews, a word that embraces canaanites as well as israelites, and suggests italian recognition of the persistence of canaanite beliefs in everyday judaism.[4] After roman defeat of carthaginian/canaanites of Africa in 143 BCE, and roman destruction of the israelite temple in Jerusalem in 70 CE, jews in diaspora came to Italy, becoming the oldest uninterrupted community of jews in Europe, leaving an indelible imprint on italian culture.[5]

The modern history of jews evokes the unbearable sound of a fingernail across a blackboard, beginning with expulsion of jews from the spanish realm in 1492, a date coinciding with Cristoforo Colombo's setting sail for the new world. Some jews, fleeing persecution, shipped with Columbus. In the early modern era after moors were subjugated, jews were forcibly converted to christianity, under threat of violence or death.

What happened to suppressed beliefs of those forcibly christianized ? In the case of the jews, the answer is complex but it has something to do with similar pagan premises in everyday beliefs of jews and christians in Italy. The similarity is brilliantly evoked in Carlo Levi's description of the pagan beliefs that pulse beneath the catholicism of peasants of Italy. Martin Scorsese's films offer a glimpse of shared heretical beliefs of italian jews and christians. Kinship of jews and christians of Italy is suggested in Primo Levi's remembrances of the holocaust wherein he pointed out that there had never been a pogrom in Italy.[6] Carlo Ginzburg, italian jewish historian studying inquisition court records has found that persecuted beliefs of jews and christian peasants were similar, and that beliefs of persecuted male and female heretics were remarkably like everyday beliefs of most people today.[7]

Common beliefs of jews and christians of Italy, in my view, ultimately refer to african origins as well as to canaanite transmission of african beliefs in Italy, discussed in chapter two of this book. Later, israelite jews, probably via Egypt and its cosmopolitan african capitol, Alexandria, came to Italy.[8] In the roman era, particularly after 70 CE, colonies of jews from Palestine and Egypt migrated to Syria, Cyrenaica, Mesopotamia, the Black Sea, islands of the Mediterranean, coasts of the Aegean sea, and Rome, a diaspora enlarged by jewish prisoners of war enslaved during roman conquests in west Asia. *Oracoli sibillini* stated that jews were found in "every land and every sea."[9] Many lived in port cities of Italy: e.g., Ostia outside Rome, and Pozzuoli near Naples, Salerno, Taranto, Otranto in south Italy, et al.

In the first centuries of the common era, many jews were attracted to the gospel of Jesus, whom they perceived as a martyred jew.[10] Paul gathered many who called themselves cristiani-ebrei (christian hebrews).[11] This fluidity across what later became boundaries tended to come to an end after roman capture of Jerusalem in 134 CE when jews ceased being a nation, becoming una religione lecita, a tolerated religion of the roman empire.[12] Jewish revolts in west Asia and in Egypt were severely put down by Trajan, yet under late roman emperors, christians, not jews, were the major targets of roman persecution.

According to Attilio Milano's excellent study, jews were low on the socio-economic scale, mostly liberated slaves, small merchants, and artisans; about 70,000 lived in Rome and about 20,000 in south Italy and the islands. In Rome, they lived in Trastevere[13] and in Ostia, port city of old Rome, where ruins of the large jewish community include a synagogue.[14] In the first millennium of the common era, major communities of jews lived in Rome, Naples, and Palermo.[15] In Sicily, besides Palermo, jews lived in Syracuse, Ragusa, Catania, and Agrigento. In the long succession of foreign rulers of Italy—greeks, romans, byzantines, lombards, normans, et al.,—jews, according to Milano, played an equilibrating role.[16] .

We know little about the history of the moors in Europe because the inquisition burned thousands of books written by "their geographers, scientists, poets, historians and philosophers." Columbus' voyage in 1492 marked not only the extension of european hegemony to the new world but the extinguishing of eight hundred years of moorish rule in Spain, when jews and moors, who physically resembled each other, lived peaceably alongside one another, in strikingly similar cultures.[17]

Africa was the origin of inhabitants of the arabian peninsula, as discussed in chapter two. Kush (Nubia) home of african veneration of the dark mother Isis, was the african region later inhabited by arabs. Interchange between Africa and Asia, a theme of prehistory, was resumed "when the 'Arabs' began to spread westwards into Egypt and across the Red Sea," and were "largely absorbed into the gene pools of the peoples of the Nile, the Sahara and the northern Mediterranean and Middle Eastern colonies scattered across the northern rim of Africa."[18]

The span of moorish culture at its height in the 9th century was wide: "...the moorish empire in Africa stretched from the western half of Algeria through Morocco and as far south as Ghana." The african empire of moors in Europe "extended from the Atlantic coast of Portugal, through Spain and across the Pyrenees to the Rhone Valley in France."[19]

This area of Europe is dense today with icons of black madonnas. Moorish intellectual centers in Spain, Toledo, Cordova, Seville and Granada, are contemporary sites of very passionate easter rituals. The song, *Granada*, Ira Pilgrim advises, invokes a dark mother.

After 827 of the common era, moors of Africa renewed the prehistoric tie of Africa with Sicily, bringing a beneficial interval into the lives of subordinated classes of that island, a golden hiatus that came to an end when normans took Sicily in 1060 CE. Before 827 CE, Sicily was ravaged by northern european invaders who sacked, looted, and raped, then ruled by patriarchal byzantines of Constantinople. After 1060, sicilians suffered under normans hired by the pope to impose canonical christianity on south Italy and Sicily—thereby keeping peoples of south Italy and Sicily under the thumbs of northern lords and bishops. In between northern european sacking and raping, byzantine rule, and domination by normans and the vatican, the interval of more than two centuries of moorish rule in Sicily, in the view of contemporary italian historians, was good for the common people.

Islam in Arabia and in Africa displaced a popular religion with goddesses and a variety of marriage customs, according to Leila Ahmed in her valuable study of women, gender, and islam.[20] In the 9th century when moors of Africa arrived in Sicily, the island was part of the world of north Africa and the frontier area of the west asian byzantine empire. At Palermo, capitol of Sicily, where ships sailed to Africa and Asia, the city was covered with islamic mosques presiding over moorish Sicily. Under the inquisition, mosques were forcibly turned into christian churches. From the standpoint of feminist muslim historian Leila Ahmed, the islamic interlude was characterized by the "more humane and egalitarian laws" of african moors in contrast to "the patriarchal customs" of "European overlords."[21]

In her comparative study of african and european cultures, Ahmed points out that the civilization of Egypt dates from 3100 BCE to greek conquest in 333 BCE. At the time of greek conquest, and for some time thereafter, Egypt was "remarkably liberal and egalitarian."[22] Why"male dominance took such an apparently benign course in Egypt, compared to the course it took in Greece and Mesopotamia," and "why it was the misogynist and oppressive models for treating women that eventually won over the entire region," are questions, for Ahmed, that need to be explored.[23] Under official islam there was regression for women, but Greece, Rome, and institutionalized christianity "had already brought about major losses in women's rights and status." Denigration of women, initiated by male elites of Greece, Rome, and then continued by the catholic church, simply was copied, according to Ahmed, by dominant male elites of islam.[24]

In the early common era, veneration of Isis blended with Cybele and Astarte was everywhere in the known world, but worship of the dark mother was "most deeply rooted in Egypt and the Middle East."[25] At the time of the rise of islam, a variety of marriage customs were practiced in west Asia and Egypt,[26] while christianity had already institutionalized women's subordination. The ethical vision of islam, "which is stubbornly egalitarian," Ahmed insists, "including with respect to the sexes," is thus "in tension with, and might even be said to subvert the hierarchical structure of marriage pragmatically instituted in the first Islamic society."[27]

The difference between official doctrines of established religions and popular beliefs and customs may be seen in islam, as well as in judaism and christianity. Official abbasid islam institutionalized the isolation of arab women as well as harems whose concubines were guarded by eunuchs, yet the popular culture of islam, according to Ahmed and others, was egalitarian in regard to women. Historians have not noted islamic egalitarianism, perhaps, because the gender equality that characterized popular cultures was not of interest to scribes writing for the dominant classes.

Although suppressed by official patriarchal islam, the dark mother persisted in islamic popular culture where women and men put her symbols in carpets, tiles, and other art. In dominant islamic culture, the dark mother has remained submerged, and distorted, but her power can be glimpsed right up to the 1990s, when an islamic ruler declared a "mother of a war" in the Persian gulf against the United States.

Under moorish rule based in Tunis and Egypt, jews of Sicily had some civil rights, including the right to maintain synagogues. In accordance with the medieval custom of identifying people by dress, jews were required to wear a yellow belt and a special turban. In addition they were required to pay certain taxes, not permitted to carry arms, and excluded from the army. Yet during moorish governance of Sicily, jews and moors knew one another's customs and spoke one another's languages. Under moorish dominion before 1000 CE, a "golden age" of jewish culture flourished in Sicily, Puglia, and the rest of south Italy, a golden age marked by talmudic study at Bari and the founding of the renowned medical school, in which jews were active, at Salerno.

O

In the early modern period, modern states initiated racist policies of pitting "white against black and brown." Yet official racist policies were resisted by the undertow of european popular culture that had absorbed african beliefs, notably the african belief in the dark mother and african sun worship. The latter was documented in 10,000 years of rock art of Italy.[28] In the early 20th century in the United States, the persistence of ancient african beliefs may be documented in the popular songs of italian/Americans. The most popular was *O Marie!* The second was *O Sole Mio!*

Everyday beliefs of moors, jews, and christians were, and remain, probably more similar than different. This needs to be emphasized because historians who write history for the dominant classes stress differences. History from the standpoint of popular cultures can not dismiss the obvious shared beliefs of the three major world religions, judaism, christianity, and islam. All claim descent from Abraham, share the same early history, the same moral code, and very similar popular beliefs.

According to Raphael Patai, whose work is indispensable to this subject, belief in spirits is shared by all three faiths: there are "male and female jinn; Muslim, Jewish, Christian, and pagan jinn....In general it can be stated that belief in the jinn has assumed identical forms among Jews and Moors/Muslims down to small details."[29] Jinn, in islamic culture, refer to spirits who are a rung below angels. They can take human or animal form, and influence humanity for good, or evil. Analogues of jinn in italian christian culture are saints. In protestant countries, the belief has been secularized, and politicized into veneration of founding fathers, presidents, popular celebrities, et al.

The popular belief in the "evil eye" was, and is, shared by jews, christians, and muslims. The belief may refer to the anxiety of dominant cultures who banished the dark mother, but who continued to be unsettled by the riveting eye of the dark mother.[30] In the popular cultures of north Africa, moors and jews wore protective amulets and considered fire and water prophylactic agents against the evil eye. Jews adopted the star of David as a protective symbol against the evil eye. Moors adopted protective grafitti of crescents, or the hand of Fatima, daughter of Mohammad. Today in islamic Turkey, blue eye amulets—protecting against the evil eye—are everywhere, on visors of buses and taxis, on clothing, on houses, et al. In my sicilian/catholic childhood in Kansas City, children wore scapulars to protect them against the evil eye; older women practiced rituals of oil and water to learn if someone were afflicted with the mal'occhio, and used incantations, including christian prayers, to exorcise the evil eye. Perhaps the point about amulets that protected against the evil eye is that they transmitted a shared anxiety of patriarchal jews, christians, and muslims that remembered the dark mother's piercing eye of judgment, while people in popular cultures indicated a continuing belief in the dark mother by wearing amulets with her eyes to protect themselves.

The patriarchal marriage custom attesting to the virginity of a bride by displaying the blood-stained nuptial sheet, was shared by christians, jews, and muslims.[31] Interechangeability of customs among jews and muslims may be seen in that men of both faiths tend to have hebrew names; jewish woman tend to have arabic names. Perhaps, Patai suggests, the fathers named the sons, the mothers named the daughters.[32] In the popular culture of sicilian catholicism, names were chosen from jewish, islamic, and christian traditions, as names in my own family demonstrate (see chapter eight).

Similarity in popular rituals of the three religions suggests to Patai that they "could have originated in an ancient pagan culture." Popular belief in the dark mother, as we shall see in the discussion below, appears to have survived rabbinical judaism, canonical catholicism, and official islam.[33]

Despite differences emphasized by clerics, continued by scribes, and manipulated by politicians, women's lives in popular cultures of major religions of the world were, and remain, very similar. In islam, polygamy and concubinage "were relatively uncommon" outside the ruling class.[34] Women's work, "sewing, embroidery, and other forms of textile production,"[35]—a major vehicle of transmission of the memory of the civilization of the dark mother—has been similar in cultures of judaism, christianity, and islam. Over the centuries, jewish, christian, and islamic women have had similar social activities. All three visit one another at weddings, births, and funerals; all three shape pastries as crescents, circles, and triangles, forms that remember the dark mother.

All three religions shared similar mediterranean cultures, notably in diet, clothing, and architecture.[36] "As for language, the Jews in all Arab lands spoke Arabic, as did the Muslims." This leaves official religions of judaism, christianity, and islam, in contrast to the popular beliefs of the three religions, as the area in which differences existed.[37] Differences pale alongside the many commonalities in belief that accompanied christian co-optation of a good deal of judaism and islamic embrace of much of judaism and christianity.

In the common era, the parallel flowering of cultures in Syria, Iraq, Egypt, Morocco, Spain, and Sicily probably "owed more to Arab than to Jewish initiative," according to Patai. "But once they followed in the footsteps of the Arab grammarians, exegetes, philosophers, poets, doctors, and scientists, the Jews excelled in all these fields to no lesser a degree than the Arabs, and in some, such as translation and cartography, even eclipsed them."[38]

Despite official suppression of the belief, perhaps the deepest commonality of jews, christians, and moors may be the ultimate belief in the dark mother. She originated among africans, and whatever the official islamic doctrine, the belief appears to have persisted in everyday cultures and symbols of muslims of Africa and Asia. Her jewish form, the shekinah, has been called the "feminine face of God." The unsubjugated dark mother may be glimpsed in Lilith, who in jewish popular belief would not lie beneath Adam, and ran away. In popular christianity the dark mother is glimpsed in images of black madonnas.

In the popular culture of Italy, in addition to ubiquitous icons of black madonnas, the dark mother was called "Matronit," as well as "Teacher, the Greek Mistress, the Wise Sibilla." During the inquisition, women of Palermo and Ragusa said that the Matronit and her followers could cure the spellbound. In 1640 a woman from Palermo, Caterina Buni, "who went at night with the women from outside," was tried and sentenced. As late as the 19th century, Carlo Ginzburg has found Donni di fuora (women from outside), Donni di locu (local women), Donni di notti (night women), Donni di casa (housewives), Belli Signuri (beautiful ladies) and Patruni di casa (mistresses of the house) to be "ambiguous figures, generally beneficent but ready to cause trouble for those who did not pay them due reverence."[39] These women, who embodied the memory of the dark mother in patriarchal times, may be considered direct ancestors of contemporary feminists who express autonomy.

On the popular level of judaism, the shekhina, according to Patai, "came dangerously close to an image of a feminine deity, distinct from, and occasionally even contraposed to, God, the masculine divine king."[40] Elinor Gadon, tracking the presence of the shekinah, found her in "the writings of the rabbis, authoritative commentators on the biblical tradition, during the early years of the Jewish exile following the destruction of the second temple by the Romans in the first century C.E."[41] The shekhina, for Patai, is "direct heir to such ancient Hebrew goddesses of Canaanite origin as Asherah and Anath,"[42] variants of Astarte.

Banished by official rabbinical judaism, the shekhina persisted in jewish popular culture in metaphors that demonized and exalted her. She re-emerged, according to Elinor Gadon, in the medieval cabbala.[43] For artists like Gilah Hirsch, the shekhina is the "boundless light that emanates from the source of creation, female like the Hindu Shakti," as well as the "dance of life that is the movement of every living cell." Hirsch, in a convergence with a theme of this book, finds the shekhina imprinted "in the double helix of the DNA, the genetic code of life."[44] Contemporary jewish feminists celebrate the shekhina in new moon, succoth, and other popular rituals that have kept her memory alive over millennia. Retrieving the submerged female in judaism is considered by many contemporary jewish feminists to be part of the work necessary to restore and heal the planet.[45]

Asphodel Long, scholar of hebrew scriptures, has placed the dark mother in historical perspective. She considers the words of Isis inscribed on the temple at Sais in ancient Egypt, "I am all that is, was or ever will be, " similar to the proclamation of Jahweh in Exodus 3:14,"I am that I am."[46] Conventionally, states Long, "Judaism is identified with an absolute monotheism," a monotheism inherited by christianity. "Such monotheism is centered on God, Jahweh (Jehovah) who is always referred to in the masculine gender." Yet, states Long, current scholarship indicates that "the ancient goddess Asherah was worshipped not only in the setting of the Canaanite religion as wife of El and mother of Baal and Anat, but quite disparately, as the consort of Jahweh. This would have been part of what is called the 'popular religion' of the Hebrews and it is the one that the Deuteronomists and their successors were trying so hard and so unsuccessfully to stamp out."[47]

Deuteronomists called her a "harlot," yet recent archeological excavation indicates that "not only the women but the whole family and whole communities who joined in her worship...were Hebrews...[who venerated] the Queen of Heaven...."[48] "The Lady Asherah, a Canaanite goddess, became part of the religion of the Hebrews and appears to have been worshipped as the partner or consort of Jahweh," according to Long. The dark mother in the jewish tradition has held a variety of names, but her "worship continued over several millennia, always condemned by the leadership and always retained by the popular will."[49] In the book of wisdom of Solomon, the female figure was "co-fashioner with God, of the universe."[50] One way official Judaism was able to cope with this popular woman figure, sometimes called Sophia of the wisdom tradition, was to identify her with the torah.

In doctrinal christianity this popular woman figure, according to Long, was subsumed to Jesus; in popular culture she melded, in various ways and times, "with the Holy Spirit and the Virgin Mary."[51] On the popular level of sicilian christianity, Mary and Jesus were both considered saints.[52] Equality of mother and son was evident in the iconography of the popular culture of italian/americans in the first half of the 20th century. On the mantle of the fireplace of our home in Kansas City, Missouri , the statue of mother Mary stood equally tall alongside her son Jesus.

The african matrix of popular religious beliefs of Europe may be traced to the fact that christianity was born in an era when the most "influential" religion was african, as discussed in chapter one, a religion of "the goddess Isis of Egypt which had spread throughout the 'known world,' and which continued for something like three millennia, ending only when destroyed about 500 C.E."[53] Isis was formidable.

I am Isis, I am she who is called goddess by women

I gave and ordained laws for humans which no one is able to
change
I divided the earth from the heavens
I ordered the course of the sun and the moon
I appointed to women to bring their infants to birth in the
tenth month
I established punishment for those who practise injustice
I am Queen of rivers and winds and sea
I am in the rays of the sun
Fate hearkens to me
Hail Egypt that nourishes me.[54]

In summary, the considerable genetic and cultural interchange among religious groups of the world[55] has been obscured by hegemonic beliefs of world religions. On the popular level, despite religious fences, there seems to have been a persistent veneration of the prehistoric dark woman divinity of multiple names throughout the historical epoch. The valence of the dark mother seems to have informed the everyday lives of canaanites, israelites, christians, muslims, as well as of heretics. Whatever the differences emphasized by canonical christianity, rabbinical judaism, official islam, and political rulers, over the long span of time, jews, christians, and muslims of Europe, as well as of west and the rest of Asia, and of Africa seem to have shared similar popular beliefs, at whose center, it has been my finding, is the dark mother, and her values of justice with compassion, equality, and transformation—values which patriarchal male elites of all three religions have attempted to silence, leave out of their histories, and try to obliterate.

My research in the popular culture of Italy has uncovered that not only christians but jews and muslims were drawn to icons of black madonnas. Embodying the dark mother, the black madonna was a figure in whom dark others in a repressive environment could project private pains and hopes. Black madonnas of Italy, although subsumed to christianity, are found in places of historical communities of jews and moors, for example, at Trastevere, Livorno, Lucera, Bari, Naples, Salerno, Siponto, et al.

How did the religions fare under the dominance of one or the other? Patai concludes that the jews fared better under islamic rule than they did under christian hegemony. "Life in the House of Islam had for the Jews pleasures and pains....However, from this point of view, compared to what Christian Europe did to the Jews, culminating in the Nazi holocaust, Jewish life under Islam must appear as infinitely better than under the Cross."[56] In Sicily, christians and jews prospered under moors of Africa who divided large land holdings, introduced agricultural reforms, citrus fruits, and bequeathed the incomparable cassata and other dolci (sweets) to the island.[57]

In a campaign that began with catholic crusades against moslems and the pope engaging the normans to take Sicily away from the moors, the church after 1100 embarked on a campaign to force jews to convert to christianity. In what Milano describes as a "psychosis of desperation among the Jews" of south Italy, forcible conversion was often carried out by christian authorities simply by turning synagogues into churches. "About half of the Jews of the south" of Italy, when presented with the choice of conversion or flight, chose conversion.[58] Some jews who converted to christianity, became "part of the most elevated nobility of the kingdom."[59] Jews who did not convert could not hold public office, sell medicine, or be familiar with christians, although in the north, and in the vatican, jewish doctors were sought after by the nobility and the clergy.[50]

Before the expulsion edict of 1492, there were large jewish communities all over Italy—in Sicily at Palermo, Termini, S. Marco, Castroreale, Santa Lucia, Messina, Taormina, Randazzo, Nicosia, Paterno', Augusta, Syracuse, Ragusa, Comiso, Noto, Scicli, Licata, Naro, Nicosia, Polizzi, Geraci, Castelnuovo, Caltabelotta, Sciacca, Salemi, Marsala, and Trapani.[61] Looking over the names of the towns, not only do I note that these jewish communities include my own ancestral places, I am reminded that canaanites, in the millennium before the common era, had earlier settled in many of the localities where israelites later came—confirming that it is very difficult to tell the difference between canaanites and israelites in their everyday lives and beliefs.

On the italian peninsula, there were large jewish communities (from south to north) at Reggio Calabria, Cosenza, Taranto, Rossano, Otranto, Lecce, Brindisi, Bari, Trani, Salerno, Napoli, Benevento, Capua, Roma, Ancona, Siena, Urbino, Florence, Pisa, Bologna, Ferrara, Reggio Emilia, Venice, Padua, Mantua, Cremona, Verona, and elsewhere.[62] For fifteen centuries, jews had lived in the mezzogiorno, land of the noonday sun south of Rome, as doctors, bankers, merchants, artisans. After 1541, there were almost no jews left in the south of Italy. Half of them converted, according to Milano, and half went elsewhere. In the south, many who remained jews lived in Naples, a curious place to choose because Naples was a capitol of the spanish inquisition, suggesting that whatever the formal policy, an implicit modus vivendi may have been worked out so that most jews were left alone so long as they kept their religious beliefs to themselves, and made external obeisance to dominant christianity.

What happened to the other jews of south Italy and Sicily who were made to subscribe to christianity? Sal Salerno, italian/american historian, went to San Fratello, his grandfather's ancestral town near Messina in Sicily, to study the easter Festa dei Giudei,the very enigmatic "easter festival of the jews." San Fratello is located near the black madonna of Tindari as well as close to the site of the historical trade in obsidian, associated with the dark mother, on the offshore Lipari islands.

In San Fratello the black madonna is venerated in small niches on outside walls of homes. On good Friday, San Fratello's celebrants of the festival of the jews wear masks, reminding me of the masked participants in 17th and 18th century pilgrimages to the black madonna, described earlier. Masking what beliefs? A local historian has described the multivalent easter ritual at San Fratello. "Hundreds of masked men, dressed in shocking colors,...turn the town upside down, doing things that the most permissive carnevale would not allow. Making noises with their trumpets, singing vulgar songs and making erotic gestures, they travel the streets, piazzas and alleys in small groups, noisily assaulting stores, homes, gardens, while the wine flows freely."[63] The festival of the jews at San Fratello reminds me of rituals of priests of Cybele in late antiquity, discussed in chapter three. What seems to be at hand are rituals of resistance to the dominant culture, rituals that seem to have persisted, perhaps subconsciously, from late antiquity through two millennia of popular culture.

At San Fratello at easter, barefoot women in black shawls follow the large wooden crucifix while men masked as jews gather in groups. "The intense emotional charge accumulated in the long wait, exasperated by three days of inebriation and exalted from transgression, explodes. They assault the procession and transform the celebration in what in the Christian vision is the most mournful and penitent moment into an explosion of pirouette dances, positioning themselves closer and closer to the people in the procession, intimidating them as they dance, sing and blow on their trumpets." The festival turns the christian day of mourning into a "huge happy uproar."[64]

From the perspective of judaism as a submerged culture in dominantly christian Europe, the festival of the jews at San Fratello may be interpreted as a memory of the *Hebrew goddess,* (Patai's book) as well as a ritual of the popular jewish festival, purim, whose christian analogue is carnival. Purim dates back to the fifth century BCE when the first temple was destroyed by Nebuchadnezar of Babylonia, when jews fled in diaspora into Persia. Esther (whose name recalls canaanite Astarte) hid her jewish origin and was chosen by the persian king to be his queen. Haman, the prime minister, manipulated the king into taking revenge on the jews who had attempted a coup. Whereupon Esther prevailed on the king to kill Haman. Ever since, jews celebrate the festival of purim with masks, gift-giving, and the pastry hamentaschen, named for Haman's pocket. Haman's pocket is shaped like the pubic triangle symbol of the dark mother; filled, suggestively, with poppy seeds or with apricot marmalade.

"Things are not as they seem," was the theme of an article in a recent issue of *Confronti*, Italy's journal of liberation theology, discussing masked celebrants of purim as well as carnival laughter at authorities of church and state. If doctrinal catholic meaning of easter as the death and resurrection of christ is put to one side, the festa at San Fratello may be understood as a ritual of resistance of subaltern jews and christian peasants to patriarchal christianity. Resistance also suggests the kinship of dark others; the name of the town, San Fratello, means holy brother, Holy brother, in this case, refers to moors, jews, and christians.

Throughout peasant history, Bakhtin reminds us, on the holiest days, notably easter and christmas, there has been peasant laughter. During the easter season, laughter and jokes were permitted even in church. The priest would tell amusing stories and jokes from the pulpit. Jokes and stories especially concerned material bodily life. Permission to laugh was granted simultaneously with the permission to eat meat and to resume sexual intercourse which was forbidden during lent."[65] I am reminded of a contemporary sicilian feminist ritual at Pietraperzia, described in my *Black Madonnas,* of women interpreting good Friday as a spring festival, in which the cross becomes a maypole.[66] Celebrants of the easter festival at San Fratello may be remembering the dark mother in her image as canaanite Astarte/Esther.[67] Pasqua, the italian word, refers both to Esther (whose origin is Astarte) and to the christian holy day, easter.

Commonality of shared submerged beliefs, expressed in everyday and festival rituals of the three religions, was paralleled by commonality of inquisition persecution of jews, heretical christians, and autonomous women. Women called witches were made to wear the inquisition costume of jews. In what may have been a conscious, or unconscious, effort on the part of church and state to prevent coalition of the persecuted and exploited, anti-semitism was promoted to prevent solidarity of others. At easter after 1100, clerics recited an anti-semitic story of the crucifixion that whipped up hatred of jews. Yet in popular rituals in San Fratello, sicilians identified with jews, in a pattern that may be seen throughout the history of italian popular christianity. This last is evident in historic italian celebration of the jewish martyr, Eulalia as a popular christian saint.[68] Identification of christians with persecuted jews was evident during world war two, when italians saved most of the jews of their country from murder by the nazis.

Jews, in the Festa dei Giudei at San Fratello, are not jews. At least they are not jews today. When Salerno asked about the festival, Toto, the town scholar, showed him a list of families of the town who had been called heretics, including converso jews, who were burned at the stake. Toto pointed to the family name Salerno on the inquisition index; Sal searched the document but could not find out what had happened to his relatives during the inquisition. "Toto carefully scrutinized my reaction."[69]

Jews of Europe were often given names of their towns as surnames; Milano's history lists Salerno as an early jewish community of Italy.[70] Under norman rule there were 600 jewish families living in Salerno,[71] a city with a famous medical school in which jews participated and an important commercial port where they worked. In 1278 the church instigated agitation against jews of Salerno.[72] Under threat of violence, 150 heads of families converted to christianity.[73]

After the 1492 edict expelling jews from the spanish realm, many fled Sicily. Some went to Reggio Calabria, Salerno, and Naples on the italian boot After 1550, when the effect of the expulsion edict had settled, there were no jews (who professed to be jews) left in Salerno, or anywhere else in south Italy. After 1550 , the only palpable evidence that jews had lived in south Italy were synagogues that had been forcibly turned into churches. The main synagogue of Naples became the church of Santa Maria della Purificazione; synagogues of Trani became the churches of Sant'Anna, mother of Mary, and Santa Maria dei Martini, a madonna with african/semitic facial characteristics.[74]

Milano, describing the "crypto Jews" of south Italy after the conversion campaign of 1290-94, said that jews coped with forced conversion to christianity in several ways. Some stoically accepted the renunciation of judaism, others regarded conversion as a temporary expedient, others resigned themselves to live on the margins between the two religions, as some did for centuries. Some children of conversos did not know that their grandparents had been jews forcibly converted to christianity. "New Christians" tended to aggregate in Puglia at Bari, at Lucera, around Naples, and particularly at Salerno—all are places of black madonnas.[75] At Lucera, where there was a settlement of moors as well as of jews, the church whitened the black madonna, yet the people continue to consider her black.[76]

The easter festa of jews of San Fratello acts out the meaning of the city's name, brotherhood, in identifying with persecuted others. Moors are recalled in the arabic embroidery of festival costumes. Heretics are remembered in the whip used by inquisitors to flail them. Women, heretics, and jews are recalled in the tail of the devil, with whom the inquisition identified all three. The festival of the jews at San Fratello also suggests how persecuted others sought protection from clerical persecution by putting on protective symbols of the christian church. Sal Salerno found that when the expulsion edict was proclaimed, jews from Palermo, Messina, and Catania took refuge in small mountain towns. "In San Fratello they probably asked to be converted to Catholicism and asked to adorn themselves with this mask during the passions of Easter week."[77]

All of which is boggling to a researcher. The more I study the history of Sicily, the more uncertain I am as to who is a jew, who is a christian, who is a muslim, who is a heretic, and what sicilian women believe, not to speak of trying to determine who is white and who is black in the receding mirrors of that island's history. This uncertainty is accompanied by the feeling I am treading in deeply submerged private waters, where, historically, one's beliefs could get one into deep trouble.

Research is often difficult to pursue in Sicily, as Sal Salerno and I have discovered. When he asked about the festival of the jews at easter in San Fratello, Sal was asked, "Why do you want to know?" Tracking down my family name in Ragusa Ibla some years ago, I found a man named

Chiavola who bore a striking resemblance to my uncle Jim. "No," he closed the discussion, when I asked if he knew, or had heard of, my relatives with the same name. "Why do you want to know?"

In Ragusa, many jews who were expelled went to live in Puglia.[78] I have been told that before 1492 there was a synagogue halfway down the steps from upper Ragusa to Ragusa Ibla, a synagogue that became the church Santa Maria delle Scale during the inquisition. This synagogue, forcibly turned into a catholic church, is located a few yards from my ancestral paternal home dug into the iblean mountains named for the dark mother at Ragusa Ibla. Did my grandmothers—were they jews, or moors or christians?—come to pray in this synagogue turned into a catholic church?

O

The patron saint of San Fratello is saint Benedict the Moor, a name that recapitulates the african/semitic/christian history of the Mediterranean, particularly of Sicily, a history that was brought to the United States. Today in italian Harlem, in New York City, a church is dedicated to saint Benedict the Moor, patron saint of San Fratello, whose festa dei giudei has been described above. In the spiral of history, saint Benedict the Moor of Sicily has become the patron saint of african americans in the United States.

Anthony D'Angelo who has researched the story of this saint found that he lived at the crest of the inquisition, 1526-1589.[79] Saint Benedict the Moor was born in 1526 in San Fratello, Sicily to Christopher and Diana Manasseri, black slaves from Ethiopia owned by the Manasseri family. After Christopher and Diana Manasseri converted to christianity, the Manasseri family granted freedom to their slaves' first born son, Benedict. Working as a day laborer, Benedict shared his earnings with the poor, and became known as "the Holy Negro." He joined a group of hermits who lived in the hills near San Fratello, eventually becoming religious superior of the community.

When the pope required hermit groups to join an established order, Benedict, a lay brother, chose the franciscan Order of Friars Minor of the Observance. Thereafter he worked in the friary, St. Mary of Jesus, in Palermo, becoming master of novices. He died on April 4, 1589 at the age of 63. Beatified in 1743 and canonized in 1807, saint Benedict the Moor is venerated in Italy, Spain, Latin America, Africa, and in the United States.

For D'Angelo, saint Benedict indicates "the widespread presence of a black Catholic population in southern Europe at the beginning of the modern period."[80] I am reminded of the mirrors and masks of sicilian history, and the long memory of the dark mother. In the late 20th century, saint Benedict the Black is remembered in the United States by Robert Lentz whose haunting paintings identify black madonnas with the poor, the persecuted, and the homeless. The story of Saint Benedict the Black when it was recounted in *Street Spirit. Justice News & Homeless Blues* was accompanied by a Robert Lentz painting of the black saint offering loaves of bread to the poor.[81]

O

The memory of heretics in Europe begins with the earliest christian heresy, the gnostic gospels of Africa, which sounded many african themes: e.g., god is both mother and father. The mother's voice sounds like that of Isis : "For I am the first and the last…." The voice reflects the continuing veneration of the dark mother as well as persecution of the dark mother in the christian epoch. "I am the honored one and the scorned one…the whore and the holy one…the wife and the virgin…I am the silence that is incomprehensible…." Church fathers condemned the gnostic gospels.

A thousand years later, the cathar heresy, also known as albigensianism, emerged in an area in France close to the Pyrenees on a primordial path of africans walking across Europe. The pope sent a crusade against the cathars, but he did not stamp out cathar heresies. Afterward the heresies could be found in the folklore of France, Italy, the Balkans, and elsewhere. Emmanuel Ladurie, in his widely-read classic, *Montaillou*, pointed out that the cathar pastoral world "derived from the early Neolithic age," that the basic principles of the heresy were laid down well before the 14th century. Cathars may be regarded as a case of the persistence in the historic epoch of the memory of the dark mother and her values, when the beliefs were branded pagan or heresy, and were murderously put down.

Cathar heretics considered themselves "good Christians" in contrast to official christians. This cathar way of believing has persisted to the present day; contemporary catholics critical of the pope say, "Noi siamo chiesa (we are church)."[82] Historians who write for the dominant classes have emphasized cathar belief in the parfait, or pure elite, but for vernacular history, the significance of catharism inheres in the credenti, or simple believers, who dined on bread, fish and wine, and regarded fasting as a ritual of faith. Like peasants in Sicily and elsewhere, cathars had doubts about the immaculate conception, the resurrection of Jesus, and the infallibility of church dogma. Today in Italy (and elsewhere) people who do not subscribe to doctrines of official catholicism, but consider themselves christian, prefer to call themselves credenti, the term used by cathars. The word credente refers to any believer—jewish, christian, muslim, buddhist, hindu, agnostic, atheist, pagan, et al. In the 14th century, however, cathar believers were mightily persecuted.[83]

Like women since the beginning of time, cathar women were responsible for "water, fire, the garden, cooking and gathering kindling." A peasant in cathar country, like peasants the world over, "worked with his hands, and often very skillfully too." Cathar elders, like jewish elders, promulgated dietary prohibitions, forbidding "bacon and butcher's meat" and credenti chose to obey the prohibitions, or not.

In the cathar region of France, as in all of christian Europe, the inquisition was everywhere. Rich churchmen behaved like arrogant secular authorities. Nobles and bishops who oversaw the inquisition employed police, notaries, and spies to do the dirty work of finding and punishing heretics. Unwillingness to pay church tithes often merged with religious heresy: "The resulting alienation was both spiritual and temporal."[84] Deference to the dominant religion was expressed by going to church; heresy throve in the family, in the neighborhood, and in the custom of godparenthood: commeres and comperes of France who are analogous to comari and compari, or godmothers and godfathers, of Italy[85]

As in other peasant christian cultures, cathars honored the madonna, locally embodied in the Virgin Mary of Montaillou, while they held heretical beliefs,[86] doubting, for example, that the madonna was immaculate. Cathar continuum with pagan beliefs is evident in the ubiquity among cathars of the name Sybille. Agents of the inquisition defined the meaning of Sybille as "Bad mother, devil!"[87] Peasants called heretics "goodmen," and respected them because "they walk in justice and truth."[88] "Saracens," as muslims were called, lived in cathar regions. So did franciscans, who believed in the goodness of the earth and all its creatures. The franciscan ideal of voluntary poverty merged with cathar beliefs in an ideal community "where great and small live together and rub shoulders freely." Cathars, like peoples of north Africa, west Asia, and Spain, shared a belief in fate, a belief compatible with beliefs of saracen shepherds who lived in their midst, as well as with beliefs of moors of Africa and Spain,.[89] The cathar belief in fate was also shared with italians who believe in la forza del destino (the force of destiny). Cathars were also friendly with jews in this period when the church was inciting hatred against them.[90]

Peasants of the upper Ariege liked to say, "The soul of man is bread," or "What one has kneaded, that one must bake." Or, "After death, the human body dissolves and is transformed into earth. That which comes from the earth must go back to the earth."[91] Ultimate beliefs are glimpsed in oaths; inquisitors made their victims swear on a sacred book, while cathar peasants swore "on their own head, or on bread and wine or on flour."[92] The cathar peasant Pierre said, "God and the blessed Virgin are nothing but the visible world around us; nothing but what we see and hear." (Pierre's wording is heretical, suggesting that god and the virgin are equal divine figures in a sacred, not fallen, world). Echoing the civilization of the dark mother of Africa, cathars believed that "souls of animals were just as good as those of men, since all souls were merely blood."[93]

Sometimes cathar beliefs were expressed in earthy bodily terms that outraged church persecutors: "God was made fucking and shitting."[94] In heretical cathar belief, priests rode everyone; "They sleep with women. They ride horses, mules and she-mules. They are up to no good."[95] A good heart, in cathar belief, was what is important, reminding me that the main journal of the student resistance of Italy in the 1990s was named *cuore* (heart). In cathar belief, it is not the act, but the intention, that counts "A lady who sleeps with a true lover is purified of all sins…the joy of love makes the act innocent, for it proceeds from a pure heart."[96] It is evident how cathar belief melded in the Languedoc with that of trouboudours who sought pure love, considering authentic love incompatible with the institution of marriage.

Inquisitors imposed their double standard of sexual conduct on heretics as well as other people. If inquisitors caught cathar heretics in acts of "irregular unions," they would imprison the man as well as the woman, but it was the woman, who when let out of prison, was made to wear the double yellow cross of shame.[97] Sexuality was comparatively free in Montaillou, but promiscuity was not condoned. Incest, deflowering virgins, and adultery were prohibited. Marriages were comparatively stable; fidelity was to the domus, or the home where the couple and the family dwelled. The analogous peasant belief in Sicily is fidelity, not to the marital bond, but to the casa and to the famiglia. The pattern of free sexuality in peasant cultures of France and Italy was similar, "reserved chiefly for widows or poor girls and maidservants, for whom a career as a concubine was available until they managed to find a husband."[98]

Even when they were heretics, cathar men could be patriarchal, sometimes violently so. Cathar women may have loved their men, but they also feared them. And, like women the world over, sought their friends among women, their commeres. Many a strong-minded Sybille took over the inn when her husband was out of sight or dead.[99] Sometimes a son tried to retrieve lands confiscated when his cathar mother was burned at the stake.[100] But among cathars, as among sicilian popular classes, customarily a son's love for his mother was(is) fervent. Sons might refer disrespectfully to the virgin Mary, but to their mothers they said "vous." Daughters in peasant society, heretics or not, as we say in sicilian culture, are "good to their mothers."

Cathar women were held to the dominant culture's patriarchal notions of dishonor and shame. In the upper Ariege of France, as in Sicily, the uppermost popular value for women was "honesty," whose meaning referred not to property but to a woman remaining inviolate, or not dishonored sexually. The perennial strength of women was illumined in cathar areas of France; e.g., "in Aix-les-Thermes, Sybille Baile the Cathar drove out her husband, Arnaud Sicre the elder, a catholic notary."[101] When Jaquette den Carot was told that the doctrine of the resurrection of the body was true because "Minorite friars and the priests have found it written in the books and records," she invoked Sancta Maria and said she did not believe a word of it.[102] A little girl, a priest's maidservant, heard Jacquette say this, and denounced her as a blasphemer.

Like heretics elsewhere, cathars of France often went to church. Beatrice, for example, offered "coloured candles" to the altar of the virgin, men offered fleeces to saint Anthony, patron saint of animals. Receptivity to heretical beliefs, according to Ladurie, was already present in cathar culture in "the pagan elements attached to the worship of the Saints and the Virgin."[103] Cathars loved feast days of saints, who were considered "friends of the workers, including farmers and agricultural labourers."[104]

Sometimes peasant priests in France disseminated the heresy of disbelief in the resurrection of the body, as was the case in Sicily, too.

The simultaneity of the past, the present, and the future, was visible in cathar beliefs, as it is in Sicily; e.g., the use of the present tense to refer to the future as well as to the present. Ancient beliefs suffuse the meaning of words. The word "earth" in cathar France, as in Sicily and other peasant cultures, held political implications of radical justice: the earth can not belong to an individual because the earth is the common inheritance of everyone.

Cathars fleeing persecution went to Lombardy in north Italy, to Sicily, and to Catalonia, Valencia, and Majorca in Spain. Ladurie calls the cathar heresy "an Italian, Mediterranean and Balkan heresy." I agree with him with the proviso that we keep in mind that mediterranean culture is originally african, and that african memories informed mediterranean cultures of west Asia, and cultures of Italy, France, and Spain.[105] In Montaillou, peasants had an inheritance of many mediterranean cultures. They relied, as did africans, on astrology, looked to "spells supplied by a converted Jewess," and read predictions "in a book written in Arabic characters." More ancient was the practice of studying the flight of birds, especially owls and magpies—both symbols of the dark mother. A cathar woman also respected magical devices "learned from some witch or baptized Jewess" which could "help her win her lawsuits, to make her daughters' love affairs prosper and to cure epilepsy."[106]

Perhaps a helpful way of understanding heresies is to see them as popular beliefs that challenge hegemonic religious concepts of upper social and economic classes, as Antonio Gramsci and others have pointed out. Ladurie concluded his study of cathar heretics saying, "Christian piety was always the attribute of an elite in the Middle Ages…urban rather than rural, and did not include the mountain dwellers."[107]

The cult of the virgin Mary, fervently preached by saints Bernard and Dominic, ascended in the high middle ages. The Council of Albi in cathar country in 1254, raised the *Ave Maria* to rank with the *Credo* and the

Lord's Prayer. Cathar veneration of Mary, like that of other peasants, did not look to the Pieta,' the passive and obedient whitened madonna of the vatican. Pilgrims in cathar country walked to the black madonna of Montserrat in Spain, and to black madonnas of Le Puy and Rocamadour in France.[108] Mary of the cathars was not a transcendental woman, but of the earth, with whom "fertility cults both human and agricultural" melded.[109]

Just as peasants in the countryside held subversive views while deferring outwardly to religious authority, lower classes in cities kept noncanonical religious and political beliefs while living under repressive religious and secular authority. For a palermitan who had a stall in the Vucciria, market where cries of vendors lauded the bounty of the earth and the color black,[110] *his* history was not the history of the dominant classes. Living under invaders for millennia, it mattered little to this vendor that Sicily belonged, at the time of the inquisition, to the kingdom of Spain. "I have always minded my own business. For me, Spanish, Piedmontese, Austrians, it's always been the same. The important thing is to keep out of danger...."[111]

The market vendor, Master Giurlannu, said that after the vespers in the 13th century, sicilians had gotten on well with the spanish, with whom they shared saints James, Dominic, Ignatius of Loyola, Francis Xavier, Eulalia, Teresa of Jesus, and the black madonna of Montserrat. This is a revealing list of saints: it includes an inquisitor (for protective covering?), a nun of a jewish conversa family, a jewish martyr considered a saint in popular christianity, and a black madonna.

Keeping out of danger was not easy, because agents of repression were everywhere in the age of the inquisition. Popes granted indulgences not only to inquisitors and their followers, but also to "familiars," people whose task it was to keep an eye out for heretics, denounce them, and help inquisition agents imprison them. In return, familiars were given exemption from the jurisdiction of ordinary courts and from payment of taxes, a wicked self-generating commerce that perpetuated persecution of heretics and political dissenters. Spanish authorities made the auto da fe (ritual of forced public confession of the faith) a public spectacle to scare people into conformity by making them watch beheadings or burnings of heretics. Sicily early appealed for removal of jews from the jurisdiction of the inquisition, but the pope, invoking defense of the faith, denied the request. On March 31, 1492 when Ferdinand issued the expulsion edict, hebrews had lived in Sicily since the time of the canaanites in the millennium and a half before the common era. After the 70 CE israelite diaspora to Italy, hebrews lived as a prosperous and large minority in christendom for nearly 1500 years. In 1492 after citizens of Palermo failed to secure exemption of the city from the expulsion order—by signing a petition that jews of the city had never committed a sacrilege—sicilians figured out ways of foiling the inquisition.

A jewish woman, Eulalia Tarmarit, who had come to Sicily after expulsion from Spain, was burned at the stake by the inquisition. Sicilians turned the burned jewish martyr into a popular christian saint. Eulalia is not listed in the official saints calendar of Rome; she is listed in the saints calendar of Carthage. The story of jewish Eulalia is similar to stories of early christian martyrs; she denounced the authorities and was tortured, and killed. Another Eulalia, an early christian martyred at the time of Diocletian, melded in popular perception with the later jewish martyr Eulalia killed for her beliefs during the inquisition. Both women were popularly identified with suppressed beliefs associated with the ancient dark mother. The celebration of sant' Eulalia is at the time of the winter solstice.

Isidoro La Lumia, in his study of jews of Sicily, analyzing inquisition violence against those regarded as other, found that persecution of jews in Sicily did not emerge from the people, but was incited by clerical and secular authorities.[112] Two sicilian cases of heresy that ended in burning were those of friar Romualdo and the nun, sister Geltruda, both from Caltanisetta, earlier a moorish town. Although Romualdo feigned madness, inquisitors said that he denied the incarnation ("just like the Jews");

and had called the holy office "a deception of the devil." Friar Romualdo went unrepentant to the stake. Sister Geltruda, like Romualdo, was a follower of the 17th century spanish priest and mystic, Miguel de Molinos, who preached suppression of the will, withdrawal from worldly interests, and sustained meditation on god. When brought before inquisitors, Geltruda flew into a rage and denounced her persecutors.

Both the friar and the nun went to death in Palermo in an auto da fe attended by most of the secular authorities of Sicily, and all of the catholic orders, an example of inquisition use of public spectacles to instill fear of nonconformity in the populace. Like condemned jews, heretics wore yellow habits, carried an unlighted candle of yellow wax, and wore conical caps on which their alleged sins were painted.[113] After the auto da fe, "Everybody, knights, officials of the Tribunal, lawyers, Senators, Praetor and ladies, dined abundantly; with the Inquisition meals were always splendid."[114]

In the era of the inquisition, the accused who repented were allowed to approach the inquisitors' throne on their knees, to recant loudly, and then be beaten. Brother Romualdo and sister Geltruda, who would not recant, were put on a cart with hands tied to a pole and dragged by oxen to the stake (an inquisition inversion of the popular story of oxen who took the black madonna to the place she wanted her sanctuary to be built). Sister Geltruda was put to death slowly, first by burning her hair, then by setting fire to her tarred surcoat, then by lighting the wood below the stake. After Geltruda, Romualdo was burned.[115] Protestant reformers and catholic clerics of the counter-reformation were the main instigators, according to recent research, of the witch panic that swept Europe and north America in the 16th and 17th centuries. In german lands, the witch craze involved "excessive use of violence inflicted primarily by men against women and the sexual nature of much of that violence."[116] In Spain and Italy, persecution of women and heretics resulted in fewer executions, perhaps because after the first convulsions, other methods (e.g., expulsion and social control) worked, notably the social control of forcing people to renounce beliefs. Or worked well enough: in Italy and elsewhere, people with pagan, jewish, or muslim beliefs could feign catholicism, covering their beliefs with catholic ritual, as many peasants, particularly women, had done for more than 1500 years.

Persecution of women was apparently propelled by the drive of both protestant reformers and clerics of the catholic counter-reformation to control women's sexuality, as we have seen in the story of Rosa in chapter three. "Heavy penalties for illegitimate births and irregular marriages, and the death penalty for abortion and infanticide, placed new limits on women's control over their bodies and their lives."[117] The 17th century marks a dividing line in gender history. Until this time premarital sex was not unusual and premarital pregnancy not condemned.[118] Heresies, and lenient attitudes toward sexuality, earlier tolerated, were now condemned by male clerics of the protestant and catholic reformations. Most persecutions of women in lands controlled by the inquisition were of women healers, lesbians, or mystics, all of whom were called witches. Carlo Ginzburg reports the trial of "the witch of Ghiai" in which the accused, whose name was Lucia, was condemned for witchcraft. In self-defense she held that she was practicing countermagic, protecting from witchcraft. Covering pagan beliefs with catholic rituals, Lucia made signs over people "with two rosaries and two crucifixes" and escaped prosecution.[119]

From his study of folklore and inquisition records, Carlo Ginzburg concludes that a women's religion existed all over Europe, from the beginnings of christianity to the present. This subterranean women's religion, grounded in the earth and centered on a woman of many names,[120] for Ginzburg, was a "belated descendant of the Celtic divinities." Ginzburg's case for the celtic connection may be tenuously argued for a later period in northern Italy but his own research of inquisition witch trials in Sicily, beginning in the second half of the 16th century, points out there were trials of "companies" of women from my ancestral cities of Palermo and Ragusa with no celtic connection, places where, in the historical epoch, beliefs in the dark mother were transmitted by peasant women.[121]

Anne Llewellyn Barstow, in a definitive history of the witch craze, evaluated the trial of Sibilla and Pierina (1384-1390) in northern Italy. "In trying these women, the Inquisition had stumbled across, not the usual heretics, but members of an old fertility cult (hence the reverence for animals) who rode out at night on the 'wild ride,' dedicated elsewhere to the goddess Diana but centered here on a living woman, Oriente."[122] Ginzburg's research is invaluable but his celtic thesis is not sustained, even for north Italy: Diana and Oriente point to west Asia.

Spanish authorities initiated the burnings in Sicily; austrian officials continued the burnings in 1726, 1727, 1731 and 1732. Vito Canzonieri was burned as a heretic because he said that Jesus was a clown, the law of christ was for madmen, and the virgin Mary was a "magara" (witch). At the last minute he recanted.[123] Today advanced italian left catholics regard genuine christianity as a special madness, authentic christian teachers as holy clowns, and the task of true christianity to be untying the bonds of holy mad people like Francis.[124] Feminist scholars, excavating layers of popular beliefs underneath dominant patriarchal culture, are finding that women burned, or hanged, as witches were women whose wisdom revering all life remembered the ancient dark mother .

Max Dashu, founder of Suppressed Histories Archives in Oakland, California has brought to light many stories of women called witches, sharing some with me. Bellezza Orsini, a healer in Perugia Italy who was tried as a witch in 1540, was accused of killing with sorcery and poisons. She said, "I am not a sorceress, and I treat everything and do it all with a flower oil of mine." Inquisitors wanted her to confess she had diabolical powders and killed babies. She defended witches as healers, and thwarted inquisitors by slitting her own throat in her prison cell. Another "old witch," this one of the russian peasantry, has been rescued by Max Dashu, Vyed'ma Baba. She was a keeper of pagan rites and festivals that preserved the wisdom of the earth and seasonal cycles. Baba, whose name in yiddish means grandmother, knew healing herbs and told mythic tales, or stories, to teach "transformative quests and initiatory encounters with animals."

O

In this historical context, a remarkable nun devised a way of keeping private beliefs away from persecution by inquisitors. In 1515, at the crest of inquisition violence, Teresa di Gesu' was born in Avila, Spain, place of a black madonna. Thirty years earlier, her grandfather Juan Sanchez had been forcibly converted to christianity, and then persecuted as a converso accused of "Judaizing." Juan, son of Alonzo and Teresa, had prospered in the wool and silk trade; as a philanthropic activity he managed church finances, and collected taxes. In 1485, forced by torture, "he confessed to having committed many grave crimes and offences against our Holy Catholic faith." It is unclear what "grave crimes" he committed because inquisitors in their persecution of jewish conversos considered anything a grave crime from putting on a clean shirt on Friday night (the jewish sabbath) to refusing to eat pork, to reciting a psalm without adding the christian gloria, as "Judaizing."

Teresa's grandfather, with his infant son (who became Teresa's father) in his arms, was one of the accused in autos de fe in Toledo in 1485. Victims were "paraded through the streets, naked to the waist and barefoot" to a scaffold, where those deemed "reconciled to Mother Church" were sentenced to parade again for the next six Fridays, stripped naked to the waist, and whipped as they walked from church to church. Other penalties included giving one fifth of all their possessions to finance the crusade against Granada, the last moorish kingdom in Spain. Juan Sanchez, it is reported, was given the additional punishment of wearing a sambenito, a garment of shame with green crosses back and front, name and alleged offenses, that was hung up in the parish church.

Thereafter, as persecution in Spain flamed with burnings of jews and heretics, the Sanchez family changed their name to Cepeda. The father continued to help church authorities manage their finances, gave his sons a catholic education, and, in a second marriage, wedded a woman of "old Christian stock." His son Alonzo did also, marrying Dona Beatriz, settling in Avila, and recording on the 28th of March, 1515 the birth of his daughter Teresa.[125] The child was given the name of her jewish grandmother.

During Teresa's childhood in Avila, people were sent to fight in spanish wars in Italy, France, Germany, the Netherlands, north Africa, and the new world. Teresa and her brother dreamed of going to Africa, "land of the Moors," and of being beheaded as martyrs. When the Cepedas aspired to "hidalgo" (gentleman) class, the episode of the grandfather's persecution in Toledo came up. It is unknown if the children knew about the family's earlier history of persecution. In later writings, under the eyes of clerical monitors, Teresa carefully described her family, not as old christians, but as "God-fearing." Disliking her mother's submission to her husband and continual child-bearing, Teresa early vowed to become a nun.

Near Teresa's childhood home was an old jewish cemetery on whose site a convent of the order of Carmel had been built. The order claimed descent from Elijah and "sons of the prophets," early christian hermits who had lived on Mount Carmel, site close to the present border of Africa with the Levant where there is archeological evidence of primordial human life.[126] Perhaps attracted to the practice of mental prayer and contemplation, Teresa entered the carmelite order, an order very close to the "alumbrados" of Spain who practiced mental prayer, a practice that the inquisition regarded suspiciously. Mystics, believing they were under direct guidance of the holy spirit, had little interest in sacraments and rituals of papal catholicism. The inquisition, viewing alumbrados as similar to lutherans of northern Europe, considered both dangerous.

Teresa, in the first part of her life, was a mystic with ecstatic experiences in which she considered Jesus her brother, "culminating in the supreme grace of the Mystical Marriage, symbolized by a vision in which Christ placed a wedding-ring on her finger."[127] This striking statement evokes Isis married to her brother, as well as the heretical popular jewish belief that Jahveh's consort was Asherah. In 1559, many people suspected of protestant and alumbrista heresies at Valladolid were sent to the stake. About this same time Teresa initiated an ambitious campaign founding seventeen reformed carmelite houses for women and discalced carmelite monasteries for men. First she limited the number of people in monastic communities to fifteen, a number that may have referred to the twelve apostles in addition to Jesus, Mary, and Joseph. Then she limited the number to thirteen. Who were the figures in her perfect holy community? She called herself Teresa de Jesus. Was she bypassing christian figures Mary and Joseph for a new holy community founded by herself and Jesus?

The life of Teresa de Jesus brings up many questions. Did she hold heretical beliefs that harked back to Africa and to west Asia ? Like Isis, who had a brother/spouse, Teresa sometimes called Jesus "brother," other times she called him "spouse." Was Teresa's elaborate mysticism, whose practice she taught her nuns, a way of keeping heretical beliefs away from inquisitors? Why do italian feminists find "la grande Teresa" so fascinating? Feminists praise Teresa's ability to combine mysticism with work in the world. But wasn't her work in the world establishing rigorous monastic orders encouraging more people to withdraw from the world?[128]

In what may have been an elaborate cover for heretical beliefs, Teresa adopted the misogynist language of the inquisition, constantly speaking of "my grave sins and the wickedness of my life."[129] Teaching mysticism as withdrawal from the world, Teresa left extraordinary passages describing the many rooms in the interior castle. *The Life of Saint Teresa of Avila by Herself* is a masterpiece and, after *Don Quixote,* the most widely read classic of Spain.[130] Penning some of the most stunning passages in world literature, Teresa said, "There is another kind of rapture—I call it flight of the spirit—that, though substantially the same as other raptures, is interiorly experienced very differently. For sometimes suddenly a movement of the soul is felt that is so swift it seems the spirit is carried off, and at a fearful speed especially in the beginning. This is why I have told you that strong courage is necessary for the one to whom God grants these favors...."[131]

Teresa was indeed a woman of strong courage. As one of her namesakes (Teresa is my middle name), with african and probable canaanite, israelite, moorish, as well as christian antecedents, I am intrigued by the possibility Teresa may have feigned doctrinal christianity to hide ancient beliefs. Perhaps, in her mystical perspective, she saw no difference between judaism and christianity. Teresa, in any event, may be considered a precursor of contemporary feminist theology wherein christianity is regarded as an offshoot of the "Jesus reform movement within Judaism."[132]

By 1582 when Teresa died, Spain had "discovered" America, a continent already inhabited by indigenous peoples who surprised invaders because they did not bear arms and believed in sharing. Columbus and his crew roamed "looking for gold, taking women and children as slaves for sex and labor."[133] In two years, half of the 250,000 native americans on Haiti were murdered, or committed suicide. By 1515, date of Teresa's birth, native americans were being worked to death on large estates. Bartolome de las Casas denounced spanish atrocities, but Teresa in Spain, (suggesting why mysticism is inadequate by itself for creating a just society) simply repeated established christian doctrine and prayed for christian conversion of the natives. Genocide of native americans continued with Cortes against aztecs of Mexico, Pizarro against incas of Peru, and english puritans against pequots and powhatans of New England.

The meaning of spanish invaders who brought christianity to the new world may have been caught in the title of an authoritative book, *When Jesus came, the corn mother went away*. The corn mother in America, like pagan women deities of Africa, Asia, and Europe, signified the spiral of life in a just civilization in which men and women were equal. "The Pueblo Indians viewed the relations between the sexes as relatively balanced. Women and men each had their own forms of wealth and power, which created independent but mutually interdependent spheres of action. The corn fetish every child was given at birth and the flint arrowhead with which boys were endowed symbolized these relations....Corn and flint were food and water, but they were also the cosmic principles of femininity and masculinity."[134]

Franciscans in the new world, intent on personal sanctity, sought to lead indians "out from the darkness of paganism" into the "Father of Light."[135] After Francis, their founder, died, the history of the franciscans becomes cloudy; some became inquisitors, persecuting others in an inversion of the franciscan belief that the world and all its creatures are sacred. Many native americans, after they were forcibly converted to christianity, became patrilineal, but the hopi, the zuni, and the keres at Acoma resisted christianization and remained matrilineal. Christian missionaries suppressed native american women's fertility societies, condemned dances celebrating sexuality as sinful, and forbade rituals celebrating the fecundity of the earth and life as "demonic."[136] Indians in North America entered spanish households as slaves between 1693 and 1846. Stripped of their own names, they were called "Mary of the Trinity," "Francis of the Holy Spirit," and "Ann of the Incarnation."[137] Patriarchal attitudes led to sexual intimacies of spanish men with indian women. Although intimate with dark native american women, the white male elite married lighter spanish women, and a color line developed in spanish america.

In the 19th century, Mexico declared its independence from Spain, Male politicians of the United States declaimed "manifest destiny" and led the country to war in 1846, a war of the United States, a nation with slaves, "to extend democracy" to "popish" Mexico, a nation that had abolished slavery. Anti-slavery people of the U. S. considered it a war to extend slavery. The upshot of the war was that the U. S. took the southwest part of the country away from Mexico.

In the 1840s during the U.S. war against Mexico, many newly arrived immigrants from Ireland served in the U.S. army, becoming americans by participating in the conquest of darker peoples,[138] a pattern of upward mobility by doing the killing in wars that benefited the dominant white male elite, a pattern that would persist for other migrants, and other wars, to the present. Noel Ignatiev has analyzed the american journey of irish immigrants in a book with a revealing title, *How the Irish Became White.*[139]

O

This chapter, concerned with commonalities of belief and common persecution of moors, jews, heretics and women refers to the early modern period described in textbooks in chapters entitled, "The Age of Discovery" and "The Age of Faith." With the multifocal vision of many cultural perspectives, students now regard the "Age of Discovery" as initiating the massacre of native americans, the enslavement of african americans, and the burning and hanging of women as witches. The "Age of Faith," scarcely a glorious demonstration of the splendid achievements of protestantism and catholicism, was realistically described, in a contemporary student's paper, as an "age of degredation" when atrocities were committed in the name of religious faith.[140]

Notes

1   Part of this chapter, in another form, was published as "Dark Others: Jews, Moors, Heretics, and Women," in *Metis: A Feminist Journal of Transformative Wisdom*, June 1997.

2   Quoted in Edward Said, *The only alternative* (San Francisco, Ca., Freedom Archives, 2001).

3   These groups, by no means, exhaust the list of dark others persecuted in christian Europe. Gypsies, to whom I have referred in chapter 4, whose ultimate beliefs are associated with the ancient dark mother, have been persecuted throughout the christian epoch to the present. See David M. Crowe, *A History of the Gypsies of Eastern Europe and Russia* (New York, St. Martin's Griffin, 1994, 1996).

4   This chapter refers to jews, moors, and others not as racial categories, as earlier chapters have emphasized, but as ethnic groups. Raphael Patai and Jennifer Patai have written an excellent analysis of why it is impossible to refer to jews as a race, an analysis applicable to other ethnic groups. See Raphael and Jennifer Patai, *The Myth of the Jewish Race*. Rev. ed. (Detroit, Wayne State University Press, 1989). In biblical times "Abraham had Ishmael by his Egyptian handmaid-wife Hagar" (93). Esau married "Hittite Canaanite women" and Jacob's sons "married either Canaanite women or, after their descent to Egypt, Egyptian women." (93). In the common era, conversion and intermarriage characterize jewish history, notably the absorption of canaanite/phoenicians in the jewish diaspora (65-66). A fascinating case of intermingling of ethnic groups is that of the Khazars, "a Turkic, and to some extent Mongoloid," people from central Asia who adopted judaism in the 8th century C.E. Jewish Khazars were described as white in complexion, with blue eyes and reddish hair." (70). "The process of absorbing genetic influences as a result of interbreeding has been part of the anthropological history of the Jews from the earliest times to the present. Jewish-Gentile interbreeding has resulted from intermarriage, concubinage, extramarital relations, slavery, prostitution, rape, and possibly also the exercise of the jus primae noctis." (91)

5   An excellent history of the jews of Italy, written by an italian jew, is Attilio Milano, *Storia degli ebrei*, Loc. Cit. See also Arnaldo Momigliano, "The

Jews of Italy," chapter 16, *On Pagans, Jews, and Christians* (Middletown, Ct., Wesleyan University Press, 1987). See Marc Shell, *Marranos (Pigs), or from Coexistence to Toleration.* Reprinted for private circulation from *Critical Inquiry,* Vol. 17, No. 2, Winter 1991 (University of Chicago, 1991).

6   See Birnbaum, *Black Madonnas,* Loc. Cit., p. 123. Susan Zuccotti, *The Italians and the Holocaust. Persecution, Rescue & Survival* (Lincoln, University of Nebraska Press, 1987).

7   Carlo Ginzburg, *Ecstasies. Deciphering the Witches' Sabbath.* Tr., Raymond Rosenthal (New York, Penguin Books, 1981).

8   Milano, *Storia,* Loc. Cit 5. See also Ginzburg, *Ecstasies,.* Loc. cit.; Elaine Pagels, *The Gnostic Gospels* (New York, Vintage Books, 1979, 1989), xvii, 57.

9   Milano, *Storia,* Loc. Cit., 5-6

10   Ibid., 15.

11   Ibid.,. 16.

12   Ibid., 19.

13   Ibid. Perhaps remembering Astarte, jewish women, according to Milano, were sought after for love filters.

14   Milano, *Storia,* Loc. Cit.21-22

15   Ibid.,22, 28, 50. See Martin Goodman, "Jews and Judaism in the Mediterranean diaspora in *the* late-roman period: the limitations of evidence," *Journal* of *Mediterranean Studies. History, Culture and Society in the Mediterranean World,* Vol. 4, Number 2, 1994.

16   Ibid., 25-28, 52.

17   Ivan Van Sertima, ed., *Golden Age of the Moor.* See chapter, Jan Carew, "Moorish Culture-Bringers: Bearers of Enlightenment." (New Brunswick, N. J. and London, Transaction Publishers, 1992).

18   Ibid., 252.

19   Ibid., 253.

20   Leila Ahmed, *Women and Gender in Islam. Historical Roots of a Modern Debate* (New Haven and London, Yale University Press, 1992), 4.

21   Ibid., 31

22   Ibid., 31.

23   Ibid., 33.

24   Ibidem.

25   Ibid., 34.

26   Ibid., 43.

27   Ibid., 63.

28   Emmanuel Anati, *Arte Rupestre. Il Linguaggio Primordiale.* Vol. 12, *Studi Camuni*, Edizioni del Centro, Valcamonica, Brescia, 1994.

29   Raphael Patai, *The Seed of Abraham, Jews and Arabs in Contact and Conflict* (New York, Charles Scribner's Sons, 1986). 132. An evocative journey of a sephardic jew is Victor Perera, *The Cross and the Pear Tree* (New York, Alfred A. Knopf, 1995) which analyzes the intermingling of christians, jews, and others,

30   See Lawrence DiStasi, *Mal'occhio. The underside of vision* (Berkeley, North Point Press, 1981).

31   Patai, *Seed*, Loc. Cit.

32   Ibidem.

33   Ibid., 186.

34   Ahmed, *Women and Gender*, 107.

35   Ibid., 112

36   See V. L. Atrosheniko & Milton Grundy, *Mediterranean Vernacular. A Vanishing Architectural Tradition* (New York,Rizzoli, 1991). Authors of this book locate the style of mediterranean vernacular in buildings of southeastern Spain and Ibixa, Morocco in Africa, Tunisia in Africa, Italy, Greece, and the greek islands, an architecture that remembers the dark mother in rounds, local stones, dwellings dug into the ground or into the hills so that homes and earth are organically related. The memory is visible in spirals, the diamond of the double vulva, the color blue of the sea, dark spaces accentuated by white stucco, arches, portals that draw one inward, natural wood, greenery against white stucco, windows framed in red ochre, closeness to the sea, natural stone boulders, red bougainvillea, spiky flax, fig trees, and fichi d'india. Le Corbusier built in this style. So does Tim Ward, who designed the mediterranean vernacular house in Berkeley in which we now dwell after our home burned down in 1991.

37   *Mediterranean Vernacular*, Loc. Cit., 189.

38   Patai, Seed, 332. See also, Raphael Patai, *The Jewish Alchemists. A History and Source Book* (Princeton, New Jersey, Princeton University Press, 1994). In this remarkable study of a popular belief, Patai tracks the meanderings of the

belief in alchemy (whose spiritual meaning was transmutation, or healing) from africans to jews.

39   Carlo Ginzburg, *Ecstasies, Loc. Cit.,* 122-123.

40   Patai, *Seed.* 334.

41   Elinor Gadon, *The Once & Future Goddess. A Sweeping Visual Chronicle of the Sacred Female and Her Reemergence in the Cultural Mythology of Our Time* (HarperSanFrancisco, 1989),. 242.

42   Quoted in Gadon, *Once & Future ,* Loc. Cit., 242-3.

43   Ibidem.

44   Gadon, *Once & Future,* Loc. Cit., . 244.

45   Ibid. , 244-245.

46   *The Absent Mother. Restoring the Goddess to Judaism and Christianity,* edited by Alix Pirani (London, Mandala/Harper Collins, 1991),. 31.

47   Ibid., 41-42.

48   Ibid., 44-45.

49   Ibid., 45-46.

50   Ibid., 48.

51   Ibid., 53.

52   See chapter 6, this work.

53   Ibid.,. 51.

54   Quoted in Long, *In a Chariot,* Loc. Cit., 51.

55   This does not imply a bland ecumenism flattening the passion out of all religions. Close attention to the distinguishing characteristic of each religion, as Simone Weil pointed out, may transform the world. Also helpful is close attention to the similarities in vernacular beliefs of religions of the world.

56   Patai, *Seed,* Loc. Cit., 340.

57   Milano, *Storia,* Loc. Cit., 66

58   Ibid., 104.

59   Ibid., 104.

60   Ibid., 168.

61   Ibid., passim.

62   Ibidem.

63   Salvatore Salerno, "Easter in my Grandfather's Sicilian Village," text accompanying exhibit Minneapolis, Minnesota, 1996.

64   Quoted in Salerno, "Easter..."

65   Mikhail Bakhtin, *Rabelais and His World*. Tr., Helene Iswolsky (Bloomington, Indiana University Press, 1984),.78-79. Art is an excellent indicator of submerged beliefs. See Salvatore Boscarino, *Sicilia barocca. Architettura e città* 1610-1760. Exuberance in baroque art, in the constrictive period of the counter-reformation, may be regarded as subversive architecture.

66   See Birnbaum, *Black Madonnas.*, Loc. Cit

67   Mirna dell'Ariccia,"Allegria nella festa di Purim," *confronti. Mensile di fede, politica, vita quotidiana,* marzo 1997.

68   An example of a heretical ritual of christians and jews brought to the new world is the popular celebration of santa Eulalia, jewish martyr adopted by christians as a saint. How this heretical european ritual blended with indigenous traditions in the new world is suggested in a description of the festival. "To the recorded sound of church bells ringing, two young girls...dressed in colorful hand-embroidered Mayan apparel reverently carried the framed image of Saint Eulalia in procession. It was the feast day of the third-century Spanish martyr who is patroness of Santa Eulalia, a small town in the western highlands of Guatemala." "Remembering those back home," *Maryknoll*, September 1997.

69   Sal Salerno, " Easter..." Loc. Cit.

70   Milano, *Storia*, 27.

71   Ibid., 84.

72   Ibid., 101.

73   Ibid., 104.

74   Ibid., 234.

75   Ibid., 609.

76   See Birnbaum, *Black Madonnas.* Loc. Cit.

77   Salerno, "Easter..." Loc. Cit.

78   Milano, *Storia*,. 231.

79   Anthony D'Angelo, "Italian Harlem's Saint Benedict the Moor," *Through the Looking Glass. Italian & Italian/American Images in the Media, Selected Essays.* The 27th Annual Conference, American Italian Historical Association, editors, Mary Jo Bona and Anthony Julian Tamburri (Staten Island, N. Y., American Italian Historical Association, 1996).

80   Cyprian Davis, quoted in "Italian Harlem's Saint Benedict the Moor." Loc. cit.

81   *Street Spirit. Justice News & Homeless Blues in the Bay Area*, Vol. 3, No. 8, August 1997. "Compassion on Trial in Buena Park."

82   See "Appello dal Popolo di Dio," January 6, 1996,an international lay catholic appeal whose offices are in Palermo and Naples. This "Appeal of the people of God," has also been distributed for signatures in the United States.

83   Emmanuel Le Roy Ladurie, *Montaillou. The Promised Land of Error.* Tr., Barbara Bray (New York, Vintage Books, 1978). See introduction. See also Ladurie's *Jasmin's Witch* (Worcester, Great Britain, Scholar Press, 1987).

84   Ladurie, *Montaillou*, Loc. Cit., 23.

85   See chapter six, this book, and *Black Madonnas*, Loc. Cit.

86   *Black Madonnas*, . 63.

87   Ladurie, *Montaillou*,. 82.

88   Ibidem.

89   Ibid., 132.

90   Ibid., 347.

91   Ibid., 134.

92   Ibid., note, 240.

93   Ibid., 242.

94   Ibid., 144.

95   Ibid., 156.

96   Ibid., 159.

97   Ibid., 168.

98   Ibid., 190.

99   Ibid., 195

100 Ibid., 190.

101 Ibid., 202.

102 Ibid., 252.

103 Ibid., 279

104 Ibidem.

105 See chapter two, this work.

106 Ladurie, *Montaillou*, Loc. Cit., 296.

107 Ibid., 305.

108 Ibid., 307.

109 Ibid., 308.

110 See chapter eight, this work, for vendor songs of Sicily.

111 Calogero Messina, *Sicilians Wanted the Inquisition.* Tr., Alexandra and Peter Dawson (Brooklyn, New York, Legas, 1993).

112 Isidoro La Lumia, *Gli ebrei siciliani* (Palermo, Sellerio editore, 1984, 1992). 37

113 Ibid.,. 41

114 Ibid.,. 45

115 Ibidem.

116 Anne Llewellyn Barstow, *Witchcraze. A New History of the European Witch Hunts* (San Francisco, Pandora/Harper Collins, 1994). 2. See also Mircea Eliade, *Occultism, Witchcraft, and Cultural Fashions. Essays in Comparative Religions* (Chicago, University of Chicago Press, 1976).

117 Barstow,. *Witchcraze.* Loc. Cit., 69.

118 Ibid. 138

119 Barstow, lll

120 Carlo Ginzburg, *Ecstasies. Deciphering the Witches' Sabbath,* Tr., Raymond Rosenthal (New York, Viking Penguin, 1991).

121 Ibid. 122-3.

122 Barstow, *Witch Craze,* Loc. Cit., 118.

123 Ibid. 51-54.

124 See Birnbaum, *Black Madonnas.*

125 See the excellent biography of Teresa by Stephen Clissold, *St Teresa of Avila* (New York, The Seabury Press, 1982). Chapter l.

126 See Mario Carniani, *Santa Maria del Carmine e la Cappella Brancacci* (Firenze, Becocci Editore, n.d.).

127 Ibid., 66.

128 See *Women in Praise of the Sacred. 43 centuries of Spiritual Poetry by Women,* ed., Jane Hirshfield San Francisco, HarperPerennial, 1994).

129 See *The Collected Works of St. Teresa of Avila,* Vol l. *The Book of Her Life. Spiritual Testimonies, Soliloquies,* (Washington D.C., Institute of Carmelite Studies, 1976). translated by K Kavanaugh, o.c.d. and Otilio Rodriguez, o.c.d.

Vol three, *The Book of Her Foundations. Minor Works* (Washington, D. C., Institute of Carmelite Studies, Washington, D. C.)

130 *The Life of Saint Teresa of Avila by Herself* (New York, Penguin Books, 1957). 21.

131 Teresa of Avila, *The Interior Castle*, Tr., Kieran Kavanaugh, O.C.D. and Otilio Rodriguez, O.C,.D. (New York, Paulist Press, 1979). An excellent italian evaluation of Teresa is that of Ida Magli, *Storia laica delle donne religiose* (Milano, Longanesi & Co., 1995. 176 ff.

132 Elisabeth Schussler, Fiorenza, *In Memory of Her. A Feminist Theological Reconstruction of Christian Origins* (New York, Crossroad, 1992). See chapter 4, "The Jesus Movement as Renewal Movement Within Judaism."

133 Howard Zinn, *A People's History of the United States* (New York, Harper Perennial, 1980). 4.

134 Ramon A. Gutierrez, *When Jesus Came, the Corn Mother Went Away. Marriage, Sexuality, and Power in New Mexico*, 1500-1846 (Stanford, Stanford University Press, 1991). 13.

135 Gutierrez, *When Jesus Came*, Loc. Cit.,

136 Ibid., 79.

137 Ibid., 180.

138 Ronald Takaki, *A Different Mirror. A History of Multicultural America* (Boston, New York, Toronto, London, Little, Brown and Company, 1993), 166-167.

139 *How the Irish became White*, (New York and London, Routledge, 1995). The irish, who were regarded as "the blacks of Europe," took on racist attitudes as soon as they became american. Frederick Douglass in 1853 pointed this out. The irish, who in their homeland identified with the oppressed everywhere, "are instantly taught when they step upon our soil to hate and despise the Negro....Sir, the Irish-American will one day find out his mistake.":

140 Paper for a class in the Women's Spirituality program of the California Institute of Integral Studies, San Francisco, Winter, 1995.

29. Bellezza Orsini
Italy
Painting by Max Dashu

30. Vyed'ma Baba
Russia
Painting by Max Dashu

part three
comparative beliefs United States and Italy

chapter eight

United States—white elites and dark others case of sicilian/americans

manifest destiny and "bedda matri!"

In this chapter I summarize the history of U. S. violence against dark others beginning with first settlements in New England. This backdrop is necessary for understanding the dominant U.S.attitude to dark others at the turn of the 20th century when "new immigrants" from south and southeast Europe arrived. To explore the difference in beliefs of dominant patriarchal culture in the United States from subaltern cultures of dark others, I have referred to my own ethnic group, sicilian/americans, as a case in point.

Confirming the case for U. S. "exceptionalism," first european settlements of spaniards and english in North America were accompanied by genocide of native americans and genocidal enslavement of africans. In spanish inquisitor and english puritan cosmologies of sin, violence to dark others was related to theologies that separated people into the saved and the damned, a theology that descended into the racism of white people who considered themselves saved and dark others whom whites considered damned, as well as the sexism of males regarding women as damned.

In the perception of dominant white male elites, the dark and the damned were conflated.

In the late 19th century, earlier violence of dominant white male elites to native americans and african americans was extended, with varying degrees of cruelty, to jews, mexicans, the irish, and asians. In the 20th century these white male elites believed it their "manifest destiny" to launch imperial conquests in the Philippines and Cuba, subjugating and "cleaning up" dark others whom they considered lower on the evolutionary scale. As we shall see in the next chapter, imperial conquest abroad was accompanied by "scientific" techniques of "social control" of dark others at home.

O

The uniquely american attitude of dominant white male elites toward dark others was evident in 1630, soon after arrival of the english on the north american continent. A New England puritan divine described the burning of captured native americans: "frying in the flyer, and streams of blood quenching the same, and horrible was the stinke and sent there of, but the victory seemed a sweet sacrifice, and they gave the prayers thereof to God...." The puritan minister thanked god that "600 Pequot souls...[were] brought down to hell that day."[1]

The "peculiar institution" of african slavery in the United States may also have been uniquely american. In what may have been the cruelest form of slavery in history, enslavement was steamed by capitalist drive for profits. First the dutch, then the english, dominated the african slave trade to America; by 1815 ten to fifteen million africans had been wrested from their homeland and enslaved in the new world.

The racism that fueled the capture of africans brought in chains to the new world is described by historian David Brion Davis who points out that in the ancient world slaves included light as well as dark peoples. "Not until the fifteenth century, when slavery increasingly became linked with various peoples from sub-Saharan Africa, [did] the stereotype began to acquire specific racial connotations. As slavery in the Western world became more and more restricted to Africans, the arbitrarily defined black 'race' took on all the qualities, in the eyes of many white people, of the infantilized and animalized slave."2

Self-delusion may have been the significant dynamic in american exceptionalism. Liberty and equality in the american revolution were themes of national rhetoric, but liberty and equality did not pertain to native americans, african american slaves, unpropertied classes, or to women of any condition. After the revolution, white male elites, enfervored by what they regarded as a religious "errand in the wilderness,"3 considered it their "manifest destiny" to over-run native americans and mexicans in their expansion across the continent in the 19th century, into the western hemisphere after 1890, and across the planet after 1945.

Violence, energized by self-deluding beliefs, has characterized political and cultural governance of patriarchal male elites from the beginning. Saint Paul said, "In Christ there is neither man nor woman," just as church fathers were excising any mention of the dark mother from the bible, leaving her out of the trinity, and identifying women with evil. The protestant reformation declared the priesthood of all believers, but the priesthood was limited to male magistrates whose self-ascribed mandate to rule was a covenant designed by those who considered themselves saved to govern those they considered damned. In the convoluted calvinist theology of 17th century magistrates in New England, the damned included native americans, african americans, and all dark others, including women.

Treatment of women in any society may throw the true nature of that society into relief. In the United States, enslaved black women were raped, native american women mutilated and violated in the drive to push them into enclaves. White women were a special case of patriarchal violence. According to 17th century puritan magistrates of Massachusetts, women had an "inferior nature and weak mind" and were "neither to teach, nor to usurp authority over the man, but to be in silence."[4] When Anne Hutchinson exposed the self-delusion of puritan male magistrates, she precipitated the antinomian crisis. A brilliant woman who knew the bible well, she so scattered the wits of male magistrates they described her as a woman "whose stern and masculine mind...triumphed over the tender affections of a wife and mother."[5]

Salvation, said Anne and her followers, was a matter of god's grace. With this statement, Anne shook the authority and self-assurance of male magistrates, who castigated her for "a very proud spirit" and "familiarity with the devil." Puritan magistrates forbade women to "meddle" in "matters of religion." Women who listened to Anne Hutchinson were chastised for being "notoriously infected with Mrs. Hutchinson's errors," and branded as witches. If women continued to think for themselves and to speak out, puritans put them to death by hanging.

Anne Hutchinson, mother of thirteen children and healer with herbs, applied the protestant belief that anyone can interpret the bible to herself and to other women. Clerics put her on trial for heresy and the government charged her with challenging the authority of magistrates. Pregnant at the trial, she was not allowed to sit down until she was about to collapse; so much for the puritan doctrine of the sanctity of the family. Banished, she left for Rhode Island in 1638, followed by thirty-five families. In a poignant turn of history, Anne Hutchinson was killed by native americans who saw her as the white enemy destroying them and their society. Mary Dyer, one of her followers, was later hanged by puritan magistrates, along with two other quakers, for "rebellion, sedition and presumptuous obtruding themselves."[6]

Sex, as it did in witch trials of northern Europe, entered puritan prosecution of Anne Hutchinson in New England. John Cotton, erstwhile supporter, said "though I have not herd, nayther do I thinke, you have bine unfaythful to your Husband in his Marriage Covenant, yet that will follow upon it." A revealing statement, the covenant-binding people in marriage and in society, as puritans saw it, was "his covenant," a male document of marriage and society without the consent of the woman to the marriage covenant, nor analogously, the consent of subordinate classes to their governance. The puritan covenant was a magistrates' document that did not have the consent of the governed. Anne Hutchinson was banished "as a Leper to withdraw yourself out of the Congregation,"[7] regarded as a threat to the puritan religion and the patriarchal family, the state, and society.

After she was banished, other women were prosecuted for "obstinate persisting in sundry Errors" or whipped for "speaking against the magistrates." Other women were punished for "disorderly singing and...idleness and saying she is commanded of Christ to do so."[8] Anne and other women were called witches driven by lust. Men who agreed with the dissenting women were subjected to derisive impugning of their masculinity. Before she was killed, Anne aligned herself with Samuel Gorton, religious freethinker and defender of universal justice. Her disbelief in magistrates led to her espousing passive resistance to authority. When she was killed by native americans, the Massachusetts clergy rejoiced at the death of the "American Jesabel." The 1648 legal code of Massachusetts Bay Colony, claiming the bible as authority, mandated the death penalty for witchcraft, well as for homicide, and a series of other crimes, including "blasphemy, bestiality, sodomy, adultery, rape, and...rebelliousness of son against parents."

In 1692, Massachusetts Bay colony was again thrown into turmoil by women whom puritans called witches; the episode involved 334 persons, of whom 35 were put to death. Among the accused, 78% were women, 80% of whom were executed. The women were "mostly poor, mostly married or widowed, between the ages of forty and sixty."[9] At Salem where 165 were prosecuted, most of the accusers were young girls; most of the witnesses for the prosecution were men. Women who had inherited money, women in business for themselves, and single and postmenopausal women were particularly at risk of being tried as witches, and punished.[10] If a woman accused of witchcraft had an instance of adultery or abortion in her past, this was considered sufficient evidence for persecutors to kill her. When Alice Lake confessed that she had become pregnant and tried to abort the fetus, she was called "a murderer in the sight of God." convicted of witchcraft, and sent to death, leaving four small children bereft.[11]

Most clearly, perhaps, the nature of colonial society of the U. S. may be seen in the condition of enslaved black women. Tituba, a caribbean slave, was caught up in the Salem witch persecutions, apparently because her dark skin led to the presumption she practiced witchcraft. She has been left out of histories of witchcraft trials of Salem. Maryse Condé, in an effort to render historical justice to this black woman who was called a witch, has written an account to make up for what Angela Davis calls the "silences, omissions, distortions, and fleeting, enigmatic insinuations" of this case, whose only sentence in the chronicles of the Salem witch trials was that Tituba was a slave from the West Indies who probably practiced "hoodoo."

Condé, writing in "a suppressed black feminist tradition," carefully researched the case.[12] Tituba was the child of a woman slave raped by an english sailor on a ship named Christ the King. bound for the Barbados. There she learned african traditions, "everything lives, has a soul, and breathes…everything must be respected…man is not the master riding through his kingdom on horseback." She learned the african belief in the protective spirits of the dead.[13]

She fell in love with John, an indian, who called her a witch. Why, Tituba wondered, was "the ability to communicate with the invisible world, to keep constant links with the dead, to care for others and heal," not respected and admired? John was the slave of Susanna Endicott, widow of a wealthy planter who "although she hated Negroes…was strongly opposed to slavery." John told Tituba that in order to survive she had to pretend to believe whatever slave-owners taught them…one god in three persons…satan…all of it…otherwise she'd get in trouble. Neither John nor Tituba could understand white people who called themselves religious yet saw evil everywhere. Samuel Parris told Tituba, "I know that the color of your skin is the sign of your damnation, but as long as you are under my roof you will behave as Christians. Come and say your prayers!" Similar to Anne Hutchinson in belief, Tituba answered, "What goes on in my head and my heart is my business." The puritan slave owner struck her.

John Indian told Tituba about the hidden world of puritan fanatics, how they mingled with "whores, sailors with rings in their ears....Bible-reading gentlemen with a wife and children at home. They all get drunk and swear and fornicate. Oh, Tituba, you can't imagine the hypocrisy of the white man's world."[14] Tituba took care of little girls whose "eyes conveyed all the contempt of their parents for those of our race. And yet they needed me to season the insipid gruel of their lives" with stories. When the witch craze swept Salem, the little girls turned on her; their elders accused Tituba of bewitching the children.

A good woman named Hester, whose eyes were "black like the benevolent shadow of night," helped Tituba. A good man, a jewish merchant, Benjamin Cohen d'Azevedo, bought her out of slavery. He told Tituba that his family had come from Portugal, where persecution made them flee to Holland. A branch of the family had gone to Brazil, then to Curacao, then to the american colonies. Tituba thought, "I couldn't have fallen into better hands." Cohen d'Azevedo told Tituba about persecution of jews in France and Britain, as well as Spain. Tituba said, "And what about us? Do you know how many of us have been bled from the coast of Africa?" He responded, "In 1298 the jews of Rottingen were put to the sword and the wave of murders spread to Bavaria and Austria. In 1336 our blood was shed from the Rhine to Bohemia and Moravia."[15]

After 1945, in the flush of a victorious war, U. S. historians praised the puritan foundations of the U.S., glossing over the murder of native americans, enslavement of african americans, and persecution of women, jews, and others. In Condé's reconstruction of the New England world of puritans, she imagined that they looked at one another, and asked, "Did we leave England for this? To see Jews and niggers multiply in our midst."

They burned Benjamin Cohen d'Azevedo's house, murdered his children while they slept,[16] and torched his ships. Cohen gave Tituba her freedom papers and set out for Rhode Island with a prayer on his lips.

Tituba could "only feel tenderness and compassion for the disinherited and a sense of revolt against injustice."[17] Declaring she "did not belong to the civilization of the Bible and Bigotry," Tituba vowed to keep the memory of her people in her heart without the written word.[18] Maryse Condé, who wrote Tituba's story, is a native of Guadalupe who lived for many years in France. Now teaching in the United States, she said recently, "In terms of narrow-mindedness, hypocrisy, and racism, little has changed since the days of the puritans."[19]

Racism was part of puritan self-righteous religious beliefs, yet all the founding fathers of the United States held racist beliefs. Benjamin Franklin, enlightenment deist, expressed the view that dark skin color was linked to mental and moral inferiority.[20] Thomas Jefferson, who penned "all men are created equal" in the Declaration of Independence, did not believe in the equal innate intelligence of whites and blacks, leaving statements in his *Notes on Virginia* that John Hope Franklin has called the curse of racism on U. S. history.[21]

Racism in late 19th century United States was heated by the fright that freed african americans might exercise their new legal rights and given intellectual justification by northern european theorists, who were read by white male elites of the U.S. For Gobineau, racist extraordinaire, later to be cited by Hitler, "The black variety is the lowest and lies at the bottom of the ladder."[22] Intellectual racism appropriated darwinian theory to justify european imperialism in Africa and U. S. expansion into the Philippines and Cuba.

Scientific racism, at the end of the 19th century when U.S. scholars founded professional associations, was an unexamined premise of U. S. and european scholars of theology, history, linguistics, and the social sciences. Scholars, upholding the hegemony of dominant white classes of the United States and Europe, elevated high greek culture (credited to aryans) to the apex of western civilization, and thought they were denigrating egyptians and canaanites by calling both africans and semites.[23] Gobineau affirmed anglo-saxon superiority to justify domination of native americans and african americans. The racist theorist described late 19th century migration to the U.S. of jews, italians, and slavs as a modern-day case of "Carthage" corrupting white civilization.[24]

After the civil war the U. S. federal government sent the army to massacre native americans, culminating in the surreal episode of a ghost dance among native americans dreaming of a world without whites, and U. S. troops pursuing and killing the dancers.[25] Native americans were forced onto reservations, their children taken from them and put into boarding schools for an education that took away their culture—a rehearsal for 20th century educational policy that obliterated the history and culture of all U. S. groups not male, white, anglo-saxon, and protestant.

Racists before the civil war used the bible to justify slavery; racists, after the war cited darwinian science to legitimate the racial superiority of white hegemonic elites and subordination of dark peoples considered racially inferior. By the 1890s the "Mississippi way" of segregation of african americans had become the "American way." After 1900, in what was called the progressive reform period, as african americans left the south for northern cities, lynchings of african americans averaged one a week.[26]

After the civil war the protestant social gospel movement, arising in response to worker unrest as well as to the ugliness of industrialization and urbanization,[27] provided some leavening. But the cosmology of the dominant white protestant elite of the U.S. at the end of the 19th century was that of a masculine god conceptualized as "mind," and a theology whose puritan derivation was evident in continuing the separation of the saved from the damned. Influenced by german philosophic idealism, the dominant philosophy of the U. S. white male elite considered the saved to be white anglo-saxon protestant males who had access to the ultimate mind—the damned (everyone else) did not.[28]

This hegemonic elite of the U. S. confirmed their access to the ultimate mind by the high social and economic level of their own ethnic and gender group. They insured longevity for themselves and their beliefs, simultaneously sedating pangs of conscience and quenching the radicalism of those at the bottom—by allowing a small number of correctly educated ethnic minorities to join the dominant white elite—once they had learned the proper attitudes...attitudes which included racism to dark others left behind.[29]

Among italian/americans and other darker "new immigrants," the pattern became upward mobility to "white," with complicity in the dominant racism toward darker others left behind. This american ideology, learned by upwardly mobile immigrant children in public schools (my own education), was to guarantee the domestic tranquility of white anglo-saxon protestants and capitalists—up until the 1960s.

Italian/americans were to become the largest "white" ethnic minority of the United States. Not considered white when they arrived, the dominant class early placed them in the category, "people of color." "New immigrants"—jews italians, greeks, and slavs from south and southeastern Europe—were considered different from earlier lighter-skinned migrants from northern Europe. South italian immigrants were needed for hard labor but were regarded with worry. The upper social and intellectual class of Boston, descendants of puritans, liked to take the grand tour of Italy for its high culture, but when they looked at italians in Boston, they uneasily considered the women sensual and the men sullen.[30]

Yet, as David A. J. Richards has pointed out, italian/americans early made a faustian pact, wherein "Italian Americans sell themselves into moral slavery in return for the price of a decent job, and the right to call themselves white people." In return for a piece of white privilege, "many italian/americans accepted racist attitudes and sometimes active racism toward those they could consider darker than they are." Today some italian/american organizations, notably IAMUS (Italian Americans for a Multicultural United States), IAWA (Italian American Writers

Association), and AIHA (American Italian Historical Association) are intent on breaking the silence on the subject of italian/american racism toward darker others.

Arriving at the turn of the 20th century, italian americans, predominantly from the south and the islands, observed white anglo-saxon democracy in action subjugating dark peoples, and kept silent. The blessings of american democracy were extended to italian/americans in lynchings at worst, patronizing by social workers at best, in a "progressive" campaign to clean up and educate italian and other dark immigrants so that they would fit into a society that white anglo-saxon protestant male elites considered at the evolutionary top of world civilization. And theirs.

For millennia, new immigrants from south italy and the islands, had learned to survive under violent elites; in the United States they kept a protective silence about U. S. imperialist and racist policies toward dark others. Yet, underneath the protective silence of new immigrants were beliefs that differed from beliefs of the U. S. white hegemonic elite. Beliefs of sicilians are a case in point.

For sicilians, the unification of Italy in 1870 meant continuing colonial dependence on the north, and deepening poverty. In 1890 the economic gap in Italy between the industrialized north and the impoverished agrarian south provoked socialist uprisings—in which women participated. After the national government suppressed the revolt, south italians and sicilians migrated to North and South America. For the most part, they kept their ultimate values in silence while they upwardly ascended toward "white"—up until the 1960s, when the american consensus held together by racism began to unravel. (See chapter ten).

O

To explore the beliefs sicilians brought with them to the United States, I have considered names as artifacts of cultural beliefs, and fastened this inquiry to names of my sicilian relatives who migrated to the United

States at the end of the 19th and beginning of the 20th centuries. For their ultimate beliefs, it has latterly occurred to me that it is revealing that the favorite exclamation of sicilian/americans, especially women, was bedda matri! (beautiful mother!). Sicilian vendor songs suggest that this popular invocation to "beautiful mother" held an implicit theology of a dark mother in a harmonious universe who gives her fruits to everyone.

Cultural baggage, like genetic inheritance, may be packed by history, but the traveler takes out what she/he needs at the time, often leaving a great deal unpacked. Left unpacked, for the most part, by sicilian migrants and their children, was the history of Sicily, to which I have alluded in previous chapters, and summarize here attached to my own family. Palermo, where my maternal grandfather was born, and close-by Termini Imerese, birthplace of my maternal grandmother, were places of prehistoric migrating africans. After 15,000 BCE, neolithic farmers came to Sicily (and elsewhere) from Anatolia. In the millennium before the common epoch, canaanite traders came to Sicily from the Levant and from Carthage in Africa.

Sicilian folk stories affirm the complexity of prehistoric african migrations. Stories about the sicani, regarded as the oldest inhabitants of the island, recount that they walked out of Africa to west Asia, turned around and walked to Spain, turned again and walked through France and Italy— before settling in western Sicily ca. 10, 000 BCE. This story is confirmed by contemporary geneticists' patterns of african migration.

Ca. 800 BCE Palermo was founded by west asian canaanite traders (originally african, later from the area called Palestine today)—from their base in Carthage, Africa. Palermo, part of a large network of entrepots and settlements around the Mediterranean, remained a stronghold of canaanites until romans conquered Carthage in the third century BCE. My nannu Joe's african and west asian ancestors were visible in his levantine/carthaginian face.

In the early common era, vandals and goths from northern Europe invaded Sicily, followed by byzantine rulers based in west Asia—until moors of Africa arrived and stayed for 240 years, presiding over a splendid era of sicilian history. In the 10th century of the common era, Palermo was an african/west asian/european city whose multicultural inhabitants included moors of Africa, jews, slavs, persians, and tartars of Asia, germans of north Europe, and lombards of north Italy. The moorish period of Sicily, marked by hundreds of minarets and mosques in Palermo, can still be glimpsed in mosaics of Monreale created by moorish artisans, as well as by catholic churches that look like mosques. Analogously, the jewish history of Palermo must be researched in the synagogues forcibly turned into catholic churches by inquisitors.

Palermo's northern european legacy has been emphasized by western historians who praise the normans who expanded into Sicily in 1060 (and into Great Britain in 1066). Normans were ancestors of the english puritans who settled in New England in 1630. Descendants of these normans founded the american empire described in the beginning of this chapter, an empire built on the bodies of massacred native americans, enslaved african americans, and other exploited dark others. Suggesting that social traits can evolve progressively (which geneticist L. Luca Cavalli-Sforza considers possible), many descendants of normans in scandinavian lands are leaders today of world peace and justice, just as many descendants of puritans in the United States, particularly in the 20th century, have worked against injustice.[31]

Names in my sicilian/american family reveal a popular interpretation of catholicism that retained african and semitic memories of the beautiful dark mother (bedda matri!) and her values of justice and equality. The maternal family name, Cipolla—onion in vernacular understanding—connotes the vulva, prehistoric symbol of the woman divinity painted on prehistoric african caves. Nannu Joe, exemplifying sicilian judeo-christianity, was named for Joseph, jewish father of Jesus. Contemporary italian men of the left, remembering that he was a workman, identify with

Joseph. The association of Joseph with workers and with the dark mother is suggested in italian celebration of saint Joseph day on March 19, the spring equinox, and on May 1st, international festival of workers of the world for justice and equality.

Justice in the United States was quashed in 1919 when forces of the federal government crushed the left. Equality was quashed in 1924 when discriminatory immigration laws were passed limiting entry into the U.S. of dark others, including italian immigrants. First and second generations of my sicilian/american relatives voted for the Democratic party; today some of them vote Republican.

Yet italian american immigrants of the first generation, despite a hostile environment, continued to transmit the dark mother's values—a transmission that can be tracked in names. My grandfather's name, Joseph, patron saint of orphans, as well as workers, conveys nurturance with a sardonic dart at the church, in whose canon Joseph, although he brought up Jesus, is *not* his father. When they were both very young, my grandfather Joe, in a marriage arranged by Za Teresa, married orphaned Giuseppina. My grandparents embodied the sicilian blend of african/west asian/european peoples. If nannu, who was dark, looked levantine and carthaginian, nanna, born in Termini Imerese, looked lombard (she had blue eyes) and greek. Greeks had, indeed, founded her town, Himera Imerese. Lombardo was her maiden name. Lombards of northern Italy came with the normans to conquer Sicily. Some recent lombards (e.g., the Northern League) vaunting a celtic (read aryan) heritage have sought a federation separating wealthy northern Italy (considered celtic) from south Italy and the islands—regions described by northern italian racists (in what they consider denigration) as " african and arab."

Lives of my maternal grandparents spanned the late patriarchal era of Italy and the United States, yet they do not easily fit categories of overbearing male and subordinated female, suggesting why gender theory needs to be studied in specific historic and cultural context, as well as with attention to class. Sicilians were a case of a subaltern people. Nannu arose before dawn to meet farmers to purchase fruits and vegetables to sell in his stall in the city market of Kansas City. When he came home late at night, nanna would take off his boots and serve him babbaluci (snails) and homemade pasta.

Yet she was not a subordinated wife; she supervised the construction of homes that nannu's good earnings provided, held ultimate family governance of seven spirited daughters and a son—and always maintained an assured sense of self. On Sundays, nanna would invite her married daughters and son to the mediterranean house on Benton Avenue for pasta cu sugu and cannoli—foods in sicilian popular culture that celebrate the dark mother and sensuality. Sugu was the color ochre red, early sign of the dark mother. Pasta carried the association of the dark mother with wheat. Cannoli were tubular pastries filled with ricotta. Nanna, when she tired of her argumentative daughters and noisy grandchildren, would tell everyone to go home.

My mother's name indicates how cultural baggage—in this case african/semitic/ asian—may be packed by history, but is unpacked by choice. A brunette sicilian/american beauty, she was named Catarina after the early christian martyr born in Alexandria, Egypt whose monastery is located in the Sinai of west Asia. "Dancer on the Fiery Wheel at the hub of the universe," Catarina was associated with the 8th century CE greek convent whose priestess/nuns called themselves Kathari (pure ones), resembling temple dancers of India who celebrated Kali, dark goddess of the karmic wheel. My mother used to say, "When you dance, you keep dancing," expressing her belief that in life one should not be an observer, but a dancer. Even in her 80s, she was an extraordinary dancer, performing a sensual african american "black bottom" that astonished observers.

The name kathari recalls medieval cathar heretics of France who revered saint Catherine "almost as a female counterpart of God." After the pope's crusade against the cathars, the papacy tried to eliminate Catherine from the canon, but her legend would not go away. Described as a beauty so intelligent she could outsmart scores of philosophers, she refused the emperor's offer of marriage. Whereupon he imprisoned her and tried to break her on the fiery wheel, but a sudden bolt of lightning saved her. Later, when she was beheaded, Catherine was said to have bled milk, not blood.[32]

My mother, caring little for saints' stories taught by stern priests and nuns (although she might have liked this one had she heard it), only knew she had been named for her father's mother, Catarina, an autocratic woman who had owned a macaroni factory in Palermo. In Kansas City, my great grandmother Catarina would extend her hand to be kissed by her grandchildren. Instead of Catherine, my mother chose to be called Kate, a name that may have revealed a touch of upward mobility; in our italian/american neighborhood, the irish, called "paddies," were considered a rung above italians on the immigrants' upward-mobility ladder to white.

Kate was her father's favorite. She would don an expensive dress from Harzfeld's and go down to help him in his stall in the city market where he was called "Horseradish and Coconut King" and she reigned as "Queen of the North End." On Sundays she played the organ in church. Courted by wealthy and powerful men, some in the mafia in the wide-open economy of Little Italy in Kansas City in the first quarter of the 20th century, she made a disastrously romantic decision when she married my father. On her wedding day, circled by bowers of flowers and a court of attendants, she wore a daring see-through wedding gown of chiffon and sequins. Beautiful young daughter/queen, nurturing/fierce mother who nuzzled her children like a lioness, and jealous Hera/wife, she was, in my view, a latter-day image of the dark triple goddess.

She became an incredibly intuitive crone. When I became consciously feminist, she advised she did not care for feminists. Why? "I don't think women ought to work for men," a statement, I realized later, that delivered a telling judgment on liberal feminism in the United States. Kate did not need the name—she *was* a feminist. The January midnight I was born, nanna Lucia announced that if I had been a boy she would have paid for the christening party. Just because she is a girl, my mother retorted, she'll have a great baptismal party. Whereupon she paid for the party with her own earnings, selling wine she illegally made in the basement during the U. S. era of prohibition of wine and liquor.

My father's brother Jim called her la cipuddu, dialect for onion, alluding to the vulva. Kate waited. For the christening party of Jim's second daughter Mary (he had wanted a son) she took bread dough, fashioned male genitalia (evoking Isis fashioning Osiris' genitalia) that she wrapped as a gift. My mother's gift to her taunting brother-in-law may be considered an implicit creation story. Replacing the biblical account that god created Adam and then created woman out of Adam's rib, my mother's gift implied that woman created man out of bread dough. Momma Katie's story, that of a sicilian/american woman who seemed to have carried a memory (largely preconscious) of the dark mother, is being written by my sister, Joie Chiavola Mellenbruch.

Names of my sicilian/american maternal aunts and uncles suggest the baggage of popular catholic beliefs that sicilians brought to Kansas City. After my mother Kate, the next sister was Mary, named for the mother of Jesus. Sisters who both carried names of powerful saints—one identified with heresy, one with the church—Kate and Mary were in a constant joust for authority in the family. Yet my mother chose Mary to be my godmother when I was baptized.

The sister next to the eldest was Anne, named for Mary's mother. Evoking prechristian history, the name Anne may go back to the Anu of Africa and to Inanna of Sumer. An untamed spirit, Anne as a child, played dangerously near the horses, and as a young woman danced dangerously near the edge of social conventions.

Rose, named for the flower associated with the madonna in the middle ages, was sensual, beautiful, and nurturant. Jennie americanized the name Giovanna, feminine version of saint John. In popular beliefs, John was venerated by sicilians who combined John the Baptist (precursor of Jesus) and John the evangelist (whom Jesus asked to look after his mother Mary).

Jennie, no-nonsense and hard working, in later years took the anglo-saxon name Jane.

Pearl as a young woman resembled Van Gogh's painting, *l'Arlesienne*. Her greek/ roman/christian/muslim name referred to feminine moon, feminine water, and the pearl—sacred to Aphrodite of the greeks, and sacred to christians and muslims as Mari, mother of the sea. Lottie's name remembered Lot and his wife, whose story in hebrew scriptures was interpreted to mean that one should never look back (Lot's wife did and turned to salt). Lottie during world war two married a cuban air officer of a wealthy family and never looked back on her sicilian inheritance. Teresa, who died at the age of four, was named for Teresa—jewish conversa and saint of dark others. I was given the middle name of Teresa in memory of saint Teresa—today almost a patron saint of italian feminists—and my aunt Teresa who died as a child. Frank, the only son to survive, was named for Francis, patron saint of Italy, whom his mother dressed in a franciscan robe for festivals. Francis celebrated the beauty of the earth and all its creatures; his namesake in Kansas City tried to be a peaceful influence on his spirited sisters. Frank later became a protestant nazarene.

In Kansas City public schools in the North End, my mother and her siblings were taught the american ideology that english puritans in search of religious freedom came to the new world and founded the United States; other migrants came to the U. S. for "materialistic" reasons. In the version of american history they were taught, grim paragraphs about killing native americans and the horrors of african slavery were omitted for paeans to the "superior race" who founded the United States, whose mission was to uplift "lesser breeds." I have wondered about the effect on my mother and her sisters and brother when they learned in school that italians, and other dark others, were "inferior races."

In 1914 when Woodrow Wilson took the U. S. into a war to "make the world safe for democracy," Kate remembered that she and her sisters banged kitchen pans on the front porch. Mostly, however, the Cipolla family—with enough money that enabled them to stay away from protestant settlement workers intent on telling immigrants how to cook and how to bring up their children—lived in their sicilian enclave in Kansas City, Missouri close to neighborhoods of jewish and african americans, and not far from the "bottoms" of the Missouri River where bordellos and black jazz beckoned, and where the mafia threatened nannu Joe, and other people.

Chaula (or ciavola) my original paternal family name means black bird, symbol of the ancient dark mother Isis of Africa. The norman french who invaded Sicily in the 11th century frenchified Chaula to Chiavola, in the manner that clerks at Ellis Island americanized italian names. The particular bird, to which my name refers, italian scholars have told me, is a magpie that feminist sources identify with the dark mother. In Italy this black bird has a streak of red and a dash of amber yellow on its wings. In my research stays in Italy, I have often seen this particular black bird just before we come upon something that opens my research to another dimension. In the excerpt from Ted Andrews' study of the spiritual meaning of birds sent to me by Joan Clair, the black bird is connected to the level of Binah in the Quabalistic Tree of Life. "This is the level associated with the Dark mother and the primal feminine energies...all of the creative forces of Nature." In the Tree of Life, black is the color for Binah, red is for energy, amber yellow is the "path of Cancer, the mother sign of the zodiac...associated with the stellar energies of Cancer."[33] My mother's sign was Cancer; she died of cancer.

In my childhood my mother would play "Bye Bye Black Bird" on the piano. Was this resistance to her husband, whose name meant black bird, who brought masculinist ideas from the old country? Or was she (unconsciously) conveying the loss of the dark mother in the protestant culture of the U.S?

The peoples who historically inhabited my ancestral paternal Ragusa Ibla unroll sicilian prehistory and history, and my own multicultural history—africans, sicani, siculi, anatolians, canaanites, greeks, israelites, romans, vandals, byzantines, moors, normans, lombards, french angevins, german swabians, spanish and austrian bourbons, and northern italians. I was named Lucia in accordance with the sicilian custom that first daughters are named for the father's mother. All four of nanna Lucia's sons named first daughters for her, as did her eldest daughter. The name Lucia holds continuing appeal in our family; it has been given to girls of the third and fourth generations, one of whom is our grand-daughter, Jessica Ann Lucia, named for herself and her two grandmothers, a remarkably grounded, and radiant young woman who, at this writing, is studying ecology in the rain forest of Australia.

Nanna Lucia's name recalls the young woman of Syracuse whom the church calls an early christian virgin martyr, whose popular rituals transmitted african beliefs of the dark mother's nurturance and vision (see chapter five) In nanna Lucia's region of Sicily, as late as the 19th century, women bonded with the dark mother by baring their breasts and pressing them to the earth. Her maiden name, Poidomani (meaning "and then tomorrow") connotes the spiral of time and a survivor's faith in the future. In 1912, in an impoverished Sicily, nanna Lucia bundled up her children and migrated to Kansas City, Missouri, leaving her husband Luigi behind—unable to travel because he was ill and then unable to come because world war one intervened.

Nannu Luigi always seemed to have lived elsewhere. In Ragusa Ibla when his children were little he lived in the local castle with descendants of the french nobility who had come a millennium earlier with the normans. In the castle, he worked as game warden and falconer, visiting his family nearby who lived in a house dug into the iblean mountains. After his family migrated to the U. S., nannu stayed in Sicily until after world war one when his eldest son came for him. In the United States, nannu Luigi wore a romantic long black cape, called the women in the family cherie, and regarded with bemusement the new country to which he had been brought. A family photo of nannu has him looking under the hood of an automobile, remarking that in America even cars had running water. Poet and romantic, nannu Luigi scarcely fit the category of patriarch;

when he came to the U.S. he brought many meters of crocheted lace to his wife Lucia, lace that I have inherited.

Nanna Lucia, on the other hand, whose personality was formed by millennia of rule by foreign patriarchal elites and of women who looked to their own resources, was close to being a matriarch in the patriarchal negative sense of the word. In the United States every Sunday each of her four sons visited her, bringing money and gifts (my sister Joie describes the gifts as "tribute") and reports on their families. Not endearing herself to her daughters-in-law, nanna Lucia told them that the closest human bond was the blood relationship of mother and son. Wives, she declaimed, were related to her sons only by "signed pieces of paper." A striking woman whom I am said to resemble, nanna Lucia evoked the dark mother as crone. I remember her parrot, the center of the household, who spoke sicilian dialect.

Names of nanna Lucia's sons suggest sicilian popular religious beliefs. Turiddu, my father, carried the diminutive affectionate name for Salvatore or Jesus, who in sicilian popular catholicism was not the christ, but saint saviour. In the apostle's creed taught to sicilian/american children by irish priests and german nuns in catholic instruction for first communion and confirmation, Jesus was the son of god the father, and savior. The doctrine differed from the belief sicilian/american children learned at home, where Gesù was considered his mother's son. A pervasive theme of italian folklore is that the son is very close to his mother and does her errands, a closeness that may reach back to the intimacy of african dark mothers and their sons/consorts. My father, very close to his mother, was called Sam by my mother's family. The name was an americanized version of Samuel, judge and prophet of hebrew scriptures, an inappropriate name for Turiddu, a nonjudgmental spirit who wept when he listened to italian opera, loved learning and beauty (including all beautiful women), and crumpled before the exigencies of life.

The paternal side of my family identified with the norman and subsequent french rulers who held Ragusa after the 11th century. Figuring in this branch of my family history are lawyers close to the french nobility, as well as writers and poets. Nannu Luigi, named for king saint Louis of France of crusader notoriety, was born and lived in the french castle in Ragusa Ibla whose lords were originally norman, later angevin. He spoke french in the castle and sicilian dialect at home with his family. Suggesting that invaders bedded and sometimes wedded the people they conquered, my father had a norman visage; my sister Joie and I have the blue/green eyes of norman invaders, eyes that sicilians call strega, or witch, eyes.

My father's eldest brother George was named for the patron saint of the normans who in return for vanquishing african moors and imposing canonical doctrine on south italians and sicilians, were given land and beatification of their patron saint. George. In church iconography, George slew the dragon (symbol of the dark mother) and became the personifica-tion of christian chivalry, and patron saint of England. Although his name connected him to the dominant class, uncle George as a youth was active in the 1890s socialist ferment in Sicily—a family political legacy I have inherited. George, who had considered the priesthood, scratched his name on the bell of the baroque church of san Giorgio in Ibla, and transferred his religious beliefs to socialist hopes.

Uncle George married Concettina, whose diminutive affectionate name refers to the immaculate conception of the madonna, to whom she was very close. Names of George and Concettina's daughters encapsulate sicilian cultural history: George, Lucia's first son, named his first daughter for his mother. The second daughter was named for her mother, Concettina, and given the diminutive affectionate name, Tina. Their third daughter was named Edea for the "idea" of socialism to which George was early committed. Wanda, suggesting the romantic streak in Chiavola men, was named for a beautiful actress of Poland. In honor of George's father, Louisa was given the feminine equivalent name of Luigi.

Success in the United States eroded uncle George's socialist beliefs; he rose to the presidency of the retail grocer's association of Kansas City, Missouri. Like my father, uncle George read Dante, was proud of his sicilian heritage, and founded the ethnic organization, Società Ragusa Americana, in Kansas City. When I told him I had married a young man studying for the doctorate in physics, uncle George said, "Remind him that Archimedes was a Sicilian!"

When I told nanna Lucia that the young man I'd married was a jewish student from New York, she exclaimed approvingly, "San Isidoro!" Her exclamation evoked the male name associated with african Isis—Isidore means gift of Isis. The name also connotes the history of the hebrews in nanna Lucia's part of Sicily: Canaanites founded Ragusa Ibla in 800 B.C.E. In the punic wars, canaanites based in Carthage, fought greeks and romans at Camarina, port of Ragusa. Israelite jews came to Sicily in diaspora after 70 C E. Martyred jews (e.g., Eulalia) were regarded as saints in sicilian popular catholicism. Jews of Ragusa who chose to remain after the spanish expulsion edict of 1492 often chose the name Isidoro, proximately for the scholarly saint of Seville, ultimately (and unconsciously, no doubt) for african Isis.

Uncle Jim was named for the spanish saint James to whose shrine at Campostella in the Pyrenees, pilgrims in the middle ages walked from France to Spain stopping along the way at sanctuaries of black madonnas. In the United States, Jim was a rebellious young man who wore his cap backward and married red-headed irish catholic Lillian (irish version of hebrew Lilith? And Ann, mother of Mary?). They named their stunningly beautiful sicilian/irish daughters Lucia and Mary. "Why," uncle Jim would later ask me, was I so interested in the "old country?"

Uncle Joe, black sheep of the family, expressed the anticlerical attitudes of sicilian peasants, spitting when he saw a priest. He cooked large pots of pasta cu lenticchi (lentils) and stew with pig's snouts and feet. During the depression in the 1930s uncle Joe would hop freight trains to Chicago, where he married Esther, whose name remembers canaanite Astarte. They named their children Louis and Lucia after his parents. His granddaughter Kathy Chiavola is today a folk and bluegrass singer, acclaimed in Nashville, Tennessee and in Europe.

Aunt Georgia was given a patriarchal name, and married Cheve', sicilian with a french name. Nanna Lucia lived with them and their daughter Anna. Aunt Serafina, whose name recalled all the seraphim of baroque Sicily, married John; they had two daughters, Lucia and Concetta, and a son Andrew, a doctor, who was killed at Guadalcanal during world war two.

The french thread winds around my brother Louis, writer and artist named for his paternal grandfather and french king saint Louis, successor of Charlemagne, who led crusaders into the holy lands. The name's history does not fit this Louis who identifies not with crusaders or kings, but with dark others—as a youth he won a prize for best Camel Walk dancer in Kansas City. Crusaders are satirized in sicilian puppet theater. When we took our son Stefan, then nine years old, to a puppet show in Palermo, he chose the puppet Orlando to take home. Scarcely a conquering hero, Orlando is a comical and cross-eyed puppet, conveying sicilian sardonic appraisal of crusaders as manipulated comical figures. Recently, we gave a cross-eyed Orlando puppet to Stefan's son Jake.

The french connection also winds around my sister Joie, nurturant and gifted, who replaced her name Giuseppina (after our maternal grandmother), with a name that connotes joy of life, and identifies with the french. Her godmother gave her the middle name, Leona, perhaps remembering Isis' cat; recently we discovered that my mother had put her own name Catarina as middle name on Joie's birth certificate.

My blonde cousin Luce also identifies with the french connection, in her case perhaps sensing her celtic (french and irish) inheritance. She early designed a life style that bypassed italian and irish catholic constriction of women. A striking blonde who now calls herself Lucy, she seems in continuum with the values of the ancient dark mother. Like a comare of traditional Sicily, Lucy nurtures anyone who needs care

The french connection early drew me to study the french language and history, an interest that may have been conveyed to our elder sons, both of whom have lived in France. Marc studied french troubadour poetry at the

Sorbonne; he and Nancy were married in Paris. Today he is a professional translator of french commercial documents. Naury and Barbara took infant son Joshua to France, where daughter Sabrina was born. Like her sister Jessica, Sabrina has a clear sense of self. An M.I.T. engineering graduate, she plans to enter politics to change an educational system that marginalizes poor kids. She is learning italian and plans to keep her french citizenship.

Youngest son Stefan, who identifies as a jew, recalls my husband's, and my own, connection with central Europe (Austria-Hungary in Wally's case; german and austrian rulers of Sicily in mine). Our family tapestry shines with multicultural threads. Barbara, of german and methodist inheritance, is married to eldest son Naury, who considers himself a jew. Nancy, who keeps her japanese and buddhist traditions, is married to Marc Turiddu, who identifies as a jew. Names of our grandchildren are a multicultural medley:—Joshua/ Sabrina/ Jessica—Matthew/Nicolas—Courtney/ Jake/ Stefanie.

My own case supports my feeling that ethnic identification is a matter of choice as well as inheritance. In the early 70s when I retrieved Lucia, the name on my birth certificate, I aligned my study of history with womanist/feminist values, and my study of sicilian history with the study of others—africans, jews, moors, heretics, peasant women, nonviolent men, and rebellious students, who work for a better world.

O

In the sicilian region of the Monti Iblei where Ibla Nera had been venerated in prehistory, a collection of vendor cries and songs of Noto, as they must have existed for centuries was published in 1896 in Palermo, just about the time my maternal grandparents left for the U. S., and a few years before my paternal grandmother and her children, including my father, arrived. Late 19th century sicilian vendor cries reveal the persistence across the millennia of the memory of the dark mother, a memory that all four of my grandparents, and my father, brought with them to the United States, a memory that my mother, born in the U. S., seemed to act out.

In the collection of sicilian vendor songs, a little girl of six or seven years of age sang of the enchantment of green fave, beans that connote, for sicilians, regeneration and the bounty of the earth. Other vendors praised the goodness of wild cicoria, asparagus, and artichokes. In Kansas City, my nannu Joe would sing the goodness and beauty of fruits and vegetables in his stall at the city market and in his vendor cry for a radio greengrocer program. My sicilian/american mother planted fig trees in her back yard and took us on outings to Cliff Drive Park, where she would dig up wild cicoria for summer salads.

Revealing ultimate beliefs, sicilian vendors lauded the goodness and beauty of the earth and all its fruits, and identified the earth and its bounty with the dark mother. In a song of grape vendors, black grapes were called madre maltrattata, or the mistreated mother, perhaps referring to the abuse of the dark mother in greek, roman, and christian history. Revealing sicilian beliefs, vendors sang that if grapes are white they connote misfortune, if black, they bring joy,[34] implying that the true mother is black and brings joy, while the whitened mother of the church brings misfortune.

Per Diana! was a favorite expletive of Corrado Ferrara, collector of these vendor songs. The cry invoked west asian dark mothers Inanna, and Astarte, whom romans called Diana. For Ferrara, songs of the vanniaturi, or vendors, were a daily praise giving of the bounty of the earth, a bounty symbolized by "figs, apples, grapes, pears, fichi d'India."[35]

Vendors in horse-drawn carts in Sicily, and in carts and trucks in Kansas City sang the spiral of the seasons. Summer was proclaimed in the call for "tomatoes, potatoes, cucumbers, and artichokes." Feast days were announced in the vendor call for la calia, the roasted chick peas identified with the dark mother. Ceci were always eaten at Noto for the festa della madonna del Carmine (an african/semitic dark madonna), as well as for feast days of san Giovanni and san Corrado, patron saint of Noto. Itinerant summer vendors lauded the taste of sweet oranges and the patience of their aging donkeys.

In autumn, pescivendole (fish sellers) rhapsodized on the incomparable taste of sicilian pesci spada (sword fish), a taste that is incomparable. Vendors of lupini promised the camaraderie of taverns where peasants ate salted lupin beans, drank red wine, and planned carnival pageants that satirized the clergy and the nobility. In rainy weather, umbrella vendors in velveteen jackets sang in melancholy tones of having to return home without a sale. In winter when the sun was a golden disk but the wind shook the trees, vendors sang of a warm hearth and pasta cu broccoli.

Christmas, in the popular catholicism of Italy, is a celebration of the mother's holy birthing (natale), in contrast to the son-centered holiday of protestant countries. In my sicilian/american family, the holiday was anticipated by ciuciulena, a sweet of sesame seeds and honey (male seeds/female honey?) that aunt Serafina prepared for children and visitors during the month of the holy birthing.

Before and after natale in Sicily, old women sold dried flowers, and sang the life spiral of birth, youth, maturity, death, and regeneration. After natale, vendors sold matches for new year's eve bonfires when peasants proclaimed capo d'anno with cries of fiammiferi! to burn the old year. In winter, young men promising spring offered violets to young women. In February, tambourines of the dark mother Cybele and of Miriam (Moses' sister) announced the festa of san Corrado, accompanied by the song of the salt sellers.

Fruit and vegetable vendors in summer would celebrate sensuality with songs about peppers, onions, tomatoes, and cucumbers; groups of people gathered around vendors jesting in double entendre about the biggest pepper, the best cucumber. Summer nights, the comical song of the vendor of boiled potatoes floated on the perfume of jasmine and tuber roses. Autumn days, vendors of black coal for warmth and cooking sang of pane bianco e cipuddi ruossi (white bread enlivened by zesty dark red onions, connoting the menstruating vulva), sang of the warmth of black madonnas, and of another spiral of seasons of earth and life.

O

The ultimate belief in the dark mother and her bounty carried by vendor cries, and the multicultural history sicilians brought in their names and in names they gave their children, were almost completely destroyed by education for "americanization" in the dominant racist culture of the United States…until the 1960s, when african americans drew the young of all ethnic groups to their vision of a just and equal world, and inspired other dark others to search for their roots.[36]

Negated cultures are never completely obliterated; they may be suppressed by schooling designed by purveyors of the dominant culture, yet their values persist in folklore, in spontaneous expressions, and in the personalities of people who embody the memory. I remember my mother's sense of self, that could create havoc all around her. She never lost it. At the age of 89, still assured she was beautiful, she continued to dye her hair black—until the week in late November, month of african/semitic santa Catarina, that she died.

Notes

1   Quoted in Howard Zinn, *A People's History of the United States* (New York, Harper Perennial, 1980), 15. See also, James W. Loewen, *Lies my teacher told me. Everything your American history textbook got wrong* (New York, Touchstone Press/Simon & Schuster, Inc., 1996). See also Sacvan Bercovitch, *The Puritan Origins of the American Self* (New York and London, Yale University Press, 1975).

2   David Brion Davis, "At the Heart of Slavery," *The New York Review of Books,* October 17, 1996.

3   See Perry Miller, *Errand into the Wilderness* (Cambridge, Ma., The Belknap Press of Harvard University Press, 1956, 1984).

4   Quoted in *Women's America .Refocusing the Past.* 2nd edition edited by Linda Kerber & Jane De Hart-Mathews (New York and Oxford, Oxford University Press, 1987), 53,

5   Quoted in *Women's America,* Loc. Cit. 52.

6   Ibid., Loc. Cit., 108.

7   *Women's America,* Loc. Cit., . 59.

8   Ibid. 60.

9   Anne Llewellyn Barstow, *Witchcraze. A New History of the European Witch Hunts* (New York, Pandora/A Division of HarperCollinsPublishers, 1994),. 78.

10   Ibid., 104, l12.

11   Ibid., 134.

12   Maryse Condé, *I, Tituba, Black Witch of Salem* (New York, Ballantine Books,1992, Angela Davis, Foreword.

13   Condé, *I, Tituba,* 9.

14   Ibid., 46.

15   Ibid., 127.

16   Ibid., 132.

17   Ibid., 151.

18   Ibid., 176.

19   Ibid., 203.

20   See Martin Bernal, *Black Athena. The Afroasiatic roots of classical civiliza-tion.* Vol I., *The Fabrication of Ancient Greece 1785-1985* (New Brunswick, New Jersey, Rutgers University Press, 1987). 203.

21   Winthrop D. Jordan, *White over Black. American Attitudes toward the Negro 1550-1812* (Baltimore, Md., Penguin Books Inc., 1968, 1969), 441 ff.

22   Ibid., 241.

23   See Bernal, *Black Athena,* Vol 1 Loc. cit. An excellent exploration of racism and sexism in late 19th century England (with whom dominant classes of the U. S. shared cultural views) is Anne McClintock's, *Imperial Leather. Race, Gender, and Sexuality in the Colonial Context* (New York and London, Routledge, 1995).

24   McClintock, *Imperial Leather,* 354.

25   Ana Castillo, *Massacre of the Dreamers. Essays on Xicanisma* (New York, Penguin/Plume, 1994).

26   Zinn, *A People's History,* Loc. Cit., 339.

27   See Henry Farnham May, *Protestant Churches and Industrial America* (Chicago, 1949).

28   See George Santayana, *The Last Puritan. A Memoir in the Form of a Novel* (New York, Scribners, 1936).; See also Ronald Takaki, *A Different Mirror. A History of Multicultural America* (Boston, et al., Little Brown and Company, 1993).

29   See Henry Louis Gates, Jr. And Cornel West, *The Future of the Race* (New York, Vintage Books, 1997) for a contemporary view of Du Bois's concept of the "talented tenth" of african americans.

30   A significant source of contemporary italian/american historiography is *Via, Voices in Italian Americana. A literary and cultural review,* editors Anthony J. Tamburri, Paolo A. Giordano, and Fred L. Gardaphe. For the faustian pact that italian/americans, and other "white" ethnics made with the dominant racism of the U. S., see David A. J. Richards, *Italian American: the Racializing of an Ethnic Identity* (New York, New York University Press, 1999).

31   See Henry F. May, *Protestant Churches and Industrial America.* Loc. Cit.

32   Barbara Walker, *The Women's Encyclopedia of Myths and Secrets* (San Francisco, Harper & Row, 1983) 151.

33   "Blackbird, Keynote: Understanding of the Energies of Mother Nature,"
Animal-Speak. The Spiritual and Magical Powers of Creatures Great & Small, (St.
Paul, Minnesota, Llewellyn Publications, 1996), 119-120.

34   Corrado Ferrara, *La musica dei vanniaturi. gridatori di Piazza Notigiani*
(Noto, Off. Tip di Fr. Zammit, 1896; Ristampa anastatica e cura della Edizioni e
Ristampe Siciliane s.r.l. Palermo, Agosto 1980, .19. See also Corrado Ferrara,
L'Ignota Provenienza dei Canti Popolari in Noto (Noto, Tipografica Zammit,
1908).

35   Corrado, *La musica,* Loc. Cit., 23.

36   The rescue of negated cultures of the United States is proceeding on sev-
eral levels; a minimal list of important studies would include Howard Zinn, *A
People's History of the United States* (New York, Harper Perennial, 1980), works of
Toni Morison, Alice Walker, et al. See *Unsettling America. An Anthology of
Contemporary Multicultural Poetry,* ed., Maria Mazziotti Gillan and Jennifer
Gillan (New York, Penguin, 1994). For italian/americans see *From the Margin.
Writings in Italian Americana,* edited by Anthony Julian Tamburri, Paolo A.
Giordano, Fred L. Gardaphe (West Lafayette, Indiana, Purdue University Press,
1991. For italian/american women, see writings of Diane Di Prima, Rose
Romano, Louisa Calio, et al.

31. Joe Cipolla's stall, City Market
Kansas City, Missouri
Photograph by Lucia Chiavola Birnbaum

32. Triad of wheat. Festival of Demetra/Cerere, August 15, 2000.
Church holy day of assumption of Mary into heaven.
Gangi, Sicily
Photograph by Wallace Birnbaum

chapter nine

empire abroad and social control of dark others at home
United States in the 20th century

> *"Enlightened behaviorists, in effect, offered a social science tech-*
> *nique of conditioning the public to attitudes of racism, sexism,*
> *homophobia, and imperialism, attitudes useful to hegemonic capi-*
> *talist elites, who have employed advertisers, social scientists, and*
> *media consultants to condition these attitudes in everyone, ever*
> *since."*

In the last chapter I summarized the history of the United States from the perspective of dark others. First settlers to the United States, like european inquisitors, continued killing, enslaving, and exploiting dark others. This was refined in the 20th century to scientific methods of "social control" of dark others.

This chapter, focusing on the movement for social control in the United States, called **behaviorism** in the social sciences, may be considered a paradoxical tale of how one branch of the hegemonic male elite in the U.S., many of them benign men close to the religious movement called the protestant social gospel—who hoped for socialist revolution—

adopted scientific ways of legitimating their credentials as the "vanguard," and scientific methods to manipulate the beliefs of the dark "masses."

During world war one, the hope for socialist revolution in the U. S. did not—as it had in Russia—come about. In the 1920s, behaviorists and enlightened behaviorists engaged in a large controversy whose implicit debate was on the meaning of democracy in the United States. In the early 1930s, the matter was resolved by legitimating **enlightened behaviorism**, a settlement that sustained the values of the old stock american elite, and a few correctly schooled upwardly mobile ethnic outsiders admitted to hegemonic circles. In effect, the settlement legitimated the U. S. puritan legacy of separating people into the saved and the damned, institutionalized this calvinist premise in the social sciences, and negated mother-centered cosmologies of subordinated outsiders—native americans, african americans, asian americans, and immigrants from subaltern european cultures.

After radicalism was suppressed in 1919, the mission of education in the United States became the "americanization" of new immigrants and other dark others. In the late 20s, in the debate between strict behaviorists and enlightened behaviorists (all of them males; not one woman was involved) analyzed in my doctoral dissertation, I was closer to Watson's egalitarian strict behaviorism than to the elitist and manipulative premises of enlightened behaviorism. Yet neither psychology was relevant to me, a sicilian/american woman whose (not yet conscious) cosmology circled a dark mother connoting justice with compassion, equality, and transformation.

Perhaps this chapter should be read as a cautionary tale of what happens when significant decisions, including decisions in the social sciences, are left solely to males who consider themselves white. Consequences of enlightened behaviorism are still with us, notably in intelligence and other tests which, in effect, validate the dominion of white hegemonic male elites over dark others and perpetuate an unventilated assumption that elites in a democracy may manipulate the religious and political beliefs of everyone else. One long term consequence in the United States of the establishment of enlightened behaviorism has been the continuing hostility of subordinated peoples toward elites, a hostility that may have been a major variable in the failure of socialist spokemen to engage the trust of exploited dark others.

An underlying theme of this chapter is how a sicilian/american woman was educated so well in "americanism" that she did not recognize racism all around her, including racism directed at her own ethnic group. In 1922 an M.A. thesis written at the University of California at Berkeley was entitled, "Inferiority of the Italian immigrant."[1] Racism pervaded my sicilian/american childhood and youth in Kansas City, yet somehow I did not notice it. Why didn't I notice it? Perhaps because of the assured sense of self I inherited from my sicilian grandmothers and my sicilian/american mother whose cosmology circled a dark mother. And my success as a model product of the U. S. educational system.

When I won a scholarship to the University of Kansas City, the protestant principal of my elementary school, who took a kindly interest in my scholarly achievements, took me aside. He urged me to give up the scholarship and go to a junior (subsequently called community) college. Why? Italian americans did not, he advised, do well in the university. This should have given me pause, but it did not. Ethnic and feminist awareness were not to surface until after I had spent a decade closely studying the history of the United States for the doctorate, and exploring hidden recesses of institutionalized white male anglo saxon protestant racism in research for my dissertation.

O

"Behaviorist psychology and U. S. social theory, 1913-1933" was the title of my doctoral dissertation, which I finished in 1964, just as the civil rights movement and campus uprisings were sparking into flame. An intellectual historian, I was intrigued by John Broadus Watson's proposal in 1913 to put psychology on a scientific basis by eliminating "consciousness," and using animal laboratory stimulus/response methods on humans.

Prevailing methods of psychology in the United States in 1913 were introspection of consciousness and the new science of intelligence testing. The latter awarded top intelligence quotients to New England white anglo-saxon protestant male scientists, descending scores to midwestern and southern protestants, sharply descending scores to "new immigrants" (jews, southern italians, greeks, slavs), even lower scores to native americans, latin americans, and asian americans. African americans were sometimes left off the charts.

Philosophers and social scientists who welcomed Watson's behaviorism in 1913 did not, for a moment, consider giving up the concept of consciousness, nor the flattering, culturally determined, results of intelligence tests, for themselves. They looked to a scientific psychology useful for manipulating the beliefs of the masses. Watson's dismissal of the concept of consciousness was fine—when it applied to dismissing the consciousness of dark others.[2]

Watson, a southerner who had studied for the baptist ministry, was an outsider to dominant New England elites in fields of philosophy, psychology, and sociology. Considering intelligence tests useless for measuring moral characteristics, Watson's version of behaviorist psychology looked to conditioning methods of animal psychology to train everyone to good work habits. He accepted Freud's theory of the significance of sexuality, but as a baptist, identified sexuality with human "defects." He proposed replacing the prevailing educational psychology of "stamping in learning with pleasure" with the orthodox protestant motivation of fear.

Unlike enlightened behaviorists, Watson was open about his methods, saying he would use "suggestion" (in this case the positive stimulus of science) to promote training to "vocational and individualistic habits," not only in the dark lower classes, but in white elites, thereby "untraining" what Watson called intellectuals' habit of "conceit." The clever strategem of an outsider, Watson claimed behaviorists had the "right" to use consciousness in the same way as did New England functionalist psychologists, who placed their religious and socialist beliefs in the concept of consciousness.

Saying he was returning to a non-reflective use of consciouness,[3] Watson said the "instrument of belief" could be "properly or improperly" used by scientists.[4]

John Dewey, significant theorist of liberalism and democracy, as well as leading educational theorist of the United States in the 20th century, was the major **enlightened behaviorist.** Keeping a transcendental consciousness, and the high scores of intelligence tests, for himself and his New England colleagues in philosophy and functional psychology, Dewey looked to behaviorist psychology as a way of detaching religious beliefs of the lower classes and attaching them to beliefs defined as "science" by his own group of pragmatist philosophers. Dewey's beliefs were ballasted by his hope for socialism.

In the "natural man," said Dewey, referring to the darker skinned peoples whom his colleagues in psychology put at the bottom of intelligence scales, "suggestion" functioned as a stimulus that offered a technique of "deliberate social control to modify belief and desire."[5] Social control, in Dewey's elitist socialist thinking, was to be exercised by an intellectual class of scientific inquirers who worked at "knowing," as other classes worked in factories or in farming. Effective communication, said the philosopher, used "science, schools, and central agencies of the national government" to educate everyone to "like-mindedness of belief, aspiration and knowledge."[6]

Hoping for socialist revolution, Dewey urged U. S. entry into world war one, advocated "force" as a legitimate educational instrument, praised social efficiency, and promoted education for "americanization" to insure the conformity of "new immigrants." After the war, this indoctrination program became educational policy in U. S. public schools, for the next five decades.[7]

During world war one, a committee of psychologists and philosophers administered intelligence tests to army recruits, confirmed their belief that dark lower classes were unintelligent, and devised the propaganda that demonized the germans and conditioned americans to believe that the massacre of a generation of young men was a war "to make the world safe for democracy." During the war, Dewey censured pacifists and spoke of "practical political psychology" as the technique of "expert manipulation of man en masse for needs not seen clearly by them." Manipulation of beliefs of lower class dark others was legitimate in a democracy, said Dewey, because the governing group held the "consent" [albeit manipulated] of the lower orders. In an article entitled, "Propaganda," Dewey pointed out how easy it is to control democracies with propaganda disguised as news.[8]

The ease with which enlightened behaviorists moved from socialist hopes to theories resembling fascism was evident in the writings of F. H. Giddings, son of a New England congregationalist minister and political sociologist. In 1918 Giddings embraced an "enlightened and pluralist behaviorism" that proposed to apply stimulus/response conditioning to everybody except white "variates" like himself. Describing his political sociology as "Puritan," Giddings said that extension of democracy under the leadership of english-speaking peoples was inevitable at home and abroad. His master principle, "consciousness of kind," (his own kind) meant democracy "for the people," not by the people. This was democracy led by a "natural aristocracy" whose credentials were confirmed in the high intelligence test quotients of New Englanders.[9] And, as it historically developed, the ethnic outsiders who joined them.

During the war, when ethnic outsiders accelerated the momentum for socialist revolution, Giddings became worried about the "illegitimate aims of the proletariat" he saw embodied in the large influx of non-anglo-saxon immigrants. In 1918, anxious about the "menace of anarchism," Giddings replaced his principle of "consciousness of kind" with the postulate, "the few always dominate." The master form of all types of government, even democracy, for this sociologist, was "protocracy," wherein a small group of men, usually wealthy, coped with the "Jacksonian" belief that all men should have equal power. Giddings advocated a strong centralized state and a stratified society wherein intelligence tests selected the governing elite who used methods of behaviorist psychology to condition the electorate to beliefs defined as correct by white male elites.[10]

In the 1920s this elitist and manipulative **enlightened behaviorism** was embraced by modernist protestant theologians, philosophers, psychologists, sociologists, political theorists, and educators—most of them descendants of puritans. Ralph Barton Perry, enlightened behaviorist at Harvard, attracted more manipulators in the 20s with his authoritative study, *Puritanism and Democracy*. "Democracy," for the New England presbyterian, could be used as a symbol to inculcate *any* beliefs in the lower dark classes desired by the governing elite. Defending the "new moral technology" as a way to "cure" racial differences, Perry advocated eugenics to preserve "superior races" and government by a small elite to manipulate the beliefs of the many, preserving the "words" of democracy while bypassing the "tyrannies and vulgarities" of the majority, exercising "human engineering through knowledge of psychology."[11]

Consciousness, in Perry's definition, was "conscience" embodied in "appointed agents of God and society" [he did not explain the process of appointment] who communicated with the masses using "stereotypes," "propaganda," and "useful lies." In addition to useful lies, social controllers could induce "benevolent cooperation" by manipulating techniques of conditioning, and using social legislation to distribute rewards and punishment.[12]

At this point in 1924, with the charisma enlightened behaviorists had bestowed on him as "America's most distinguished scientist," Watson promulgated a **strict behaviorism** discarding consciousness, intelligence tests, instincts, and "mind" from scientific psychology. Calling enlightened behaviorists "medicine men," Watson repudiated all "half way behaviorists" who kept the doctrine of consciousness for themselves while manipulating the religious and political beliefs of others. He made it very clear that his psychology was particularly applicable to elitist intellectuals, and proclaimed a radical egalitarianism. Training a child to good work habits, declared Watson, would enable any child to become a "doctor, lawyer or Indian Chief."[13]

Watson's strict behaviorism removed the foundation posts supporting modernist protestantism,. wherein consciousness was the chief proof of the existence of the idea of god, the eugenics movement that aimed to preserve new englanders and eliminate the "unfit," John Dewey's version of state socialism led by a leninist vanguard of manipulating intellectuals, and Ralph Barton Perry's enlightened behaviorism whose philosophy of "puritanism and democracy" held considerable resemblance to fascism. After 1945, the inherently contradictory coupling of "puritanism and democracy" was to enjoy large academic afflatus, fitting in well with cold war aims of U. S. white male elites.

Watson's strict behaviorism discarded the notion of race, holding that everyone was born equal in responses of fear, rage, and sex. Intelligence tests did not reveal moral characteristics, said Watson. No one, including scientists, was "free of defects." He held out a utopian hope: "For the universe will change if you bring up your children, not in the freedom of the libertine, but in behavioristic freedom…until the world finally becomes a place fit for human habitation."[14]

In the field of psychology, enlightened behaviorists were, for the most part, modernist protestants whose theology, based on the mind, was dependent on the confirming evidence of intelligence tests as evidence of mind. These enlightened worthies looked to stimulus/response psychology to detach the religious beliefs of the dark underclass, attaching the religious beliefs of the dark underclasses to "scientific" ideas defined by themselves and a few correctly educated outsiders whose intelligence quotients, in effect, became admission tickets to the hegemonic elite.

Enlightened behaviorists in sociology were led by C. H. Ellwood, leader of the protestant social gospel movement who pinned religious faith and socialist hopes on the good instincts and high intelligence of New England leaders in manipulating the religious beliefs of the dark underclass. Strict behaviorist in sociology was W. I. Thomas, southerner and close friend of

Watson, who found "social instability" in the racist attitudes of enlightened behaviorists. With the sardonic tone of an outsider, as well as the sexism that pervaded both parties to the behaviorist controversy, Thomas proposed using the same conditioning methods on victorian ladies of the upper classes and prostitutes of the lower classes. Yet Thomas respected the beliefs of new immigrants from subaltern cultures of Europe. With Florian Znaniecki, he wrote a pioneering study of the religious beliefs of immigrants from Poland.[15]

A few upwardly mobile ethnic outsiders joined the protestant magistracy of enlightened behaviorists. In 1929, Walter Lippman, upper class jewish intellectual, and subsequent dean of american journalism, proposed a moral philosophy of humanism for the great society, reserving freudian and gestalt psychologies for controllers and mechanist and determinist behaviorist psychology for the controlled. Lippmann praised the "puritan" insight that regeneracy was attained by rigid suppression of the "carnal" emotions. He described the rulers of the new society as guardians of morality who, with disinterested realism, practiced the "high religion incarnate" of scientific rationalism.

Like other enlightened behaviorists, Lippmann considered conditioning methods useful for manipulating the beliefs of darker people, whom he described as inherently stupid, beset by "childish religious beliefs," and driven by "greed, sex, and pride." Upward climber and rapid learner, Lippman joined latter-day puritan magistrates in their desire to rule with "high disinterestedness," manipulating stimuli of rewards and fear of punishment to disabuse the masses of their religious beliefs, teaching dark others to want what the white elite willed them to want.[16] Not all jewish intellectuals. Horace Kallen, lower class and jewish, took Watson's side, finding strict behaviorism consonant with his beliefs in equality and cultural pluralism, as well as with good child training.[17]

Two outsiders intervened in the U.S. controversy over "enlightened vs. materialistic behaviorism." Bertrand Russell, free-thinking british philosopher who said he was offended by Dewey's "cosmic impiety," and George Santayana, catholic philosopher who taught at Harvard until he left the U. S. forever for Italy. Both took the side of Watson's materialistic behaviorism in opposition to the puritanism of enlightened behaviorists.

Declaring his rejection of theological religion, disbelief in free will, and suspicion of formal morality, Russell advised puritans that ethics can not be bent to the mold of logic. For the british philosopher, whose ultimate beliefs appeared to be grounded on the golden rule and Hume's premise that the truths of religion are not demonstrable to reason, Dewey's views were not compatible with individual liberty nor with any belief in "final excellence." Enlightened behaviorists, said Russell, camouflaged love of power as love of doing good.[18]

Santayana, whose unease with the puritan legacy to U. S. culture provoked him to write the novel *The Last Puritan,* sent missives to the controversy from Rome. Dewey sounded as if he accepted the principle that the mind was reducible to mechanical habits, said Santayana, but Dewey was not a "true behaviorist." Dewey's pragmatist philosophy was a "half hearted and short-winded naturalism similar to that of Emerson and left Hegelians." Dewey's enlightened behaviorism, for Santayana, was a parochial, patriotic, and pious philosophy wherein consciousness was a transcendental absolute for the mystic who believed it, while the accompanying social philosophy reduced other people to their social functions.[19] Santayana's critique was to leave a lasting imprint on my thinking.

Dewey responded that Santayana's was a "broken-backed naturalism." Declaring that Hegel's doctrine of spirit was now validated by the physics concept of indeterminacy, he led the 1930's closure movement of modernist protestant theologians, philosophers, social scientists, and educators who, exempting themselves, appropriated Watson's stimulus/response techniques to apply to others.

Banishing Watsons' "destructive treatment of mind" to protect the hegemony of lighter-skinned controllers, the "unique" characteristics of consciousness, said Dewey, were to be recognized by behaviorist psychology, not because there was a "scientific reason" for doing so, but because of the "exigencies of social control."[20] Affiliating his views with George Herbert Mead's social behaviorism, Dewey urged "social education" to detach the traditional religious attitudes of lower class dark others and attach their religious attitudes to "science," thereby suffusing scientific intelligence with religious numinosity. In his call for a "common faith" in scientific intelligence, Dewey said that "God" might be described as the active relationship of conscious intelligence with the "ideal and the actual in the movement toward a more just society."[21] No wonder Bertrand Russell described Dewey's views as cosmic impiety; and religious fundamentalists of the United States have been suspicious of liberalism, science, and socialism ever since.

Santayana, in a 1930 anthology of critics of Watson's "materialism," declared that his catholic religious philosophy was wholeheartedly in accord with Watson's behaviorism. The passions of the heart, not the mind, determined a person's beliefs and conduct; the mind was an epiphenomenon of the body. Both religion and science are myths, said Santayana, but myths are far from signifying nothing.[22]

After 1930, the closure movement in academic circles banished Watson's egalitarian (albeit reductive) psychology, and established elitist enlightened behaviorism wherein intelligence tests were used to legitimate the elite of controllers, and conditioning techniques adopted to indoctrinate the dark lower classes. Enlightened behaviorists, in effect, offered a social science technique of conditioning the public to attitudes of racism, sexism, homophobia, and imperialism, attitudes useful to hegemonic capitalist elites, who have employed social scientists, advertisers, and media specialists to condition these attitudes in everyone, ever since.

In an article for the *Encyclopedia Britannica* article, Watson revealed his religious premises. He described behaviorism as an "objective" psychology based on the laboratory experiment that humans at birth responded to loud sounds and loss of support with fear.[23] True to his "vocational bent" as a baptist minister, Watson had devised a scientific psychology that demonstrated the existence of god by inferring cause from effect—inferring god from the inborn response of fear in all humans—while eroding the scientific under-pinning of the concept of "mind" of modernist protestant theologians.

In 1932 H. Richard Niebuhr, protestant theologian of realism, who considered the marginal sects (quakers and baptists) of the protestant ref-ormation the carriers of genuine christianity, credited realistic psychology with eroding anthropomorphic beliefs of modernists, and for refounding american protestantism on realism.[24] After 1945, H. Richard Niebuhr's religious realism was appropriated, and distorted, by government elites for the uses of cold war propaganda—for the next half century.

Watson's "puerile behaviorism," with his proclamation that all men and women are born equal, and dismissal of parochially defined concepts of consciousness, mind, instincts, and intelligence tests from scientific psy-chology, was banished from academic respectability in the early 1930s. Established were enlightened behaviorism and an operationalist method-ology, conservative in political implication, that Morris Raphael Cohen declared would remove "illusions."[25] Operationalism banishes the study of possibilities, limiting the social sciences to study of what has happened in the past.

The establishment of scientific methodology in the social sciences did not, as Dewey hoped, lead to socialism. Watson's exposure of all "medicine men" implanted a distrust of social planners that became visible in the New Deal era, a distrust that has haunted social planners ever since. In the dem-ocratic decade of the 1930s, popular critics applied premises of mechanism and determinism to controllers as well as the controlled, often leading to a loss of will on the part of planners—the loss of will that controllers had hoped to inculcate in subordinated dark masses.[26]

Criticism of puritans in the 1920s and 1930s was not as far from his-torical accuracy as subsequent academic apologists have led people to believe.[27] The puritan attitude of violence to dark others may be the one continuous thread of dominant U. S. history right up to 1960s, when the pentagon daily reported the number of dark vietnamese killed by U. S.

forces, in the same manner that early new england puritan divines gave thanks to god for the number of native americans they had killed.

In the 1990s the first Bush administration's war in the Persian Gulf was a chilling display of the military uses of enlightened behaviorism, manipulating the U. S. public into viewing the killing of dark-skinned others as a video game. Ralph Barton Perry's enlightened behaviorism has subsequently proven useful to social scientists, publicists, and focus group pollsters aiding imperial presidents and their spin doctors to condition the word democracy to the preponderant role of the United States in the world.

An ironic, and vicious, institutionalization of Dewey's enlightened behaviorist (and state socialist) idea of a central intelligence agency to manipulate the beliefs of the public was institutionalized after world war two in the Central Intelligence Agency. In the cold war from 1945 to 1989, the C.I.A. countered grass roots democracy, populism and democratic socialism, with stimulus/response methods of negative conditioning to banish ideas that threatened the hegemony of white anglo saxon protestant political and economic elites—and those outsiders who made a faustian pact to join them.

Enlightened behaviorist use of intelligence tests to separate an elite of controllers from the controlled many remains an unexamined premise of public discourse. Since the 1930s, standards of objectivity have largely been determined by white men of dominant elites, along with the few upwardly mobile ethnic, and even fewer gender outsiders who have joined them. In ways I would not have understood when I wrote the doctoral dissertation, I realize now that the story of enlightened behaviorists in the United States is one that Stephen Pfohl calls the "economic exchange of anomalous fears and almost magnetic fascinations...a story of the sacrificial actions of predatory elites and the forms of contemporary social science which must serve these elites...."[28]

Hegemonic elites have institutionalized inequality in the United States with intelligence, and other tests, and enforced inequality by seeing to it that subordinated dark-skinned others do not, as Jonathan Kozol has demonstrated, receive an equal education. Beliefs in racial inferiority, as Howard Zinn has pointed out, "whether applied to blacks or Jews or Arabs or Orientals, have led to mass murder."[29]

In the late 90s the legacy of enlightened behaviorists was visible in the national debate evoked by publication of *The Bell Curve*[30], a study that muffled undemocratic ideas with the authority of quantitative science. Given a great deal of publicity by establishment media, the book postulated contemporary puritan and capitalist dogmas—widening inequality in the U. S. and in the world is inevitable because of "human nature" and the "market."

In 1996, a group of social scientists responded to the book with scientific data aimed to "crack the bell curve."[31] Scarcely utopian, the group of sociologists of the University of California at Berkeley concluded, "It is not that low intelligence leads to inferior status; it is that inferior status leads to low intelligence test scores."[32] Inferior status, and low test scores, are connected to how people are treated. In every country of the world, people who are treated as other do less well on intelligence tests.

The sociologists concluded that the United States has "the most economically unequal society in the industrialized world," an inequality protected by policy decisions and methodologies in the social sciences that insure inequality.[33]

Notes

This chapter is excerpted from my unpublished doctoral dissertation: Lucille Terese Birnbaum, *John Broadus Watson and American Social Thought, 1913-1933* (Ph.D, Dissertation, University of California, Berkeley, 1964). Footnotes that refer to this dissertation are in the style of the 1964 dissertation, citing place of publication, and date.

1   I am indebted to Dr, Rose Scherini for bringing this thesis (written at my alma mater, the University of California at Berkeley) to my attention: Edna L. Desseny, *A Study of the Mental Inferiority of the Italian Immigrant*, M.A. thesis, University of California, Berkeley, 1922.

2   John Broadus Watson, *Behavior. An Introduction to Comparative Psychology* (New York, 1914), Chapter X,. 62, 94, 105, 109, 256-262, 263-4, 267, 276. See Edward L. Thorndike, *The Original Nature of Man*. Vol 1 (New York, 1913), 171.

3   This is the epistemology of traditional religious realism.

4   Watson, *Behavior,*, 166, 167.

5   John Dewey, *Essays in Experimental Logic* (Chicago, 1916), Dover ed., 4, 6, 66, 10-13, particularly 47, 50, 51, 56.

6   Ibid,. 440-442. See also Dewey, *Democracy and education. An Introduction to the Philosophy of Education* (New York, 1960, Macmillan pb, 1961,. 21-26.

7   See Lucia Chiavola Birnbaum, "Education for Conformity. The Case of Sicilian American Women Professionals," *Italian Americans in the Professions. Proceedings*, the Twelfth Annual Conference of the American Italian Historical Association, 1983.

8   See Dewey, "Propaganda," *The New Republic*, December 1918.

9   Franklin Henry Giddings, *Democracy and Empire. With Studies of their Psychological, Economic, and Moral Foundations* (New York, 1900). . 50, 53, 242-245. Giddings, "Americanism in War and Peace," *Publications of the Clark University Library*, May, 1917, 1-16. Giddings, *The Responsible State. A reexamination of Fundamental Political Doctrines in the Light of World War and the Menace of Anarchism* (Boston and New York, 1918), 18-19.

10   Giddings, *Responsible State*, 20-22, 29, 46-48, 75-90, 103.

11   Ralph Baron Perry, "A Modernist View of National Ideals," *University of California Press Publications in Philosophy*, 1925, . 183-204. Perry, *General Theory of Value. Its Meaning and Basic Principles Construed in Terms of Interest* (New York, 1926), . l, 10-12, 197, 694.

12   Perry, *General Theory of Value*, 187-193, 263-269.

13   Watson, *Psychology from the stand-point of a Behaviorist*, 1924 edition. See also Lucille Terese Birnbaum, *John Broadus Watson*, Loc. Cit, Chapter 10.

14   Watson, *Psychology from the Standpoint*. vii, l-4, l13-l15, 10, l13-l15, 10-16, 194-41, 185, 180-201, 58-68, 42-73, 46, 74-107, 217, 216-248, 220-234, 248.

15   W. I. Thomas and Florian Znaniecki, *The Polish Peasant in Europe and America* (1910) Dover edition, 1958.

16   See Walter Lippmann, *A Preface to Morals* (New York, 1929, Beacon edition, vi-vii, ix, 253, 155, 1822-183, 192-198, 201, 209, 231.

17   Horace Kallen, *Culture and Democracy in the United States. Studies in the Group Psychology of the American Peoples* (New York, 1924), 24-28, 34, 43, 66, 187-189, 339.

18   See Bertrand Russell, "Professor Dewey's 'Essays in Experimental Logic," *Journal of Psychology (1919)*. 5-26. Russell, *The Analysis of Mind* (London and New York, 1921), 212. Russell, *Icarus or the Future of Science* (London, 1924. Russell, "Materialism, Past and Present," in *The Basic Writings of Bertrand Russell*, 1903-1969, eds. R. E. Eger and L. E. Denonn (New York, 1961), 238-245. Russell, *Sceptical Essays* (London, 1928), Chapter VII, . 84-88, 139-147.

19   George Santayana, *Scepticism and Animal Faith. Introduction to a System of Philosophy* (1923, Dover ed., 1955. 304, 298, 125, 219, 286. *The Letters of George Santayana*, ed, Daniel Cory (New York, 1955, 183, 206-209, 224-226, 390. Santayana, *The Last Puritan. A Memoir in the Form of a Novel* (New York, Scribner, 1936), 61-84, 510. Santayana, "A General Confession," in Charles Frankel, *The Golden Age of American Philosophy* (New York, 1960) 264-284.

20   Ibid.

21   See Dewey, "Conduct and experience," *Psychologies of 1930* (Worcester, Ma., 1930) 410, 411, 414-415, 421, 418. Dewey, "George Herbert Mead," *Journal of Philosophy*, 28 (1931) 309-314, 311. See also Dewey, *A Common Faith* (New Haven, Conn., 1934) paper ed., 26, 51.

22   Santayana, *A General Confession*, Loc. Cit., 264-284.

23   See D. C. Macintosh, "Experimental Realism in Religion," in *Religious Realism*, ed., D. C. Macintosh (New York, 1931, 307-409.

24   See Helmut Richard Niebuhr, "Religious Realism in the Twentieth Century," in *Religious Realism*, 413-432. See also Niebuhr, *The Social Sources of Denominationalism* (New York, 1929), l-12, 248-258.

25   Morris Raphael Cohen, *American Thought. A Critical Sketch* (Glencoe, Ill.) 298-302.

26   See Rexford Tugwell, "Human Nature and Social Economy," *Journal of Philosophy*, 27 (1930) 449-557; 477-492. Rexford G. Tugwell and Leon H. Keyserling, *Redirecting Education* (New York, 1934), 33-l12. See also John Dewey, *Educational Frontiers* (New York, 1933), chapter II. See also Rexford Tugwell, *The Democratic Roosevelt. A Biography of Franklin D. Roosevelt* (Garden City, New York, 1957).

27   See works of Perry Miller.

28   Stephen Pfohl, *Death at the Parasite Café. Social Science (Fictions) & the Postmodern.* (New York, St. Martin's Press, 1992).

29   See Jonathan Kozol, *Savage Inequalities. Children in America's Schools* (New York, 1991) and Howard Zinn, Chapter 2, "Drawing the Color Line," *A People's History of the United States* (New York, Harper Perennial, 1980). The best contemporary study of manipulation of beliefs in the United States is Noam Chomsky, *Deterring Democracy* (New York, Hill and Wang, 1991, 1992).

30   Richard J. Herrnstein and Charles Murray, *The Bell Curve: Intelligence and Class Structure in American Life* (New York, The Free Press, 1994).

31   Claude S. Fischer, Michael Hout, Martin Sanchez Jankowski, Samuel R. Lucas, Ann Swidler, and Kim Voss, *Inequality by design. Cracking the Bell Curve Myth* (Princeton, N. J., Princeton University Press, 1996.)

32   Ibid., 18.

33   Ibid., 192.

33. La Guadalupe
Mexico and the Americas

Painting by Elaine Soto

34. La Virgen del Pozo
Puerto Rico
Painting by Elaine Soto

35. Black madonna, Erzulie
Haiti
Painting by Elaine Soto

36. Carito of Cuba
Painting by Elaine Soto

chapter ten

rise of dark others
United States in the 1960s

"God is black and is she pissed!"
—Berkeley bumper sticker, 1960s

In the 1960s, millions of people protested, demonstrated, and went on strike for a better world in Italy, France, Germany, Czechoslovakia, China, Japan, Australia, Africa, South America, and the United States. The revolutionary 60s in Italy have been analyzed in my *Liberazione della donna. Feminism in Italy.*[1] To evoke that watershed decade in the United States I have chosen a piece I wrote in 1970. The essay is based on primary documents of the San Francisco State student strike against racism and imperialist violence against dark others—epitomized in the U. S. war in Vietnam. Primary documents for this chapter are my notes as a participating striking professor as well as papers and leaflets of striking students. In the latter part of the chapter I have examined the historical backdrop and legacy of Mario Savio in the context of themes of this book. Mario was the sicilian/american student who became a catalyst of the Free Speech Movement at the University of California at Berkeley in 1964.

her story of the San Francisco State strike

Because the 60s have been analyzed by theorists who were not swept by the great hope, or by people who had regrets later, it is important that sources written at the time be relied on for an account of what, up to that time, may have been the most visionary and egalitarian decade in United States history. Mira is, of course, me. In 1970 when I wrote this, choosing a pseudonym that connotes observer, I was numb from having lived through the hope, and the crash of hope, at the end of the decade. To keep the authenticity of this primary document, I have not changed wording, or capitalization. Concluding the chapter is a note on the 1988 anniversary honoring strike participants for "courageous contributions to the development of the School of Ethnic Studies, San Francisco State University 1965-1970." And a note on my later thinking.

O

In 1970, fending off confrontation with self, she began a draft, "A few years after the Revolution, historians began compiling source materials on the Great Campus Uprisings." Sleepless one night, she typed another beginning, "At some point in the 60s, Mira's world view shattered."

Shattering, she realized, began during the 1964 Free Speech Movement at the University of California at Berkeley when Mario Savio inspired 800 students, including most of the students in her American Studies honors class, to occupy the administration building on the issue of free speech. And were jailed. Free speech, for students at the University of California at Berkeley in 1964, connoted the right to express opposition to racism and its global face, imperialism.

The passion of students' commitment had shaken her into writing, "The Unkempt Prophets of Berkeley."[2] Afterwards she taught U. S. history at San Francisco State while the country careened toward apocalypse punctuated by assassination. Faces of her students became etched on her consciousness. Some were to die in Vietnam, others were journeying to death of hope for their country, most were headed for heartbreak.

For a brief season Mira was able to navigate on the wave of hope created by helping to place an anti-racist, anti-imperialist political party on the ballot. On the way to a Peace and Freedom conference for Dick Gregory's independent presidential candidacy, the car in which she traveled, crashed. Charles Herrick, early spokesman for ecology, and editor of *The Modern Utopian*, was killed. Mira, asleep in the back seat, was critically hurt; she survived.

September 1968 she returned to teaching at San Francisco State. November 5, the nation elected Richard Nixon president. November 6, Black Student Union leaders called a strike against the institutionalized racism of admissions and curriculum policies of the college. The chairman of the history department inquired; she responded she would not cross the picket line against racism. In retrospect the cracking of her professional mind-set is apparent: she paid no prudential attention to the datum her tenure was to be decided the very week she went on strike along with a small ad hoc committee of professors. The sole striking professor in the history department, denial of tenure came immediately. The special delivery letter from S. I. Hayakawa, governor Ronald Reagan's appointee president of San Francisco State, arrived on Thanksgiving day, 1968.

The strike at State holds many meanings, but in the small of the night Mira knew that, for her, it would always evoke the memory of Chuck Koloms, graduate student in history who signed his letters "love, peace, freedom." Born in 1945, the year the U. S. dropped an atomic bomb on non-white people, Chuck volunteered in the 60s for Vista—the Kennedy program to assist subordinated groups. He opposed the war in Vietnam, set his bearded chin ("That's wrong!") against professorial apologetics for U. S. imperial policies, participated in the counter culture's festival of life at the democratic national convention in Chicago in 1968, and became spokesman for striking history students at State. In the spring of 1969, at a San Francisco intersection, Chuck was struck by a vehicle, and died at the age of twenty-four.

On the faculty-student dialogue day in December 1968, Chuck presented the position paper of history students. The history department had already passed resolutions opposing an open admissions policy, and calling for maximum police force on campus. History students analyzed the historical roots of the strike, censured "faculty indifference," "academic tower-sitting," and the "neither reasonable nor just authority" of the trustees. From the students' perspective, faculty unwillingness to face the underlying issue of racism was precipitating a revolutionary crisis. Students invited professors to join in building "a new community;" demands of the Black Students Union and the Third World Liberation Front were "self-evident" and "legitimate." College doors should be opened to everyone, higher education should be directed toward initiating rapid and responsible social and political change.

Mira listened to her colleagues respond. One professor dismissed the dead seriousness of strike demands by downgrading the diction of the Third World Student who had explained strike demands to his class. Another professor refuted the student statement that the crisis was revolutionary. Pulling rank, he pronounced, "There is no revolutionary situation because no Lenin has emerged." A Chicano student wondered aloud, "Lenin?" To direct questions posed by students, professors returned elegant, convoluted sentences on the paradoxes and ironies of the strike. Others disposed of strike demands by sending them back to "proper" bureaucratic channels, where they had weltered for eighteen months while student frustration mounted.

Mira noted that the dominant cognitive style of the professors was functional and operational, a style that bars the intrusion of ethical norms, and manages conflict by legitimizing the existing structure of power. The chairman of the history department gave a lecture on "professionalism:" follow established procedures, do one's "duty" as defined from above, accept given "realities." Faces of history students began to blanche. Mira felt an impulse of compassion for her professorial colleagues who could not help but notice the disintegration of their credibility, the erosion of student respect. A student asked the chairman of the history department, "Don't you have any standards of right and wrong?" She was reminded of Dick Gregory's saying, "It isn't a generation gap, it's a moral gap."

Recognizing she would have difficulties with an "objective" historical analysis, Mira fell back on her training. She'd kept boxes of documents during the strike. Notes she wrote shortly after the dialogue of professors and students revealed deepening despair, deepening anger of students. "December 1968. Afterwards, students gathered in the cafeteria to explore the realization that their professors seemed perfectly willing to teach classes indefinitely surrounded by police on a campus under martial law, amidst shrieks of students, community leaders, and ministers being beaten by police." The next day, a student who had asked, "Why can't they hear?". banged a trash can in classroom corridors to disrupt non-striking classes.

"Christmas season 1968 at S.F.State: Police again dispersed the students, this time with gunshots in the air, gunshots that resonated in the terror and despair of those who believe that if this crisis cannot be settled peaceably and equitably in a college community of 'enlightened' people, that it is unlikely that the crucial issues can be resolved in the United States without a bloodbath."

Mira found a December 1968 student handbill that suggests why Third World student demands at S.F.State expanded into a large movement encompassing all ethnic groups—becoming the longest campus struggle in U. S. history: "We have struck for these demands not because we are some kind of militant charity doing our best to help get a better education for our deprived black brothers....We support the strike because what they want, we want too. We are tired of being assimilated in the culture of the blue people: police, puppets, trustees, corporations, and racist legislators and politicians....What we learn in class is how to adopt their viewpoint, how to solve their problems, how to run their errands, how to create ourselves in their image. We want an education that teaches us the true history and real situation of our communities so that we can go back to them to serve them, and if need be, to lead our people in revolution. We are the majority of the poor, the majority of the plastic and alienated, the majority of the Americans wasted in Vietnam."

A January 1969 editorial in the student newspaper *Open Process* put the strike at S. F. State in the context of late 60s campus uprisings throughout the United States. "Colleges are not enlightened or rational places. Their existence reinforces the same social conditions that have always governed our lives—racism, social stratification, poverty, injustice, violence….The article probed student alienation: "If he can't 'adjust' to the prevailing cultural standards of society he'll spend most of his time in school being told that his own cultural standards and his own experiences aren't legitimate, unless, of course, they're redefined and fed back to him in 'acceptable form' by some patronizing, smart-ass professor."

S. I. Hayakawa, the Reagan appointee sent to "clean up the mess at State," described striking students as mindless nihilists. Mira found a remarkable degree of self-awareness. A student reflected, "Unable to control their own education, they are alienated from it; alienated from it they find it is irrelevant to their needs. Instead of enlightened men and women, they are helpless pawns in a huge game of fear, authoritarianism, manipulation, exploitation, personal fragmentation and individual isolation."

Early in January 1969, the hundred or so professors on strike since November were joined by other members of the American Federation of Teachers, Local 1352. Among the anomalies of the AFT strike at State, professors not only endangered their jobs by striking, they continued teaching. After a day on the picket line, striking students turned in papers that were due and striking professors read them. An essay, "On Revolution," written by Claire in January conveyed searing dilemmas.

"I have spent the best part of this semester

thinking about revolution.
'You say you want a revolution.
Well, you know, we all want to change the world.'
....
Is there going to be a revolution? Or, has it already begun?"

"When I was nineteen," wrote Claire, "I fell in love with Prince Peter Kropotkin. I love his supreme humanity and I want to believe in his revolution, spontaneous, joyous, a revolution of life not death. Bakunin was a creep by comparison, but who was right?" Ethical self-examination followed: "Can I kill someone? In self-defense? . I spend a lot of time trying to figure out how to get the police helicopter without killing anyone. It would be relatively easy to shoot it down with a high-powered rifle, but anyone aboard almost certainly would have been killed. Maybe next semester...if they begin firing on crowds."

Claire's revolutionary hope—visibly influenced by the Beat Poet Diane Di Prima ("We are not alone: we have brothers in all the hills. We have sisters in the jungles and in the Ozarks....They gather arms. They multiply.")—plunged into despair in late January when hundreds of strikers, peaceably assembled, were entrapped and arrested. "The number to call in San Francisco is 552-2811, Jerry Parrish Bail Bonds, pay 10% and feed the hand that shoots you."

Non-striking professors accused striking students of not knowing history. On the contrary, papers of striking students were steeped in history. Claire wrote: "My husband thinks I think like 6 million dead Jews, Gypsies and social nonconformists....I still remember the closed boxcars crossing in the night and I see no refuge, none, no escape, no avoidance....It's easy to go underground—you just cut your hair and shave your beard and change your skin to approved, standardized medium ivory."

Claire thought about her own ethnic heritage: "Can you imagine what Irish women lived with for so long, all their men that were worth anything dead before they were thirty? Birthing and raising sons to be martyrs and daughters to be widows?.... Did you know IRA meant Irish Republican Army or Irish Revolutionary Army interchangeably?"

"I want to change the world. Can I? Are we just one generation after another pushing the rock of progress up a hill so it can roll down and give the next generation something to do? Have we gotten anywhere? Haymarket, cossacks, agents provocateurs, Black & Tan, red flags, torture, tyrants, mangled bodies, dead souls. The study of history teaches us that the study of history doesn't teach us....Give you everything I've got for a little peace of mind."

The history teacher hoped that Claire's essay "On Revolution" might be found by a post-revolution archivist because the student had listed her "sources" in the bibliography:

John Lennon, *Revolution*
I Ching
Louise Pauwels and Jacques Bergier, *Morning of the Magicians*
Diane di Prima, *Revolutionary Letters*
W. B. Yeats, *Easter, 1916*
Tommy Makem, *Freedom's Sons*
John Lennon, *I'm So Tired*

Mira wrote a political analysis for a local newspaper. "At San Francisco State, an unprecedented alignment is being formed.of professors and students, of the American Federation of Teachers and off-campus unions, of Third World students and community groups, of Third World and white students...." Spring 1969 the strike was settled—equivocally. Dan planted a tree for Chuck at the speaker's podium at State and another in People's Park Annex in Berkeley.

The atmosphere in the immediate aftermath of the strike is suggested in the journal of the English Students Union. Ernie's prose-poem, "From Ghosts to Fists," traced a path from English major to revolutionary, revealing that, for some, revolutionary commitment deepened after the strike "settlement." .I saw how culture embedded people with fence-straddling by bathing them in continual ambiguities so you never had to take a stand or take a risk or take a chance…and they told you to take all sides into consideration and keep your objectivity while they hid the side of the people who were getting stomped on…and the strike brought out the hidden side.

> 50% of the men from California killed in Vietnam are Chicano.
>
> Over 50% of the kids in public schools in San Francisco are Third World and less than 10% go to State College.
>
> 80% of the people in California prisons are Third World.

Ernie remembered childhood comic books "racist to the core" and racism at S. F. State: "and when you brought up the question of racism, people preferred not to look at it and a flunky Tom…became a national hero…he could say 'the most exciting day of my life' while Dave Gordon was in the hospital in critical condition, they had to take out his spleen…"

He described a battle at State: "…dark blue moved slowly towards us…slowly closed in…we held our ground hundreds of us and then began to move back slowly steady together…and later turning up Holloway the mounted horses chasing us…and later that night at the mass meeting we packed the church to overflow and the next day we marched around the campus in the thousands…."

"I understood," said Ernie, that "the greatest moments in life are people standing up together and fighting back and struggling, people from two on up struggling either about staying together or splitting up or struggling over a friendship and most of all struggling against the State."

In his piece, "Amy's Boss," Ernie caught a revealing conversation:

> "You in school?"
> "Yeah."

312 • *dark mother*

"Where?"

"State." His eyes narrowed.

"You one of them people causing all that trouble?"

"I'm on strike if that's what you mean."

He sipped his coffee.

"I want to tell you something, buddy.

I have three rifles in my office.

You should get one yourself."

He sipped his coffee.

"Learn to use it. Because when the time

comes, me and plenty like me are gonna

use ours on you, and we shoot good."

Later the district attorney said, "Guys like you should be gassed." "Sounds German to me," said Ernie. The state exercised violence, he thought, while controlling a public education that taught people to be "sensitive cowards and romantic weaklings" encouraging "the scabs' MeMeMe." The strike at State had revealed that "freedom of speech" was "fastened to a fist that when you come right down to it gives nothing and hunts, jails, exiles, and kills all who oppose it."

While people were saying "how we were destroying the schools" we were "actually building them up and opening them up because to cure a body you have to cut away a lot of skin...ripping back the veil of 'education' and pulling up the nerve endings of racism, exposing them, fighting them."

The post-strike situation was assessed by a leader of the Black Student Union: "Since the end of the strike last March and the withdrawal of the 600 stormtroopers, S.F.State has been transformed into a fascist enclave in a suburban desert, a concentration camp decorated with a tam-o-shanter instead of barbed wires." A spreading pattern of "fascism" was visible in tanks in Berkeley during the People's Park struggle, in killing and jailing of Panthers...." S.F.State was becoming "a model for fascist control of educational institutions throughout the country."

"This kind of fascist control," said the black student leader, "depended on maintaining traditional college forms while concentrating power in the hands of appointees who doled out an occasional carrot to insurgent groups to maintain the illusion of freedom, while keeping the bulk of the campus population under control by manipulating various forms of 'fear of reprisal.'"

Mira received letters from students in jail. Paul, leader of the Asian American Political Association, was sentenced to five months incarceration for "disturbing the peace." In his letter of January 1970, Paul wrote, "State is dead, strangling in its own blood....The spirit that seemed to give State a unique quality not often found in a large state-supported institutions has departed."

Paul left an epitaph for the strike at S. F. State: "Through the ignorance and stupidity that seems to be the history of man, there are the rare brilliant flashes when people for a few moments are able to come together to plant a seed of hope....Unfortunately these seeds have fallen onto barren ground...."

The student's revolutionary beliefs remained intact. "The institutions that are in existence now are temporary and will fall....The old slavemaster will laugh no more." Sadness lined revolutionary belief: "Little comfort to those who are oppressed today. No words or prophecies can feed an empty stomach, give life back to the body that lies crumpled on the ground." "Yet", said Paul, "If I had to do it over again I'm pretty certain, I would do it the same way."

Her last day of teaching at State, Mira gave a packet of seeds to each of her students. "Paul's letter from jail said that last year's seeds fell on barren ground. Some one else reminds us, all of the flowers of all the tomorrows are in the seeds of today. Tomorrow...."3

Lucille Birnbaum. 1970

O

In 1978, Louisa Calio wrote "Children of the Sixties:"

Born on a soil already ravaged, defiled and scraped
Of its fecundity
We
The homeless children of sinning parents
Bear on our heads the marks

Of three centuries of racism, oppression, and greed.

Into the mouth of the monster we rode
Head on
Aching with fear and desire
Trying to escape our fates
We journeyed west
Stomping through ancient Indian burial grounds
Retracing our roots.

Lost in a mad fury
We raced Helter Skelter
Hitting the Pacific
Hurling ourselves East
Hoping to be born again.

We opened our eyes to a newer vision
Electronically alive with hallucinogenic wisdom:
We were rootless, boundless and free
We believed.[4]

O

[In October 1988, I wrote an afterword to my 1970 essay.]

Almost twenty years later, it seems to me that one meaning of the 1960s was that it was a decade of crisis in identity, and belief, not only in the United States but around the world. Implicit in confrontations of 1968 in the U. S., France, Italy, Czeckoslovakia, and China, Africa, and elsewhere were the questions "Who am I?" "What kind of country do I live in?" "What kind of world do I want?"

In the United States the truth of third world students' demand for their own history resonated in the consciousness of other ethnic groups. After 1968, my career in teaching foreshortened by being fired at San Francisco State, I was free to travel frequently to Italy. Convergence of moral, ethnic, feminist, and political values is evident in the book I researched in the 1970s and wrote in the 1980s, *Liberazione della donna. Feminism in Italy.*[5] "Offering a mirror to other women's movements, feminists of Italy have drawn on a long history for their vision of a new society where terrorists 'of all types' throw away arms and abuse gives way to respect for the beauty and diversity of human life."

My need to understand the connection between religious and political beliefs pulled me to write *Dark Wheat and Red Poppies: Women and Italian Socialism, a Study in Popular Beliefs.*[6] [editorial note: Dark Wheat became *Black Madonnas. Feminism, religion, and politics in Italy*, (1993, 1997, 2000)]. The shattered world view described at the beginning of the 1970 essay is being replaced by an emerging multicultural vision. My search for an Italian component for multiculturalism in the United States adopts a radical use of the ethnic consciousness that I learned in the 60s, probably from African American and other Third World students.

In a provocative essay, "red, a little white, a lot of green, on a field of pink,"[7] I upturned conventional categories of "western civilization" courses. Instead of a "high culture" emphasis on the Graeco-Roman heritage and the Renaissance—justifiably criticized by Third World students who point to the narrowness of the euro-centered curriculum, and by feminists who note male dominance in classical and renaissance cultures—my design for an Italian contribution to a multicultural canon for the United States suggested (a) relevance of Mediterranean history, (b) folklore of Africa and Asia as well as folklore of Europe, (c) 20th century writings of the Italian political left, particularly world war two resistance to nazis and fascists, (d) postwar Italian literature and film focusing on the other, (e) "unedited" interpretation of hebrew scriptures and the christian bible, and an unedited understanding of marxism, today called liberation theology, (f) signs of a new civilization discernible in writings of independent nonviolent radicals, and (g) vision and work of Italian, and other, feminists for a new world."

[In 1997 I wrote another afterword to my 1970 essay.]

Rereading this after three decades I am struck by the suppressions of memory. I wonder why I did not mention what seems strikingly significant to me today—the rise in the 1960s of Africa in the consciousness not only of african americans, but in the consciousness of all the diverse people who were forming an american counter culture. We wore afro hair styles, liked african textiles (I remember I danced in a dress of african cloth in 1969), we carried amulets of the african carthaginian dark mother Tanit."

—Lucia Chiavola Birnbaum, Berkeley, April 1997

Mario Savio, sicilian/american radical

[In May 1997 I presented a paper to the conference of the American Italian Historical Association, "The Lost World of Italian American Radicalism. Labor, Politics, and Culture," whose concluding session was a memorial to Mario Savio.][8]

The memory of 22-year old Mario Savio in Sproul Plaza at the University of California at Berkeley in the fall of 1964—in that halcyon time when many of us hoped to change the world—is lined with the pain of his death in November 1996. And also lined with a need to understand why, after Martin Luther King, Jr. and Malcolm X, Mario Savio seems to me to have embodied the transformative 1960s.

In the fall of 1964, I was a lecturer in History and American Studies at the University of California at Berkeley, and participant/observer of Free Speech Movement demonstrations. My students, a sophomore honors class in American Studies, participated in the uprisings that opened the University of California at Berkeley to freedom of speech. In 1965, deeply moved, I wrote "The Unkempt Prophets of Berkeley."[9]

After 1965 I had a few intense conversations with Mario, once when he wanted to discuss my research in Italy, once in the 80s when he was about to leave for Italy, where he had been invited to speak at a Festa dell'Unità. I've looked into his papers at Bancroft library at UCB, attended the session, "Mario Savio and the 1960s," at the 1997 conference of the Organization of American Historians, and discussed Mario with my long-time friend, Reginald Zelnik, professor of history at the University of California, Berkeley, who knew him better than anyone on campus. Zelnik considers Mario Savio an american radical more influenced by Henry David Thoreau than by european left theorists, including Antonio Gramsci, whom he did not read until the 70s.

Was Mario Savio an italian/american radical? Because ethnic identification, after the 60s, has been critically important to me, I would like to think so. My consciousness that I am a sicilian/american woman has molded my recent life and informed my scholarly research and writing.[10] Yet in the early 60s african americans were the only minority (whom I remember) who publicly expressed ethnic consciousness. Ethnic awareness in other americans existed, but open and public declarations of ethnic consciousness of other minority groups followed that of african americans; e.g., the American Italian Historical Association was not founded until 1966. It was not, Gil Fagiani reminds us, until the 1980s that Mario said in public, "I am a Sicilian American."[11]

In the early 60s, Mario seemed to have been motivated by what was then called the Negro Civil Rights movement. Recent scholarship places the Free Speech Movement at the University of California at Berkeley in the historical context of african american voter registration in the south and early 60s' demonstrations for equal job opportunity in San Francisco. Mario participated in both, loaning weight to the view that the immediate backdrop to the Free Speech Movement was the african american struggle. The precipitating variable in the eruption of the Free Speech Movement was the UC administration's ban on campus political tables whose leaflets opposing racism demanded better working conditions for chicano farm workers.

Arthur Gatti, who knew Mario in high school and accompanied him on a catholic-sponsored mission to help the poor in Mexico, has told us that in the 50s, Mario was a devout catholic. By 1964 he had come out of the church. Although his activities against racism and inequality in the United States resemble those of Father James Groppi[12], italian/american catholic priest who worked against racism in the 60s, the roots of Mario's radicalism seem to me deeper—and more ancient—than catholicism.

In my view, for Mario and the 800 students arrested on the issue of freedom to express deep beliefs, it was the subordinate condition of african americans that sparked identification and fervent protest. Discussing this with my Berkeley women's study group, another italian/american woman said it was Martin Luther King who inspired her in the 60s. Neither the history of radicalism in Italy nor italian/american radicalism in the 20th century seem to have molded Mario Savio—or other italian/american radicals of the 1960s. The education we had received in U. S. schools left out everyone's history except that of white anglo-saxon protestants. Pre-world war one italian/american (and other) radicalism was effectively suppressed by government raids in 1919 and by executions of Sacco and Vanzetti in the late 20s. During world war two, relocation of italian/americans as possible subversives "iced" italian/american culture, as Lawrence DiStasi tells us.[13] After 1945, the era when Mario was growing up, U.S. official anti-communism branded anything threatening to hegemonic white male elites…from grassroots democracy, populism, to free speech, as communist. This successful use of conditioning techniques in the 20th century in the United States, explored in a previous chapter of this book, is a striking example of how well male elites have learned to use techniques of enlightened behaviorist social control.

Trying to understand how Mario became a symbol of student radicalism of the 60s, I have thought about my own itinerary from somewhat conformist italian/american scholar to radical of the 60s. A generation older than Mario, we both retrieved our italian names in the period, 1960-1970. When he graduated from high school, Robert Mario Savio chose to become Mario Savio. After I was fired in 1970 for participating in the strike against racism and imperialism at San Francisco State, I replaced Lucille with the name on my birth certificate, Lucia. Retrieving my name, in my case, meant that I wanted to be identified as a sicilian/american woman scholar/activist. It is unclear what Mario's decision to be known by his italian name meant.

Yet I was a radical of the 60s before I retrieved my italian name…supporting the civil rights movement of african americans, the free speech movement at the University of California, the movement against the war in Vietnam, helping to found the anti-racist, anti-imperialist Peace & Freedom Party in 1967, participating in the San Francisco State strike against racism and the Vietnam war in 1968. My radicalism of the 60s emerged, insofar as I can track it, from living in the United States at a point in history when the disparity between the country's rhetoric, whose history I had closely studied in graduate school, and the reality of injustice and poverty of submerged groups, notably african americans, became intolerable. Igniting my radicalism was the completion in 1964 of my doctoral dissertation on social control of dark others (discussed in the previous chapter), a ten-year project researching institutionalized racism in the social sciences in the United States, just as the african american struggle was reaching fever intensity, and the free speech movement at Cal burst into flame.

Not until after 1969, when I had been fired at San Francisco State and gone to Italy in search of my roots, did I learn there was a very relevant radical, indeed revolutionary, tradition in Italy, and a contemporary italian revolutionary movement that included a passionate feminism. The revolutionary fervor I discovered in Italy after 1969 was associated with a liberation theology that resonated for me—an unedited theology inspiring social activism that combined writings of hebrew prophets, christian gospels, and what italians call "unedited marxism." Arthur Gatti has told us that in the early 60s Mario was aware of the liberation theology then emerging in Latin America and in Italy. Yet liberation theology does not seem to exhaust the "why" of Mario's radicalism. Nor, as my books since 1969 suggest, the deep "why" of my own radicalism.

To support his premise that Mario was an american radical, Reg Zelnik has referred me to a paper Mario wrote (which I cannot find) entitled, "Why I am not a marxist." Karl Marx said something similar. This document, it seems to me, must be put in the context of marxism as it was then understood in the United States, when official anti-communism put marxism in opposition to religion. In Italy, in contrast, marxism in the 60s was associated with the openings to the poor that pope John XXIII created, openings known as liberation theology. The passion of the revolutionary generation of 1968 in Italy, analyzed in my *Liberazione della donna*, was an explosive amalgam of unedited judeo-christianity and "marxismo inedito."[14]

Central to understanding italian marxism is Antonio Gramsci, 20th century sardinian marxist theorist who widened the meaning of exploitation beyond economics to encompass negation of cultures of subordinated peoples, or dark others. Founder of the italian communist party, Gramsci early pointed to the racism of northern italians who considered southern italians ignorant dark others, a racism that informed the premises of the early italian socialist party. Mario did not read Gramsci until the 70s. Did he know that in the late 60s that left wing catholics were at the forefront of marxist revolutionary activity in Italy? Or that in the 80s italian feminists placed two significant codicils into policy documents of the italian communist party: religious/spiritual beliefs take priority over politics; nonviolence is the way to socialism. Or that contemporary italian leftists consider racism the first barrier to overcome in the work to create a just world?

Mario Savio clearly identified with the strategy of nonviolent civil disobedience, but he seems to have learned nonviolent civil disobedience not from Thoreau, but from african americans in the Student Nonviolent Coordinating Committee when he went south in the early 60s to help with voter registration. Did he know the writings of Aldo Capitini, italian nonviolence theorist of the 60s, who looked to secular as well as to religious prophets, a perspective that has shaped the contemporary nonviolence consciousness of italians, including that of the italian left?

There is the matter of ultimate beliefs. Mikhail Bakhtin, russian theorist of popular culture, stated that during periods of upheaval, or celebration, a great rush of deep beliefs from the unconscious rises to the surface. Deep beliefs, in my considered opinion, inspired 60s demonstrations, not only in the United States, but around the world .We know little about deep beliefs, but their transmission seems to have more to do with a mother's lullabies, a family's remembered history, and early childhood experience, than with reading books later. What cannot be dismissed from the attempt to understand Mario Savio's radicalism is that he was a sicilian/american in the United States when white anglo protestant culture was hegemonic. I do not know if he knew about Sacco and Vanzetti as an upwardly mobile italian/american child (who became an Eagle Scout), but we do know that Mario's mother taught her children that racial discrimination is wrong, and that his father is careful to identify the family's origin as Sicily, not Italy.

Sicily, historically, was an oppressed colony of Greece, Rome, northern Europe, and northern Italy. In the modern era, the Kingdom of the Two Sicilies, based at Naples and Palermo, comprised the regions of south Italy and Sicily, whence the majority of italian migrants to the U. S. came at the end of the 19th and beginning of the 20th centuries. Northern italian denigration of southern italians continued in the United States. Elites of the dominant white male protestant culture of the U. S. categorized italian americans, in the late 19th and early 20th centuries—period of brutal racism toward african americans—as "people of color."

Sicilians were the pre-eminent dark others among the "new immigrants"—italians, jews, slavs, other south europeans—in the early 20th century when the dominant white male political elite of the U. S. expanded the nation into an empire by subjugating dark others in the Caribbean and the Pacific, and looked, at home, for methods of social control of dark others. White social control of dark others—ranging from intelligence testing to public education for "americanization"—remained in place until the 1960s, when the consensus of racism toward dark others—abetted in the 20th century by upwardly mobile white ethnics—began to unravel.

Unraveling was evident in papers my American Studies honors students turned into me on December 2, 1964, the day they were arrested. In their papers, even more in their actions, students of all ethnic groups—including the young of the dominant wasp culture—identified with dark peoples of negated cultures of the United States, a nation, they were coming to realize, built on genocide of native americans, slavery of african americans, exploitation of the labor of latin americans, asian americans, south europeans, subordination of women, and suppression of dissenters.

Consciously identifying with dark others, the passion for justice of my students in an honors class at the University of California at Berkeley heretically exceeded conventional patriotic and religious boundaries. Students scored racist hypocrisies of the founding fathers of the United States along with bureaucratic hypocrisies of liberals of the U. C. administration. Remembering the long line of crushed martyrs of world history, students the same age as Mario identified with african americans and with jews in the nazi holocaust.[15] Mario's papers during the Free Speech Movement held overtones of apocalypse; one was entitled, "The End of History." Although FSM leaflets were models of logic and learning, the word hypocrisy, in Mario's and other students' papers, kept rising, from what seems to be deep strata of belief.

Some decades ago when I was an "intellectual historian," I might have written a paper on Mario Savio that traced his intellectual antecedents to Giordano Bruno of Naples, burned at the stake for his hermetic/cabalistic belief that the most ancient and true religion was that of Africa.[16] Today Giordano Bruno's statue as a free speech martyr hovers over political demonstrations of the left in Rome in the Campo di Fiori.

Yet neither Giordano Bruno for submerged south italian religious beliefs, nor Antonio Gramsci for italian marxism, nor Vito Marcantonio, italian/american congressman of the 1950s from italian Harlem—who insisted that freedom means inclusion of all points of view, including that of communists—apparently influenced Mario Savio.[17] Discarding that favorite verb of intellectual historians, I have come to the conclusion that Mario's radicalism was not influenced by anyone, that his radicalism may have emerged from a well of deep unverbalized beliefs that Mario shared with Giordano Bruno, Antonio Gramsci, Vito Marcantonio, sicilian peasants, and contemporary italian leftists.

To understand my hypothesis of Mario's deep unverbalized beliefs, we may need to go beyond Italy and beyond the recent experience of italian/americans, farther back in time, to Africa, where life began, to prehistoric migrations out of Africa that early arrived in Sicily, and to african migrants bringing their beliefs in the dark mother with them to every continent of the earth after 50,000 BCE.[18]. To understand nonverbal beliefs in justice and equality held by common peoples of the earth from time immemorial—what Gramsci calls the "buon senso"of all peoples—we may need to enlarge memory beyond cognition to bodily resonance. This is the bodily resonance, I am often reminded by young people, that one feels instantaneously when listening to african or african/american music...music that transmits the memory of the african dark mother who nurtured all living creatures in a harmonious universe, a memory that survives, in the folklore and rituals of the world.[19]

We may need to remember that Mario was born in December, winter solstice month of the african dark mother Isis of many names, whose hebrew name was Miriam, whose christian name was Maria—name, in male equivalence, that Mario carried. To understand the particular geographical context of Mario's beliefs in justice and equality, we should remember, with Mario's father, that the origin of the family was Sicily. Ancestors of sicilians were africans, blended later with african descendants in west Asia, and african descendants in Europe from regions later called Germany, France, Scandinavia, Spain, and north Italy, whose bedding and/or wedding of our grandmothers lightened the skin of dark others of south Italy and Sicily.

When Mario Savio said in the 1980s that he was a sicilian/american he may have been referring to knowing that to be a sicilian is to have been a dark other from the beginnings of the common era to the late 19th century when sicilian immigrants came to the U. S. To be a conscious sicilian/american, in my view, means knowing that yours is the history of a conquered and oppressed people who yet preserved—in their images of black madonnas, stories, rituals, vendor songs, and exclamations—a deep memory of the harmonious age of the dark mother, and a deep hope for a just world.

Mario's defining characteristic may have been that he held a deep belief in justice and equality for the subordinated, the negated, the poor. His early participation in the struggle of african americans was followed by the free speech movement when he became a martyr, in effect, of freedom to express beliefs. Later, a lecturer in physics at California State University at Sonoma, he braided his hair in chinese peasant style, and worked to help the poor. He died the day after the November 1996 California election whose outcome was a set-back to his work against the anti-immigration law aimed at poor mexican workers. The day before his heart stopped, he met with the president of Sonoma State College to urge lower tuition for poor students.

What is Mario Savio's legacy as a sicilian/american radical ? Not, in my view, a narrow italian/american ethnicity, but a remembering of all of our ancestors—primordial africans, west asian hebrews of african origin, moors of Africa, and northern and southern europeans who were, also, ultimately african in genetic origin.

Bypassing easy notions of ethnicity in a world whose history is that of very complex migrations from Africa, authentic sicilian/american radicalism, in my view, is grounded on a complex story. During the inquisition (1480 to the 18th century) moorish minarets and jewish synagogues were forcibly turned into christian churches. A synagogue-turned-church where my grandmothers prayed, located a few yards from my family's ancestral home in Ragusa Ibla, has provoked me to wonder—after the african dark mother of everyone—were my grandmothers jews or moors or christians?

To be a sicilian/american radical means, in my case, being conscious of my african origin and my multicultural inheritance of many dark others—not only peoples of darker skin of Africa and Asia, but dark others perceived as threatening to ruling white male elites—women, jews, moors, heretics, et al. Perhaps being a sicilian/american radical means a deep knowing—a knowing ultimately located in the DNA energy we inherit from our mothers—that we are dark others, whose origin is Africa. This knowing is deepened by learning from history that our ancestral inheritance also includes the lighter-skinned northern invaders and persecutors (also ultimately african), who raped or married our grandmothers.

A sicilian/american consciousness means, in my view, working for justice for everyone. Perhaps Reginald Zelnik is correct: Mario was an american radical, more precisely a sicilian/american radical, who carried the yet unfulfilled american promise of "liberty and justice for all" beyond the manipulative rhetoric of the dominant few, to freedom of deep belief—so that the promise can come true.

Lucia Chiavola Birnbaum
Primo maggio 1997
Berkeley, California

Notes

1   Lucia Chiavola Birnbaum, *Liberazione della donna. Feminism in Italy* (Middletown, Ct., Wesleyan University Press, 1986, 1988).

2   Lucille Terese Birnbaum, "Unkempt Prophets of Berkeley," *issue: those who make the waves* (Berkeley, University Church Council, 1965). Reprinted in *renewal,* Oct.-Nov., 1965.

3   Letter to author. The best analysis of the San Francisco State strike was written by a leading student participant: William Barlow, *End to Silence. The San Francisco State Strike* (New York, Pegasus, 1970). A good account of the student movement at the University of California, Berkleley, flawed by retrospecive cynicism, is David Lance Goines, *The Free Speech Movement. Coming of Age in the 1960s* (Berkeley, Ten Speed Press, 1993).

4   Louisa Calio, *In the Eye of Balance* (Manhasset Hills, New York, Paradiso Press, 1978).

5   Middletown, Ct., Wesleyan University Press, 1986, American Book Award of the Before Columbus Foundation, 1987, paperback edition 1988.

6   November, 1993. *Black Madonnas. Feminism, religion, and politics in Italy* (Boston, Northeastern University Press, 1993).Bari, Palomar Editrice 1997, Salerno, Premio Internazionale di Saggistica, 1998, iUniverse edition, 2000.

7   "red, a little white, a lot of green, on a field of pink: a controversial design for an Italian component of a multicultural canon for the United States," *From the Margin. Voices in Italian Americana,* edited by Anthony J. Tamburri, Paolo A. Giordano, Fred L. Gardaphe, Purdue University Press, 1989).

8   The international conference sponsored by the John D. Calandra Institute of Italian American Culture and the Graduate Program of the City University of New York in May 14-15, 1997 may be regarded as a marking point when italian/americans came out of defensiveness to claim their radical tradition, replacing upward mobility to "white" with solidarity with peoples of colors, a theme continued in the November 1997 conference of the American Italian Historical Association, Cleveland, Ohio. "Encounters in black and white. "

9   Lucille Terese Birnbaum, "The Unkempt Prophets of Berkeley," Loc. Cit.

10   Birnbaum, *Liberazione della donna.* Loc Cit.. Birnbaum, *Black Madonnas.* Loc. Cit.

11   Gil Fagiani, "A Memorial to Mario Savio," Conference, The Lost World of Italian American Radicalism, City University of New York, New York City, Loc. Cit.

12   See Jackie Di Salvo, "Father James Groppi: Portrait of a 1960s Radical," in session, "A Continuing Tradition," conference, Lost World of Italian American Radicalism, Loc. Cit.

13   Lawrence DiStasi, "How World War II Iced Italian American Culture," *MultiAmerica. Essays in Cultural Wars and Cultural Peace,* edited by Ishmael Reed (New York, Viking, 1997) See. Also, Lawrence DiStasi, *Una Storia Segreta. The Secret History of Italian American Evacuation and Internment during World War II* (2001).

14   Birnbaum, *Liberazione della donna.* Loc. Cit.

15   Birnbaum, "The Unkempt Prophets of Berkeley," Loc. Cit.

16   See Frances A. Yates, *Giordano Bruno and the Hermetic Tradition* (Chicago, University of Chicago Press, 1964)

17   See chapter 8, this book.

18   See chapter l, this book.

19   See Carlo Ginzburg, *Ecstasies. Deciphering the Witches; Sabbath.* Tr., R Rosenthal (New York, Pantheon Books, 1991).

chapter eleven

godmothers and others
Italy and the "uncruel revolution"

"Today we can speak of a spiritual revolution that consists in our confronting what is partially hidden, putting it back into the current of history."
                              —Luisa Muraro, *L'Ordine simbolico della madre*

This chapter suggests a spiral view of life and of history. Not the unilinear progression of western modernism, but the spiral dance in processions of black madonnas—two steps backward before going forward, two steps backward before going forward....

The spiral theory of history is appropriate to Sicily as a metaphor for Italy in the last decade. The 1995 book, *Midnight in Sicily*, conveyed steps backward into deep darkness—revelations that right wing politicians had been in collusion with the mafia in "extortion, drugs, kidnapping, torture, murder and terrorism...[with] links to international secret services, America, corrupt financiers, and the Vatican."[1]

Yet, at the edge of the darkness, it was possible to see signs of dawn. One was the nonviolence movement—perhaps the most telling sign that the memory of the dark mother is alive today in Italy, and everywhere that people believe that nonviolence is the way to a genuinely green earth verdant with justice and human rights. In part, nonviolence in Italy is a reaction to the 1970s when some of Italy's young left pushed for violent revolution, yet nonviolence is the theme of thousands of contemporary italian initiatives concerned to nurture, not destroy, the earth and all its creatures, and to give birth to a culture of peace characterized by justice, dialogue, cooperation, and a pluralism of faiths and cultures.[2]

Contemporary nonviolence in Italy has been articulated, for the most part, by men, but nonviolent men were nurtured by italian peasant mothers who throughout the patriarchal era nonviolently resisted the violence of church and state. In the 1960s, Aldo Capitini, antifascist and religious reformer, became convinced that institutional religion could not by itself confront the violence of both sides of the cold war. He looked to hebrew prophets, Jesus, Buddha, saint Francis, Mazzini, and Gandhi for an "open religion" grounded on active nonviolence that identified with the poor and humiliated of the earth.

Nonviolence for Capitini, and the activists he has inspired, is a critical strategy that can subvert an unjust society. Nonviolence understood as not killing, not collaborating with injustice, not obeying laws that do not respect the dignity, and interests of everyone. Born in Perugia, outside Assisi, city of of saint Francis, Capitini looked to the spontaneity of festivals when the desire for a new, and as yet unimagined, society can be felt. This society was one that i nonni (grandparents) remembered in stories and celebrated in festivals. We can feel this society, said Capitini, when we tell the truth and when we resist injustice nonviolently.[3] Compresenza, is Capitini's word for a vision of a new time that encompasses the past, the present, and the future, and embraces the dead, the living, all sentient creatures, and the unborn.

Nonviolence activists met at the University of Florence in January 1993 to found a national school to educate people in strategies of conscientious objection and nonviolent defense, bonding these strategies with nonviolent resistance to the mafia, work for human rights, and nonviolent intervention in places where human rights are violated. In Italy, as elsewhere, nonviolence movements remember the values of the civilization of the ancient dark mother of Africa, values echoed by grandmothers in the world's subordinated cultures, as well as by Buddha, saint Francis, Tolstoi, Gandhi, Martin Luther King, Aldo Capitini, the Dalai Lama, Paolo Freire, Nelson Mandela, Simone Weil, and contemporary womanists and earth-bonded feminists of the world.

Azione Nonviolenta, journal of the movement in Italy, analyzes the economic disparity between peoples of the north and south of the world, but avoids labels. Economic democracy, attained nonviolently, is considered the necessary way station to a culture of peace. The harmonious civilization of the ancient dark mother is evoked by experimenting inside grottoes with sounds of reeds, walnuts, and pebbles, but tasks are here and now. Nonviolence activists have founded hostels for dark-skinned migrants, schools to teach the philosophies of Tolstoi and Gandhi, and summer nonviolence camps celebrating the beauty of shared work. The pacifist practice of fasting is combined with performance politics in the streets to encourage dialogue between different ethnic and cultural groups.

Italian nonviolence does not identify with traditional passive pacifism—which is regarded as historically having supported the status quo and the interests of dominant powers—but insists on activism for human rights and democracy as indispensable to peace. The major avatar of democracy in the contemporary world is regarded critically; *Azione Nonviolenta* has published national security documents of the United States that describe the poor dark peoples of the south of the globe as a menace to the interests of first world countries. Scoring theorists and spokesmen of U. S. foreign policy for inciting more exploitation, more destruction of nature, and prostitution of personal dignity to attain power, *Azione Nonviolenta* stated that U. S. actions, exemplified in the first Gulf war of the 90s, point to a world in which the west must safeguard its high consumption of petroleum to the point of mounting a spectacle in which bombs are proclaimed "intelligent" while they kill hundreds of people. "Invoking the principle of possession, nobody can interfere with those countries of the West who already consume four-fifths of the world's resources."[4]

Consciously antifascist, antimilitarist, and antiracist, *Azione nonviolenta* supported the May 7, 1995 international demonstration of nonviolence in Germany whose symbols, recalled the dark mother—triangles made of flowers representing the people nazis put to death as dark others: jews, gypsies, and political dissenters.[5] Aligning nonviolence with deep ecology, the nonviolence journal asked Arne Naess, norwegian alpinist, to explain mature ecosystems. Humans, living in an equilibrium of a myriad of different living species, said Naess, should live with, not work against, this equilibium. Naess hopes that the power of nonviolent direct action can rapidly transform the world.[6]

O

The contemporary women's movement in Italy, as I have suggested in previous books, may be the midwife of transformation in that country. A sicilian perspective on the italian women's movement is offered by *mezzocielo*, journal in Palermo that crosses political parties to oppose violence. Founded by Simona Mafai, daughter of a jewish mother and an italian catholic father, she became a partisan during world war two at the age of fifteen. After the war she was given the task of typing Gramsci's prison notebooks. Later, as feminist communist senator from Sicily, she carried the 1978 bill legalizing abortion through parliament. Today Simona is concerned for all peoples of the earth, from gypsies in Milan to dark children in Madagascar, but her immediate tasks are in local politics of Palermo, where she has confronted the hideous violence of the mafia that destroys sicilians and their beautiful island.[7]

Mezzocielo explores the culture of violence in which women live; e.g., at Castiglione, from childhood until they die, women embroider fine linens for mainland boutiques. In the ancient neighborhood of

Castiglione, stories are told of nymphs with the gift of prophecy, but in the historic era, women have largely been mute.[8] Yet women in Sicily, as elsewhere, are finding the courage to write about their lives and to work for an "uncruel revolution." As their grandmothers did, contemporary sicilian women use everyday tasks to cover defiance; e.g., concertedly throwing bedsheets across balconies to defy the mafia. Women often ally with courageous men, like the one who lit all the lights of his factory to give heart to those demonstrating against mafia murders. Increasingly more aware of themselves, the awareness is evident in private decisions—Italy today has the lowest birth rate in the world: 1.3 children per woman, compared with 2.1 in the U. S. and 3.3. in the world.

Italians are advantaged by one of the most advanced constitutions of the world: their 1948 charter affirms that "It is the duty of the Republic to remove economic and social obstacles that, in effect, limit the liberty and equality of citizens, impede the full development of human beings and effective participation in all political, economic, and social institutions of the country without distinction of sex, race, language, religion, political opinion."

Yet the critical variable for transformation in contemporary Italy may have been voiced by Luisa Muraro. "Today one can speak of a spiritual revolution that consists in our confronting what is partially hidden and putting it back into the current of history."[9]. Like Fernand Braudel, Levi Strauss, and Karl Marx, Muraro urges study of the long and deep history that has been submerged by scribes who record the history of the patriarchal dominant violent class.

Bringing the "symbolic order of the mother" to consciousness is not, states Muraro, a matter of choice, "we live on this earth and not in the sky. It is not a matter of choice, it is a matter of struggle. We need to give a social translation to the maternal power." For Muraro, a social rendering of maternal power is the condition of liberty; "private property and rights are secondary conditions of liberty, conforming to historic syntheses that do not include me, as they do not include the great part of women and of men."[10]

Muraro, a founder of the Libreria della Donna at Milan, as well as of Diotima, feminist theory group of the University of Verona, agrees with Luce Irigaray's analyses that the origin of western culture is not patricide, as Freud thought (pointing to the Oedipus plays of Sophocles) but matricide, as Euripides suggested in the *Orestea*. Freud was wrong in saying that the initial strong love of the baby for the mother changes into hate because the child must detach himself/herself from the mother. Love, states Muraro, does not change into hate; what happens is not knowing how to love, a lack which becomes a wound that does not heal. Recognizing the mother "who freely gave me life, gives me a sense of being and of illimitable possibilities."

When she grasped that the first task was to learn to love her mother, she felt a surprising lightness of being. Instead of unlearning patriarchal culture, Muraro realized she had not learned it that well; it wasn't that hard to unlearn it. All feminist work will be gone in a generation, states the black-haired theorist who likes to think in the kitchen, unless deconstruction of patriarchy is accompanied by affirmation of the symbolic order of the mother.

Calling herself a metaphysician whose ground is the "real and true world in which my mother put me after nine months of gestation," Muraro says that we can begin by telling the truth. Recognizing the symbolic order of the mother need not take eons of time. The change can occur in an instant, or it doesn't come about, as it hasn't, in the last two thousand years. In December, 1995, Muraro announced that "patriarchy has fallen," precipitating a large debate—which may have been what she intended.

On Women's Day 1995, women of Palermo demonstrated with banners protesting that despite legal advances for women, violence against women and children has increased all over the world, a theme that Italy's greatest woman writer, Dacia Maraini, has been exploring for three decades.[11] Suggesting that the center of gravity of italian feminism, as well as the center of the italian left, is shifting southward, women of the south in 1995 proposed a feminist editing of marxist principles, adopting the theme, "women's class consciousness."[12]

In the south, the struggle against the mafia has brought men and women together in work against violence to the environment, against the violence of fascism, and against the violence of racism and sexism—myriad forms of violence that italians consider one grotesque carnival monster. All over Italy in 1995, demonstrations remembered that the old fascism, brought down after world war two, was grounded on racism that easily becomes fascist hatred of many others, exemplified in hatred of jews, hatred of peoples of colors, hatred of homosexuals, hatred of communists, et al.

Siciliani, journal of sicilians who work against all varieties of fascism, noted that at the end of the 20th century, racist hatred was still alive in Italy, Europe, and the United States—evident in the violent zenophobia against dark-skinned migrant workers. Contemporary italian capitalism, according to *Siciliani,* has inherited fascism and racism. Capitalism the world over assumes the inferiority of the poor at home, and the backwardness of dark peoples of the south of the globe. It is possible, *Siciliani* tells its readers, to defeat fascism and racism. It is possible to have an earth without wars, without violence, without exploitation, societies in which color and ethnicity are enriching, not a cause for discrimination. A first step to a nonviolent world is "international solidarity against the violence of racism."[13]

In 1994 when the right wing came to national power in Italy, sicilians voted counter to the national trend: 115 sicilian towns elected progressive mayors. The towns were located in regions with evidence of paleolithic african presence, of veneration of Ibla Nera in the neolithic epoch, in places where canaanites brought images of the dark mother of Africa and Asia in the millennium before christianity, where, in the christian epoch, the memory of the ancient african dark mother was transmitted in lullabies and stories of peasant godmothers, and where the dark mother, in the form of black madonnas, continues to be adored to this day.

At Fiumefreddo in the Monti Iblei, the professoressa Marinella Fiume (whose names connote the sea and a river) was a newly elected mayor. She has red hair, a volcanic temperament, and knows every wild herb in in her native mountains. When she defeated the incumbent mayor, he sent her the book, *Running with the Wolves*. Fiume has closed down a mafia operation, opened a day center for older people, and shut down a polluting incinerator in an orange growing region.

Outside Palermo, Maria Maniscalco was elected mayor of a mafia-ridden town. Like african and asian goddesses who governed with spouses, Maria is married to the newly-elected mayor of a nearby town. Both work against the mafia, which has retaliated with threats and car bombings. Although put on a death list by the mafia, Maria continues her work nurturing life, e.g., building an elementary school in an impoverished area. With the sense of self that characterizes women who carry the memory of the dark mother, Maria said that after she was elected, "the mafia lost control of public works and the territory."[14]

Cuore, meaning heart, is the name of the italian student movement. Embodying nonviolent resistance, students of Italy have been clubbed and arrested, yet remain defiant to violent patriarchy in all its configurations, including residual patriarchal attitudes of politicians of left parties, whose goals they share. Grandchildren of strong peasant grandmothers and sons and daughters of feminists, the contemporary student nonviolent resistance began in Palermo in 1990, then was taken up by students at Rome and the rest of the country. Italian students have catalyzed a resistenza umana, a human resistance that has jailed mafiosi and nonviolently removed from office corrupt christian democrat and socialist leaders.

In the 1990s, students of Italy traveled around the world setting up work camps against war, repairing the environment, opening green paths from Bulgaria to Tibet. They helped refugees from ex-Jugoslovia, transformed old buildings into houses for peace, built welcoming hostels for immigrants, cleared forests, worked on native american reservations, organized ecology projects with children of Chernobyl, assisted women of Nicaragua, and fed hungry children in Palestine, the Western Sahara, the Sudan, and East Timor. In Italy, in areas devastated by the mafia, they have built camps for peace; in former nazi death centers in Poland and Germany, they have co-ordinated study groups on racism and anti-semitism. They have proposed a year's draft for everyone from 18 to 29, an army for peace to clean up the environment and to help the poor and suffering.

Restoring schools in Albania, helping children in ex-Yugoslovia, building an irrigation system in Mozambique, helping to create a Latin American artists' mural in Manchester, digging wells in Senegal, building a woman's center in Nicaragua, a handicapped children's park in Denmark, working for appropriate agriculture in Scotland, teaching non-violence to children, helping with the fruit harvest in Hungary, working in a children's hospital in Minsk, creating ecology projects in the Urals, cleaning up beaches in Siberia, restoring the historic center of Kiev, helping americans restore neighborhoods in Boston, working with palestinians, rebuilding native homes in Alaska, protecting wolves in Colorado, putting out forest fires, organizing an ecofestival at Bari, building hospices for people with terminal Aids, creating centers for abused women, students have founded centers for refugees from violence from Greece to Ukraine to New York City.[15]

Students of Italy have done all this across the world, while, on their own turf, they have worked to democratize universities, a spiral of student activism that reminds me of the catalytic effect of student movements in the 1960s. Yet movements of the 90s and first years of the third millennium are different from movements of the 60s. The italian student movement has lived through the post 1968 violent revolutionary period and insists, as do all branches of left activism in Italy, on nonviolence.[16]

In 1995 *cuore* initiated a new series, *Studenti Serpenti*, remembering the snake, symbol of the ancient mother, whose shedding of skin connotes regeneration. Serpents in *cuore* bite icons of the left; e.g., they criticise the showcase of the italian left—the red province of Emilia—for consumerism. More moral than the pope, *Studenti Serpenti* point to the pope's equivocations on the death penalty (he sanctions it for public order). They cite Gandhi who opposed violence because "when it seems to do good, this good is often temporary, while the evil that violence does is enduring."[17]

On June 3, 1995 italian feminists held a demonstration whose themes have become their charter for the new millennium. These feminist themes, together with themes of the male nonviolence movement and student initiatives, suggest why contemporary Italy may be a laboratory in radical democracy for the third millennium.

In the 1970s italian feminists, sharing values of justice, equality, and transformation with men of the left, values that go back to the ancient dark mother, convinced their husbands, lovers, and sons to support divorce, equal family rights, family clinics, equal pay for equal work, legal abortion, et al. In the 1980s italian feminists changed the nature of the italian communist party. With a women's optic, they stipulated in party codicils that religious/spiritual beliefs are prior to politics, and that nonviolence is the way to socialism. In the '80s and '90s italian feminists quietly built a network of feminist institutions, women's universities, journals, newspapers, libraries, shelters, bookstores, professional societies, communication networks, et al.[18]

On June 3, 1995, against a backdrop of a resurgent political right, tens of thousands of women demonstrated in Rome with the theme, "women have the first and the last word on conception and abortion." For this historian, the theme evoked the 2nd century CE african gnostic poem, "Thunder Perfect Mind," and the chthonic voice of the ancient dark african mother, "I am the first and the last."[19]

In 1968 italian feminists launched the second cycle of feminism with the banner, "There is no revolution without women's liberation; There is no women's liberation without revolution." At the beginning of the third millennium, what may differentiate italian feminists from their sisters elsewhere is that they still refer to revolution. In the last two decades, they liked the word *transformation* (word that connotes the necessity of individual as well as political change), but on June 3, 1995 the word was *revolution*, understood to be nonviolent, whose bannered aims were *sexuality, liberty and self-determination*.[20] Alongside aims of earlier revolutions, Liberté, Egalité et Fraternité of the french revolution, or Peace, Land, and Bread of the soviet revolution, the contemporary revolutionary triad of italian women is different, and unprecedented, combining marxism with sexuality, liberty, and self determination. Perhaps more than any other women's movement of the world, italian women have wrestled with the contradictions between marxism and feminism. In the 1995 demonstration, they proclaimed un approccio sessuato al marxismo, a sexualized approach to marxism, a perspective that would have boggled the dialectics of earlier male marxists.

Italian women's approach to marxism was adumbrated in the 1970s by Mariarosa Dalla Costa whose provocative analysis of the unpaid work of housewives put sexual work in the category of housewives' unpaid labor.[21] In the 1995 italian feminist demonstration, women's work was equated with public happiness; women's liberty was "situated between equality and difference."[22]

Italian feminists differ among themselves, but they share a passion for a just and equal world, a hope they associate with marxism, but whose deeper ground may be an unverbalized memory of the ancient civilization of the dark mother. The vision enables them to cross barriers. In leaflets and banners of the June 3rd demonstration, cultural feminists analyzed a sexual approach to marxism, while political feminists (indicating that they have learned from cultural feminists) interpreted marxism from the perspective of women's history, identifying a just and equal communist society with diversity.

For the demonstration, Rifondazione comunista, the left group who retained the name after 1989 (when the majority of the italian left changed the name of the communist party to Partito democratico della sinistra, or Pds) enunciated feminist marxist theory from the perspective of refounded communism. Patriarchy, said women of Rifondazione comunista of Naples, did not begin with capitalism; patriarchy began long ago with the male take-over of the ancient civilization of the mother. Although capitalism did not create patriarchy, capitalism, by stipulating competition in the name of the strongest, is the expression of the omnipotent will of patriarchy.

This time, said neapolitan women, we shall not be reduced to silence, nor subordinated to masculine codes. Refounded communists of Italy have absorbed the meaning and metaphors of multiculturalism and of liberation theologies: "We want a diverse society grounded on peace and justice for new women and men."[23] Rifondazione comunista, as a political party, aspires not to exercising power but to using moral pressure to keep other parties to principles. In 1997 the refounded communist party played the determining role in administrative elections of April 1997, elections which rebuffed the racist Northern League.

"A secure woman is always destabilizing," advised a placard in the 1995 women's demonstration. Sense of self was also evident in a placard that proclaimed that abortion was not a "right," because that implies the right of the state to control women's bodies. Women's choices, asserted another placard, were not related to the "western" juridical philosophy of rights, but preceded it.[24]

Autodeterminazione was the watchword on June 3rd. Self-determination was expressed by older communist women who traveled all night to come to Rome, by dancing young women who helped organize the demonstration, It was manifested in a myriad of different ways by women parliamentarians, teachers, journalists, lawyers, writers, poets, jungian therapists, psychoanalysts, gynecologists, trade unionists, anthropologists, waldensian pastors, catholic thealogians, nuns, philosophers, refounded communists, and social democrats. Nonpolitical women of Buon Pastore, international women's center at Rome, suggested passing the microphone to each and every woman to say why she was there. Diversity was evident in the music of the 1995 italian feminist demonstration.—hymn of the communist international, partisan ballads, feminist songs of the 70s, and traditional folk songs.

Shared premises of contemporary italian feminists are that the world is inhabited by women and men, that women and men are both protagonists in creating a new society. Italian women tweaked this premise in the 1995 demonstration by proclaiming that women have the first and the last word on matters of creation and abortion, and, by analogy, the first and last word on the creation of a new society. One woman said she did not much care for speeches; it was enough to say, "we are here and we are many." This recalled the feminist record album of the 70s with Cybele on the cover, *Siamo in tante* (we are many), referring to italian feminist identification with all life, and to the forza of all women in bringing a new society into being.

What kind of society? Some banners called for "women's anticapitalism;" others for women's alignment with workers and proletarians of the earth. Self-determination was expanded to "all aspects of our lives." Freedom of choice about one's body in Italy has become freedom of choice about everything.

The memory of the self-determined dark mother is found in unexpected places. Women religious of Italy announced at the June 3rd demonstration that they were coming out of traditional subordination, liberating themselves from roles assigned to them by male clerics. Nuns demonstrated as a group with Unione donne italiane (he italian women's union), saying that italian feminists had reached a level of profonda autocoscienza. Nuns, in joining the June 3rd demonstration that supported women's decisions about creation and abortion, indicated that the italian women's movement has breached an earlier difference, removing one more dualism (between "religious" and "secular") in the work of women and others to make the earth, and all life, sacred once more.[25]

O

The woman who seems to me to embody the deepest beliefs of contemporary italians is Simone Weil, french woman of a jewish family whose life and writings escape categories. Her resonance in contemporary Italy is almost mythic. She may be the most cited theorist in Italy in contemporary discussion of a good society.[26] Her ideas, in my view, point to an unprecedented liberation theology grounded on the values of the civilization of the ancient dark mother.

Touching the deepest beliefs of italians, Simone Weil seems to embody the christian, and communist, belief that the last shall be first, as well as the belief, for which she gave her life in witness, that violence is the central evil of western civilization. An uninscribed communist, Weil was drawn to the vision, but alienated when workers shed blood in their efforts to build a just society. She admired greek civilization, but concluded from her reading of the *Iliad*, that it was a document of male violence. Combining abhorrence of violence with her belief that might is never to be admired, Weil insisted that the enemy is never to be hated, sufferers never despised.[27]

Like Ernesto de Martino, italian ethnographer of the 1930s, Weil was critical of social scientists who study myth and folklore, civilizations of antiquity, and peoples of color "without finding any trace of spirituality anywhere." By 1940, the "white races," said Weil, had "almost lost all feeling for the beauty of the world, and...they had taken upon themselves the task of making it disappear from all the continents where they have penetrated with their armies, their trade and their religion."[28]

Like contemporary italian feminists who read her writings, Simone Weil was uneasy with the concept of rights. One can not imagine, she said, Francis of Assisi talking about rights. "If you say to someone who has ears to hear, 'What you are doing to me is not just' you may touch and awaken at its source the spirit of attention and love. But it is not the same with words like 'I have the right' or 'you have no right to….' They evoke a latent war and awaken the spirit of contention."29

Justice, truth, and beauty, in the personified universe of Simone Weil, saint Francis, and italian peasants, are "sisters and comrades." Words like "right, democracy and person" are valid in their own context, but "for the sustaining inspiration of which all institutions are, as it were, the projection, a different language is needed." Weil is stating here what Gramsci at the time was writing in his prison cell, the necessity of tapping the metaphors and images that manifest the deep beliefs of ordinary people before there can be an authentic revolution.

She lived, said Simone Weil, at "the intersection of Christianity and everything that is not Christianity." She saw, as did D. H. Lawrence, that behind the virgin mother of christianity was the earlier mother, whom Weil identified with justice in a beautiful world. "When perceived as beautiful the world appears perfectly just." "The Virgin is Justice. The Virgin of the Zodiac, holding an ear of corn. Cosmic Virgin of the Apocalypse. The Virgin is the creation."30 Jesus is "our first-born brother. If Mary embodied creation and justice, the beauty of the world is Christ's tender smile…coming through matter."31

In the late 1930s, half-remembering yet unexcavated eons of prehistory and peasant history, and writing before the substantiating evidence of archeology and genetics in the 80s and 90s, Weil spoke of an "ancient people's civilization, of which we are today collecting the crumbs as museum pieces under the name of folklore," when "people doubtless had access to the treasure. Mythology, too, which is very closely related to folklore, testifies to it, if we can decipher the poetry it contains."32

At Le Puy, which has one of the oldest vierges noires (black virgins) of France, where Weil engaged in radical political organizing, the townspeople called her la vierge rouge (the red virgin),alluding to communism but also, perhaps in a deep memory that ochre red was the ancient color connoting the dark mother and life.

The italian feminist closest to the thinking of Simone Weil may be Lidia Menapace, whose radicalism may stem from a heretical left catholicism that goes back to the cathars. Menapace's writings point to a heretical communism grounded on the beauty of the universe, the order visible among differences, and a pythagorean sense of harmony. Arguing for a "feminist marxism," Menapace considers differences beautiful and the key to a good society. For this italian feminist, a "good marxism" is grounded on the belief that "the world is beautiful because it is always different."[33] The goal is a new communal socialist society that remembers the past, envisions the future, acknowledges the partiality of all views, does not exclude any, and considers women's and men's historical experience to be different, yet interdependent.[34] A new communal socialist society may be created, says Menapace, by exploring the "freely given" quality of women's work. When work is freely given, it cannot be exchanged, its value is wholly subjective and it is ribboned with pleasure, caprice, and contemplation.[35] For this central issue of work, Simone Weil pointed out that in prehistory "before slavery began there was a civilization with spirituality of labour."[36]

Inspiring contemporary italian feminists, male nonviolence activists, and students, Weil held that religious experience is not circumscribed by belonging to a church, nor by a vague ecumenism. The point is to appreciate diverse religious traditions, not subsiding into a bland ecumenism, but looking for the specific difference within each religion that can make a difference in transforming the world. For Simone Weil, the significant difference of christianity was Jesus, whom she called "our first-born brother."

At the intersection of christianity and what she called "all that was not Christianity," she found significant difference in passages of hebrew scriptures, writings of pythagorean greeks, texts of Lao-Tse, and hindu sacred books. Egyptian fragments, said Weil, were the foundation of the first ten books of hebrew scriptures. The basic truths of these diverse religions, for Weil, were "hidden in…myths and stories."[37]

Christian inquisitors would have burned her as a jew, or as a witch, for saying the holy spirit is a woman.[38] In today's Italy, Simone Weil's life and writings have attained mythic resonance, perhaps because her language is both ancient and contemporary: e.g., "The soul is the human being [the human body]."[39] She sounds simultaneous themes of hopelessness...and hope. "You could not have wished to be born at a better time than this, when everything has been lost"[40] "After the collapse of our civilization one of two things will happen, either it will perish completely or else it will adapt itself to a decentralized world."[41]

Simone Weil's ideas, which she left in fragments, have inspired a generation of scholars and seekers to search for her meaning. For some, Simone Weil implies a hidden god and a psychology of a hidden self. "Commitment to the hidden God and the hidden self is commitment to creation, the modality of God's hiddenness."[42] For this book, Simone Weil bequeathed her finding: there was, indeed, a Black Demeter.[43] In the context of themes of this study, Simone Weil's thinking offers, in my view, the possibility of a liberation theology circling the dark mother of prehistory and her values.

O

This chapter has been an implicit contrast of the feminist movement in Italy and the feminist movement in the United States. The close memory of the dark mother has molded italian feminism. The memory has been nearly completely suppressed by the dominant culture of the United States. The difference may be suggested in the way March 8, International Women's Day, is celebrated in Italy and the United States. When I was in Rome a few years ago on March 8, bouquets of yellow ginestra (mimosa) were everywhere—given by men to their mothers, lovers, wives, sisters, daughters, grand-daughters, nieces, and other women.

The poignant implication of this is evoked when one remembers that International Women's Day began in the United States in the first decade of the 20th century. The dominant U.S. patriarchal environment has been a major obstacle for feminists, although, as Ruth Rosen has splendidly documented, women in the United States have managed to accomplish a great deal despite male anxiety/hostility.[44] Perhaps cities of the United States will become celebrations of women on March 8, and every day of the year, when the memory of the dark mother, and her values of justice with compassion and equality—reaches the consciousness of everyone. Especially worried men.

Notes

1   Peter Robb, *Midnight in Sicily. On Art, Food, History, Travel & La Cosa Nostra* (Boston and London, "Faber and Faber, Inc., 1998). Flyleaf.

2   "La pace ha molti colori," *confronti. mensile di fede, politica, vita quotidiana,* luglio/agosto 1994.

3   "Aldo Capitini, 1899-1968," *Azione nonviolenta,* settembre-ottobre 1978. "Aldo Capitini," "La Festa." *Italia Nonviolenta* (Perugia, Centro Studi Aldo Capitini, 1981).

4   "Il nuovo modello di difesa," *Azione nonviolenta,* marzo-aprile 1993.

5   "Dov' eravamo cinquant'anni fa?" *Azione nonviolenta,* aprile 1995. See also, *Donne e uomini nelle guerre mondiali,* a cura di Anna Bravo (Roma-Bari, Editori, Laterza, 1991).

6   See Arne Naess, *Ecosofia* (Como, Red Edizioni, 1994).

7   "Le Protagoniste dell' Anno Uno,"*mezzocielo,* giugno 1993.

8   "Il Telaio di marmo," *mezzocielo,* giugno 1993.

9   Luisa Muraro, *L'ordine Simbolico della Madre* (Roma, Editori Riuniti, 1981).

10   Ibidem.

11   See in particular, Dacia Maraini, *Voci. Romanzo* (Milano, Rizzoli, 1994. Also Dacia Maraini, *Buio* (Milano, Rizzoli, 1999). Her masterpiece is *La lunga vita di Marianna Ucria. Romanzo* (Milano, Bompiani, 1990).

12   "marzo otto," *mezzocielo,* febbraio 1995.

13   "Per un 25 aprile antirazzista," *Siciliani nuovi,* aprile '95.

14   "Sicilia. La Nuova Resistenza. 'Noi anomali,' Vite di sindaci antimafia," *Avvenimenti,* 15 agosto 1994.

15   See *cuore,* "50 nazioni, 50 campi," *Avvenimenti,* 9 giugno 1993.

16   See Birnbaum, *Black Madonnas,* (Loc. Cit.)

17   Patrizia Roversi, "La Posta del Cuore," *cuore,* 6 maggio 1995.

18   See Birnbaum, *Liberazione della donna.* Loc. Cit.

19   See Elaine Pagels, *The Gnostic Gospels* (New York, Vintage Books, 1979), 55.

20   Carla Casalini e Marina Forti, "Il desiderio di vedersi," *il manifesto,* 4 giugno 1995.

21   See Birnbum, *Liberazione*, chapter ten.

22   Lettere, "Una festa fuori dal recinto," *il manifesto*, 3 giugno 1995.

23   "Contro il patriarcato," *le lettere, il manifesto*, 3 giugno 1995.

24   Ida Dominijanni, "Oltre la norma. Sull'aborto non serve piu' legge ma meno legge. La responsabilità femminile e il linguaggio dei diritti fra pensiero della differenza e cultura giuridica," *il manifesto*, 1 giugno 1994. An excellent guide to contemporary italian feminist literature is "Bibliomappa," in *legendaria. Libri e percorsi di lettura*. See, in particular, "Femminismo," by Ida Dominijanni, an article that cites the ten most historically significant books written by italian feminists. The list, with which I concur, includes Luisa Muraro, *L'ordine simbolico della madre* (Roma, Editori Riuniti, 1991).

25   "Diritto. Su una legge contro la violenza sessuale...." *DWpress, il notiziaro delle donne*, 22 maggio 1995.

26   A random sample of contemporary articles about Simone Weil in Italy has been collected by Guglielmo Forni Rosa, *Simone Weil. Politica e mistica* (Torino, Rosenberg & Sellier, 1996). Themes of the articles are revolution, revolutionary traditionalism, the division of labor, judaism, christianity, a new christology...The best source of writings about Simone Weil is *Cahiers Simone Weil. Revue trimestrielle publiee' par l'Association pour l'etude de la pensee' de Simone weil, avec le concours du C.N.L. et de la Ville de Paris.*

27   "The Iliad, Poem of Might," *Simone Weil Reader*, ed., George A. Panichas (Mt. Kisco, New York, Moyer Bell Limited, 1977, 183.

28   "Paths of Meditation," *Simone Weil Reader*,. 472.

29   "Human Personality," *Simone Weil Reader*,. 313 ff.

30   "Paths of Meditation. The Father's Silence," *Simone Weil Reader*, 434., 438.

31   "Forms of the Implicit Love of God," *Simone Weil Reader*, 474.

32   Ibid., 479.

33   See Lidia Menapace, *L'economia sessuale delle differenze* (Rome, edizioni Felina Libri, 1987).

34   See Birnbaum, *Black Madonnas*, 190, passim.

35   Ibidem, 182.

36   Ibid., 337.

37   Rino Bernasconi, "L'attualità di Simone Weil," *Azione nonviolenta,* dicembre 1993. See Angela Putino, *Simone Weil e la Passione di Dio. Il ritmo divino nell'uomo* (Bologna, Centro editoriale dehoniano, 1997).

38   Simone Weil, *First and Last Notebooks.* Tr., Richard Rees (London, Oxford University Press, 1970). See Gabriella Fiori, *Una donna assoluta* (Milano, La Tartaruga edizioni, 1991).

39   Weil, *First and Last Notebooks*, . 31.

40   Ibidem

41   Ibid., 51.

42   Robert McKibben, "Simone Weil and Progress," 16th Annual Colloquy on Simone Weil, Simone Weil Society, Graduate Theological Union, Berkeley, California, April, 1996.

43   Ibid., 190.

44   Ruth Rosen, *The World Split Open. The modern women's movement changed America* (Viking, 2000).

part four
L'Ordine simbolico della madre

chapter twelve

dark mothers and others of the world

"Enter here. You are all my children."
—black madonna of Tindari, Sicily

The memory of the dark mother was palpable in the 1995 Beijing world conference, the largest gathering of women in history. Women of the world remembered the values of the primordial dark mother, even as they cited statistics of continuing violence against women and children. In the culture of globalization, seventy percent of the world's poor (1.2 to 1.3 billion people) are women, and children dependent on women, who live in cultures of violence—violence against the earth, violence against all life implicit in pollution, militarized economies, wars, violence of exploited labor, and violence against those perceived as dark others.

Rain outside the global tribunal on domestic violence and tears inside the auditorium, provided a chorus for testimonies of women raped and battered from Bosnia to Ireland, Uganda to New York City, a poignant escalation of violence against women that has accompanied legislation for women's equality. The international group, Women in Black, with lights, candles, lanterns, shammas, lamperas, and placards, remembered "our sisters and mothers who have been subjects of violence…we stand for peace for all." Strategies for abolishing violence were explored in

353

many workshops whose major themes were women's economic independence, education of the girl child, and all women taking immediate responsibility for transforming a violent world into peaceful cultures.

An emerging feminist liberation theology circling the dark mother and others was glimpsed in the brazilian workshop on women's spirituality. Brazilian culture, remembering its african roots, showed a film with a black mother, her black child, and african/brazilian water rituals. The implicit theology of the workshop was that a dark mother loves all her children, all of them dark others in one way or another. Criticizing established world religions for doctrines that denigrate women and others, the workshop held all religions responsible for the social consequences of their doctrines, declaring that the aim of all religions should be social justice.

Women from Lake Baikal in Siberia, place of paleolithic evidence of the dark mother, declared, "We can not leave reconversion of military economies of the super powers to the men, because most men seem unable to give up war weapons." Women must begin the change to a peaceful world. "We can start," they said, with "clean water for our children." Siberian women brought liters of clean water to the workshop, and invited the world's women to an international conference "to save the earth," a conference held in Siberia in July 1996.

Music in the Africa tent, quiet of the Asia healing tent, african american women singing on the buses, italian women kissing everyone, the ambiance of a great bazaar, yet the prevailing tone of the conference was very serious. "Nobody is safe, anywhere," warned a banner linking toxic substances from manufacturing, military activities, nuclear explosions, land mines, nuclear dumping, traffic, and corporate agriculture to the deterioration of the health of the earth and all its creatures.

French women denounced globalization for widening the breach between rich and poor countries, a system that "generates discrimination and excludes large sectors of the population and especially women." "Globalization," a plenary concluded, has resulted in profits of a few transnational corporations of the superpowers while bringing greater exploitation of peoples, "especially to women of the third world." Sounding the tocsin that was to be heard in 1999 in the streets of Seattle, in 2000 in the streets of Washington D.C., and in 2001 in the streets of Toronto and Genoa, demanding democratizing all decisions that affect all the people of the world—the world's women urged "sharing of wealth and democratization of international economic institutions, including the World Bank and the International Monetary Fund."

The relative conservatism of the U.S. women's movement was thrown into high relief by placards carried by the rest of the world's women challenging the inequality of wealth and power in the world. Directly addressing the group of seven who dominate the world economy (United States, United Kingdom, Japan, France, Italy, Canada and Germany), women of the world demanded, "Stop structural adjustment policies in the south! Stop destroying social programs in the north!"

Emboldened in the supportive environment of women of the world, a woman economist of the large U.S. mainstream organization, United Methodist Women, chaired the session on exploitative practices of transnational corporations. Japanese women held their government responsible for using "comfort women" in world war two, and demanded reparations. Women of the Philippines stretched long banners denouncing sex trafficking in women. Australian feminist marxists demanded valuing the work of all women—prostitutes, house workers, domestic workers, home care workers, and unwaged as well as waged workers. Exemplary women of Sweden and Norway, who have institutionalized 50/50 gender representation in their political institutions, were criticized for not including in their statistics the unwaged work of housewives.

The sheer courage of Wings, organization of iranian women, numbed observers. Iranian women denounced islamic fundamentalists for abusing women, distributing a photo of a woman flogged and imprisoned for attending a birthday party where men were present. Women of the United States held their government accountable for unsigned human rights treaties. Women of Europe for a Common Future declared that all women must take full responsibility for a sustainable future, starting with the global threat to health and survival caused by environmental pollution. Every women's group of the world, was urged, to take responsibility for a healthy planet, while simultaneously working for gender-balanced participation in politics, and women's participation in all major scientific and military decisions affecting the lives of everyone.

A film of the life of Fannie Lou Hamer, great civil rights worker of the United States, followed by songs of the 60s sung by women of the world, left me with the conviction that the finest contribution of the United States to the world in the last century was the civil rights movement of the 1960s. In China in 1995, women of Africa, Asia, Europe, and North and South America wept while we sang, "We shall not be moved."

The metaphor of the dark mother for an emerging international feminist network was implicit in the congress of Wedo, organization founded by the late courageous Bella Abzug. Called Daughters of the Earth, the congress was dedicated to Songi—great african mother of Bantu; Nu Kwa—great mother goddess of China; wise Athena; Tara rooted in nonviolence and peace; buffalo woman and medicine woman of the kiowa people of North America (intriguingly dedicated "in honor of Passover"); Aditi—hindu goddess of regeneration; and Nanshe—mesopotamian dark mother who judges humanity.

The story of the dark mother of a thousand names, and the women who kept her memory in the historical epoch, was told in a leaflet distributed by Streelekha, feminist book store of Bangalore, India. "There once and forever lived a woman/ who spun words of wisdom/ from gossamer thread so fine/ that the eye could not see/ so soft/ that only the breeze could hear/ so strong that it cut through eons of hard silence."

The flyer of the Asian Women's Human Rights Council put the conference platform of action (poverty, political inequality, democratization of national and international institutions and the mass media, human rights, care of the environment) into a story honoring the women who dwelled at the edges of time and memory for more than 2,000 years. "Once upon a time in the great global village where life was a madness called civilization, there once and forever lived a woman dwelling on the edges of time and memory...a woman who belonged to the forgotten tribe of village idiots...[who] laughed at scientists and shamans, priests and professors, mullahs and medicine men.

For she refused to be the handmaiden of all holy men. She and her man knew that in the world they lived, nothing was holy, yet everything was sacred....And so together they laughed at immutable wisdoms and wondered at the endless possibilities of most ignorance....She nurtured many knowledges. And so every wrinkle on her face sparked with the intensity of forgotten wisdoms; her soft touch sought out the familiar source of every pain to soothe and heal....She was consumed with anguish over the violence...armed with nothing more lethal than compassion...she had the security of an unfettered inner peace...possessed of a power that knew how to care...a power that found 'political' expression [in] ethical governance in which leadership was responsibility to all, not subservience to a few....She raged against wrongs and spoke of the right to be human...sought justice for the poor and powerless....She was Anabiti, Inanna, Isis, Demeter, Prakriti...."

Chinese women declared "Let us unite under the banner of Women and Environment." If each of us is "a piece of green leaf...we shall become a vast green forest....[stopping] strong winds and sand storms. If each of us is a small stream...we shall be a vast and mighty river [with] more water to irrigate the arid land and crops. In order to keep the mountains green, clean water flowing forever, and keeping our Earth, our beloved Mother...."

On the second night of the conference, in the confusion of more than 35,000 women gathered in one place, I took the wrong bus. After two hours of wandering in unknown neighborhoods of Beijing, bedraggled in the rain, I reached the hotel. African women of the Transvaal welcomed me, asked what I was doing at the conference, and promised to help in my workshop on black madonnas and other dark mothers of the world.

They did. Women who have worked in the unspeakable conditions of mines of South Africa, spent their lives in the bloody struggle against apartheid, and now work in african health services, Rosemary and Alba skipped a session on constitutions for new african free states to participate in the workshop on the dark mother. Women of central and south Africa, where modern humans and world civilization originated, live today in the toxic backwash of colonialism where first world countries profit selling arms that incite murderous tribal rivalries, western development policies that often take power away from women, where sometimes half the population has Aids, and where girls have to prostitute themselves to survive. Yet, women of Africa work for a better continent and a better world.

During the workshop on the dark mother, Rosemary and Alba revealed the source of their strength. "We always knew," said Rosemary, "that god was a woman." Indoctrination in patriarchal dogmas of christianity, islam, and imperialism have not, apparently, obliterated the ancient african belief in the dark mother. Alba wrote "Dark Mothers of the World" on the blackboard, and shaded the letters in red, black, yellow, and green, colors of Africa and life. Red for women's childbirth and menstrual blood, primordial sign of the mother who created and sustained life. Black for dark women divinities who transmitted the memory of the dark mother in the epoch of patriarchy. Yellow and Green for the spiral of death and regeneration.

O

Elsewhere, ancient beliefs associated with the dark mother have also, apparently, withstood 2,000 years of patriarchal indoctrination. Editors compiling the 1997 *Dictionary of Global Culture*[1] discovered that chinese people, for example, consider the spring festival celebrating regeneration more important than doctrines of Confucius. The implicit message of this dictionary reminded me of the spiral dance of pilgrimages when people carry the icon of the dark mother, and dance two steps backward before moving forward. The global dictionary and the dance convey the wisdom that all of us need to remember the everyday and festival beliefs of our ancestors before we can move forward to a green world of justice with compassion.

Everydayness—the images, colors, taste, and wonder—was conveyed by Luciana Polney in a poem inspired by her journey to her maternal grandmothers, who lived near the black madonna of Tindari.

The small brass female fertility statue is faceless
on the window sill,
next to a tall green unlit candle
facing the sun,
a statue of Buddha
and an Inca God with defined faces
seven power beads,
from a Puerto Rican botanica.
Seven orange, seven green, seven yellow, seven red, seven brown,
seven white, seven turquoise
wrapped around its body

Thinking I was protected
I slept dreaming of elephants
retrieving the collective memory
recalling the one hundredth morning.
This morning was different
I lost an earring and
tasted coffee made in a new pot,
watered flowering plants
made no phone calls
as I lit a red candle,
burnt sage scented incense
the prayer beads around my neck

broke. Seeds fell and dispersed everywhere.
I stopped chanting
searched for meaning in the scatter of the seeds,
wondered
why the fertility Goddess has no face.[2]

Thinking about her ancient great grandmother, and wondering why italian/americans can not trace their families farther back than their immediate grandparents, Rose Romano traveled from Brooklyn to Trapani in Sicily. "It never even occured to me until after I arrived in Sicily to ask for the word for great grandmother. In fact, even then it didn't really occur to me. Instead, it finally came to me, slowly, when I was being shown pictures of the family and they told me about my great grandparents. It took me a while to understand what the word meant and I felt the word in my whole body."[3]

After a year and more of silence, Rose wrote "invocation to the great grand mother."

great grand mother
your water is the font
that brings my life
up from the dark
of the womb
great grand mother
take me home

great grand mother
your fire is the blood
that spirals up through
the three corners of
my own eternity
great grand mother
take me home

great grand mother
your sirocco is the word
that inspires every prayer
even before I knew
families go back so far
great grand mother
take me home

great grand mother
your earth is my mother, America
my grand mother, Sicilia
my great grand mother, Africa
the font, the blood, the word
lost when I left home
bisnonna
take me home.

O

Men, as well as women, have embarked on the journey. John Heuser, in my class on the dark mother thought aloud. "Confront, say, a white male christian, or a U. S. politician," with the statement that the dark mother is a metaphor for the new millennium, he wrote, "and you will no doubt be met with stiff resistance if not violent disagreement." For John, student of Jung, the huge pornography market is related to "men's driving need and longing for experiences of the feminine." He offers a jungian lens to men to help them refocus three unconscious "scorned pieces of [their]own femininity—virgin/whore, mother/nourisher, and terrible mother."

John creates altars to the dark mother embodying "the sacred and the profane." He contemplated the dollar store icon he'd spray painted black and enshrined in a bed pan. Feeling her energy in the limbs of a nearby willow and oak, "A saying came to me, as if whispered from some ancient

Kali: 'As I freeze your bones, so shall I embrace your soul in the warmth of my arms.' I slept there, under the open stars, all night."

Rob Brezny captures the irreverence/reverence, playfulness/seriousness that all of us may need in the turbulent voyage to a green and just world.

I am starting to pray right now to the God of Gods,
the God beyond all
Gods, the Girlfriend of God, the Teacher of God, the
Goddess who invented
God, and what I pray is:

Oh Goddess Who Never Kills But Only Changes:
I pray that my exuberant, suave, and accidental words might
move You to
Unleash ferocious blessings on all the beauty and truth fans
who've tuned in
I pray that You'll grant them what they don't even know they
want. Not
Just the boons they think they need but everything they've
been afraid to even
imagine or wish for....

Arouse the Wild Woman within them—even if they're men.
Give them bigger, better, more original sins and wilder, wet-
ter, more
interesting
problems....[4]

Remembering helps students surmount artificial barriers: "the masculine and the feminine are both sacred mysteries." Their journeys, often a
great circle backward, are not easy expeditions. Tracking Lilith, Deborah
Grenn-Scott found "she mocked me with her laughter, disappearing in a
windstorm every time I thought I was getting close on her trail."[5] They

encounter resistance, often inside themselves, resistance that often dissolves with the realization that tentacles of "othering" clutch racism, imperialism, homophobia, demonization of women, and that everyone in the third millennium, in some way or another, is a marginalized dark other.

Questions mark their journeys. "Have we," asked Mary Patricia Ziolkowski, "been like Isis, searching the world over for the missing parts of the beloved? Is Magdalen a link to the divine feminine so long lost to us? Is she the other half of the archetypal 'divine pair,' heralding a new balance between the feminine and masculine? As we bring her back from her long stay in the underworld, and re-member her, are we resurrecting her, the divine feminine, or ourselves?"[6]

"She's been with us all along," concluded Donna Ray Erickson; "we must sit still, pay attention, stop the wars, end the violence, and feed the children."[7]

O

A friend told me that her reading group that meets in a church was discussing a feminist study of prehistory, when the cleric poked in his head and jocularly asked, "How is Heresy 101 doing?" Which provoked me to think about heresies and that the hypothesis of this book might well be Heresy 202, offering dominant cultures of the world a heretical metaphor for transforming the planet...the dark mother as a unifying and healing metaphor...offering subaltern cultures what they may already know....

We continue on our journeys. Louise Paré, whose doctoral dissertation in the women's spirituality program was captured by a serious health crisis, went into a deep spiral backward. At the end of cancer treatment, she wrote:

Smile—walk
Stretch—sound forth
Breathe in the garden

Pruned
New shoots emerging.

Live large
Grounded in breath flowing from
Love of life
Sound
Words
Movement
Color
Touch
I'm moving again.[8]

Sometimes, meditated Kalli Halvorson, the spiral dance of two steps backward before going forward causes one to "fall to the floor." Yet the spiral dance, and the spiral view of history, help you to "stand up again." and, as Louise Paré advises, "move again."[9]

Our ancestors knew what we may have forgotten. Gian Banchero, in his poem, *Saeculum*, remembers:

Under the EveningStar,
The day harvesters
Gather in Prayertime for
The Dead, and
In anticipation of the World
To come;
Thanking, thanking, and rethanking
The Fruitfulness
of
Daily Life.

Every spring, as they do every year, doves have flown up from the south to nest in the eaves of our home in Berkeley.

As the new century commences, nonviolent children of the dark mother are rising again, at Seattle, Toronto, Genoa, and Berkeley—embodying her values of justice with compassion, equality, and transformation.

bedda matri!

Notes

1   *The Dictionary of Global Culture*, edited by Kwame Anthony Appiah and Henry Louis Gates, Jr. (New York, Alfred A. Knopf, 1997).

2   Luciana Polney, "To Lucia Chiavola Birnbaum on Tour in Sicily," *Voices in Italian Americana.* Vol. 6, No. 1 (1995)

3   Communication to author, 1997.

4   Rob Brezny, *The Televisionary Oracle* (Berkeley, California, Frog, Ltd.,2000). 479-480.

5   Deborah Grenn-Scott, "Lilith's Dark Tree of Life." Paper for my class on the Dark Mother, California Institute of Integral Studies, San Francisco, Spring 2000.

6   Mary Pat Ziolkowski, "The Dark Mother," paper for my class on the Dark Mother, California Institute of Integral Studies, San Francisco, Spring 2000.

7   Donna-Ray Erickson, "African origins of the European and feminist Enlightenments," paper for my class on the Dark Mother, California Institute of Integral Studies, San Francisco, California, Spring, 2000.

8   Louise Paré, *Unpublished Poems.* (Oakland, 2001)

9   For Kalli Halvorson, see *The Herstar Report*: March 2001.

37. Black madonnas on Red Square, Moscow
Photograph by Louise Paré

38. Shango of Brazil
Painting by Elaine Soto

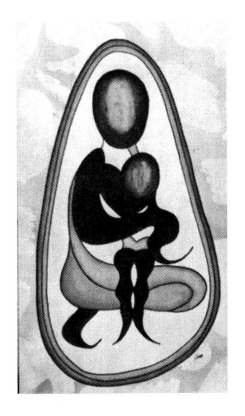

39. Contemporary asian dark woman divinity
Cloth painting purchased at Beijing women's conference, 1995.

Photograph by Wallace Birnbaum

40. Sarasvati, India

Painting by Elaine Soto

41. african sculpture

by Stephanie Romeo

42.Black madonna of the Andes
Banner by Lydia Ruhle

43. Dark mother

Painting by Eleanor Dickinson

about the author

Lucia Chiavola Birnbaum's maternal and paternal grandparents, and her father, migrated from Sicily to the United States at the turn, and first years, of the 20th century. She received the Ph.D. in intellectual history of the United States, and early modern and modern history of Europe, from the University of California at Berkeley, where she has taught U. S. history and American Studies. Lucia has also taught U.S. history, and the humanities, at San Francisco State University. Later, as an independent feminist scholar of cultural history, she has been affiliated with the Graduate Theological Union of Berkeley, and the Institute for Research on Women and Gender of Stanford University. In 2001 she is a professor in the department of Philosophy and Religion, program in Women's Spirituality, of the California Institute of Integral Studies, San Francisco.

Her books include *Liberazione della donna. Feminism in Italy* (Wesleyan University Press, 1986, 1988, American Book Award of the Before Columbus Foundation, 1987). And *Black Madonnas. Feminism, religion, and politics in Italy* (Northeastern University Press, 1993). In its italian edition (Bari, Palomar Editrice, 1997), *Black Madonnas* won a Premio Internazionale di Saggistica in 1998. .She has .lectured in a variety of venues in the United States, Europe, Australia, et al., contributed to several anthologies and many scholarly journals, and in 1996 was inducted into the African American International Multicultural Educators Hall of Fame.

Lucia's professional work has developed from that of a traditional historian to the continually widening methodologies of a feminist cultural scholar concerned with submerged beliefs. Intercultural, as well as interdisciplinary, she has studied everyday and celebratory rituals, saints' stories, the lives of her sicilian grandmothers/godmothers, and other dark others, including canaanites, moors, jews, heretics, and witches. Adopting comparative history, she has juxtaposed european and U. S. history and beliefs of the italian women's movement with beliefs of women of the world.

As she sends this book to the publisher in the perilous, yet liminal, days of October 2001, Lucia hopes that this study will hearten those working for a new world civilization grounded on the dark mother's values of justice with compassion, equality, and transformation.

selected bibliography

This selected bibliography does not include all the sources for chapter 9 on the social control of dark peoples. For fuller documentation see Lucille Terese Birnbaum, *John Broadus Watson and American Social Theory, 1913-1933*, Ph.D. dissertation, University of California, Berkeley, 1964.

To supplement this selected bibliography, see extensive bibliographies in the other two volumes of this trilogy: Lucia Chiavola Birnbaum, *Black Madonnas. Feminism, religion & politics in Italy* (Boston, Northeastern University Press, 1993; *Black Madonnas. Femminismo, politica, e religione in Italia* (Bari, Italy, Palomar Editrice, 1997, iUniverse, 2000) and *Liberazione della donna. Feminism in Italy* (Middletown, Ct., Wesleyan University Press, 1986, 1988).

À Santa Lucia. Profili della vita del culto della vergine e martire sirucusana (Siracusa, Emanuele Romeo Editore, 1994).

Adams, Henry *Mont Saint-Michel and Chartres* 1904. (Reprint, New York, Viking/Penguin, 1986).

Saint Augustine, *Confessions*. Tr., Edward B. Pusey, D.D. (New York, Simon & Schuster, Touchstone Edition, 1997.

African Folktales. Selected and Retold by Roger D. Abrahams (New York., Pantheon Books, 1983).

African History from Earliest Times to Independence, ed., Philip Curtin, Steven Feierman, Leonard Thompson, Jan Vansina (London and New York, Longman, 1978, 1995).

African Presence in Early Europe, ed., Ivan Van Sertima (New Brunswick and London, Transaction Publishers, 1993).

African Presence in Early Asia, ed., Runoko Rashidi, co-edited by Ivan Van Sertima. (New Brunswick and London, Transaction Publishers, 1993, 1995).

African Sculpture Speaks (New York, Da Capo Press, 1969, 1975).

Ahmed, Leila *Women and Gender in Islam* (New Haven and London, Yale University Press, 1992).

Alla ricerca di Iside. Analisi, studi e restauri dell'Iseo pompeiano nel Museo di Napoli (Soprintendenza Archeologica delle Province di Napoli e Caserta), 1992).

D'Alessandro, Vincenzo *Terra, nobili e borghesi nella Sicilia medievale* (Palermo,Sellerio editore, 1994).

D'Aversa, Arnaldo *La donna etrusca* (Brescia, Paideia Editrice, 1985).

Amin, Samir *Eurocentrism.* Tr., Russell Moore (New York, Monthly Review Press, 1989).

Anati, Emmanuel *Palestine before the Hebrews. A History, from the earliest arrival of man to the conquest of Canaan* (New York, Alfred A. Knopf, 1963) .

———. *Arte Rupestre. Il Linguaggio dei Primordi* (Brescia, Italia, Edizioni del Centro Camuno di Studi Preistorici, 1994).

———. *Brescia Preistorica. 300 mila anni di presenza umana nel territorio bresciano.* (Capo di Ponte, Italia, Edizioni del Centro Camuno di Studi Preistorici, 1995).

———. *Esodo tra Mito e Storia. Archeologia, esegesi e geografia storica* (Capo di Ponte, Italia, Edizioni del Centro Camuno di Studi Preistorici, 1997).

———. "Har Karkom. La Montagna di Dio," *Archeologia Viva*, marzo-aprile 1995).

———. *Har Karkom. 20 Anni di Ricerche Archeologiche.* (Capo di Ponte, Italia, Edizioni del Centro Camuno di Studi Preistorici, 1999).

———. *La Religione delle Origini* (Capo di Ponte, Italia, Edizioni del Centro, 1995).

———. *Les Racines de la Culture* (Capo di Ponte, Italia, Edition Francaise, 1995).

———. *Il Museo Immaginario della Preistoria. L'arte Rupestre nel Mundo* (Milano, editoriale Jaca Book SpA, 1995).

———. *Spedizione Sinai. Nuove Scoperte ad Har Karkom* (Brescia, Edizioni del Centro Camuno di Studi Preistorici, Brescia, 1994).

———. *La Religione delle Origini* (Brescia, Edizioni del Centro Camuno di Studi Preistorici, 1995).

————. *Valcamonica. Una Storia per L'Europa. Il Linguaggio delle Pietre.* (Capo di Ponte, Edizioni del Centro Camuno di Studi Preistorici, 1995).

Anati, Emmanuel, Luigi Cottinelli, and Federico Mailland, "Il santuario piu' antico del mondo." *Archeologia Viva,* marzo/aprile 1996

Ancient Anatolia. Aspects of Change and Cultural Development. Edited by Jeanne V. Canby, et al. Essays in Honor of Machteld J. Mellink, (Madison, University of Wisconsin Press, 1986).

Anthony, Sharon *The Courage to Burn: Following Jeanne d'Arc and the black madonnas* (unpublished manuscript).

Antalya Museum Guide (Antalya Museum Publication, 1966)._

Antiche Genti d'Italia, a cura di Pietro Giovanni Guzzo, Sabatino Moscati, Giancarlo Susini (Rimini, Edizioni De Luca, 1994).

L'Antico Egitto. Archeologia di una civiltà (Trieste, Electa/Gallimard, 1992).

Anzaldua, Gloria *Borderlands: La Frontera; The New Mestiza* (San Francisco, Spinster/Aunt Lute, 1987)._

Appiah, Kwame Anthony and Henry Louis Gates, Jr. *The dictionary of global culture. The global citizen's guide to culture, emphasizing the achievement of the non-Western world, what every American needs to know as we enter the next century* (New York, Alfred A. Knopf, 1997).

Apuleius, The Golden Ass. The Transformations of Lucius Otherwise Known as A new translation by Robert Graves (New York, Farrar, Straus & Giroux, 1951).

The Archaeological Museum of Syracuse Paolo Orsi, Text by Giuseppe Voza, Photographs by Mimmo Jodice (Siracuse, Ediprint, 1987).

Aries, Philippe and Georges Duby, General Editors *A History of Private Life. From Pagan Rome to Byzantium* (The Belknap Press of Harvard University Press, Cambridge, Ma. , 1987).

Art et Civilisations des Chasseurs de la Prehistoire 34000-8000 ans av. J.C. (Paris, Laboratoire de Prehistoire du Musee de L'Homme et Musee des Antiquites Nationales de Saint-Germain-en-Laye, 1984).

Art of Rome, Etruria, and Magna Graecia. Text by German Hafner (New York, Harry N. Abrams, Inc., 1969.

Archeologia Viva. Bimestrale, Florence, Italy.

Asante, Molefi Kete *The Afrocentric Idea* (Philadelphia, Temple University Press, 1987).

Assmann, Jan *Moses The Egyptian. The Memory of Egypt in Western Monotheism* (Cambridge, Ma., Harvard University Press, 1997).

Assyrian Sculpture, ed., Julian Reade (London, British Museum Press, 1983).

Atroshenko, V. I. And Milton Grundy *Mediterranean Vernacular. A Vanishing Architectural Tradition* (New York, Rizzoli, 1991).

Aubet, Maria Eugenia *The Phoenicians and the West. Politics, Colonies and Trade.* Translated from the Spanish by Mary Burton (Cambridge, Cambridge University Press, 1996).

Austen, Hallie Iglehart. *Art, Myth and Meditations of the World's Sacred Feminine* (Berkeley, Wingbow Press, 1990.

d'Aversa, Arnoldo *La Donna Etrusca* (Brescia, Paideia Editrice, 1985).

Badone, Ellen, Ed., *Religious Orthodoxy & Popular Faith In European Society* (Princeton, New Jersey, Princeton University Press, 1990).

Bakhtin, Mikhail *Rabelais and His World.* Tr., Helene Iswolsky (Massachusetts Institute of Technology, 1968).

Balibar, Etienne and Immanuel Wallerstein *Race, Nation, Class. Ambiguous Identities* (London and New York, Verso, 1991

Barber, Elizabeth Wayland *Women's Work. The First 20,000 Years* (New York, London, W. W., Norton & Company, 1994).

Barbera, Henry *Medieval Sicily. The First Absolute State* (Brooklyn, N. Y. Arba Sicula—Legas, 1994).

Baring, Anne and Jules Cashford. *The Myth of the Goddess. Evolution of an Image* (London, Penguin-Arkana, 1991, 1993).

Barlow, William *End to Silence. The San Francisco State Strike* (New York, Pegasus, 1970).

Baurain, Claude and Bonnet, Corinne *Les Pheniciens. Marins des trois continents* (Paris, Armand Colin, 1992).

Baroin, Jeanne, Josian Haffen *La Prophetie de la Sibylle Tiburtine* (Paris, Annales litteraires de l'Universite de Besancon—Les Belles Lettres, 1987).

Barstow, Anne Llewellyn Barstow. *Witchcraze. A New History of the European Witch Hunts. Our Legacy of Violence against Women* (N. Y., Pandora, a Division of Harper Collins, 1994).

De Bascher, Dom Jacques de *La Vierge noire de Paris. Notre Dame de Bonne Deliverance* (Paris, Tequi, 1979).

Bastid, Jean-Pierre *Notre-Dame des Negres. "Les pauvres sont les negres de l'Europe"* (Paris, Editions Gallimard 1996).

Bazin, Germain *Baroque and Rococo* (New York and Toronto, Oxford University Press, 1964).

Beastiary of Christ, Tr. D. M. Dooling (New York, Penguin Books, 1992).

Begg, Ean *The Cult of the Black Virgin* (London, Arkana, 1985, 1996).

Behar, Ruth *The Vulnerable Observer. Anthropology that breaks your heart.* (Boston, Beacon Press, 1996).

Bevilacqua,Piero *Breve storia dell'italia meridionale dall'Ottocento a oggi* (Roma, Donzelli Editore, 1993).

Bell, Diane *Daughters of the Dreaming* (Minneapolis, University of Minnesota Press, 1993).

Bellah, Robert, "The Five Religions of Modern Italy," *Varieties of Civil Religion* (San Francisco, Harper & Row, 1980).

Berger, Pamela *The Grain Goddess Obscured: Transformation of the Grain Protectress to Saint* (Boston, Beacon Press, 1985).

Berman, Morris *Coming to our senses. Body and spirit in the hidden history of the west* (New York, Simon and Schuster, 1989).

Bernal, Martin *Black Athena. The AfroAsiatic Roots of Classical Civilization* (New Brunswick, New Jersey, Rutgers University Press,). Volume I *The Fabrication of Ancient Greece l785-1985,* 1987. Volume II *The Archaeological and Documentary Evidence,* 1991.

Berton, Hugues *Sorcellerie en Auvergne. Sorciers, guerisseurs, medicines magiques et traditionneles* (Cournon d'Auvergne, Editions de Boree, 1995).

Biaggi, Cristina *Habitations of the Great Goddess* (Manchester, Ct., Knowledge, Ideas & Trends, 1994).

———. *The Goddess Mound.* With Mimi Lobell (Palisades, N. Y., Biaggi/Lobell, 1994).

Biale, David Gershom Scholem *Kabbalah and Counter-History* (Cambridge, Ma. and London, Harvard University Press, 1984).

Bijou, Jacqueline "Antistructure and the Feminine in Roman Catholicism and Tibetan Buddhism," M.A,.Thesis, California State University, Bakersfield, June 1996.

Birnbaum, Lucia Chiavola *Black Madonnas. Feminism, religion, and politics in Italy* (Boston, Northeastern University Press, 1993; iUniverse reprint edition, 2000).

————. *Black Madonnas. Femminismo, religione e politica in Italia* (Bari, Palomar Editrice, 1997).

————. *Liberazione della donna. Feminism in Italy* (Middletown, Ct. Wesleyan University Press, 1986, 1988).

————. *Report on the Fourth World Conference on Women, Beijing, China* Unpublished manuscript. (San Francisco, Ca., Women's Heritage Museum Archives, 1995).

————. *John Broadus Watson's Behaviorist Psychology and American Social Theory, 1913-1933* (Ph.D. Dissertation, University of California, Berkeley, 1964). Revised, 1994, *Behaviorists, Enlightened Behaviorists, and Democracy in the United States.*

————. "The Long History of Sicilians," *Proceedings*, the 27th annual conference, American Italian Historical Association, November, 1994.

————. "The Unkempt Prophets of Berkeley," *issue: those who make the waves*, University Church Council, Berkeley, California, 1965. Reprinted in *renewal*, Oct.-Nov. 1965.

————. *La religione e le donne siculo americane* (Siracusa, Italia, Editrice-Minori Cappuccini, 1981).

————. "Education for Conformity. The Case of Sicilian American Women Professionals," Italian Americans in the Professions. Proceedings, the Twefth Annual Conference of the American Italian Historical association, 1983.

————. "Analisi comparativa delle donne italiane ed italo americane dagli anni 1890 agli anni 1980," *Atti del Convegno: Le società in transizione: italiani ed italoamericani negli anni ottanta,"* (Philadelphia, Balch Institute, 1985).

————. "la famiglia italiana e la famiglia statiunitense: A comparative historical study," Italian Ethnics, Their Languages, Literature and Life,

Proceedings, Conference of the American Italian Historical Association, Nov. ll-l3, 1987, eds. Dominic Candeloro, Fred L. Gardaphe, Paolo A. Giordano, eds. (Staten Island, New York, The American Italian Historical Association, 1990).

————. "red, a little white, a lot of green, on a field of pink: a controversial Italian design for a multicultural canon for the United states," *From Margin to Mainstream: Writings in Italian Americana,* ed., Anthony J. Tamburri, Paolo A. Giardano, Fred L. Gardaphe (Purdue University Press, 1991).

————. "African Heritage of Italian and other European Americans, and of all Peoples of the Earth," *MultiAmerica. Essays in Cultural War and Cultural Peace,* edited by Ishmael Reed (New York, Viking, 1997).

————. "Marija Gimbutas and the Change of Paradigm," *From the Realm of the Ancestors. Essays in Honor of Marija Gimbutas.* Ed., Joan Marler (Manchester, Ct., Knowledge, Ideas, Trends, 1997).

Bloch, Marc. *Feudal Society.* Vols. 1 and 2, Tr., L. A. Manyon (Chicago, University of Chicago Press, 1961).

Bocchi, Gianluca Mauro Ceruti *Origini di storie* (Milano, Feltrinelli, 1993).

Bonfante, Larissa, ed. *Etruscan Life and Afterlife. A Handbook of Etruscan Studies* (Detroit, Wayne State University Press, 1986).

Bonanno, Anthony *Malta. An Archaeological Paradise* (Valletta, M. J. Publications, Ltd. 1991, 1995).

Bornstein, Daniel and Roberto Rusconi *Women and Religion in Medieval and Renaissance Italy.* Tr., Margery J. Schneider (Chicago and London, The University of Chicago Press, 1996).

Boscarino, Salvatore, *Sicilia barocca. Architettura e città 1610-1760* (Roma, Officina Edizioni, 1981, 1986).

Bowman, Alan K. *Egypt after the Pharoahs 332 BC – AD 642 from Alexander to the Arab Conquest* (Berkeley and Los Angeles, University of California Press, 1986).

Brand, Stewart *The Clock of the Long Now. Time and Responsibility. The Ideas Behind the World's Slowest Computer* (New York, Basic Books, 1999).

Brandes, Stanley *Metaphors of Masculinity. Sex and Status in Andalusian Folklore* (Philadelphia, University of Pennsylvania Press, 1980).

Braudel, Fernand *Il Mediterraneo. Lo spazio, la storia, gli uomini, le tradizioni* (Milano, Bompiani, 1985).
———. *A History of Civilizations.* Tr., Richard Mayne New York, Penguin, 1993).
Bravo, Anna, a cura di *Donne e uomini nelle guerre mondiali* (Bari, Editori Laterza, 1991).
Brentjes, Burchard *African Rock Art.* Tr., A. Dent (New York, Clarkson N. Potter, Inc., 1965).
The British Museum Book of Ancient Egypt, eds., Stephen Quirke and Jeffrey Spencer (London, British Museum Press, 1992).
Brooke, Rosalind and Christopher, *Popular Religion in the Middle Ages. Western Europe l000-l300* (New York, Barnes & Noble Books, 1984).
Brown, A. C. *Ancient Italy before the Romans* (Oxford, Ashmolean Museum, 1980).
Brown, Peter *The cult of the saints. Its Rise and Function in Latin Christianity* (Chicago, University of Chicago Press, 1982).
———. *The Making of Late Antiquity* (Cambridge and London, Harvard University Press, 1978).
Brown, Shelby "Perspectives on Phoenician Art," *Biblical Archaeologist,* March 1992.
Buckton, David, ed., *Byzantium. Treasures of Byzantine Art and Culture from British Collections* (London, British Museum Press, 1994).
Burke, Peter *The Renaissance* (Atlantic Highlands, Humanities Pess International, Inc. 1989, 1990).
Buttita, Antonio and Silvana Miceli *Percorsi simbolici* (Palermo, S. F. Flaccovio Editore, 1989).
Byzantium. A World Civilization Edited by Angeliki E Laiou and Henry Maguire (Washington, D. C., Dumbarton Oaks Research Library Collection 1992).
Byzantium. Treasures of Byzantine Art and Culture. Ed., David Buckton (London, British Museum Press, 1994).
Cacciari, Massimo *Geo-Filosofia dell'Europa* (Milano, Adelphi, 1994).
Calio, Louisa. *Journey to the Heart Waters* (Unpublished mss., 1999).
———. *In the Eye of Balance* (Manhasset Hills, New York, Paradiso Press, 1978).

Calzoni, Umberto *Museo Archeologico Nazionale dell"Umbria-Perugia.* Sezione Preistorica (Roma, Istituto Poligrafico dello stato, MCMLXXI).

Campbell, Joseph *The Mysteries. Papers from the Eranos Yearbooks* (Princeton University Press, 1955).

————. *The Flight of the Wild Gander. Explorations in the Mythological Dimensions of Fairy Tales, Legends, and Symbols* (HarperPerennial, 1990).

Cantarella, Glauco Maria, *Le Sicilie e i Normanni. Le fonti di mito* (Bologna, Patron Editore, 1989.

Capel, Anne K. and Glenn E. Markoe, Editors *Mistress of the House. Mistress of Heaven* (New York, Hudson Hills Press, 1996).

Capitini, Aldo *Elementi di un'esperienza religiosa* (Bologna, Cappelli Editore, 1990).

Capodieci, C. Ottavio Garana *Santa Lucia nella tradizione, nella storia, nell'arte* (Siracusa, Deputazione della cappella di S. Lucia, 1992).

Caputi, Jane *the age of sex crime* (London, The Women's Press Ltd, 1987).

————. *Gossip, gorgons & crones. The Fates of the Earth* (Santa Fe, New Mexico, Bear & Company Publishing, 1993.

Carbonaro, Antonio and Arnaldo Nesti, *La cultura negata: Caratteri e potenzialità della cultura popolare* (Florence, Guaraldi Editore, 1975).

Carbonaro, Gino *La donna nei proverbi. Tradizioni popolari siciliane* (Ragusa, Thomas Editore, 1981, 1982).

Carniani, Mario *Santa Maria del Carmine e la Cappella Brancacci* (Firenze, Becocci Editore, n.d.).

Carletti, Sandro *Guide to the Catacombs of Priscilla.* Tr., Alice Mulhern (Vatican City, Pontifical Commission for Sacred Araeology, 1982).

Carniani, Mario *Santa Maria del Carmine e la Cappella Brancacci* (Firenze, Becocci Editore, n.d.)

Cashford, Jules *The Myth of Isis and Osiris* (Boston & Bath, Barefoot Books, 1993).

Cassell's Encyclopedia of Queer Myth, Symbol and Spirit covering Gay, Lesbian, Bisexual and Transgender Lore. Foreword by Gloria E. Anzaldua. Randy P. Conner, David Hatfield Sparks, Mariya Sparks (London, Cassell, 1997).

Castillo, Ana *Massacre of the Dreamers. Essays on Xicanisma* (New York, Penguin/Plume, 1994).

Cassagnes-Brouquet, avec la collaboration de Jean-Pierre Cassagnes *Vierges Noires. Regard et fascination* (Passage des Macons, Editions du Rouergue, 1990).

Le Catacombe Romane e L'Origine del Cristianesimo , Introduzione di Umberto M. Fasola (Firenze, Scala, 1981).

Cassagnes-Brouquet, Sophie *Vierges Noires. Regard et fascination* (Passage des Macons, Editions du Rouergue, 1990).

La Cathedrale de Monreale. Testo di Sandro Chierichetti (Milano, Co.Graf. Editrice, n.d.).

Cavalieri, Grace *Poems. New & selected* (Pensacola, Fla., Vision Library Publications, 1993).

Cavalli-Sforza, L. Luca and Paola Menozzi, Alberto Piazza *The History and Geography of Human Genes* (Princeton University Press, Princeton, New Jersey, 1994). (See also Louise Levathes, "A Geneticist (Cavalli-Sforza) Maps Ancient Migrations," *New York Times, Science Times*, July 27, 1993. And Sribala Subramanian, "The Story in Our Genes." Science, *Time,* January l6, 1995. Luigi L. Cavalli-Sforza, Paolo Menozzi, and Alberto Piazza, "Demic Expansions and Human Evolution," *Science,* 29 January 1993. Vol. 259).

Cavalli-Sforza, Luigi Luca *Genes, Peoples, and Languages* (New York, North Point Press/A division of Farrar, Straus and Giroux, 2000).

Cavalli-Sforza Luca e Francesco *Chi Siamo. La Storia della Diversità Umana* (Milano, Arnoldo Mondadori Editore, 1993).

———. *The Great Human Diasporas. The History of Diversity and Evolution* (Reading, Ma., et al. , Addison-Wesley Publishing Company, Inc. Heliz Books, 1995).

De Cepeda, Stor*ja tal—Madonna ta' Atocja* ((Malta, Giov. Muscat, 1953).

Charbonneau-Lassay, Louis and Emmanuel Ciaceri *Culti e Miti nella storia dell'antica Sicilia* (Catania,Clio, 1910, 1993).

Chiavola, Louis G. *A Sicilian American Youth in Kansas City* (unpublished manuscript).

Chomsky, Noam *Powers and Prospects. Reflections on human nature and the social order* (Boston, South End Press, 1996).

Chiat, Marilyn J. and Kathryn L. Reyerson, *The Medieval Mediterranean. Cross-Cultural Contacts* (St. Cloud, Minnesota, North star Press of St. Cloud, Inc. 1988).

Chomsky, Noam *Deterring Democracy* (New York, Hill and Wang, 1991, 1992).

Cipolla, Carlo M. "The South Italian Question: It's the Fault of the Normans," *Il Sole*, May 1, 1996.

Clissold, Stephen *St. Teresa of Avila* (New York, The Seabury Press, 1982).

Colafemmina, "Cesare *Gli Ebrei in Benevento," Estratto da Italia Judaica. Gli ebrei nello Stato pontificio fino Ghetto (1555)*. (Roma, Pubblicazione degli Archivi di Stato, Saggi 47).

———. "Una nuova epigrafe ebraica altomedievale a Lavello," *Estratto da Vetera Christianorium* 29, 1992, 411-421.

———. "Dagli dei a Dio. Parole Sacre e Parole Profetiche sulle Sponde del Mediterraneo." *Atti del Convegno Internazional di Studi promosso dall'Associazione Biblia*. Bari, 13-15 settembre 1991, a cura di Cesare Colafemmina (Cassano, ItaliaMessaggi, 1997).

Colinon, Maurice *Les saintes Maries de la Mer. Ou les pelerins du clair de lune* (Paris, Editions S.O.S., 1975).

Coetzee, J. M. *In the Heart of the Country. A Novel* (New York, Penguin Books, 1977).

Collins, D. Jean "The Message of Meroe" *Gnosis,* Spring 1990. No. 15.

Comte, Louis Notre-Dame du Puy. *Histoire. Art. Message. Notre-Dame de France* (Lyon, Lescuyer, 1988).

Conde', Maryse *I, Tituba, Black Witch of Salem*. Tr., Richard Philcox, Foreward by Angela Y. Davis (New York, Ballantine Books, 1992).

Con Lucia a Cristo (Siracusa, Cappella di S. Lucia, Festa di Maggio, 1994).

Conde', Maryse. *I, Tituba, Black Witch of Salem*. Tr., Richard Philcox (New York, Ballantine Books, 1992).

Confronti. Mensile di fede, politica, vita quotidiana. Roma.

Conner, Randy et al. *Cassell's Eycyclopedia of Queer Myth, Symbol and Spirit, Gay, Lesbian, Bisexual and Transgender Lore* (London, Cassell, 1997).

Connag, Graham *African civilizations. Precolonial and states in tropical Africa: an archaeological perspective* (Cambridge University Press, 1987, 1994).

Consiglio, Carlo *Una società a misura di natura* (Catania, Alfa Grafica Sgroi, 1981).

Conti, Carmelo *Il Vento a Corde dagli Iblei. Autori del novecento* (Ragusa and Catania, Criscione Tecnoplast Graficarta s.r.l, Edizioni Greco s.a.s., Catania, 1987).

Corbin, Alain, ed. *La violenza sessuale nella storia* (Roma-Bari, Gius. Laterza & Figli Spa, 1992).

Cordelier, Pierre, *Les Gitans* (Rennes, Editions Ouest-France, 1983).

Corradi, Laura *When Night is Day. Women, Everyday Life and Nightshift Work.* Published in Italy as *Il Tempo Rovesciato. Quotidianità femminile e lavoro notturno* (Milan, Franco Angeli, 1991).

Cottrell, Leonard *Hannibal. Enemy of Rome* (New York, Da Capo Press, 1992).

Cross, Frank Moore *Canaanite myth and Hebrew Epic. Essays in the History of the Religion of Israel* (Cambridge, Harvard University Press, 1973).

Customs and Habits of the Sicilian Peasants. Edited and translated by Rosalie N. Norris. Translated from *Costumi e Usanze dei Contadini di Sicilia* di Salvatore Salomone-Marino 1897) (Teaneck, New Jersey, Fairleigh Dickinson University Press, 1981).

D'Alessandro, Vincenzo *Terra, nobili e borghesi nella Sicilia medievale* (Palermo, Sellerio editore, 1994).

Davidson, Basil *The Lost Cities of Africa* (Boston, New York, Toronto, London, little Brown and Company, 1959, 1970, 1987).

———. *African Civilization Revisited. From Antiquity to Modern Times* (Trenton, N J. , Africa World Press, Inc., 1991).

———. *The African Genius. An Introduction to African Social and Cultural History* (Boston, Little, Brown and Company. An Atlantic Monthly Press Book, 1969).

Davis, Angela Y. *Women, Culture, & Politics* (New York, Random House, 1984, 1989).

Davis, Natalie *Zemon Society and Culture in Early Modern France. Eight Essays* (Stanford, Ca., Stanford University Press, 1965).

"Dawn of Art: A New View," *The New York Times*, June 8, 1995.

Delaney, Carol *The Seed and the Soil. Gender and Cosmology in Turkish Village Society* (Berkeley, Los Angeles, Oxford, University of California Press, 1991).

Delarue, Louis o.m.i. *notre dame de lumieres* (Lyon, E.I.S.E., 1973).

Dewey, John *Essays in Experimental Logic* (Chicago, 1916).

————. *Democracy and Education. An Introduction to the Philosophy of Education,* (New York, 1916).

————. "Propaganda," *The New Republic,* December 1918

Diana's Hunt. Caccia di Diana. Boccaccio's First Fiction. Edited and Translated by Anthony K. Cassell & Victoria Kirkham (Philadelphia, University of Pennsylvania Press, 1991)

Demas, Jean *The Hawaiian Volcano Goddess Pele v. the United States Constitution: The Dilemma of Earth-Based Religion and the First Amendment.* (Paper, CIIS, 2000)

Desert Wisdom. Sacred Middle Eastern Writings from the Goddess through the Sufis. Translations & Commentary by Neil Douglas-Klotz (HarperSanFrancisco, 1995).

Dexter, Miriam Robbins, edited and supplemented *Marija Gimbutas. The Living Goddesses.* (Berkeley, Los Angeles, London, University of California Press, 1999

Diamond, Jared *Guns, Germs, and Steel. The Fates of Human Societies* (New York and London, W. W. Norton & Company, 1997).

Dictionary of global culture, edited by Kwame Anthony Appiah and Henry Louis Gates, Jr. (New York, Alfred A. Knopf, 1997).

Diop, Cheikh Anta, *Civilization or Barbarism. An Authentic Anthropology* (Presence Africaine, Paris, 1981; Brooklyn, New York, Lawrence Hill Books, n.d.).

———— *The African Origin of Civilization. Myth or Reality.* Edited and translated by Mercer Cook (Chicago Ill., Lawrence Hill Books, 1974).

————. *Precolonial Black Africa. A Comparative Study of the Political and Social Systems of Europe and Black Africa, from Antiquity to the Formation of Modern* States Tr., Harold Salemson (New York, Lawrence Hill Books, 1987).

Diotima. Il cielo stellato dentro di noi. L'ordine simbolico della madre (Milano, La Tartaruga edizioni, 1992)

Di Prima, Diane *Pieces of a Song* (San Francisco, City Lights Books, 1973, 1990).

DiStasi, Lawrence *Mal'occhio. The Underside of Vision* (Berkeley, Ca., North Point Press, 1981).

Dixon, John "Michelangelo's Carnal Spirituality," *Cross Currents: Religion & Intellectual Life,* Summer, 1991.

Donne nel Sud. Il prisma femminile sulla questione meridionale, a cura di Nella Ginatempo (Palermo, Gelka, 1993).

Doresse, Jean *The Secret Books of the Egyptian Gnostics An Introduction to the Gnostic Coptic manuscrits discovered at Cheoboskion. With an English translation and critical evaluation of the Gospel According to Thomas.* (Rochester, Vt., Inner Traditions International, Ltd., 1986).

Drewel, Margaret Thompson *Yoruba Ritual. Performers, Play, Agency* (Bloomington and Indianapolis, Indiana University Press, 1992).

Drews, Robert *The Coming of the Greeks. Indo-European Conquests in the Aegean and the near East* (Princeton University Press, 1988).

Du Bois, W. E. B. *Autobiography. A Soliloquy on Viewing My Life from the Last Decade of Its First Century* (New York, International Publishers, lst edition, 1940. Reviised edition 1968).

———. *Darkwater. Voices from Within the Veil* (New York, Schocken Books, 1920, 1969)

Durkheim, Emile "Religion and Ritual," *Selected Writings,* Edited, translated, and with an introduction by Anthony Giddens (Cambridge at the University Press, 1972).

Dwpress. Il notiziario delle donne, Roma.

Ebla. la città rivelata (Paris, Electa/Gallimard; Italian edition, Trieste, Editoriale Libreria, 1995).

Ebla to Damascus. Art and Archaeology of Ancient Syria (Seattle and London, Smithsonian Institution in association with University of Washington Press, 1985).

Egypt and the Ancient Near East. The Metropolitan Museum of Art, New York (Tokyo, Dai Nippon Printing Co. Ltd., 1987).

Eichman, William Carl "Catal Huyuk. The Temple City of Prehistoric Anatolia." *Gnosis*, Spring 1990, No. 15.

Einsiedeln (Einsiedeln, Beat Eberle, Publisher, 1993).

Eisler, Riane *Sacred Pleasure. Sex, myth, and the politics of the body. New paths to power and love* (HarperSanFrancisco, 1995).

Eliade, Mircea *Occultism, Witchcraft, and Cultural Fashions. Essays in Comparative Religions* (Chicago and London, The University of Chicago Press, 1976).

Ennabli, Abdelmajid, "Cartine. Civiltà Risorta," *Archeologia Viva*, Luglio/Agosto 1995.

Egypt and Nubia. Ed., John H. Taylor (London, British Museum Press, 1991).

Egypt: Land of the Pharaohs. Lost Civilizations, (Alexandria, Virginia, Time-Life Books, n.d.).

Egyptian Art in Munich, ed., Sylvia Schoske (Munich, Sgaatliche Sammlung Agyptischer Kunst Munchen, 1993).

Egyptian Museum, Cairo (Cairo, Art Publishers Lehneert & Landrock, Cairo, 1995).

Ennen, Edith *The Medieval Woman (Oxford, Basil Blackwell Ltd, 1989).*

Etruscan and Roman Antiquities (Paris, Scala Publications, 1991).

Euripedes, *Medea* (reprinted New York, Dover Publications, Inc. 1993)

Fanon, Frantz *The Wretched of the Earth*. Preface by Jean-Paul Sartre. Translated by Constance Farrington (New York, Grove Press, 1963).

————. *A Dying Colonialism* (New York, Grove Press, 1965).

Farmer, David Hugh *The Oxford Dictionary of Saints* (New York, Oxford University Press, 1992).

Fasola, Umberto *Maria Le origini cristiane a Trastevere* (Roma, Fratelli Palombi srl, 1991).

"I Fenici e il Mare. Lilibeo e la colonizzazione della Sicily." *Archeologia Viva* Video, 1991.

Ferrara, Corrado *La Musica dei Vanniaturi o Gridatori di Piazza Notigiani. Impressioni* (Noto, Off. Tip. Di Fr. Zammit, 1896).

————. *L'Ignota Provenienza dei canti popolari di Noto* (Noto, Tipografia Zammit, 1908).

Fiorenza, Elisabeth Schussler *In Memory of Her. A Feminist Theological Reconstruction of Christian Origins* (New York, Crossroad, 1983, 1992).
———. *Jesus. Miriam's Child. Sophia's Prophet. Critical Issues in Feminist Christology* (New York, Continuum, 1994).
———. *Discipleship of Equals. A Critical Feminist Ekklesia-logy of Liberation* (New York, Crossroad, 1993).
Fiori, Gabriella *Simone Weil. La biografia interiore di una delle intelligenze piu' alte e pure nel nostro secolo* (Roma, Garzanti Editore s.p.a. 1981, 1990).
Fitton, J. Lesley *Cycladic Art* (London, British Museum Publications, 1989).
Flinders, Carol Lee *Enduring Grace. Living Portraits of Seven Women Mystics* (HarperSanFrancisco, 1993).
Folklore Religioso nella Contea di Modica. Testo di Giuseppe Iacono. Prefazione di Antonino Buttitta (CTG. Criscione Tecnoplast Graficarta srl—Ragusa, 1989).
Four Centuries of Jewish Women's Spirituality. A Sourcebook. Ed., Ellen M. Umansky and Dianne Ashton (Boston, Beacon Press, 1992).
From the Margin. Writings in Italian Americana, ed., Anthony J. Tamburri, Paolo A. Giordano, Fred L. Gardaphe (W Lafayette, Indiana, Purdue University Press, 1991).
Ford, Clyde W. *The Hero with an African Face. Mythic Wisdom of Traditional Africa* (New York, Bantam Hardcover, 1999).
Fraser, Angus *The Gypsies* (Oxford U K & Cambridge USA, Blackwell, 1992, 1995).
Frauen Museum, Sprache der Gottin. Annaherung an das werk von Marija Gimbutas. Katalog zur ausstellung (Wiesbaden, Frauenwerkstatt, 1994).
Fredrickson, George *The Black Image in the White Mind. The Debate on Afro-American Character and destiny, 1817—1914* (Middletown, Ct., Wesleyan University Press, 1971).
———. *The Arrogance of Race. Historical Perspectives on Slavery, Racism, and Social Inequality* (Middletown, Ct., Wesleyan University Press, 1988).
From the Realm of the Ancestors. An Anthology in Honor of Marija Gimbutas, ed., Joan Marler (Manchester, Ct., Knowledge, Ideas, & Trends, Inc.,1997).
Fuiani, *Pasquale Santa Lucia. Profili della vita e del culto della virgine e martire siracusana* (Siracusa, Flaccavento, 1994. Originally published 1886).

Fox, Robin Lane *Pagans and Christians* (HarperSanFrancisco, 1986).

Gadon, Elinor W. *The Once & Future Goddess. A Symbol for Our Time. A Sweeping Chronicle of the Sacred Female and Her Reemergence in the Cultural Mythology of Our Time* (HarperSanFrancisco, 1989).

Galland, China *Longing for Darkness. Tara and the Black Madonna* (New York, Penguin, 1990).

Garofalo, Filippo, *Discorsi sopra L'Antica e Moderna Ragusa* (Ragusa, Libreria Paolino Editrice, 1980).

Garana, Ottavio *Santa Lucia. V. e M. Sirucasana nella Tradizione, nella Storia, nell'Arte* (Siracusa, Cappella di S. Lucia, 1992).

Gates Jr., Henry Louis and Cornel West *The Future of the Race* (New York, Vintage, 1997).

Gebara, Ivone and M. Clara Bingemer *Maria Madre di Dio e madre dei poveri* (Assisi, Cittadella Editrice, 1987).

Getty, Adele *Goddess. Mother of Living Nature* (London, Thames & Hudson, 1990).

Gianfreda, Grazio *Iconografia di Otrantro tra Oriente e Occidente* (Lecce, Edizione del Grifo, 1994).

Giddings, Franklin *Henry Democracy and Empire* (New York,, 1900).

———. *The Responsible State. A reexamination of Fundamental Political Doctrines in the Light of World War and the Menace of Anarchism* (Boston and New York, 1918).

Gillon, Werner *A Short History of African Art* (London, Penguin Books, 1984).

Gohary, Jocelyn *Guide to the Nubian Monuments on Lake Nasser* (American University in Cairo Press, 1999).

Grove, Margaret, *An Iconographic and Mythological Convergence: Gender Motifs in Northern Australian Aboriginal Rock Art.* (Doctoral Dissertation, CIIS, 2000).

Gilroy, Paul *Black Atlantic. Modernity and Double Consciousness* (Cambridge, Ma., Harvard University Press, 1993).

Gillan, Maria Mazziotti and Jennifer Gillan, eds., *Unsettling America. An Anthology of Contemporary Multicultural Poetry* (New York, Penguin, 1994).

Gimbutas, Maria *The Language of the Goddess* (HarperSan Francisco, 1980).

————. *The Civilization of the Goddess* (HarperSan Francisco, 1989)

————. *The Goddesses and Gods of Old Europe 6500-3500 BC* (Berkeley, Los Angeles, New York University of California Press, New and updated edition, 1982, 1992).

Ginzburg, Carlo *Ecstasies. Deciphering the Witches' Sabbath* (Originally published in Italy as *Storia Notturna,* 1989; New York, Penguin Books, 1991).

————. *Night Battles. Witchcraft & Agrarian Cults in the Sixteenth & Seventeenth Centuries.* Tr. John & Anne Tedeschi (New York, Penguin Books, 1983).

————. *The Cheese and the Worms: The Cosmos of a Sixteenth-Century Miller* (Johns Hopkins University Press, 1980).

The Glory of Byzantium. Art and Culture of the Middle Byzantine Era A.D. 843-1261. Ed., Helen C. Evans and William D. Wixom (New York, The Metropolitan Museum of Art, 1997).

Goddess of the Americas. Writings on the Virgin of Guadalupe, edited by Ana Castillo (New York, Riverhead Books, 1996).

The Gods and Symbols of Ancient Egypt. An Illustrated Dictionary. Ed., Manfred Lurker (London, Thames and Hudson, 1974).

Gonzalez-Wippler *Santeria. African Magic in Latin America* (New York, Original Publications, 1981, 1992).

Gordon, Cyrus H. *the ancient near east* (New York and London, W. W. Norton & Company, 3rd edition revised, 1965).

Gottner-Abendroth, Heide *The Dancing Goddess. Principles of a Matriarchal Aesthetic.* Tr., Maureen T. Krause (Boston, Beacon Press, 1982).

————. *The Goddess and Her Heros* (Stow, Ma. Anthony Publishing Company, 1995).

Gottwald, Norman K. *The Hebrew Bible in its Social world and in Ours* (Atlanta, Georgia, Scholars Press, 1993.

Gould, Stephen Jay, "So Near and Yet So Far,' *The New York Review of Books,* October 20, 1994.

Grahn, Judy *Blood, Bread, and Roses. How Menstruation Created the World* (Boston, Beacon Press, 1993).

————. *Metaformic theory and menstrual rituals of Kerala* (Doctoral Dissertation, CIIS, 1999)

Gramsci, Antonio *The Southern Question.* Translation and introduction by Pasquale Verdicchio (West Lafayette, Indiana Bordighera Incorporated, 1995).

———. *Prison Notebooks.* Vol. L, Ed, Joseph A. Buttigieg (New York, Columbia University Press, 1975).

———. *Antonio Gramsci. Selections from the Prison Notebooks.* E.d., Hoare and G. N. Smith (New York, International Publishers, 1971).

———. *Pre-Prison Writings.,* Ed., Richard Bellamy (Cambridge University Press, 1994).

———. *Lettere del carcere,* ed., Paolo Spriano (Turin, Einaudi, 1971).

———. *Folclore e senso comune* (Roma, Editori Riuniti, 1992).

Grant, Michael *The Ancient Mediterranean* (New York, Penguin Books, 1969).

———. *The Visible Past. Greek and Roman History from archaeology* (New York, Charles Scribner's Sons, 1990).

Grasso, *Mario Lingua delle Madri. Voce e pensiero dei siciliani nel tempo* (Catania, Prova d'Autore di N.L.)

Greco, Sabino *Miti e leggende di Sicilia* (Palermo,Dario Flaccovio Editore, 1993).

Guastella, Serafino Amabile L'Antico Carnevale della Contea di Modica. Schizzi di. costumi popolari. (Ragusa, Piccitto 7 Antoci Editori, 1887) s.a.s. 1994.

———. *Le Domande Carnescialesche e gli scioglilingua del circondario di Modica.* Raccolti e annotati da S. A. Guastella (Ragusa, Piccitto & Antoci, 1888).

———. *Le parità morali* (Ragusa, 1884. Reprint. San Casciano, Cappelli Editore, 1968).

Guidi, Oscar *Gli Streghi, Le Streghe. Antiche credenze nei racconti popolari della Garfagna* (Lucca, Maria Pacini Fazzi Editore, 1990).

Guthrie, W. K. C. *Orpheus and Greek Religion. A Study of the Orphic Movement* (Princeton, N. J., Princeton University Press, 1993).

Gutierrez, Ramon A. When Jesus Came, the Corn Mother Went Away. Marriage, Sexuality and Power in New Mexico, 1500-1846) (Stanford, Stanford University Press, 1991.)

Hafner, German *Art of Rome, Etruria, and Magna Graecia* (Baden Baden, Germany Holle Verlag GmbH, 1969, 1994).

Hamel, Pasquale *Breve storia della società siciliana l790-1980* (Palermo, Sellerio, n.d.).

Hamer, Mary, *Signs of Cleopatra. History, politics, representation* (Routledge, London and New York, 1993).

Haraway, Donna J. *Simians, Cyborgs, and Women. The Reinvention of Nature* (New York, Routledge, 1991).

———. *How Like A Leaf. An Interview with Thyrza Nichols Goodeve* (New York and London, Routledge, 2000).

Harding, Sandra *Feminism & Methodology* (Bloomington, Indiana, Indiana University Press, 1987).

———. *Is Science Multi-cultural? Postcolonialisms, Feminisms, and Epistemologies* (Bloomington and Indianapolis, Indiana University Press, 1998).

Harkless, Necia Desiree *Heart to Heart* (Lexington, Kentucky, Heart to Heart and Associates, 1995).

Haarmann, Harald *Early Civilization and Literacy in Europe. An Inquiry into Cultural Continuity in the Mediterranean World* (Berlin and New York, Mouton de Gruyter, 1996).

Haruach, Miri Hunter *The Queen of Sheba: An Ancient Woman for Modern Times.* (Doctoral Dissertation, CIIS, 2000).

Harrison, Jane *Prolegomena to the Study of Greek Religion* (London, Merlin Press, 1962, 1980).

Haskins, Susan *Mary Magdalen. Myth and Metaphor* (New York, Riverhead Books, 1993).

Haynes, Joyce L. *Nubia. Ancient Kingdoms of Africa* (Boston, Museum of Fine Arts, 1994).

Herm, Gerhard *The Celts* (New York, St. Martin's Press, 1975).

Hey Paesan! Writings by Lesbians & Gay Men of Italian Descent, edited by Giovanna (Janet) Capone, Denise Nico Leto and Tommi Avicolli Mecca (Oakland, Ca., Three Guineas Press, 1999).

L'Heuereux, Conrad E. *Rank among the Canaanite Gods El, Ba al and the Repha* (Harvard Semitic Monographs, No. 21, 1979).

Higgins, Reynold *Minoan and Myceneaean Art* (London, Thames and Hudson Ltd, 1967, 1981).

Higham, John *Strangers in the Land. Patterns of American Nativism, 1860-1925* (New York, 1966).

Hirshfield, Jane, ed. *Women in Praise of the Sacred. 43 Centuries of Spiritual Poetry by Women* (New York, Harper Perennial, 1995).

Hoffman, Michael A. *Egypt Before the Pharaohs* (New York, Alfred A. Knopf, 1979)

Holub, Renate *Antonio Gramsci: Beyond Marxism and Postmodernism* (London, Routledge, 1992).

Homer, The Iliad. The Story of Achilles. Translated by W. H. D. Rouse (A Mentor Book, n.d.).

hooks, bell and Cornel West *Breaking Bread. Insurgent Black Intellectual Life* (Boston, Ma., South End Press, 1991).Egypt). Tr. John Baines (Ithaca, N. Y., Cornell University Press, 1971, 1982, 1996).

Hornung, Erik *History of Ancient Egypt.* (Ithaca, New York, Cornell University Press, 1999).

———. *Conceptions of God in Ancient Egypt. The One and the Many.* Tr. John Baines. (Ithaca and London, Cornell University Press, 1999).

———. *The Ancient Egyptian Books of the Afterlife* (Ithaca and London, Cornell University Press, 1999).

Hourani, Alaberet *A History of the Arab Peoples* (New York, Warner Books Edition, 1992).

Houston, Drusilla Dunjee *Wonderful Ethiopians of the Ancient Cushite Empire* (first published in 1926. Baltimore, Md., Black Classic Press, 1985).

Hubbs, Joanna *Mother Russia. The Feminine Myth in Russian Culture* (Bloomington and Indianapolis, Indiana University Press, 1993).

Hurston, Zora Neale *Their Eyes Were Watching God* (First published 1937. New York, Harper Perennial, 1990).

Huynen, Jacques *l'enigme des vierges noires* (Chartres, Editions Jean-Michel Garnier, 1972, 1994).

Iacono, Giuseppe *Folklore Religioso nella Contea di Modica.* (Ragusa, Criscione Tecnoplast Graficarta srl, 1989).

"Identities in Conflict: The Jews and Jewish Communities in the Mediterranean," *Journal of Mediterranean Studies. History, Culture and Society in the Mediterranean World* (Malta, Printwell, Ltd., 1994).

Il Messaggio della Santa Casa (Loreto, Italia).

In all Her Names. Explorations of the Feminine in Divinity. Ed., Joseph Campbell, Riane Eisler, Maria Gimbutas (HarperSanFrancisco 1991).

Irigaray, Luce *This Sex Which is Not One* Tr., Catherine Porter (Ithaca and New ork, Cornell University Press, 1985).

————. *J'aime à toi: Esquisse d'une felicite' dans l'histoire* (Paris, Bernard Grasset, 1992).

————. *The Irigaray Reader*, ed., Margaret Whitford (Oxford, UK, Basil Blackwell, 1991).

Istanbul Archaeological Museum (Istanbul, A Turizm Yaymlari, 1996).

Italia Nonviolenta (Perugia, Centro Studi Aldo Capitini, 1981).

Jacobsen, Thorkild *The Treasures of Darkness. A History of Mesopotamian Religion* (New Haven, Ct., Yale University Press, 1976).

James, Peter, *Centuries of Darkness* (New Brunswick, N. J., Rutgers University Press, 1993).

Jameson, Fredrick *Postmodernism. Or, the Cultural Logic of Late Capitalism* (Durham, Duke University Press, 1995).

Jenett, Dianne *Red Rice for Bhagavati/Cooking for Kannaki: an Ethnographic/Organic Inquiry of the Pongala Ritual at Attukal Temple, Kerala, South India* (Doctoral Dissertation, CIIS, 2000).

Joan, Eahr, *Re-Genesis: The Mother-Line Archive of Feminist Spirituality* (M.A. Thesis, CIIS, 2000).

Jordan, Winthrop D. *White Over Black. American Attitudes toward the Negro l550-l812* (Baltimore, Md., Penguin Books, 1968).

————. *The White Man's Burden. Historical Origins of Racism in the United States* (London, Oxford, New York, Oxford University Press, 1974).

Journal of Mediterranean Studies (The Mediterranean Institute, University of Malta)

.Kack-Brice, Valerie *Silent Goddesses: A Study of Elder Breton Women and Sainte Anne, Grandmother of Jesus* (Doctoral Dissertation, CIIS, 2000).

Kamen, Henry *The Phoenix and the Flame. Catalonia and the Counter Reformation* (New Haven & London, Yale University Press, 1993).

Kamil, Jill *Coptic Egypt. History and guide.* Rev. Ed. (The American University in Cairo Press, 1987, 1990).

————. *The Ancient Egyptians. Life in the Old Kingdom* (The American University in Cairo Press, 1984, 1996).

————. *Upper Egypt and Nubia. The Antiquities from Amarna to Abu Simbel* (Cairo, Egyptian International Publishing Co., 1996).

Kaplan, Temma *Anarchists of Andalusia 1868 1903* (Princeton, N. J., Princeton University Press, 1977).

Keddie, Nikki R. and Beth Baron *Women in Middle Eastern History. Shifting Boundaries in Sex and Gender* (New Haven and London, Yale University Press, 1991).

Kerenyi, Carl *Eleusis. Archetypal Image of Mother and Daughter* (Princeton University Press, 1967).

Kertzer, David I. and Richard P. Saller, editors *The Family in Italy from Antiquity to the Present* (New Haven and London, Yale University Press. 1991).

Kinsley, David *Hindu Goddesses: Visions of the Divine Feminine in the Hindu Religious Tradition* (Berkeley and Los Angeles, University of California Press, 1988).

Knappert, Jan *African Mythology. An Encyclopedia of Myth and Legend,* (London, Diamond Books, 1995).

Kozol, Jonathan *Savage Inequalities. Children in America's Schools* (New York, Crown Publishers, Inc. 1991).

Kraemer, Ross Shepard *Her Share of the Blessings. Women's Religions among Pagans, Jews and Christians in the Greco-Roman World* (New York and Oxford, Oxford University Press, 1992).

Kramer, Samuel Noah *History Begins at Sumer. Thirty-Nine Firsts in Man's Recorded History* (Philadelphia, University of Pennsylvania Press, 1956, 1981).

Kreutz, Barbara M. *Before the Normans. Southern Italy in the Ninth & Tenth Centuries* (Philadelphia, University of Pennsylvania Press, 1991).

Ladurie, Emmanuel Le Roy, *Montaillou. The Promised Land of Error* (New York, Vintage Books Ed., 1979).

La Lumia, Isidoro *Gli Ebrei siciliani* (Palermo, Sellerio editore, 1984, 1992).

LaMonte, Willow *Sicilian Goddess Chronicles. A Journal of Women's Mysteries* (Malta, 1995)

Lange, Judith "ll00 anni di Tunisia," *Archeologia Viva*, Luglio/Agosto 1989.

L'antico Egitto. Archeologia di una civiltà (original edition, A la recherche de l'Egypte oubliee', Ed. Martine Buysschaert (Paris, Gallimard, 1986. Italian edition, Electa/Gallimard, 1992).

L'Antica e Moderna Ragusa. Discorsi sopra. Con una biografia di Giovan Battist. (Ragusa, n.d.).

Lefkowitz, Mary. *Not Out of Africa. How afrocentrism became an excuse to teach myth as history* (New York, A New Republic Book. Basic Books. A Division of HarperCollins, Publishers,. 1996).

Lefkowitz, Mary R. and Guy MacLean Rogers, *Black Athena Revisited.* (Chapel Hill and London, University of North Carolina Press, 1996).

Leggio, Giuseppe *Ibla Erea* (Ragusa, Tip. Leggio e DiQuattro, 1978).

Levi, Carlo *Cristo si e' fermato a Eboli* (Turin, Einaudi, 1945).

Lewis-Williams, David and Thomas Dowson, *Images of Power. Understanding Bushman Rock Art* (Johannesburg, Southern Book Publishers Ltd., 1989).

Long, Asphodel *In a Chariot Drawn by Lions. The Search for the Female in Deity*(n.d.).

Loreto. Nuova guida della città e del santuario della S. casa (Rimini, Pama Graphicolor, 1990).

L'Utopia di Francesco si e' fatta Chiara (Assisi, Cittadella Editrice, 1994).

The Louvre. Greece, (Avenel, N. J., Gramercy Books, 1994).

The Louvre. Greek, Etruscan and Roman Antiquities (Paris, Scala Publications, Ltd., 1991).

Lurker, Manfred An Illustated Dictionary of The Gods and Symbols of Ancient Egypt (London, Thames & Hudson Ltd., 1980)

Macmullen, Ramsay *Paganism in the Roman empire* (New Haven and London, Yale University Press, 1981).

Mackenzie, Donald A. *Egyptian Myths and Legends* (New York. Avenel, Gramercy Books, 1978).

Mackey, Mary *The Year the Horses Came. A novel* (HarperSanFrancisco, 1993).

Macmullen, Ramsay *Christianity & Paganism in the Fourth to Eighth Centuries* (New Haven, Ct., Yale University Press, 1997).,

Magli, Ida *Storia laica delle donne religiose (*M. Longanesi & Co., 1995).

Maempel, Georg Zammit *Ghar Dalam Cave and Deposits* (Malta, Maempel, 1989).

Mallory, J. P. *In Search of the Indo-Europeans. Language, archaeology and Myth* (London, Thames and Hudson, 1989).

Maltese Prehistoric Art 5000—2500 BC. Fondazzjoni Patrimonju Malti in association with the National Museum of Archaeology, ed., Anthony Pace (Valletta, Malta, Parimonju Publishing Limited, 1996).

Mancinelli, *Le Catacombe Romane e l'origine del Cristianesimo* (Firenze, Scala, n.d.)

Marable, Manning *Beyond Black and White. Transforming African-American Politics* (Verso, London & New York, 1995).

Maraini, Dacia *La lunga vita di Marianna Ucria: Romanzo* (Milan, Rizzoli, 1990).

———. *Voci* (Milano, Rizzoli, 1994)

De Martino, Ernesto *Sud e magia* (Milan, Feltrinelli, 1959).

Masaccio, ed., Ornella Casazza (Firenze, Scala, 1990)

Matthiae, Paolo *Ebla. An Empire Rediscovered.* Tr., Christopher Holme (London, Hodder and Stoughton, 1977).

Marx-Engels Reader, Edited by Robert C. Tucker (New York and London, W. W. Norton & Company, 1978).

Masaccio e la Cappella Brancacci, ed., Ornella Casazza (Firenze, Scala, 1991).

Masters, Robert *The Goddess Sekhmet. Psycho-spiritual exercises of the Fifth Way* (St. Paul, Minnesota, Llewellyn Publications, 1991).

May, Henry Farnham *Protestant Churches and Industrial Am*erica (Chicago, 1949).

———.*End of American Innocence* (New York, Alfred A. Knopf, 1959).

Maulucci, Francesco Paolo *Il Museo Archeologico Nazionale di Napoli* (Naples, Carcavallo Editore, 1988).

Mazar, Amihai *Archaeology of the Land of the Bible—10,000—586 B.C.E..* The Anchor Bible Reference Library (New York, et al., Doubleday, 1990).

McCall, Andrew *The Medieval Underworld* (New York, Barnes & Noble Books, 1979).

McClintock, Anne. *Imperial Leather. Race, Gender, and Sexuality in the Colonial Context* (New York & London, Routledge, 1995).

McKissack, Patricia and Fredrick *The Royal Kingdoms of Ghana, Mali and Songhay* (New York, Henry Holt and Company, 1994).

Meador, Betty DeShong *Uncursing the Dark. Treasures from the Underworld* (Chiron Publications, 1994).

———*Inanna: Lady of Largest Heart. Poems of the Sumerian High Priestess Enheduanna* (Austin, University of Texas Press, 2000).

Mellenbruch, Joie *Momma Katie. Twentieth Century Earth Mother* (Unpublished manuscript).

Menapace, Lidia *L'economia sessuale delle differenze* (Roma, Edizioni Felina Libri, 1987).

Mesopotamia, ed., Julian Reade (Cambridge, Harvard University Press, 1991).

Il Messaggio della Santa Casa (Loreto, Italia)

Il messaggio di Aldo Capitini. Antologia dagli scirtti. A cura di Giovanni Cacioppo (Manduria, Lacaita, 1977).

Messina, Calogero *Sicilians Wanted the Inquisition.* Tr., Alexandra and Peter Dawson. Italian edition, *Volevano l'Inquizione.* Edizioni Italiane di Letteratura e Scienze, Roma; U. S. edition (Brooklyn, Legas, 1993).

Metzner, Ralph *The Well of Remembrance. Rediscovering the Earth Wisdom Myths of Northern Europe* (Boston & London, Shambhala, 1994).

Meyer, Marvin W. , editor, *The Ancient Mysteries. A Sourcebook. Sacred Texts of the Mystery Religions of the Ancient Mediterranean World* (HarperSanFrancisco, 1987).

Mifsud, Marie *Temples* (Malta, Marie Mifsud, 1999)

Milano, Attilio *Storia degli ebrei in Italia* (Torino, Giulio Einaudi, 1992).

Miller, Francesca *Latin American Women and the Search for Social Justice* (Hanover & London, University Press of New England, 1991).

Miller, Perry *Errand into the Wilderness* (Boston, Harvard University Press, 11th printing 1993).

Missione a Malta. Ricerche e studi suilla preistoria dell'arcipelago maltese nel contesto mediterraneo. A cura di Ariela Fradkin Anati, Emmanuel Anati (Milano, Jaca Book, 1988).

Mitchell, Timothy *Passional Culture. Emotion, Religion, and Spciety in Southern Spain* (Philadelphia, University of Pennsyylvania Press, 1990).

Modrzejewski, Joseph Meleze *The Jews of Egypt from Rameses II to Emperor Hadrian* (Princeton, N. J., Princeton Univesity Press, 1997).

Momigliano, Arnaldo *On Pagans, Jews, and Christians* (Middletown, Ct., Wesleyan University Press, 1987).

Moreau, Roger *Walking in the Paths of the Gypsies* (Toronto, Ontario, Key Porter Books, 1995)

Moscati, Sabatino, Direzione scientifica *I Fenici* (Milano, Bompiani, 1988).

————. *Antichi imperi d'Oriente*. (Roma, Grande Tascabili Economici Newton, 1997).

————. *Ancient Semitic Civilizations* (New York, Capricorn Books, G. P. Putnam's Sons, 1957).

————. *La Bottega del Mercante. Artigianato e commercio fenicio lungo le sponde del Mediterraneo* (Torino, Società Editrice International, 1996).

————. *Chi Furono I Fenici* (Toriino, Società Editrice Internazionale, 1992).

————. *Italia Punica* (Milan, Rusconi, 1995)

————. *Il Tramonto di Cartagine* (Torino, Società Editrice Internazionale, 1993).

————. "Some Reflections on Malta in the Phoenician World," *Journal of Mediterranean Studies*, 1993. Vol. 3, No. 2: 286-290.

Moorey, P. R. S., *Ancient Egypt*. (Oxford, Ashmolean Museum, 1992).

Morison, Toni *Song of Solomon. A novel* (New York, Penguin/Plume, 1977)

MultiAmerica. Essays on Cultural Wars and Cultural Peace, ed., Ishmael Reed (New York, Viking/Penguin, 1997).

Muir, Edward and Guido Ruggiero *Microhistory & the Lost Peoples of Europe*. Tr., Eren Branch (Baltimore, *Md.*, Johns Hopkins Press, *1991*.

Muraro, Luisa *L'Ordine simbolico della madre* (Roma, Editori Riuniti, 1991).

————. *Guglielma e Maifreda: Storia di un'eresia femminista* (Milan, La Tartaruga, 1985).

————. *La Signora del Gioco: Episodi della caccia alle streghe* (Milan, Feltrinelli, 1976).

Murphy, Edwin *The Antiquities of Egypt*. A translation, with notes, of Book I of the *Library of History of Diodorus Siculus* (New Brunswick and London, Transaction Publishers, 1990).

Museé de la Nubie (Assouan, Republique Arabe Unie Egypte, n.d.

404 • *dark mother*

Museo Archeologico Firenze. Testi di Francesco Razeto e Marino Marini (Firenze, Becocci Editore, n.d.).

Museo Archeologico Regionale Paolo Orsi. Text by Giuseppe Voza, Photographs by Mimmo Jodice n.d.).

Museo Egizio, ed., Anna Maria Donadoni Roveria. n.d..

Museo Preistorico dei Balzi Rossi. Itinerari Ventimiglia , No. 39), (Roma, Istituto Poligrafico e Zecca dello Stato, 1996).

Mystery Religions of the Ancient Mediterranean World (HarperSanFrancisco, 1987.

Naess, Arne *Ecosofia* (Como, Red Edizioni, 1994).

The Nag Hammadi Library. James M. Robinson, General Editor. Revised Edition (HarperSanFrancisco, 1978, 1988).

National Museum. Sculpture-Bronzes-Vases (Athens, Clio Editions, 1993).

Neumann, Erich *The Great Mother.* Tr., Ralph Manheim (Princeton University Press, 1963, 1983).

Nigra sum. Iconografia de Santa Maria de Montserrat (Barcelona, Publications de L'Abadia de Montserrat).

Nobecourt, Jacques *Un Archeologo nel suo tempo. Georges Vallet.* Immagini di Mimmo Jodice (Siracusa, Ediprint, 1991).

Noble, Vicki *Shakti Woman. Feeling our fire. Healing our world. The new female shamanism* (HarperSanFrancisco, 1991).

Nocerino, Kathryn *Candles in the Daytime* (West Orange, N. J. Warthog Press, 1985).

di Nola, Alfonso *Gli aspetti magico-religiosi di una cultura subalterna italiana* (Torino, Biringheri, 1976).

Nubia. Ancient Kingdoms of Africa Ed., Joyce L. Haynes (Boston, Museum of Fine Arts, 1994).

Occhipinti, Maria *Il carrubo e altri racconti* (Palermo, Sellerio editore, 1993).

Oden, R. A. Jr. *Studies in Lucian's De Syria Dea* (Cambridge, Scholars Press for Harvard Semitic Museum, 1977).

Odjik, Pamela, *The Phoenicians* (The MacMillan Company of Australia, 1989).

Oduyoye, Mercy Amba *Daughters of Anowa. African Women & Patriarchy* (Maryknoll, N. Y., Orbis Books, 1995).

Oppenheim, A. Leo *Ancient Mesopotamia. Portrait of a Dead Civilization* (Chicago and London, University of Chicago Press, 1964).

Other Histories, edited by Kirsten Hastrup (London and New York, Routledge, 1992).

Otieno, Nicholas, *A Flight into the Unknown. Contemplating the Hidden Meaning of Life* (Sparta, New Jersey, Multi Media Design, 1999).

Otte, Marcel *Le paleolithique inferieur et moyen en Europe* (Paris, Amand Colin, 1996).

Oya. Kala. Dao. Die macht des weiblichen in stammes-kulturen. Katalog zur ausstellung (Wiesbaden, Frauen Museum 1995).

Pagan Rome to Byzantium (Cambridge, Ma., The Belknap Press of Harvard University Press, 1987).

Pagels, Elaine *The Gnostic Gospels* (New York, Vintage Books, 1979, 1989).

———. *The Johannine Gospel in Gnostic Exegesis: Heracleon's Commentary on John* (Nashville & New York, Abingdon Press, 1943).

———. *The Origin of Satan* (New York, Random House, 1995).

Pantel, Pauline Schmitt, ed., *A History of Women in the West. From Ancient Goddesses to Christian Saints* (Cambridge, Ma., The Belknap Press of Harvard University Press, 1992).

Paré, Louise *Moving Between the World She Brings Forth All Things from Within Her Body: Intrinsic Movement Practice as Treansformative Spiritual Practice and Expression of Women's Spirituality* (Paper, CIIS, 2001).

Parke, H. W. *Sibyls and Sibylline Prophecy in Classical Antiquity*, ed., B. C. McGoing (London and New York, Routledge, 1988).

Pasquier, Alain *Greek, Etruscan and Roman Antiquities. The Louvre* (Paris, Scala Publications Ltd, 1991).

Patai, Raphael *The Hebrew Goddess.* Third enlarged Edition. Foreword by Merlin Stone (Detroit, Wayne State University Press, 1967, 1978, 1990).

———. *The Children of Noah. Jewish Seafaring in Ancient Times* (Princeton, N.J. , Princeton University Press, 1998).

———. *The seed of Abraham. Jews and Arabs in Contact and Conflict* (New York, Charles Scribner's and Sons, 1986).

———. *The Jewish Alchemists. A History and Source Book* (Princeton, N. J., Princeton University Press, 1994).

Patai, Raphael and Jennifer Patai *The Myth of the Jewish Race.* Revised edition(New York, Charles Scribner's Sons, 1975;.Detroit, Wayne State University Press, 1975. Revised edition, 1989).

Pelikan, Jaroslav *Mary Through the Centuries. Her Place in the History of Culture* (New Haven and London, Yale University Press, 1996).

The Penguin Encyclopedia of Ancient Civilizations, ed., Arthur Cotterell (London, Penguin books, 1980).

Perera, Silvia Brinton *Descent to the Goddess. A Way of Initiation for Women* (Toronto, Canada, Inner City Books, 1981).

Perera, Victor *The Cross and the Pear Tree. A Sephardic Journey* (New York, Alfred A. Knopf, 1995).

Perrin, Joseph-Marie *In Dialogo con Simone Weil. l'attesa dell'uomo* (Roma, Città Nuova Editrice,1989).

Perry, Ralph Barton *General Theory of Value. Its Meaning and Basic Principles Construed in Terms of Interest* (New York, 1926).

Perry, Mary Elizabeth *Gender and Disorder in Early Modern Seville* (Princeton, N J. Princeton University Press, 1990).

Petrement, Simone *Simone Weil. A Life* (New York, Random House, 1976).

Petrioli, Emiliana, "Hal Saflieni. Gli antichi abitanti di Malta," *Archeologia Viva,* maggio-giiugno 1989.

―――. "Miti e Megaliti. Monumenti di pietra nella civilta dei Celti" (*Archeologia Viva Video,* 1972).

Pettinato, Giovanni *Ebla. Un impero inciso nell'argilla* (Milano, Arnaldo Mondadori Editore, 1979).

Pfohl, Stephen, D*eath at the parasite café. Social science (fictions) & the postmodern* (New York, St. Martin's Press, 1992).

Piper, David *Treasures of the Ashmolean Museum* (Oxford, Ashmolean Museum, 1990).

Pirani, Alix *The Absent Mother. Restoring the Goddess to Judaism and Christianity* (Mandala/HarperCollins, 1991).

Pitré, Giuseppe *Fiabe, Novelle e Racconti Popolare Siciliani.* Vol. IV (Gruppo Editoriale Brancato-Clio-Biesse-Nuova Bietti, Siracusa, Italia, 1993).

―――. *Spettacoli e feste popolari siciliane:* Biblioteca delle tradizioni popolari siciliane, Ed., Aurelio Rigoli (Palermo, l870-1913).

Plaskow, Judith *Standing again at Sinai. Judaism from a Feminist Prespective* (HarperSanFrancisco, 1990).

Pomeroy, Sarah B. *Goddesses, Whores, Wives, and Slaves. Women in Classical Antiquity* (New York, Dorset Press, 1975).

Ponce, Charles *Kabbalah. An Introduction and Illumination for the World Today* 4th Quest Printing, 1986, (Theosophical Publishing Company, 1986).

Powell, T. G. E. *The Celts* (London, Thames and Hudson Ltd., 1958, 1980).

Pritchard, James B. *Recovering Sarepta, A Phoenician City* (Princeton, N. J., Princeton University Press, 1978).

Puleo, Mev *The Struggle is One. Voices and Visions of Liberation* (Albany, N. Y., State University of New York Press, 1994).

Quatriglio, Giuseppe *A Thousand Years in Sicily. From the Arabs to the Bourbons.* Tr., Justin Vitiello (Brooklyn, N. Y., Legas, 1991.

Radford, Michele *Turning the Heart Inside-Out: The Vision of Reality according to Kashmir Shaivism and Vajrayana* (Doctoral Dissertation, CIIS, 2000).

Ragusa, Giovanni *Chiaramonte Gulfi nella storia di Sicilia (dalle origini ai nostri giorni)* (Modica, Franco Ruta Editore, 1986).

RAI, Milan *Chomsky's Politics* (London, Verso, 1995).

Rashidi, Runoko Co-edited by Ivan Van Sertima. *African Presence in Early Asia* (New Brunswick and London, Transaction Publishers, 1995).

Reade, Julian *Mesopotamia.* British Museum (Cambridge, Harvard University Press, 1991).

Reed, Holly *An Inquiry into the Meaning of Descent and Ascent in Women's Psychological Development Research contributing to the theories of Women's Development* (Doctoral Dissertation, CIIS, 2000).

Religion in Ancient Egypt. Gods, Myths, and Personal Practice. Ed., Byron E. Shafer, John Baines, Leonard H. Lesko and David P. Silverman (Ithaca and London, Cornell University Press, 1991).

The Renaissance in National Context. Ed., Roy Porter & Mikulas Teich (Cambridge, Cambridge University Press, 1992).

Renda, Francesco *Il Primo Maggio l890* (Palermo, Sellerio editore, 1990).

———. *I fasci siciliani l892-94* (Torino, Einaudi, 1977).

Renfrew, Colin *Before Civilization. The Radiocarbon Revolution and Prehistoric Europe* (New York, Alfred A. Knopf, 1974).

Redford, Donald B. *Egypt, Canaan, and Israel in Ancient Times* (Princeton, N. J., Princeton Univ Press, 1992).

Richards, "David A. J. *Italian American. The Racializing of an Ethnic Identity* (New York and London, New York University Press, 1999).

Rizzo, Laura *Che Donna, La Sicilia. Ritratti e riflessioni al femminile* (Catania, Prova d'Autore, 1993).

Roberts, David "Age of Pyramids. Egypt's Old Kingdom," *The National Geographic,* January 1995).

Robins, Gay *Women in Ancient Egypt* (Cambridge, Ma., Harvard University Press, 1993).

Rogin, Michael *Blackface, White Noise. Jewish Immigrants in the Hollywood Melting Pot* (Berkeley, Los Angeles, London , University of California Press, 1996).

Rolzinski, Katarzyna *Seeing Mother Home: An Inquiry into the Experience of Daughters as Caregivers for their Dying Mothers (*Doctoral Dissertaition, CIIS, 2000)

Romano, James F. *Daily Life of the Ancient Egyptians* (Pittsburgh, Pa., The Carnegie Museum of Natural History 1990).

Romano, Rose *Vendetta* (San Francisco, malafemmina press, 1990).

Roscoe, Will "Priests of the Goddess: Gender Transgression in the Ancient World, " Paper, Institute for Research on Women and Gender, Stanford University, 1993.

Rossi, Maria Luigia *L'Aneddoto di tradizione orale nel comune di Subbiano. Novelle, barzellete, bazzecole* (Firenze, L. S. Olschki Editore, 1986).

Runciman, Steven *The First Crusade* (Press Syndicate, University of Cambridge, 1980).

Russo, John Paul, "From Italophilia to Italophobia: Representations of Italian Americans in the Early Gilded Age," *Proceedings,* conference of the American Italian Historical Association, Philadelphia, November 1991).

Sacred Texts of the World. A Universal Anthology. Edited by Ninian Smart & Richard D. Hecht (New York, Crossroad, 1996).

Saggs, H. W. F. *Civilization before Greece and Rome* (New Haven and London, Yale University Press, 1989).

Said, Edward W. *Orientalism* (New York, Vintage Books, 1979).

———. *Culture and Imperialism* (New York, Vintage Books, 1994).

———. *How the media and the experts determine how we see the rest of the world* (New York, Vintage, 1997).

———. *Representatives of the Intellectual* (New York, Vintage Books, 1996).

Saliba, Marlene *Time-Faring Poems* (Mala, Formatek Lt., 1994).

Santa Maria del Carmine e la Cappella Brancacci, ed., Mario Carniani (Firenze, Becocci Editore, n.d.).

Saint Teresa of Avila. The Collected Works. 3 vols. Tr., Kieran Kavanaugh o.c.d. and Otilio Rodriguez, o.c.d. (Washington, D. C., Institute of Carmelite Studies, 1976, 1985).

Santarelli, Giuseppe *Le Leggende dei Monti Sibillini* (Montefortino, Edizioni "Voce del Santuario Madonna dell'Ambro," 1974).

Sansoni, Umberto *Le Piu' Antiche Pitture del Saraha. L'Arte delle Teste Rotonde* (Milan, Jaca Book, 1994). Prefazione di Emmanuel Anati.

Sun Stories. Tales from Around the World to Illuminate the Days and Nights of Our Lives. Carolyn McVickar Edwards, ed. (HarperSanFrancisco, 1995).

Santayana, George *Skepticism and Animal Faith. An Introduction to a System of Philosophy* (1923, Dover ed,. 1955).

———. *The Last Puritan. A Memoir in the Form of a Novel* (New York, Scribners, 1936).

Sassi, Dino *Upper Egypt* (Milan, Kina Italia, 1988).

Scarre, Geoffrey *Witchcraft and Magic in 16th and 17th Europe* (Atlantic Highlands, N. J., Humanities Press International, Inc. 1987).

Schug-Wille, Christa *Art of the Byzantine World* (New York, Harry N. Abrams, Inc., 1969).

Segy, Ladislas *African Sculpture Speaks* 4th edition enlarged (New York, Da Capo Press, Inc. A subsidiary of Plenum Publishing Corporation, 1969, 1975).

Sertima, Ivan Van *They Came Before Columbus The African presence in Ancient America.* (New York, Random House, 1976).

———. *African Presence in Early Europe* (Journal of African Civilizations, Ltd. Inc., 1985).

———. *Golden Age of the Moor* (New Brunswick and London, Transaction Publishers, 1992.

Shafer, Byron E., editor *Temples of Ancient Egypt* (Ithaca, New York Cornell University Press, 1997).

Shell, Marc "Marranos (Pigs), or from Coexistence to Toleration" (*Critical Inquiry*, Vol. 17, No. 2, Winter 1991. The University of Chicago, 1991).

"Sicilia. La Nuova Resistenza. 'Noi anomali.' Vite di sindaci antimafia," *Avvenimenti*, 15 agosto 1994.

Sicilia Meravigliosa. Arte-storia-paessagio (Milano, Edizioni Kina Italia, 1985).

Siracusa. Arte-Storia-Natura (Milano, Cografa S.r..l. -Usmate, n.d.).

Siracusa. Arte-Storia-Natura (Siracusa, Co-Graf Editrice, n.d.).

Sitwell, Sacheverell *Baroque and Rococo* (New York, G. P. Putnam's Sons, 1967).

Sjoo, Monica and Barbara Mor *The Great Cosmic Mother. Rediscovering the Religion of the Earth* (HarperSanFrancisco, 1987, 1988).

Snell, Daniel C. *Life in the Ancient Near East 31-332 B.C..E.* (New Haven and London, Yale University Press, 1997).

Snowden, Frank M., Jr. *Blacks in Antiquity. Ethiopians in the Greco-Roman Experience* (Cambridge, Ma., Harvard University Press, 1970).

Solarino, Dr. Raffaele, *La Contea di Modica. Ricerche Storiche*. Vol. Primo, Vol. Secondo (Ragusa, Libreria Paolino Editrice, 1982. First published 1885).

Some, Malidoma Patrice *The Healing Wisdom of Africa. Finding Life Purpose Through Nature, Ritual, and Community* (New York, Jeremy P. Tarcher, 1999).

Soto, Elaine, Ph.D. *Black Madonnas* (Catalog, New York, 1999).

Spadaro, Tommaso *I racconti di Motya* (Marsala, La Medusa Editrice, 1989).

Spretnak, Charlene *Lost Goddesses of Early Greece: A Collection of Pre-Hellenic Mythology (Boston,* Beacon Press, 1992*)*.

Springsted, Allen and Eric O. *Spirit, Nature and Community. Issues in the Thought of Simone Weil* (Albany, State University of New York Press, 1994*)*.

Starbird, Margaret. *The Woman with the Alabaster Jar. Mary Magdalen and the Holy Grail* (Santa Fe, N. M., Bear & Company Publishing, 1993).

Stone, Merlin *When God was a Woman* (New York, Dorset Press, 1976*); Three Thousand Years of Racism.*

————. *Recurring patterns in racism, ed.*, Merlin Stone in conjunction with Women against Racism (New York, New Sibylline Books, 1981).

Takaki, Ronald T. *Iron Cages. Race and Culture in 19th Century America* (Seattle, University of Washington Press, 1979).

————. *A Different Mirror. A History of Multicultural America (Boston, Little Brown and Company, 1993)*

Talking about a Revolution, Ed., South end Press Collective. (Cambridge, Ma., South End Press, 1998).

Taylor, John H. *Egypt and Nubia* (London, British Museum Press, 1991).

Teish, Luisah *Jambalaya. The Natural Woman's Book of Personal Charms and Practical Rituals* (HarperSanFrancisco, 1985).

————. *Carnival of the Spirit. Seasonal Celebrations and Rites of Passage* (HarperSanFrancisco, 1994).

Teresa of Avila. The Interior Castle. Tr., Kieran Kavanaugh, O.C.D. and Otilio Rodriguez, O.C.D. (New York, Paulist Press, 1997).

————. *The Life of Saint Teresa of Avila by Herself* (New York, Penguin Books, 1957).

The Collected Works of St. Teresa of Avila (Washington D.C., Institute of Carmelite Studies, 1976).

Terra e uomini nel mezzogiorno normanno-svevo. Atti delle settime giornate normanno-sveve Bari, 15-17 ottobre 1985. (Centro di studi normanno-svevi, Universita' degli Studi di Bari, 1987).

Teuba, Savina J. *Sarah. The Priestess. The First Matriarch of Genesis* (Athens, Swallow Press/Ohio University Press, 1984).

Third World Women and the Politics of Feminism, ed., Chandra Talpade Mohanty, Ann Russo, Lourdes Torres (Indiana University Press, 1991).

Thomas, Keith *Religion & the Decline of Magic* (New York, Charles Scribner's Sons, 1971).

Thomas, W. I. and Florian Znaniecki, *The Polish Peasant in Europe and America* (1910) Dover edition, 1958.

Thompson, Robert Farris *Flash of the Spirit. African & Afro-American Art & Philosophy* (New York, Vintage Books, 1984).

Tramontana, Salvatore *L'effimero nella Sicilia normanna* (Palermo, Sellerio Editore, 1984, 1985).

Trialogues at the Edge of the West. Chaos Creativity and the Resacralization of the World. Ralph Abraham, Terence McKenna, Rupert Sheldrake (Santa Fe, New Mexico Bear & Company Publishing, 1992).

Trigger, Bruce G. *Early Civilizations. Ancient Egypt in Context* (Cairo, Egypt The American University in Cairo Press, 1993).

Trompetto, Mario *Storia del santuario di Oropa* (Biella, Libreria Vittorio Giovannacci, 1990).

Turner, Victor *The Forest of Symbols. Aspects of Ndembu Ri*tual (Ithaca and London, Cornell University Press, 1967).

————. *The Drums of Affliction. A Study of Religious Processes among the Ndembu of Zambia* (Oxford, Clarendon Press and the International African Institute, 1968).

Tusa, Sebastiano *La Preistoria nel Territorio di Trapani* (Siracusa, Palermo, Ediprint s.r.l. 1990).

————. *Sicilia Preistorica* (Palermo, Dario Flaccovio Editore, 1994).

————. "La Sicilia dalla Protostoria ad Augusto," *Antiche Genti D'Italia* (Rimini, Edizioni De Luca, 1994).

Unsettling America. An Anthology of Contemporary Multicultural Poetry, ed., Maria Mazziotti Gillan and Jennifer Gillan (New York, Penguin, 1994).

Vafopoulou-Richardson, C. E. *Ancient Greek Terracottas* (Oxford, Ashmolean Museum, 1991).

Veen, Veronica and Adrian van der Blom, *The First Maltese. Origins, Character and Symbolism of the Ghar Dalam Culture* (Haarlem, Holland, fia, 1992).

Venuta da Lontano. L'Antico Culto della Madonna di Gulfi. Storia e Tradizione. A cura di Giuseppe Cultrera (Chiaramonte Gulfi, Utopia Edizioni, 1990).

Vigil, Jose' a cura di Maria,. *Con I poveri della terra. Studio interdisciplinare sull' opzione per I poveri* (Assisi, Cittadella Editrice, 1992).

Villette, Jean *Guide des vitraux de Chartres* (Ouest-France, 1987)

Vitiello, Justin *Sicily Within.* Supplement to *Arba Sicula, Journal of Sicilian Folklore and Literature* (Jamaica, N. Y., Arba Sicula, 1992).

————. *Poetics and Literature of the Sicilian Diaspora. Studies in Oral History and Story-Telling* (San Francisco, Mellen Research University Press, 1993).

Voragine, Jacobus de *The Golden Legend. Readings on the Saints.* Tr. William Granger Ryan, Vol I. (n.d.)

Voss, Jutta *La Luna Nera. Il potere della donna e la simbologia del ciclo femminile* (Como, Italia, Red Edizioni, 1996).

Walker, Barbara G. *The Woman's Encyclopedia of Myths and Secrets* (HarperSanFrancisco, 1983).

———. *The Woman's Dictionary of Symbols & Sacred Objects* (HarperSanFrancisco, 1988)

———. *The Sceptical Feminist. Rediscovering the Virgin, Mother & Crone* (HarperSanFrancisco, 1987)

Weil, Simone *The Need for Roots* (New York, G. P. Putnam's Sons, 1952).

———. *Lectures on Philosophy.* Tr. Hugh Price Cambridge University Press, 1978).

———. *Formative Writings 1929-1941.* Ed., Dorothy Tuck McFarland and Wilhelmina Van Ness (London , Routledge & Kegan Paul, 1987)

———. *Simone Weil Reader*, ed., G. A. Panichas (Mt. Kisco, New York, Moyer Bell Limited, 1977).

West, Cornel *Keeping Faith. Philosophy and Race in America* New York and London, Routledge, 1993).

———. *Prophetic Thought in Postmodern Times. Beyond Eurocentrism and Multiculturalism* (Monroe, Maine, Common Curage Press, 1993). {

Wilshire, Donna and Bruce Wilshire "The Great Cosmic Mother: Openness to the Past as Openness to the Future" (Unpublished paper).

Willetts, R. F. *The Civilization of Ancient Crete* (New York, Barnes & Noble Books, 1976).

Williams, Delores S. *Sisters in the wilderness. The Challenge of Womanist God-Talk* (Maryknoll, N. Y., Orbis Books, 1993).

Williams, William Appleman *The Contours of American History* (New York and London, W. W. Norton, 1988).

——— *Empire as a Way of Life. An Essay on the Causes and Character of America's Present Predicament Along with a Few Thoughts About an Alternative* (New York and Oxford, Oxford University Press, 1980).

———. *The Great Evasion. An Essay on the Contemporary Relevance of Karl Marx and on the Wisdom of Admitting the Heretic into the Dialogue about America's Future* (New York, New Viewpoints, 1964).

Willett, Frank *African Art* (New York, Thames and Hudson, 1971, 1993).

Witt, R. E. *Isis in the Graeco-Roman World* (Ithaca, N. Y. Cornell University Press, 1971).

Women's America. Refocusing the Past. Edited by Linda K. Kerber & Jane De Hart-Mathews (New York and Oxford, Oxford University Press, 1987).

Yates, Frances A. *Giordano Bruno and the Hermetic Tradition* (Chicago and London, University of Chicago Press, 1964).

Zammit, Themistocles *The Prehistoric Temples of Malta and Gozo* (Malta, 1995).

Zappa, Vera ed., *Il passato e Noi, Le Ricette della Nonna Camuna* (Breno, Pro Loco di Angolo Terme, 1994).

Zerbst, Rainer *Antonio Gaudi, l852-1926. A Life Devoted to Architecture* (Koln, Benedikt Taschen Verlag GmbH, 1993).

Ziegler, Christine *The Louvre. Egyptian Antiquities* (Paris, Scala Publications, Ltd., 1990).

Zinn, Howard. *A People's History of the United States* (New York, Harper Perennial, 1980).

0-595-20841-X